Willie Mangum and the
North Carolina Whigs
in the Age of Jackson

Willie Mangum and the North Carolina Whigs in the Age of Jackson

BENJAMIN L. HUGGINS

McFarland & Company, Inc., Publishers
Jefferson, North Carolina

Names: Huggins, Benjamin L., 1965– author.
Title: Willie Mangum and the North Carolina Whigs
in the Age of Jackson / Benjamin L. Huggins.
Description: Jefferson, North Carolina : McFarland & Company, Inc.,
Publishers, 2016. | Includes bibliographical references and index.
Identifiers: LCCN 2016015441 | ISBN 9780786498765
(softcover : acid free paper) ∞
Subjects: LCSH: Mangum, Willie Person, 1792–1861. | Legislators—
United States—Biography. | United States. Congress. Senate—
Biography. | United States—Politics and government—1815–1861. |
North Carolina—Politics and government—1775–1865. |
Whig Party (U.S.)—Biography. | Whig Party (U.S.)—History.
Classification: LCC E340.M3 H84 2016 | DDC 328.73/092 [B] —dc23
LC record available at https://lccn.loc.gov/2016015441

BRITISH LIBRARY CATALOGUING DATA ARE AVAILABLE

**ISBN (print) 978-0-7864-9876-5
ISBN (ebook) 978-1-4766-2509-6**

© 2016 Benjamin L. Huggins. All rights reserved

*No part of this book may be reproduced or transmitted in any form
or by any means, electronic or mechanical, including photocopying
or recording, or by any information storage and retrieval system,
without permission in writing from the publisher.*

On the cover: Willie Person Mangum (U.S. Senate);
background North Carolina map © 2016 Roberto A Sanchez/iStock

Printed in the United States of America

*McFarland & Company, Inc., Publishers
Box 611, Jefferson, North Carolina 28640
www.mcfarlandpub.com*

To Adrina

Table of Contents

Preface	1
Introduction	3
1. Mangum and the Old Republicans	7
2. Young Old Republican	30
3. The Beginning of Opposition: States' Rights and the Anti–Van Buren Party	59
4. The Whig Opposition: States' Rights and the Senate	75
5. The Revolution of 1840: From States' Rights Whigs to Clay Whigs	107
6. The Whig Ascendancy: Whig Principles and Clay Whigs	132
7. The End of the Whig Ascendancy	170
Conclusion	211
Chapter Notes	219
Bibliography	244
Index	249

Preface

The political career of Willie P. Mangum, Whig senator and opponent of Andrew Jackson's Democrats, offers a focal point for analyzing the ideology and politics of North Carolina's Southern Whigs, from their origins to their fall. In the 1820s the young congressman Mangum imbibed the political philosophy of North Carolina's senator Nathaniel Macon, who has been described as the "prophet of pure republicanism"—the republicanism of Thomas Jefferson's Democratic-Republicans. From his election to Congress in 1824 Mangum was at the epicenter of both national and state politics. In the 1830s Mangum, like his mentor Macon before him, emerged as leader of a political opposition party—the Whigs.

Mangum's Southern Whigs, too little studied by scholars, were linked by a shared opposition ideology with Macon's Old Republicans. This book shows how the Old Republican ideology of opposition—Jefferson's "Principles of '98" of the Revolution of 1800—were adopted by Mangum and a new generation of North Carolina Old Republicans, who, along with other opponents of Democratic presidents Andrew Jackson and Martin Van Buren, made that Old Republican ideology the foundation of the Whig Party in the state. The opposition ideology of the North Carolina Whigs and older, but popular, Republican political ideas allowed the party to organize rapidly and capture the state from the Jackson Democrats. The Whigs' opposition to executive power was the chief aspect of their ideology, emphasized in all their campaigns from 1836 to 1844. Most important, the North Carolina Whigs evolved from a primarily Old Republican states' rights party to a coalition Whig party with a political philosophy combining the Old Republicans' creed with the National Republican economic agenda touted by Henry Clay. This evolution was critical to sustaining the ascendancy of the Carolina Whigs. At both the national and state levels of politics, though, success raised expectations of governance, increased regional and personal rivalries, and revealed ideological conflicts within the Whig coalition. Conflicts over President John Tyler's strict constructionism and President Zachary Taylor's anti-party appeal emerge as key episodes in the state's political development. A political culture of opposition could not remain ascendant under such tensions.

This book, then, seeks to account for political continuities between the decades of the early republic and the antebellum decades that most historians have ignored, particularly the links between Old Republican ideology and Southern Whig ideology. It also complicates traditional interpretations of antebellum Southern politics by showing that North Carolina's politics did not simply reflect a parochial regionalism but was the result of a negotiation between state and national political ideals. The political culture of antebellum North Carolina emerges as a complex mix of national and state politics and democratic and opposition ideologies.

Introduction

In 1954 Charles Grier Sellers, Jr., asked the readers of *The American Historical Review*, "Who Were the Southern Whigs?" Despite half a century of historiography, few historians have tackled this enormously important question and even they have not yet fully examined the Southern Whigs' ideology. In particular, they have failed to comprehend fully how much the origins of Southern Whigs' ideology lay in "old" Republican ideology—the doctrines, or, principles, of the Jeffersonian Republicans—first articulated by Thomas Jefferson, James Madison, and their fellow Republicans during their heated political struggles with the Federalists between 1798 and 1800. Because of an overemphasis on the Northern Whigs, historians of antebellum politics have largely failed to understand that the political creed of many Southern Whigs was fully as influenced by the ideas of the Old Republicans as was the ideology of the Southern Democrats.[1] A major question in a study of the origins of the Southern Whigs must be how Jeffersonian political thought was carried forward into the political ideology of the Southern Whigs and how they in turn modified that ideology to accord with the needs of their particular political situation. The Whig Party in North Carolina, from its origins in the politics of the 1820s to its demise some thirty years later, shows these ideological developments and the important interaction of state and national politics.[2]

This book focuses on North Carolina for several reasons. Because of the sway of Nathaniel Macon, one of the chief Old Republicans in Congress, on the state's politics in the Jeffersonian era, both the North Carolina Democratic and Whig parties of the 1830s and 1840s were influenced by Old Republican doctrines perhaps more than those in any other state with the exception of Virginia. Also, North Carolina was one of the few Southern states where the Whigs controlled the state government for an extended period and where the Whig Party, professing an anti-party, opposition ideology, was able to rise from political opposition to become the dominant state party. And as the home of Willie P. Mangum, who in the 1840s became a staunch ally of Henry Clay and one of the most powerful Southern senators, North Carolina came to exert a powerful influence on national affairs and party policies.

The political life of Mangum offers a focal point for analyzing the culture and politics of North Carolina's Southern Whigs. Mentored in the school of old republicanism by Macon while both were in Congress in the 1820s, Mangum soon began to take over the old senator's political mantra. His strong commitment to the Old Republicans and his political and speaking skills made him a star of the Old Republicans, and they elected Mangum to the U.S. Senate in 1830. He joined the short-lived Anti–Van Buren opposition party, and then became a leading opponent of Jackson in the Senate and a leader of the new Whig Party in North

Carolina. Mangum stood at the epicenter of both national and state politics for over two decades. A study of his career thus allows an examination of how national and local politics intersected and interacted in North Carolina. With his friend and close political ally William A. Graham, Mangum led the North Carolina Whigs in their years of ascendency, and as the political leader of one of the staunchest Whig states in the South he wielded great influence in the national Whig party as well. The leadership role held by Mangum meant that he not only acted within the political culture, he also helped to shape it. Like his political mentor before him, Mangum led an opposition revolution in state and national politics—Macon with Jefferson's Republicans against the Federalists and Mangum with the Whigs against Andrew Jackson and Martin Van Buren. The identification of both Macon and Mangum with the same "old republican principles" indicates that they lay as much at the core of Mangum's Southern Whig philosophy as Nathaniel Macon's Old Republicanism. Therefore, examining the course of Mangum's political career and the ideology that shaped it provides insight into the continuities and changes in Southern political culture from the Revolution of 1800 to the coming of the Civil War.

The Carolina Whigs' political tenets were firmly rooted in Nathaniel Macon's brand of Old Republicanism. North Carolina had been a thoroughly Republican state since the Revolution of 1800 and Macon and his Old Republican allies dominated the state during the presidencies of Thomas Jefferson and James Madison. The Old Republicans were still the strongest political faction in the 1820s—a testament to the popularity of their creed in the state. Both the seeds of union and disunion, democracy and dissent were to be found in Macon's "doctrines of '98." The ideas that Mangum and his fellow Whig leaders engrafted onto that Old Republican foundation and the political factions they melded together to make their opposition coalition shaped the difference between them and their Democratic opponents. By the 1840s the doctrines of the Carolina Whigs were a complex mix of Old Republicanism—with its proslavery and states' rights philosophy—democracy, and economic nationalism.

Two over-arching themes united this diverse political coalition. As with the Whig party as a whole, the Carolina Whigs' resistance to presidential power stood as the most important aspect of their ideology; they emphasized it in all their campaigns from 1836 to 1844 and it shaped their response to every administration. The next most important "opposition" in their political canon was opposition to Martin Van Buren. As this book will show, the Whig coalition first came together as an anti–Van Buren party. Carolina Whigs viewed Van Buren as the symbol of all that was evil in the Democratic Party: presidential usurpation of power, corruption, intrigue, and the pursuit of party "spoils." The Whig Party reached the height of its unity and its ascendancy in North Carolina with a catalogue of Van Buren's supposed sins as its central message. These two themes, well suited to opposition and popular with a people long favorable to Old Republicanism, allowed them to organize rapidly and capture political control of the state.

Strongly influenced by Old Republican principles, the ideology of North Carolina's Southern Whigs began as an opposition ideology, and their party as an opposition party. The Republicanism of Jefferson was an ideology of opposition—largely formulated by the Republican leaders in the years from 1798 to 1800 to counter the alleged wrongs of Federalism. In the years after Jefferson's first term the Old Republicans set themselves up as the defenders of the "doctrines of '98" in opposition to Republicans whom they believed to be moving too far away from the true Republican creed. Both the Republicanism of 1800 and the Old Republicanism professed by Macon and his allies in the 1810s and 1820s were ideologies for men who designed either to bring down governments or at the very least reform them. The Whigs took shape as the opposition party to the Democrats supporting Jackson—"King" Andrew as the Whigs called him. Like the Old Republicans, they were far more suited to opposition than support of presidential administrations.

Despite the Old Republicanism of the Carolina Whigs' ideology, a unique and contingent union of Old Republican and National Republican ideas made their Whig ascendancy in the state possible. The dominance of the Whig Party in North Carolina was founded on a union of Henry Clay's National Republican economic agenda and Mangum's Old Republican ideology. Old Republicanism had been the Whigs' core message in 1836, but Henry Clay became increasing popular in the state. The unexpected choice of Harrison, who embodied Old Republican traditions, by the national party and the popularity of Clay with North Carolina Whigs in the campaign of 1840 allowed the Carolina Whigs to unite Old Republicanism and National Republicanism into an effective blend of "Whig principles" and "Whig measures." With this combination, which became the foundation of their ascendancy, they won the elections of 1840, the culmination of their opposition revolution against "Jacksonism" and "Van Burenism." At both the national and state levels of politics, however, success raised expectations of governance, gave rise to regional and personal rivalries, and revealed ideological conflicts within the party.

This study is not a complete narrative of the course of American government and state politics, or even Mangum's political career. Rather, each chapter focuses on key periods and events at the level of national and state politics. As the Whig Party rose in his state, Mangum and the Southern Whigs in the Senate led the opposition fight against Jackson. Mangum's career in the Senate was important to the Whig Party—his decision to do political battle with Jackson in 1834 helped found the opposition to the Democratic Party. The Senate—where the Southern Whig legislatures were represented and where the Whigs of the Union met—became the chief opposition to presidents Jackson, Van Buren, Tyler, and Polk. The opposition between the Whig Senate and the Democratic presidents (or in Tyler's case apostate Whig) became the focal point of national politics. And that struggle had an impact on politics in states controlled by the Southern Whigs. To the Southern Whigs, states' rights, legislative supremacy, and opposition to expansion of presidential power were closely related concepts. States' rights and legislative supremacy were the Southern Whigs' defense against executive power; the Senate embodied these principles and the Southern Whigs—like the Old Republicans before them—defended the Senate as the bastion against presidential power.

The Democratic presidents from Jackson through Polk consistently sought to expand presidential powers at the expense of Congress. Democrats tended to view the president as the man above legislative control, and, from the time of Jackson, sought presidential supremacy in the federal government. The Whigs resisted this expansion of presidential power. They opposed presidents who disregarded Congress, the laws, and the Constitution to implement "the will of the people."[3] Whigs wanted a president who deferred to Congress.

Jackson's war on the Senate opposition, detailed in this book, was particularly important. Southern Whig states such as North Carolina were critical to the Whig majority in the Senate. The controversy over legislative instruction of senators that arose in North Carolina during Jackson's war on the Senate defined the ideological contest between the parties with key issues of states' rights and democracy: Was the president or the Senate the defender of states' rights? Should senators act independently on their own constitutional judgment or should they be constrained by the "people's" instructions? The controversy also showed how national and state politics interacted in the struggle between the president and the Senate.

When Mangum became a leader of the Whig Party in Congress, his position embroiled him in confrontations with three presidents—conflicts over principles and measures that placed him in opposition to their administrations. Always more comfortable in opposition than in cooperation with the administration, both Mangum and his old mentor Macon never remained long in support of any president, even one from their own party. With only two brief exceptions Mangum opposed every president from Jackson to Millard Fillmore. One could say that like Macon before him, Mangum preferred bringing presidents down to building them up. Foremost among the ideological clashes were the Whigs' internecine quarrels with two Whig presidents over political principles: John Tyler's Virginia states' rights/strict constructionist brand of Whig principles and Zachary Taylor's appeal to Whig anti-party principles. Mangum and other North Carolina Whig congressmen stood at the forefront of these battles and influenced the course of the state's Whig Party. Yet, a political culture of opposition could not remain ascendant under such tensions.

An opposition ideology made governance more difficult. The Republicans divided when Jefferson had to confront the difficult foreign policy crises of his second term. The Old Republicans were born as a distinct opposition party during those schisms. Later, Southern Whigs opposed Virginia Whig John Tyler's presidency. The Southern Whigs of North Carolina also had difficulty in power in their own state. While rising to ascendancy in North Carolina, the Whig Party remained an opposition coalition. That placed it in a difficult situation when Whigs controlled the state government *and* the presidency. Even when the Whigs were ascendant in North Carolina and controlled the state government their campaigns were most effective when they could oppose the policies of Democratic presidents. Whig oppositional ideology and rhetoric was most effective when they were *out* of the presidency; the party suffered its greatest defeats in North Carolina with nominal Whigs in the White House. Moreover, Van Buren's abrupt and unexpected departure from the political scene in 1844 removed an important unifying enemy for the Whigs' coalition. Without Van Buren to unite the Whig coalition, personal and regional rivalries in the party increased. When Mangum and the Whigs had to confront the Democrats, armed with new popular issues, with a Whig in the White House they experienced their greatest challenges—challenges that broke their ascendency. And the end of their ascendency, combined with the fall of Southern Whigs in other states, may have hastened the coming of the Civil War.

1

Mangum and the Old Republicans

To understand North Carolina politics and national politics as Willie Mangum knew them in the 1830s and 1840s one must understand the Old Republicans who in the 1820s professed Thomas Jefferson's "pure republican" creed. This philosophy originated among Jefferson and his followers during their political battles with the Federalists before the turn of the century.

In the late 1790s Jefferson's political adherents, calling themselves "Republicans," had begun to view their cause against what they believed was the mis-government of the Federalists as tantamount to a political revolution. In the election of 1800, later styled by Jefferson as the "Revolution of 1800," Jefferson's Republicans swept the Federalists from power in the national government and in 1801 inaugurated Republican rule. With Jefferson's election achieved, the Republicans would now have to convert their opposition to the Federalist program to the administration of the government by Republican principles. In line with their revolutionary conception of the election of 1800, the Republicans intended to govern the country by the political principles they had articulated over the course of the past decade.

The Jeffersonian Republicans formulated the essentials of their political philosophy in the course of the political and ideological struggle of the 1790s with the Federalists. The key period of this ideological formation, however, occurred during 1797–1800 with the tensions of the "quasi-war" with France and the political combat of the years preceding the election of 1800. The Jeffersonian Republicans reacted to the Federalists' passage of the Alien and Sedition Acts and their measures for a new army and bigger navy that increased taxes and appeared to threaten liberty. Such measures giving increased power to the federal government were bound to provoke the resistance of those who opposed the Federalist philosophy and preferred instead greater state sovereignty and strict construction of the Constitution. The political philosophy that Republicans later called "The Principles of '98," and that became the core ideology of the party, crystallized in this period.[1]

In his inaugural address Jefferson stated what he deemed to be "the essential principles of our Government, and consequently those which ought to shape its administration":

> Equal and exact justice to all men, of whatever state or persuasion, religious or political; peace, commerce, and honest friendship with all nations, entangling alliances with none; the support of the State governments in all their rights, as the most competent administrations for our domestic concerns and the surest bulwarks against antirepublican tendencies; the preservation of the General Government in its whole constitutional vigor, as the sheet anchor of our peace at home and safety abroad; a jealous care of the right of election by the people…; absolute acquiescence in the decisions of the majority, the vital principle of republics…; a well-disciplined militia, our best reliance in peace and for the first moments of war, till regulars may

> relieve them; the supremacy of the civil over the military authority; economy in the public expense...; the honest payment of our debts and sacred preservation of the public faith; encouragement of agriculture, and of commerce as its handmaid; the diffusion of information and arraignment of all abuses at the bar of the public reason; freedom of religion; freedom of the press, and freedom of person under the protection of the habeas corpus and trial by juries impartially selected.

Jefferson insisted that these were the principles that formed "the bright constellation" that had guided Americans through "revolution and reformation." "They should be," he said, "the creed of our political faith."[2] This litany indicated Jefferson's vision of how he intended to apply Republicanism to the governance of the country. Under a Republican government the freedoms of the Bill of Rights were to be respected. The civil authority would be supreme: there would be no Napoleons (or Alexander Hamiltons). State governments would administer all domestic affairs; the general government would suppress insurrection, defend the territories and overseas commerce, and conduct foreign affairs. Public opinion and "absolute acquiescence" to the majority will would lie at the foundation of government.

By 1801 the Republicans had achieved a consensus around the Principles of '98 as the way they believed the country should be governed, in contrast to the Federalists' program and style of government. Jefferson's paramount desire was "to see this government brought back to its republican principles." He was confident that "the great body of the people" were passing over to the Republicans and away from the Federalists. Though it might take several elections "it will assuredly take place," he insisted. "The madness & extravagance of their career is what ensures it," he explained to a correspondent. "The people through all the states are for republican forms, republican principles, simplicity, economy, religious & civil freedom."[3]

Whatever may have been the actual case in other states, Republicanism certainly held sway in North Carolina. In the 1790s the Anti-Federalists had dominated the state's politics. With such strong Anti-Federalist traditions, North Carolina was a prime region for the emergence of a Republican opposition to the Federalist administration. Historians have noted the distinct Anti-Federalism of the North Carolina legislature in the 1790s.[4] The majority of the state's delegation in Congress was also usually Anti-Federalist. During that decade the legislature consistently demonstrated a marked spirit of opposition to the Federal government in matters touching state sovereignty.

In North Carolina the Revolution of 1800 was not that revolutionary. The state was already predominantly Republican. The elections of 1800 turned back a brief Federalist resurgence which had taken place during the foreign policy crisis and war scare with France. In fact, in general the elections for Congress and the composition of the legislatures in 1798 and 1799 indicate that the French crisis merely moderated the state's Republicanism rather than shifted the state to Federalism.[5] When the crisis subsided, North Carolina quickly returned to its ardent Republicanism. Though four of ten districts continued to send Federalists to Congress, the legislature returned to its former strong Republicanism. The August elections for the General Assembly brought to Raleigh newly elected Republicans who had no inclination to compromise with Federalists, and they provided a solidly Republican majority.[6] Both houses elected Republicans as speaker, replacing Federalists who held the posts in the last two Assemblies. In the fall's presidential contest the state's return to solid Republicanism was confirmed. North Carolina delivered a solid electoral majority to Jefferson. Eight of twelve electoral districts voted for Jefferson electors.

At the national level, especially in matters related to foreign policy, Jefferson and his cabinet found it difficult to administer the country purely by Republican principles. Some Republicans in Congress began to criticize the president and his administration for straying from pure Republicanism. In the years following Jefferson's retirement from office, as his successors continued to govern pragmatically rather than adhere to pure Republican ideology these men began to call themselves "old" Republicans to differentiate themselves from the "new" Republican supporters of James Madison and James Monroe who they felt were becoming too nationalist in their outlook. These Old Republicans formed an opposition group. In North Carolina, the old party principles remained popular and the Old Republicans continued to hold sway as the state's dominate political faction. In the presidential election of 1824, the Old Republicans backed the candidacy of Georgia senator William Harris Crawford and joined with his supporters, called the "Radicals," against the Republican nationalism of Henry Clay of Kentucky and Monroe's secretary of war John Calhoun of South Carolina.[7] In North Carolina, with the Old Republicans the dominant political faction, the young Republicans entering politics were committed to Crawford and the Old Republican creed.

Willie P. Mangum of Orange County

On June 4, 1823, superior court judge Willie Person Mangum of Hillsboro in Orange County announced his candidacy for Congress as representative of the Eighth District composed of Orange, Person, and Wake counties. He favored western demands for a more democratic state constitution, state-funded internal improvements, and a broad educational program. Largely on the strength of votes in Orange and Person counties where constitutional revision was popular, Mangum won the election by a vote of 2,523 to 1,729 for his rival Daniel Barringer of Wake County. Thus began the career in national politics of North Carolina's ablest antebellum politician, who quickly rose to be a leader of the southern branch of the Whig Party and became the president pro tem of the U.S. Senate—de facto vice president.

Willie P. Mangum had been born May 10, 1792, in Orange County, the first son of William Person and Catherine Davis Mangum. The Mangum family had migrated to North Carolina from Sussex County, Virginia, eventually settling in Orange County where William's father, Arthur, had obtained land grants as early as 1763. William Mangum was a merchant and owner of a 2,500-acre plantation in Orange County. Willie Mangum had two younger brothers, Priestly and Walter, and one sister, Rebecca. He was schooled at the Hillsboro Academy, the Fayetteville Academy of the Rev. Colin McIver, and the Raleigh Academy of the Rev. William McPheeters before entering the University of North Carolina in 1811. After his graduation in 1815, he studied law under the direction of Duncan Cameron, a wealthy planter and influential politician from Orange County, and received his law license in 1817. Willie's law practice was moderately successful and in 1819 he married Charity Alston Cain, daughter of wealthy Orange County merchant and plantation owner William Cain.[8] Mangum seems to have had more enthusiasm for politics than law. He practiced law only two years before being elected to the state House of Commons in 1818 where he was the protégé of Duncan Cameron. Reelected in 1819, he was chosen judge of the superior court in 1820. Judge Mangum made valuable political contacts on his circuit throughout the state, but he soon found the duties of the office not to his liking and resigned in November 1820 to resume his law practice. He could not suppress his political instincts, however, and in the summer of 1823 he began the campaign that resulted in his election to Congress. For the next thirty years he stood at the center of North Carolina politics.⁹

Mangum was one of the young Old Republicans in Washington described by Norman Risjord as a group of "relatively young conservatives" that constituted the main strength of the Old Republicans in the early 1820s.¹⁰ Mangum's view of the presidential candidates reveals his Old Republican sentiments. In his election campaign, Mangum had run as a friend of William Crawford, but apparently he had refused to pledge his vote for Crawford if the election, as all expected, went to the House. Instead Mangum reserved the right to exercise his judgment regarding the political situation in Washington.¹¹ Although he did not immediately associate himself with the Old Republicans, Mangum never wavered in support of Crawford and increasingly favored the political philosophy of the Old Republicans. One of his first letters on his arrival in Washington was to his old political mentor Duncan Cameron. In it, he described the Old Republicans as a party that he had not yet joined: he had observed that the "thoroughgoing '98 men" were complaining of the "essential departures by the '23 republicans, from the good, old, orthodox, democratic republican faith."¹² Mangum quickly recognized Henry Clay's political talents but he did not adopt Clay's national outlook. He acknowledged Clay's popularity in the House of Representatives, but deprecated it as a species of popularity that was "not very enviable." While he admired the man and his political skills, Mangum thought that Clay lacked the "broad basis of moral confidence" despite his "superior qualifications" and "transcendent abilities" as a speaker. Believing that Clay was "unrivaled" as a popular speaker, Mangum reported that Clay would be a "dangerous competitor" if he received sufficient votes in the presidential election to place his name among those in the anticipated election in the House of Representatives.¹³

But by January of 1824, the young congressman was firmly associating himself with the Old Republicans in support of William Crawford, and he clearly indicated that he shared the Old Republican ideology. "Since my arrival at Washington I have become more and more confirmed in the belief that the best interests of this nation require the elevation of Mr. Crawford to the Executive Chair," he reported to a political friend in Orange County. Mangum's political associates recognized him as "the friend of Mr. Crawford."¹⁴ He supported Crawford because he thought he was "a sounder constitutionalist" than Clay and John C. Calhoun and because he believed Crawford's administration would be marked by "economy" and "rigid accountability."¹⁵ Mangum opposed, as did the Old Republicans, the Republican nationalism of Clay and Calhoun. He thought the "present fashionable ultra republicans" had gone beyond the Federalists. "The new school has taken the principles of the old Federalists but press their principles much further ... on the subjects of internal improvement etc., and especially in a latitudinous construction of the constitution generally." Calhoun, he believed, was unquestionably "at the head of the new school" and he was mortified to learn that a friend in Orange County was actively promoting Calhoun's election. Mangum had begun to associate with North Carolina's senior senator and arch Old Republican Nathaniel Macon: "Mr. Macon informs me that even [old Federalist] Rufus King told him that he was alarmed at the extent to which the new school were going, and that it had put him upon a reexamination of long established opinions."¹⁶ Opposed to the "splendid & profuse policy" of the Republican nationalists Clay and Calhoun, Mangum preferred Jackson to Calhoun. Mangum was already expressing opposition to the protective tariff as a "tribute" paid by the South to the manufacturing states of New England.[17] Thus, by early 1824, Mangum had joined the Old Republicans in Congress in adamant support for Crawford and was a decided proponent of the Old Republican ideology of economy, strict construction, opposition to both the tariff and the Republican nationalists of the "new school." The man from whom Mangum absorbed this philosophy was Macon, who perhaps more than any other man in Congress personified the Old Republican doctrines, and who had led the congressmen professing those doctrines since Thomas Jefferson's revolution of 1800.

Nathaniel Macon

In December 1800 the Age of Federalism was drawing to a close and the country was on the verge of political revolution. As a result of sweeping victories in elections that fall, Thomas Jefferson's Republicans were about to assume the reins of a government that the Federalists had wielded as their own for the first decade of the Union. When Federalists in the House of Representatives introduced a bill to fund the construction of a mausoleum in Washington City to house the mortal remains of the young republic's first president, General George Washington, Revolutionary War hero and now symbol of Federalism, Macon, then serving as a representative, opposed it. The House should take a stand against such "monument mania." "For what purpose was this great mass to be raised," he asked, "…Can stones show gratitude?" He saw no good purpose in it. If the nation wished to show its gratitude, it should do so by making the life of Washington a school book. "Our children then will learn and imitate his virtues. This will be rendering the highest tribute to his fame, by making it the instrument of enlightening the mind and improving the heart." If the representatives truly believed that by raising a magnificent monument to Washington they could give him everlasting fame or carry his name into any country it had not already reached, they were gravely mistaken. They should instead look to Egypt: "there they will behold precedents in profusion; men made gods, and statues and monuments and mausolea covering the whole face of the country; but where will they find the virtues or the talents of the men they were meant to commemorate?" Macon warned that the precedent established by the raising of the mausoleum would affect the future fate of the Republic: "If we decline raising a mausoleum to Washington, no man who succeeds him, can expect one reared to his memory. On the other hand, if we now raise one to Washington, every pretender to greatness will aim at the same distinction."[18] In Macon's view, republicans should not raise monuments to heroes. Their deeds should be their monuments.

From the Assembly of 1781, the Macon brothers, Nathaniel, John, and Harrison, from Warren County (bordering Halifax) were prominent members of Willie Jones' Anti-Federalist party. The Macons' father had been one of the original settlers of Warren County, and the family owned large plantations near the Roanoke River. Nathaniel Macon was from one of the chief families in Warren County. His father, Gideon Hunt Macon, migrated from Virginia to the area that would become Warren County, settling there about 1737 in the area south of the Roanoke River, acquiring 3,000 acres of land before 1760. He was one of the wealthiest men in the "Southside of Roanoke" region. Nathaniel, born on December 17, 1758, was one of eight children born to Gideon and Priscilla Macon at their plantation, "Macon Manor." When Gideon Macon died in 1762, Nathaniel inherited three young slaves, two boys and one girl, a tract of land on Shocco Creek, and five hundred acres lying on Hubquarter Creek about four miles south of the Roanoke River.[19] Macon preferred the remoter Hubquarter Creek lands to the far more valuable Shocco Creek tract. In 1779, at the age of twenty-one, Macon took up residence there and called the place "Buck Spring." From 1774 to 1776, Macon studied at the College of New Jersey (now Princeton University), but dispersal of the faculty and students due to the British invasion of New York in 1776 prevented his graduation. Macon joined a New Jersey militia company and served a tour on the Delaware before returning to North Carolina in 1777. He joined a Warren County militia regiment in early 1780 and served in the southern army until taking up a seat in the state senate as senator from Warren County in 1781.

Macon, not yet 23 years of age, joined the Assembly for its second session in June 1781. His service with a company of the Warren County militia which had fought at the Battle of Camden in August 1780 had prevented him from attending the first session of the 1781 General Assembly. In the 1782 legislature, Macon was again elected to the Senate and John and Harrison represented Warren in the House. All three Macon brothers appear to have imbibed Jones' pro–Confederation, state sovereignty politics.[20] From 1781 to 1786, Nathaniel Macon was a member of the state Senate and sat in that body with Jones in 1782 and 1784. In 1786, the same General Assembly that appointed Jones to the Philadelphia Convention delegation elected Nathaniel Macon to the Confederation Congress. Both declined.[21] John Macon was an Anti-Federalist at the Hillsborough Convention in 1788.[22] In 1790, Nathaniel Macon was a member of the North Carolina House of Commons and in 1791 he was elected to the United States House of Representatives and took his seat that October.

By 1796, though he was only thirty-seven years old, Nathaniel Macon had five years of experience in the House of Representatives that by seniority made him leader of the North Carolina delegation. In his speeches against the Federalist measures, Macon was a firm proponent of the Republican doctrines. Opposition to increased executive power figured in his objections to all the Federalist measures, as did economy of expenditure. Arguing that it showed "a want of due confidence" in the militia, he opposed the bill for a Provisional army. Macon, a veteran of the North Carolina militia, had no doubt "as to the bravery and power of the militia, whenever real danger approaches." He thought the bill's only object was "to get an armed force under the command of men appointed by the President of the United States, rather than under men appointed by the Executives of the States." Macon also cautioned that the Provisional Army would be expensive, and he wished to avoid "an unnecessary expense of a penny."

During the debates, Macon defined "the true distinction of party" in Congress as the difference between the Federalists' support for measures leading to "expense and patronage" and the Republicans' opposition to them. He also opposed provisions for coast fortifications, fitting out and manning the three incomplete frigates, and arming merchant ships.[23]

The Federalists' Alien and Sedition Acts gave rise to some of Macon's most heated opposition. He objected to the act concerning alien enemies because it gave the president "a very extraordinary power"; in the bill it seemed that "his proclamation, in all cases, was to be considered as law." Defense of the country, Macon argued, should be by "guns, powder, and men" not by such laws as the alien and sedition laws. He took the lead in opposition to the sedition law. His deep and strongly felt opposition to the law shows the extent to which he valued public opinion as a counter to Federalism. Early in the Sixth Congress in January 1800, Macon proposed a resolution for repealing the sedition law, and his arguments centered on republican transparency and abhorrence of secrecy: specifically, the necessity of free inquiry into the acts of government. Even though Macon was "well convinced" that the Constitution gave no power to Congress to enact such a law censoring criticism of the government, he explained why no such law should be enacted even if the power to do so existed. He asserted that discussions of government actions in the press or elsewhere were "perfectly consistent with the Constitution." And Macon asked the House, "What other means than the press could the people employ to disseminate their opinions, or of knowing the opinions of others?" The sedition law prevented freedom of inquiry, a freedom inseparable from the right of voting: "If elections are to be free, the people ought to have the liberty of freely investigating the character, conduct, and ability of each candidate to fill any place of public trust whatever." Moreover, Macon could find no reason for preventing a "free investigation" of the acts of government. The power to impeach implied the power to investigate the conduct of government officers, he insisted, "And if at any time, any officer liable to be impeached, should be guilty of malpractice in office, what so ready a way to make the discovery as a free and public investigation of his conduct?" In short, Macon argued that the law should be repealed because it impeded an open republican government.[24] He was thus in full accord with the Principles of '98; and as an ardent Republican from a solidly Republican state he was a natural leader of the Republicans in the House after they gained the majority in the election of 1800.

In addition to governing by the tenets of Republicanism, Macon wanted the political revolution of 1800 to change the style of government. The style, as well as the actions, of a Republican government should reflect the principles of Republicanism—austere, economical, and republican in spirit. Soon after Jefferson took office, Macon advised him of the changes that he believed "the people expect[ed]." Macon advised the new Republican president

> that the people expect, That Levees [formal presidential receptions] will be done way—That the communications to the next Congress will be by letter not a speech—That we have too many ministers in Europe—That some of the Collectors, perhaps all, had better receive a fixed salary, than commissions—That the army might safely be reduced—That the navy might also be reduced—That the Agents to the War & Navy might be reduced—In fact that the system of economy is to be adopted and pursued with energy.

Macon gave a further preview of Republican intentions in an early 1802 letter to a friend in which he explained "what may be expected" of the Republican government. Prime on the list was a reduction of federal power over the states, followed by government economy. The hated Judiciary Act and the internal taxes were to be repealed, the national debt was to be paid down as fast as possible, the army was to be reduced, and expenditures on the navy would be trimmed. Yet, revealing Macon's concern that the young Republic gain international respect, he wanted the navy to remain strong enough to protect the country's trading vessels from the "Tripolitans."[25] This more austere and strictly republican style of government reflected all the main Republican tenets: opposition to presidential aggrandizement; executive deference to Congress; government economy; concern for corruption; and reliance on the militia for the country's defense.

Republican Divisions

"I shall ... by the establishment of republican principles in substance and form ... sink federalism into an abyss from which there shall be no resurrection for it," declared Thomas

Jefferson to Levi Lincoln in 1802.[26] As Macon had desired, Jefferson set out to administer the federal government by Republican principles; he hoped that this would discredit Federalism and attach the people to Republicanism. By the time Mangum arrived in Congress in the 1820s Jefferson had achieved his goal—Federalism was destroyed as a national political force. But, like the young Mangum, the old prophets of the doctrines of 1800 had, by the second decade of Republican ascendancy, become dissatisfied with the philosophy of the new Republican leaders. The ideological divide created by this division had a fundamental impact on Mangum's political views and thus deserves a close examination.

Thomas Jefferson by Thomas Sully (1783–1872), oil on canvas, 1856 (U.S. Senate).

The victory over the Federalists in the election of 1800 required the Jeffersonian Republicans to put their opposition political ideology—the "Principles of '98"—into practice as they governed the nation. From 1801 to the War of 1812, they essentially attempted to govern the country with political principles born of an opposition to Federalism—principles suited to opposition but untested in governance. As the strains of governance increased, adhering to pure Republican principles became increasingly difficult.[27]

When governing consisted of instituting reform, the Republicans were largely successful in administering the county by party principles. This was the task of Jefferson's first term. The Republicans repealed the Federalists' expansion of the federal judiciary (the Judiciary Act of 1801), economized government expenditures, repealed the internal taxes, removed some of the worst Federalist appointees, and provided new territory for national expansion through the bloodless acquisition of the Louisiana Territory. Looking back, Macon always considered Jefferson's first term as the ideal of Republican government, when the nation was governed by Republican principles.[28]

The extended foreign policy crisis of Jefferson's second term that eventually led to a second war with Great Britain occasioned ideological and rhetorical tension over how the Republican principles should be translated into policies and styles of governance. Once the Republicans were in power and could no longer focus (primarily) on righting the wrongs of Federalism, as they had during Jefferson's first term, party unity became severely strained. The disagreements arose through the Republicans' effort to govern the country.[29] The Republicans' opposition ideology made governing strictly by Republican principles difficult for the Republican government—particularly for Jefferson and the administration as they dealt with foreign policy crises.

"I had always expected that when the republicans should have put down all things under their feet, they would schismatize [sic] among themselves. I always expected, too, that whatever names the parties might bear, the real division would be into moderate & ardent republicanism." Jefferson thus explained to Thomas Cooper in 1807 that he had anticipated the schism that divided the Republicans in the last years of his administration.[30] The believers in "ardent republicanism" were Macon and like-minded doctrinaire Southern Republicans who came to view themselves as "old" Republicans—defenders of the true Republican creed against the corrupting influence of newly-converted northerners and Republican pragmatists. The man who in the 1820s sought to pass his political creed to the young congressman Willie Mangum was the chief "old" Republican in 1807—Nathaniel Macon.

The divisions that emerged between Republicans during Jefferson's administration largely resulted from the tension between their ideology and the requirements of governance. The greatest issue exposed in the ideological divisions among the Republicans and the one that created the deepest divide was the question of the proper role of executive power in a republican government.

In their writings during their political struggles with the Federalists in the late 1790s, the Jeffersonian Republicans called for a clear separation of executive and legislative powers, which they believed the Federalists' Alien and Sedition Acts of 1798 had mixed. James Madison, the chief Republican essayist of the period, advocated a definite separation of powers: "It has become an axiom in the science of government, that a separation of the legislative, executive and judicial departments, is necessary to the preservation of liberty," he wrote. The Republicans also wanted greater restraints on executive power. Believing that the Alien Act had given far too much power to President John Adams, Jefferson had called in his Kentucky Resolutions for "limited Constitutions to bind down those whom we are obliged to trust with power." Madison boldly declared that Congress had acted unconstitutionally because in the Alien Act "they leave every thing to the President. His will is the law." He also expanded the opposition to executive power to include opposition to expansion of the executive's "patronage" and "prerogative."[31] In these documents, Madison and Jefferson clearly called for limited executive powers, but the pressures of governing modified this pure Republican outlook.

The greatest measure of Jefferson's first term was the Louisiana Purchase. Scholars generally agree that the acquisition of Louisiana was the most significant achievement of Jefferson's presidency.[32] The acquisition of Louisiana was unique among Jefferson's foreign policy measures because it produced no divisions in the party. Yet the Louisiana Purchase tested the ability of the administration to govern within the constraints of its ideology. All Republicans united to support enthusiastically the treaty. But in doing so they were unified in their divergence from their doctrines.

Many aspects of the Louisiana Purchase conflicted with Republican doctrine. Acquiring the territory by executive action alone conflicted with the Republican principles of strict construction and limited government. For a party dedicated to limiting executive power, the Republican Congress was very deferential to the president in regard to Louisiana. Congress, in fact, never explicitly authorized the acquisition of the territory; instead, when the dispute with Spain over rights of navigation on the Mississippi arose, the Republican Congress deferred to "the vigilance and wisdom of the Executive."[33] The Constitution did not explicitly authorize either the executive or Congress to acquire territory, and Jefferson himself had strict constructionist concerns about the incorporation of new lands into the United States. The Republicans in Congress showed no constitutional qualms and the Republican-controlled Senate ratified the treaty just three days after it arrived.[34]

Despite Jefferson's constitutional reservations, the acquisition of Louisiana did accord with his and Madison's view of a vigorous national executive in foreign affairs.[35] Additionally, Jefferson thought that the president must at times use his prerogative, even to the point of exceeding constitutional powers. This was his solution to the ideological dilemma of the Louisiana Purchase, although one he professed only privately and only after having left office. In an 1810 letter to John B. Colvin, which he asked Colvin to keep private, Jefferson set out his views on executive prerogative, which presumably had guided his actions while in office. He believed executive officers "of high trust," when acting in the high national interest could and sometimes must "assume authorities beyond the law." "A strict observance of the written laws is doubtless *one* of the high duties of a good citizen, but it is not *the highest*," he explained to Colvin, "The laws of necessity, of self-preservation, of saving our country when in danger, are of higher obligation." Executive officials acting in such cases, and only such cases, could risk themselves by "transcending the law" when the public advantage offered was "immense." The executive would then trust to Congress for "their justice for the transgression of the law."[36]

The letter confirms Jefferson's view of an active executive, but he undoubtedly wished Colvin to keep the letter private because of the conflict between principle and practice that it exposed. This then was Jefferson's final resolution to the justification for his extra-constitutional action in the Louisiana Purchase: a doctrine for the president's use of extraordinary and extra-constitutional powers: "transcending the law" when the public advantage offered was "immense." Yet Jefferson's conception still preserved deference to Congress. The president would trust to Congress for "their justice for the transgression of the law." Congress would ultimately judge the action of the Executive.

The purchase also conflicted with some Republicans' ideas of governmental economy. After a short negotiation with Napoleon's finance minister, James Monroe and Robert Livingston, respectively minister extraordinary and minister to France, were able to purchase the entire French-Spanish territory of Louisiana for $15 million. Jefferson, though, had been willing to pay much more simply to secure New Orleans, the original object of the negotiation. Jefferson and Madison authorized their representatives in France to pay up to $10 million for New Orleans and the territory to the east.[37] Although the Republicans had fought Federalist appropriations for the quasi-war with France, they were willing to spend huge sums for the acquisition of New Orleans and the territory to the east that controlled the mouth of the Mississippi River.

Macon found assent to and even admiration of the Louisiana Purchase in North Carolina. He told Jefferson: "The acquisition of Louisiana has given general satisfaction.... But if [the purchase] is within the compass of the present revenue, the purchase when the terms are known will be more admired than even now."[38] He was more concerned with economy than with acquisition of the Louisiana territory by executive action. The state legislature praised the Louisiana Purchase and associated it with the "republicanism of the General Government."[39] The Purchase was seen as a Republican measure that would further the "Republican cause." Such willingness to set aside key tenets of their ideology did not mean the Republicans were not serious about their ideology—later events would show that at least some among them were very committed to it. Rather, as the North Carolina legislature recognized, it shows that acquiring new territory was now added to the Republican doctrines. And with some Republicans, especially those of the southern states, commitment to that doctrine of expansion had the potential to displace other tenets of their ideology.

Open division in the Republican party began shortly before the start of Jefferson's second term. In January 1805, John Randolph of Charlotte County, Virginia, Republican ally of Macon in the House of Representatives, declared on the floor of the House his effective opposition to Jefferson over an administration-sponsored compromise bill intended to settle the complicated Yazoo land claims. Randolph claimed that "the spirit of *Federalism*" had entered the administration in its efforts to pass the bill. The use of government to gain privilege for the few against the interests of the many was to be expected from Federalists, Randolph explained, "[b]ut when I see associated with them in firm compact, others who once rallied under the standard of opposite principles, I am filled with apprehension and concern."[40]

But foreign policy, not domestic policies, became the chief point of contention between the administration and Randolph. Jefferson's second term was to witness no such Republican unity as earlier existed with the Louisiana Purchase. In the period 1804 to 1812, the war in Europe between Great Britain and Napoleon's France that had temporarily halted in Jefferson's first term flared into activity again. The renewal of the war forced Jefferson and Madison to confront issues of foreign policy that they had largely been able to avoid in the first term. Also, the Louisiana Purchase in 1803 involved the government in disputes with Spain over the borders of the territory. The second term was essentially one continuous foreign policy crisis. The ensuing debate over national defense resulted in ideological tensions. The need for defense measures placed strain on Republican ideology and forced Republicans to examine the compatibility of professed principles with the need to defend the Republic. The difficulties of governing through an opposition ideology were exposed.

As a cousin of the president, Randolph was a natural leader of the Republican cause in the House. With proven rhetorical skills, he had collaborated with Macon and Gallatin as the chief defenders of Republicanism against the Federalist program. Gallatin also considered Randolph a possible successor to Jefferson and Madison.[41] He was a personal friend of Macon, the Speaker of the House, and the two shared a commitment to ardent Republicanism. He became the floor leader in the House. Macon appointed Randolph to chair the Ways and Means committee, the most powerful committee in the House of Representatives. And it was John Randolph who did more than any other to exacerbate the ideological divisions among Republicans.

The first crisis of the second term involved a dispute with Spain over the territory of West Florida. The West Florida crisis grew out of the same tensions as the earlier dispute with Spain over Louisiana and the Mississippi, with the added dimension that many settlers in the new southern territories of Alabama, threatened by Indian raids from Florida, accused the Spanish of sheltering tribes that included runaway slaves. Essentially, the furor grew from an effort by the American government to impose its will in its new territory and remove the threat of Spain from the region. Tempers between Great Britain, at war with Napoleon's French Empire, and the United States had been fraying over neutral rights on the high seas since the resumption of the European war in 1805.

The Florida crisis tested Jefferson's adherence to the principle of a limited executive power, but he was careful to maintain the party principle of separation of executive and legislative power.[42] Jefferson was sensitive about how far to go in recommending measures to Congress. In an 1805 letter to Madison, Jefferson set down seven resolutions for Madison's "consideration and correction" that he intended to send to Congress in conjunction with his December annual message. Jefferson intended the last three resolutions to give him extraordinary powers to deal with the Spanish crisis. They vested the president with the execution of the resolutions, including the seizure of Spanish outposts; authorized him to use any money in the treasury "not otherwise appropriated"; and authorized him to employ armed vessels to combat privateers preying on American trading ships.[43] But Jefferson did not present the resolutions to Congress because, as the editor of his correspondence with Madison notes, he feared that such specific recommendations might encroach on the legislature's prerogative.[44]

This incident indicates the fine line that Jefferson's idea of an active executive forced him to walk between obtaining his preferred policy and maintaining the clear separation of powers demanded by Republican principles.[45] Nevertheless, Jefferson attempted to gather support for his preferred measures in Congress, and he often conveyed proposals and even draft legislation to the friends of the administration in Congress, though he always insisted that the Congressmen should exercise independent judgment.[46] In noting this use of "the president's agents" in Congress, David Mayer points out that Jefferson preferred to mobilize support for his policies in Congress through "informal, extra-constitutional tools."[47]

The Embargo Act was the most ambitious measure undertaken by the Republican administration. While reflecting it also conflicted with Republican ideology. The European war threatened United States commerce as the warring European powers—Great Britain and France—sought to block trade with their opponents. They both began to seize neutral shipping, much of it owned by U.S. merchants. The act's restrictions thus placed the administration in a confrontation with the governments of both France and Britain in an effort to securing American neutral rights on the seas. After attempts at non-importation failed, Jefferson and Madison with the support of the Republican majority in the Congress enacted the embargo, the total cessation of U.S. overseas trade, in hopes of forcing the European powers to relent for want of the U.S. trade products. Using trade as a weapon of foreign policy dated back to the Revolution and remained a preferred Republican foreign policy measure. Yet, while the embargo adhered to Republican principles about preserving peace and avoiding war, it deviated from Republican principles about federal power versus state sovereignty because of the central government's need to enforce the restrictions on the states.[48]

The embargo shows the lengths to which the Republicans were prepared to go to avoid war and its negative impact on Republicanism while still trying to secure America's neutral rights. Unlike the other divisions, the embargo found Macon and most of the conservatives on the side of the administration. The embargo provides a window into Macon's view of federal power and the limits of state sovereignty. Additionally, during this period of tension with Britain and France, an unprovoked attack on a U.S. warship tested Republican ideas about the justifications for war and the risks it posed to Republicanism. Macon was particularly concerned with the threat to Republicanism. When in June of 1807 the British frigate *Leopard* attacked and disabled the American frigate *Chesapeake* in waters off Virginia and impressed members of her crew into the British navy, the government had to decide on a response.

The reaction of Congress to the *Chesapeake* affair raised the issue of whether the militia or regulars were best able to defend the country. Republican doctrine favored reliance on the militia instead of standing peacetime armies. The militia, because it represented the people's right of self-defense and thus was an ultimate defense against centralized power, was in many respects the institutional embodiment of Republican principles. As such, it was at the forefront of Republican conceptions on the proper way to wage war. As we have seen, the Republicans had praised the militia in the battle over the Federalist measures in the late 1790s. In Republican eyes, the militia had two advantages over the standing army: it cost the government nothing in time of peace except the cost of storing arms, and the militia could only be used for defensive warfare.

In response to the attack on the *Chesapeake*, John Randolph proposed to arm the whole militia. His reaction demonstrates the high place the militia held in the Republican ideology. A measure so in accordance with Republican principles was bound to find favor with every faction of the Republican party. Virginian John Taylor of Caroline commented that the resolution was "the most effectual, principled, and grand measure, which has been introduced since the government has been in operation."[49] Any Republican who voted against such a measure would have essentially been declaring that he no longer believed in the Principles of '98. As Risjord writes of the measure, "No Republican could afford to vote against it."[50]

As part of its response to the Chesapeake affair, the administration, in February 1808, sent a bill to increase the standing army with an "Additional Army" to the House. Risjord calls this measure a "departure from party principles."[51] In 1799 Jefferson had expressed concern over the size of the army that the Federalists contemplated raising. Now, his own administration was asking for an increase in the size of the regular army the very measure the Republicans had campaigned against in 1800 when the Federalists increased the size of the army, and during a similar situation: a looming war. Significantly though, and in accord with their conceptions discussed above, the administration presented the increase as being a nucleus for the militia.

Though Macon recognized the necessity of a regular army in time of war, he left no doubt he preferred militia to defend the country; he believed militia was the only force authorized by the Constitution for national defense against invasions. The North Carolina delegation had strongly defended the militia in the debates over the Federalist war measures. During the debate over the Federalists' "Provisional Army," Macon upheld Republicans' confidence in the militia, citing the Revolutionary War battles of Cowpens and King's Mountain as showing the past effectiveness of the militia. Macon did not doubt "the bravery and power of the militia, whenever real danger approaches," and argued that the militia could repel any invasion. He preferred it as the country's primary means of defense, arguing that the militia was equal to all purposes specified for its use in the Constitution: to counter invasion and insurrection and to enforce the laws.[52] During the congressional debates over the response to the Chesapeake affair, Macon urged measures to provide arms and equipment to state militias.[53] Despite his staunch defense of the militia, Macon did realize that in time of war some regular troops might have to be raised for defense. When the administration proposed to raise 6,000 additional men for the "Additional Army" in response to the *Chesapeake* affair, Macon supported the measure. He denied charges by more doctrinaire Republicans that the current situation was equivalent to 1798; his positive vote had been, he insisted, "not produced by a departure from principle ... but by an entire change in the state of our foreign affairs then and now." Macon viewed the 6,000 men as a defensive force against raids by the British. Arguing that "our situation is a critical one," Macon declared that the 6,000 soldiers were too few for offensive war but would be enough to "render great service about the cities" as a rallying point if attacked.[54] Macon thus associated reliance on militia with Republican principles and republican government.

Macon's reaction to the *Chesapeake* affair reveals much about his conception of the relation of war and republican government. It also shows his strong belief that relying on militia was best for a republican government. Though he consistently opposed navy appropriations for new ships, since he believed the navy more a threat to liberty than a benefit and decried the establishment of a Navy Department as an unnecessary expense, Macon worried about violations of the United States' neutral rights at sea and in Congress had closely monitored the issue. His desire to preserve neutral rights was closely linked to his desire to avoid war. In 1804 Macon offered Jefferson advice on the importance of maintaining neutrality. Though the Carolina congressman believed the conduct of the warring European nations to U.S. merchant vessels had not been "so satisfactory," it did not justify war. "The U.S. will I hope for ever be neutral," he declared. Injuries to merchant vessels were "trifling" compared to "the advantage of the neutral situation."[55]

Somewhat surprisingly for someone who so little valued a navy, Macon reacted strongly to the *Chesapeake* affair. His response reflected the strong sentiments of his constituents in North Carolina and also showed his insistence that the new republic be taken seriously by the European powers. In July and August of 1807, Macon insisted to Gallatin that peace was always the best policy for the United States. Yet when the British ships refused to leave United States waters after receiving Jefferson's proclamation and some British crewmen were captured by Virginia light horse troops, Macon told Gallatin that "it now seems to me that we may be considered at war with Great Britain." Macon preferred "strong measures" if war was unavoidable. "If war must be, we ought to prosecute it with the same zeal that we have endeavored to preserve peace, and by great exertions convince the enemy, that it is not from fear or cowardice that we dread it." Macon did not believe in half measures. Yet he still preferred a negotiated settlement to war. "Peace is everything to us especially in this part of the Union." His greatest concern in the crisis was that the administration "get justice done." "But," he continued "peace, if we can have it, is always best for us, and if the Executive can get justice done and preserve it, that Executive will deserve the thanks of every democrat in the Union." A satisfactory end to the crisis would add as much to Jefferson's reputation as the Purchase of Louisiana.[56]

Still Macon saw dangers in a war, but not from the British. Republicanism would be imperiled if the country went to war. He suspected that the Federalists would again use the threat of war to further the interests of their party. And any willingness by the Federalists to serve in the army and navy was part of that conspiracy, "It affords them the best opportunity to carry on their wicked projects, and they will never cease to imagine evil while they have the least hope to execute their plans." Yet Macon reminded Gallatin that a Republican administration should resist using the war spirit generated by the crisis to build up its own importance among the people. Macon wanted no addresses and resolutions; he thought such measures were Federalist means of building support for the government; Republicans had no need of them:

> The administration is sufficiently popular and does not want the aid of addresses, nor town resolutions; These things were done in federal days, and I had vainly hoped that as Congress and the President had quit the federal practice of delivering a speech & answering that the people would also have quit the federal practice of Resolutions and addresses—they are not binding, and therefore serve only for a few men to make a noise about.[57]

Macon was concerned that the crisis would impel the return of Federalism. Deeds, not addresses, would maintain Republicanism. In a letter to friend and fellow Republican conservative

Joseph Nicholson, Macon explained that though some Federalists might use the war crisis to revive their old program of federal consolidation he was prepared to vote money to raise troops to protect "some defenceless places." "The attack on the Chesapeake was war on the part of Great Britain," he insisted, and he argued that since Congress had authorized the president to make his Proclamation, Congress had to willingly take measures to enable him to enforce it.[58] Still *Congress* must be the branch in the lead. In this view Congress makes policy; the president is an agent. Macon thus sought to avoid war if at all possible because of its negative impact on Republicanism. Yet if the administration could not obtain "justice" by any other course than war, then he wanted the government to prosecute it aggressively—a position that resembled Jefferson's.

Notwithstanding Macon's opinion that only Federalists needed addresses and town resolutions, meetings were held in towns across North Carolina to protest the British actions and declare support for Jefferson's course. On July 23, after declaring their approval of Jefferson's Proclamation, the officers and soldiers of the Fayetteville Independent Light Infantry Company volunteered their services. They declared that, although they appreciated the blessings of peace, they were "ever ready to avenge an insult offered to their country." On the same day the citizens of Hertford County called the attack by the *Leopard* on the frigate *Chesapeake* "lawless and unprecedented" and expressed their "most entire confidence" in the "wisdom and patriotism of the Executive of the United States." On August 28, the militia officers and citizens of Caswell County declared the attack "unjustifiable," "lawless," "disgraceful," and a "wanton outrage." They proclaimed their approval of Jefferson's conduct and his Proclamation, and pledged their support for the administration. When the General Assembly met in December, it overwhelmingly passed, over sharp Federalist objections, a resolution approving the course of the administration in the crisis, praising Jefferson's character, lauding his administration of the government since 1801, and requesting him to be a candidate for a third term. Blake Baker of the Warren Junto argued in favor of the address. Jefferson responded to the General Assembly's address by thanking them for their praise, but declaring it his duty in the interests of representative government to uphold the precedent set by Washington and retire from the presidency after his second term.[59]

Macon supported the embargo even though it granted great powers to the federal government to coerce the states. Strongly backing the embargo as a proper response to the attack on the *Chesapeake*, Macon viewed it as far preferable to war. Although he did not vote on the measure because he was absent from Washington in December 1807 when the Embargo Act was passed, Macon supported its passage.[60] Part of his support stemmed from the belief that it operated equally on all sections. When in March 1806 a bill on non-importation of goods from Britain was debated as a response to British violations of American neutral rights, Macon opposed it as a sectional measure; it would be "unjust and partial in its operation." (He also expressed his belief in the importance of the Union; he thought it was wrong to introduce expressions of disunion.)

The embargo divided Republicans, yet it united the administration with the conservatives. Republicans in general were thus pleased with Jefferson's response to West Florida and his policies in defense of neutral rights. Because his plans for army organization still relied on the militia, they pleased most Republicans. Yet this general satisfaction among Republicans with the administration's course did not extend to John Randolph and his Quids. The Quids, so named by Randolph, were a group of congressmen who consistently followed Randolph's leadership in the House.⁶¹ They opposed Jefferson on all policies and measures. They believed that Jefferson had led the Republicans astray and only opposition could restore true Republicanism. As a matter of course, they thus opposed any policy originating in the administration. The larger group of Republican conservatives, who might be called independents, included Macon. While Macon opposed the administration when he believed it acted against Republican principles, he was not "in opposition" as were the Quids—he supported the administration policy when it seemed wise and Republican.⁶² As Norman Risjord has noted, the real division that opened by the end of the decade was between conservative Republicans (mostly from the South), which definitely included Macon, and the administration Republicans. By the end of the decade the Southern conservatives would be calling themselves "old Republicans."⁶³

The West Florida crisis and the attack on the *Chesapeake* gave Randolph an occasion to question Jefferson's adherence to Republican principles. Although Macon and the other Republican conservatives outside the small group of Quids did not always follow Randolph in his attacks or utilize his inflammatory language, Randolph's critiques represented their concerns about Republicanism—Randolph was, of course, bidding for their support and he appealed to their ardent Republicanism to enlist their support in his attacks on the administration. With his critique of the administration's involvement in the Yazoo land claims, Randolph chose the issue of corruption for his first challenge to the administration. For his next attack, Randolph likewise used issues important to the Republican ideology: those of republican openness in government and executive influence on the legislative branch. Randolph complained about presidential manipulation of Congress, specifically Jefferson's use of agents in Congress to guide legislation in response to the diplomatic and territorial dispute with Spain over West Florida. In contrast with Jefferson's concept of the role of the president, Randolph believed that *any* executive influence in Congress was corrupting. He combined the issues of republican openness and opposition to executive influence in Congress in his bitter denunciations of the administration's course on West Florida.

Randolph argued that the administration did not openly communicate its preferred policies. In his 1805 annual message to Congress Jefferson had explained his military orders for defense of the Florida frontier and recommended various war preparations. Three days later, in a secret, special message to Congress, Jefferson announced, in marked contrast with the militaristic tone of his public message, that, although a show of force on the border was important for the "spirit and honor of the country" and the protection of American citizens, "war is not necessary—it is not probable it will follow." Jefferson also notified the legislators of France's willingness to "effect a settlement" of the differences between the United States and Spain, if Congress would provide "the command of means" the settlement required."⁶⁴ In speeches and a letter to the Richmond *Enquirer* signed "Decius," Randolph decried this secretive approach as "highly disingenuous," and declared it un-republican. Such a proposal represented "a base prostration of the national character." His larger complaint was that Jefferson did not openly ask Congress for the money. In contrast with the president's "confident and dignified" public message, the secret message required Congress to "privily ... take upon itself all the odium of shrinking from the national honor and the national defense" by voting the money to pay France. Complaining about "this double set of opinions and principles," Randolph insisted that such "wisdom and cunning" was "utterly incompatible in the conduct of great affairs."⁶⁵

Randolph's primary concern lay not so much with the content of the two messages or even with the policy pursued by the administration as with republican openness. The essence of his reaction was revulsion over the way he saw the administration preceding in the matter: public preparations for war and secret requests for what amounted to a bribe to be paid to France to facilitate the Spanish negotiations. Randolph believed that the administration was covering its reputation by keeping the request for France secret and out of the published journals. It is not clear why Jefferson used the dual-message approach unless he feared exactly the charges Randolph was making. Placing all of his communications on the negotiations with Spain in a separate and secret special message was a procedure that Jefferson had never used or ever attempted again.[66] Was his resort to it in 1805 an attempt to avoid charges of "corruption" while pursuing a policy of avoiding war, which would be hazardous to all their principles?

Randolph combined his criticism of Jefferson's secret, special message to Congress with attacks on the president's unofficial advisors and on the presidential influence that seemed to hold sway in Congress, concerns that he knew Macon and the other Republican conservatives shared. In terms of Republican divisions, this critique of the administration by the Quid opposition was most important for subsequent events. In a speech condemning the administration's West Florida policy, Randolph attacked a fellow representative for implying that the House should act on suggestions of the president: "A member in his place told you that the course recommended by a particular individual was consonant with the secret wishes of the Executive. I did then reprehend that language, as the most unconstitutional and reprehensible ever uttered on this floor." He complained about "this double dealing, the sending one Message for the journals and newspapers, and another in whispers to this House."[67] Randolph argued that the president was manipulating Congress through unofficial advisors and was using his friends in Congress as his agents.

Randolph also used the administration's efforts to formulate an effective policy defending neutral rights as an occasion to attack Jefferson for failing to adhere to the Principles of '98. Randolph criticized the bill introduced for the administration by Nicholson, like Macon an independent, for non-importation of specific manufactured goods from Britain.[68] Though Randolph's chief reason for opposing the Nicholson non-importation bill was most likely simply because it was an administration bill, he framed his objections in terms of the bill's incompatibility with Republican principles. The bill, he argued might lead to an offensive war, specifically a naval war. Randolph objected to war with Britain because it was bound to be such a naval war, and he stated that the Constitution's language was "inconsistent with offensive war." Randolph even insisted that it was incompatible with the purpose of government and, in an allusion to the danger Republicans had traditionally seen in executive power, large navies, and standing armies, he declared a foreign war endangered constitutional liberty.[69] In short, Randolph believed that the administration's policies and methods of government no longer accorded with Republican principles by 1806. He insisted that the Republicans in Congress hold the administration accountable and criticized them for not measuring Jefferson with the same principles they had used to judge Adams: "Do gentlemen flinch from this, and pretend to be republicans?"[70] Most Republicans, conservative and otherwise, did not agree.

The administration's 1808 proposal to raise an additional 6,000-man army, part of a response to the British attack on the *Chesapeake*, gave Randolph and his Quid allies another chance to use Republican ideology against Jefferson, but Macon and the conservatives did not follow them. While wishing to keep the army small, the administration also recognized the value of the regular army. The Quids and many other Republicans preferred only the militia. Randolph claimed he held to his view of 1798, the "doctrine ... that, in times of danger, reliance should be had on the militia."[71] Randolph admonished his colleagues in the House to remember "that a standing army is the death of which all Republics have died." Only in the case of actual hostilities and actual invasion of the territory of the United States would Randolph be willing to vote for raising an army of regulars.[72] In the Quid view, opposition to a standing army was thus a matter of principle and synonymous with identity as a Republican. Yet, even many of the conservative Republicans disagreed with a doctrinaire reliance on militia alone and agreed with Macon that something more substantial than arming the militia needed to be done. Thus they supported raising the 6,000 additional regular troops.[73] Forced to make a choice between the Quid's rigid adherence to principle and the need to defend the Republic, Macon and the other conservatives sided with the administration and chose a strong defense.

As noted above, Macon and the conservatives also adamantly defended the administration's most divisive measure, the Embargo Act. The Quids seemed to decry the embargo out of sheer opposition to the administration rather than defense of Republican principles. Randolph had supported an embargo policy since 1806, but when the administration proposed it he opposed the policy.[74] Macon, as in the case of the Additional Army, broke with Randolph's Quids over the embargo. The embargo was almost a measure of the conservative/independent Republicans.

Nevertheless, John Randolph's critique of the administration's methods of government shows that two different conceptions of executive-legislative relations existed by 1806. Randolph believed that Jefferson's influence in Congress and methods of private councils were un-republican; moreover, he did not find diplomatic openness occurring in the administration's actions on Florida and Spain. The controversy also reveals the Republican sensitivity about adherence to Republican principles. Both factions believed they were remaining loyal to the principles but two conceptions about proper policy are evident. Randolph opposed all the administration's actions; Macon, like the larger group of conservatives, did not so strongly oppose the administration as a matter of course, but they shared Randolph's concern about pure Republicanism.

Macon's loyalty to Randolph even as Randolph so adamantly opposed the administration's measures resulted in Macon's loss of the leadership of the House. Randolph's inflexible opposition to Jefferson and Madison drove a wedge between Macon and Jefferson, and that division was the beginning of the Old Republicans as a separate group of Republicans in Congress.

In 1806 Jefferson tried to retain Macon's support. Jefferson complained that "some enemy, whom we know not" was "sowing tares" between the two men. Jefferson sought a meeting with the Speaker. "Between you & myself nothing but opportunities of explanation can be necessary to defeat these endeavors. At least on my part, my confidence in you is so unqualified that nothing further is necessary for my satisfaction. I must therefore ask a conversation with you."[75] The sower of tares, of course, was Randolph. Randolph's friendship with the Speaker was one of the greatest supports of his opposition—Macon had consistently appointed him to the chairmanship of the Committee on Ways and Means, the House's most powerful committee. With that chairmanship Randolph was well placed to obstruct Jefferson's measures. Jefferson valued Macon as a leader in the House for the administration, but he wanted to detach Macon from Randolph. His efforts proved futile. Macon refused to separate from his friend, and Macon, though in no way as obstinately opposed to Jefferson as Randolph, favored pure Republicanism too greatly to ever renounce his independent stance.

During the Ninth Congress (1806–1807), Macon placed his loyalty to Randolph above his loyalty to Jefferson. Despite Randolph's irreconcilable opposition to the administration and the general recognition among Republicans that he would not support the administration, Macon again placed him at the head of Ways and Means. Macon's determination that Randolph head the committee defined his independence: he would not bend to Jefferson's will on the appointment. But it also showed his stubborn loyalty to his friend. At the beginning of the second session, December 1806, Macon was challenged as Speaker out of fear that he would again appoint Randolph to Ways and Means. Macon was reelected Speaker but only after three ballots.[76] Macon's loyalty to Randolph was so great that the latter's opponents moved to strip the committee appointing power from the Speaker. The motion failed by 2 votes. Even Willis Alston of the Warren Junto opposed Randolph as chairman.[77] Then, when the House was organized, Randolph's enemies took advantage of his absence and Macon's obsessive adherence to the rules of the House to block Randolph's appointment. The appointments were called for on the day when Randolph was late arriving in the House; by rule no absent member could be appointed. Anguished that he could not appoint Randolph to the committee, Macon described himself as in a "most anxious state of mind" over the decision that placed him in an "awkward and disagreeable situation." Macon told Nicholson that he could not act against the rules of the House. The rules "compelled" him to leave Randolph off though it may have "hurt the feelings of [one] I love as well as my own." Without Randolph as chairman of Ways and Means, his position as Speaker was "disagreeable." But, he explained to Nicholson, "such was my sense of duty that I could not act otherwise."[78]

Macon appointed conservative Joseph Clay of Pennsylvania in Randolph's stead. Macon chose Clay from a sense of principled adherence to the rules of the House, not loyalty to the administration or the Republican majority. Supported by his fellow conservatives and Randolph's Quids, Macon soon maneuvered to put Randolph back in charge of Ways and Means and thus thwart the designs of the Republican majority. Macon had appointed Quids and conservatives to the committee. James Garnett, Quid from Virginia, resigned from the committee and Macon appointed Randolph. Clay then declined the chairmanship, and the committee elected Randolph chairman.[79]

When Macon made it clear that Randolph would chair Ways and Means as long as he was Speaker, Macon had burned his bridges. Jefferson concluded that nothing could be done until Randolph was removed and that also meant Macon had to go as Speaker. Though he remained the choice of the Republican conservatives, Macon never again was elected to the position. At the end of the Ninth Congress, Macon was so disheartened by the animosity between Randolph and the Republican majority that he considered resigning.[80] The administration gave up hope of opposing Randolph in the Ninth Congress, though. Jefferson did not mention relations with England or war preparations against Spain in his 1806 annual message, and the Republicans approved Randolph's bill suspending the Non-Importation Act by a vote of 101–5. Macon approved of the vote, writing to Nicholson: "The doings here will hereby convince every candid man in the world that the Republicans of the *old school* were not wrong last winter."[81]

Jefferson identified Randolph as the primary obstacle to his policy. Randolph's rhetorical skills and chairmanship of Ways and Means allowed him to dominate the House, despite his Quid opposition. Except for "the little band of schismatics," all the Republicans in the House were well disposed, Jefferson wrote, "But there is no one whose talents & standing, taken together, have weight enough to give him the lead. The consequence is, that there is no one who will undertake to do the public business, and it remains undone.... A rallying point is all that is wanting."[82] After Macon's maneuvering to place Randolph on Ways and Means, Jefferson also certainly realized that Randolph's hold could not be broken until Macon was replaced as Speaker. Macon would not receive a majority vote in the House in the Tenth Congress.

Randolph's Quid opposition forced Macon to choose between loyalty to the "Republican cause" and loyalty to a friend. Too devoted to Randolph to remain loyal to Jefferson, he chose Randolph. He placed a Quid, *the* arch–Quid, opposed to Jefferson and the policy of the Republican administration at the head of the most important committee in the House, thus ensuring Republican divisions. Macon then lamented the divisions as if he had nothing to do with them. Macon showed that he would oppose the administration on appointments. Macon's removal from the leadership was of his own making, but, because it was viewed negatively by his friends and allies, it nevertheless became a major factor in the separation of the Old Republicans.

Despite his loyalty to Randolph, Macon opposed him on an important policy issue— the Embargo Act—that involved choices between war and peace. Macon supported the administration's efforts to continue the embargo. Once there was no threat of Macon being able to reappoint Randolph to Ways and Means, Madison and Jefferson welcomed Macon's cooperation. In March 1808, Macon informed a correspondent that his and the president's "sentiments have been much more in unison than two years ago."[83] Macon wanted Randolph to join him in support of the embargo but Randolph refused to back an administration measure. "It grieves me to the heart, to be compelled from a sense of right & duty to oppose him,"[84] Macon lamented to Nicholson. Macon worked with Madison and Gallatin on the renewal of the embargo in last two months of 1808.[85] Macon refused to submit to any violation of American neutral rights and clung to the embargo as the only alternative to war.

The Republican legislature of North Carolina once again demonstrated its staunch Republicanism by backing Macon and the administration during this period when Congress was considering repeal of the great party measure. The legislature of 1808 passed a set of resolutions declaring its support for the Embargo. Averring the acts of Britain and France to be "unjust and vexatious" and in violation of America's "Neutral Rights and National Sovereignty," the General Assembly indicated its approval of the measure, stated a hope that the address would "serve to strengthen the hands of those who have the management of our National Affairs." It called the Embargo "the best means which could have been devised" to protect the interests of the country.[86] The legislature thus made it clear that Macon retained the backing of his state in his strong support for continuing the embargo as the country's best course to avoid war.

"I believe we have but three alternatives—*war, embargo,* or *submission*," Macon declared in 1808 as he defended the embargo in Congress. In the 1808–1809 session of Congress when the embargo was under severe attack from Republicans and Federalists alike, Macon staunchly stood by the administration. Macon believed that the Embargo was the only alternative to war with Great Britain. "If anything can prevent war," he insisted to a correspondent, "it [must be] the continuance of the Embargo."[87] He maintained that war must be avoided if any other policy could be found.[88] And he remained adamantly opposed to war until the embargo policy had been fully tried.[89] Macon was so convinced that the embargo was the best policy for the country that he put aside his usual stand in support of states' rights and supported federal enforcement of the Embargo Act on the states as the only alternative to a dangerous war. In November Macon put forward three resolutions authorizing the continuance of the embargo and argued for it as the country's best policy.[90] Josiah Quincey of Massachusetts, opponent of the embargo, said that Macon then spoke "with zeal which did him honor." Macon later described his course as embodying "no other zeal than for the welfare of our common country."[91] Later, when a bill embodying his resolutions and placing the two European powers on equal footing of non-intercourse was put forward, Macon supported it as well.

In arguing for the continuation of the embargo, Macon appealed to unity and the need for obedience to federal laws. Macon's survey of bipartisan opinion among "well informed merchants and navigators" in North Carolina convinced him that they considered it a "wise measure." Macon called for the united spirit that had enforced the Continental Congress's non-importation resolutions before the Revolution. "Where is the spirit which enforced a simple resolution of the old Congress ... as a law from Heaven?" he asked, "Is it extinct? Is it lost to this nation?" It was, he said, a subject "in which the whole nation has a common interest." Quoting the inscription on the old Continental money, Macon praised the Union as the best defense and the best way to secure its rights: "*United we stand, divided we fall*. Nothing but a strict attention to this can secure our rights."[92] In introducing his resolutions, Macon declared that the embargo was "a law constitutionally enacted" and insisted that the states must obey the law. "I believe the embargo was right; that it was right to pass laws to enforce it." He acknowledged no parallel with the Federalists' enactment of the Alien and Sedition Acts—considered unconstitutional by the Republicans—that had also aroused great opposition and protest. He saw Federalist influence at work in the opposition to the embargo. In 1798, the Republicans had organized opposition to overturn the law (and the government). Macon now viewed such opposition by his opponents as unprincipled opposition to the majority will: "Shall the majority govern, or shall a few wicked and abandoned men drive this nation from the ground it has taken?" Macon thus cast aside state sovereignty and invoked the will of the majority as reason to enforce federal laws. Exercise of coercive federal power was acceptable to enforce an act operating equally on all sections. Macon believed that war was a danger to liberty, and he could see no alternative to war but the embargo.

By February of 1809 support for the embargo had collapsed, especially among New England Republicans. Macon feared the consequences of repealing the embargo and was sure it would lead to war. When he learned that despite his efforts Congress had turned against the embargo and repeal was certain, he privately declared, "I fear we are undone as a nation."[93] With the choice as a war that could threaten Republicanism or federal coercion of the states to enforce an alternative policy that avoided the hazards of war, Macon chose to violate the Republican principle of state sovereignty, if the federal coercive power operated equally across the Union.

By the last years of Jefferson's administration, Macon's Old Republicans had joined Randolph in viewing themselves as a distinctive party within the larger Republican party; they were the only true defenders of the Principles of '98. "New" Republicans were their chief opponents. When in opposition, the Old Republicans adopted the rhetoric of the Quid critique of the government. Doubts as to the loyalty of a future Madison administration to the "old" Republican principles drove some to support Randolph's courtship of James Monroe as an alternative successor.[94] Yet, it was the Old Republicans' opposition to "new" Republicans—younger men entering Congress during Jefferson's presidency—that most separated them from the main body of Republicans.

The ideology of the Old Republicans centered around Republicanism as it existed in March 1801. They claimed that they were the true defenders of the Republican "Principles of '98." After the political battles of 1805–1808, their critique of the Republicans' failure to adhere to principles focused on patronage, executive power, and nationalism as forms of federal "consolidation." They, of course, still insisted on strict construction of the Constitution and obedience to law. Macon declared in 1806: "I know of nothing binding in this country, except the Constitution and the laws."[95] The danger of executive power and patronage loomed paramount among their warnings. In their view the executive was the primary threat to liberty. Old Republicans adamantly opposed grants of power to the president, especially those that involved army troops. In the 1790s Macon had opposed giving the president power to raise volunteer troops for the Provisional Army.[96] And in a speech on Jefferson's proposed Additional Army in April 1808 Macon asserted: "I believe that at all times the Executive Department of the Government has too much power."[97] Macon believed that "no president ought to be trusted with troops, unless Congress were ready to vote a declaration of war."[98] This opposition to executive power extended to hatred of patronage for party-building and any and all office-hunters. Macon indicated his concern that "there are many in the world, nay in the U.S. that regard the good fat offices in the gift of the Executive more than they do the public good, and I sincerely wish that our elections may not turn on the love of office more than a respect for principles."[99]

The strains between loyalty to principle and governing led to the Old Republicans setting themselves against many administration measures. Since the Republican doctrines represented an opposition ideology, the Old Republicans' staunch loyalty to the "Principles of '98" suited their opposition position. Having set themselves as defenders of true Republicanism, the Old Republicans began to view themselves as a distinct party. As they set themselves off as a distinct faction, they claimed a purer, older Republican ideology untainted by the nationalist ideas of Republicans coming to Washington during Jefferson's second term.

Many of the Old Republicans, including Macon, began to associate the emerging Republican nationalism with Federalism. The Old Republicans viewed any nationalism as a compromise of Republican principles and thus a weakening of Republicanism. In 1810 John Taylor of Caroline, replying to James Monroe's assertion that the divisions arose in response to Jefferson's policy of commercial retaliation against Europe in his second term, argued that these divisions were of several years standing: "I think that the republican minority originated at a much earlier period than you state, and upon very different grounds." This minority believed that Jefferson had done "many good things" but had "neglected some better things" and they now viewed "his policy as very like a compromise with Mr. Hamilton's…. Federalism, indeed, having been defeated, has gained a new footing by being taken into partnership with republicanism. It was this project which divided the republican party."[100]

By 1808, Macon believed that he was isolated from the main portion of the party. Macon explained his situation to Nicholson: "I am not consulted as you seem to suppose about anything, nor do I consult anyone. I am about as much out of fashion as our grand-mothers ruffle cuffs, and I do not believe that I shall be in fashion as soon as they will." In the same letter Macon complained of the influence of the "N. E. Republicans" on the administration.[101] Macon believed the Old Republicans in Congress were a distinct party with a distinct ideology: conservatives "out of fashion," with the Republican majority. He also disliked those who claimed to be Republicans but who seemed without principles and would "be ready to join any majority in the nation" for the sake of office.[102]

Nicholson likewise viewed the Old Republicans as a distinct group, and he too complained of false Republicans without principles, but he went further. Nicholson, in particular, did not respect the young Republicans entering Congress at the beginning of Madison's administration, men who had not been in Congress during the great fight against the Federalists in 1798–1799. In an 1807 letter to Monroe he directly contrasted the two groups and portrayed them as opposites in adherence to true Republicanism:

> There is a portion who yet retain the feelings of 1798, and who I denominate the old republican party. These men are personally attached to the President, and condemn his measures when they think him wrong. They neither wish for nor expect anything from his extensive patronage. Their public service is intended for the public good, and has no view to public emolument or personal ambition. But it is said they have not his confidence, and I lament it. You must have perceived from the public prints that the most active members in the House of Representatives are new men, and I fear that foreign nations will not estimate American talent very highly if our congressional proceedings are taken as the rule ... you would be mortified at seeing the affairs of the nation in such miserable hands. Yet these are styled exclusively the President's friends.[103]

Claiming the mantra of true Republicanism, he associated the Principles of 1798 with "the old republican party." They are the defenders of true Republican principles even against Jefferson. He condemned the "new men" in Congress as untalented and implied that they were unprincipled. Reflecting the Old Republicans' self-image of persecuted true-believers, Nicholson clearly was bitter about the administration Republicans' attacks on Macon and Randolph.[104]

Both Macon and Nicholson disparaged less doctrinaire Republicans, Nicholson's "new men," and questioned their loyalty to the Republican doctrines of '98. They set themselves in opposition to these new republicans. And most of these "new men" shared a quality that all Old Republicans disparaged: nationalism. Old Republican opposition to the emerging Republican nationalism was tied to their lack of faith in these "new men." The Old Republicans believed the new Republican nationalism threatened the foundations of republican government. Macon and the Old Republicans had become a Republican opposition.

2

Young Old Republican

The Old Republicans felt that the "new men" who claimed to be Republicans did not share their principles. Worse still, they believed that some Republicans who had been with them in 1800 had abandoned "the Principles of '98" and were now adherents of the new nationalism. John Randolph reflected this view during the war of 1812:

> Is it necessary for me at this time of day to make a declaration of the principles of the Republican party? ... These principles are on record ... it is not for any men, who then professed them ... to conceal apostasy from them, for they are there—there in the book.... What are they? Love of peace, hatred of offensive war, jealousy of the State Governments toward the General Government; a dread of standing armies; a loathing of public debt, taxes, and excises; tenderness for the liberty of the citizen; jealousy, Argus-eyed jealousy, of the patronage of the President.[1]

This accusation of apostasy from true principle was the central theme of the Old Republicans' critique of the government after the War of 1812. The Republican nationalists, the "new men," were but Federalists in disguise who did not hold to the true Republican principles and threatened the continued existence of republican government. The chief defense against this threat was absolute adherence to the letter of the Constitution.

Old Republicans feared that loose constitutional construction would cede too much power to the federal government which would in turn result in "consolidation" of federal power over the states. They also opposed the commercial and economic policies of the Republican nationalists as menacing the egalitarian basis of republican society and threatening to corrupt it—Macon's rhetoric in particular focused on "aristocracy." In short, they believed the nationalists' policies were jeopardizing republican self-government.

In the post-war period the Old Republicans were not able to modify the nationalists' ideology and largely failed to stop their program. Indeed, the Old Republicans' opposition to the postwar nationalism was ineffective, as Norman Risjord has pointed out. They were a small minority in the Republican party. Only six of the prewar Old Republicans—a group he calls "the hard core of Old Republican sentiment"—consistently opposed the post-war program of the nationalists.[2]

As one might suppose, Nathaniel Macon, who the legislature of North Carolina had elevated to the United States Senate in December 1815, belonged to that "hard core of Republican sentiment." For Macon, any concession on strict adherence to the Constitution could lead to the eventual overthrow of the Constitution, even what many Southerners at the time considered its most secure guarantee: the right to property—and thus to own slaves. And because of the Tenth Amendment's reservation to the states of powers not granted to the federal government, this restriction of the power of the federal government—the "general government" as Southerners at the time called it—was directly linked to the doctrine of states' rights. From the time of the Virginia and Kentucky Resolutions, Republicans had considered state government as a counter-weight to the general government. Any stretching of federal powers, Old Republicans insisted, would eventually overthrow the state governments. In almost every instance, when Macon discussed the threat of the expansion of federal power which the policies of the Republican nationalists implied, he almost always included strict adherence to the Constitution as the counter to that threat. Perceptive historians of this period have recognized Macon's association of states' rights and strict construction, but they usually fail to notice that Macon coupled these warnings with warnings against the popular appeal of false Republicans—what he called the "fashion" of the ideas of the "new" Republicans.[3] These false Republicans were a threat because they professed adherence to Republican principles but courted popularity through patronage and corruption. This objection was another aspect of the Old Republicans' opposition to the protective tariffs and internal improvement programs put forward by the Republican nationalists.

A Republican majority in Congress, Macon held, was no protection. He feared that Republican opposition to corruption and Federalist doctrines were being set aside. A majority in Congress might change "without acknowledging that it had changed its principles, or changed at all."[4] As he explained to a young protégé in 1818:

> If Congress can make canals they can with more propriety emancipate.... I speak soberly in the fear of God, and the love of the constitution. Let not love of improvement, or a thirst for glory blind that sober discretion and sound sense, with which the Lord has blest you ... your error in this, will injure if not destroy our beloved mother N. Carolina and all the South country. Add not to the constitution nor take therefrom [sic].... Be not lead a stray by grand notions or magnificent opinions.[5]

Macon was thus convinced that the "grand notions" of the Republican nationalists that seemed to intrigue younger Republicans threatened the Republic and especially the South. The only defense was the Constitution.

In the view of such staunch Old Republicans as Macon, any profession of loyalty to Republican principles was worthless without absolute adherence to the Constitution. Thus, as Macon argued it, the Principles of '98 were now summed up in the defense of the Constitution and states' rights.

Crisis and Compromise: Old Republicans, New Republicans, and Missouri

Macon and the Old Republicans failed to modify the nationalists' ideology or stop their program in the immediate post-war years. But the years of 1819 and 1820 saw the start of a reversal of the Old Republicans' situation in the South. Two events began to change the minds of those Southern Republicans, principally in Virginia, North Carolina, and South Carolina, who had given lukewarm support to elements of the Republican nationalists' program. The first was a decision of the Supreme Court of arch–Federalist John Marshall.

The decision of the Marshall Court in the case of *McCulloch v. Maryland* turned the Republicans of Virginia back to the Old Republican doctrines. Marshall's decision held that a state tax on a branch of the Bank of the United States was invalid because it was contrary to the implied power of Congress to create a bank. Judge Spencer Roane, a chief member of the powerful "Richmond Junto," attacked Marshall's decision in Thomas Ritchie's Richmond *Enquirer* in a series of articles signed "Hampden." The Hampden essays maintained the conception of the Union as a compact between sovereign states that had delegated only a set of specified powers to the general government—the long-held position of the Old Republicans. Jefferson praised the essays.[6] With Jefferson, the Richmond Junto, and Ritchie's *Enquirer* behind them, Judge Roane's essays "became the official creed of Virginia Republicans."[7]

The second and even more decisive event to Southern Republicans was the controversy aroused by the debate in Congress over the admission of Missouri to the Union as a slave state. The controversy began in the House of Representatives in February 1819 when James Tallmadge, Jr., a representative from New York, proposed amendments to the enabling legislation on Missouri's admission to the Union. The amendments were designed to bring about gradual emancipation by preventing the further introduction of slaves into Missouri and freeing at twenty-five years of age any slaves born in the state after Missouri's admission. The controversy continued in Congress until 1821 and required not one but two Missouri Compromises to be finally resolved. Republican nationalist Henry Clay of Kentucky stood at the center of events in both compromises, particularly the Second Missouri Compromise in which his role was pivotal.[8] The controversy created great political agitation in Congress and raised several critical questions. Examination of all these issues is not required in this study; they have been adequately covered by historians.[9] However, three of the issues raised are of particular interest: the question of the constitutional authority of Congress to restrict slavery in the territories, Old Republican fears of the encroachment of federal power on the states, and the sectionalist tensions generated by the crisis.

Many Southern Congressmen believed that Tallmadge and his political allies were simply trying to use the issue of Missouri to enhance their own power and restrict that of the South. Westerners feared that other Congressmen who supported the Tallmadge amendments intended to restrict Western growth and development.[10] Such sectional divisions and suspicions ran directly counter to Macon's declarations during Jefferson's presidency for sectional unity.

The Senate rejected the Tallmadge amendment. After "a long and animated debate," the Senate defeated the gradual emancipation clause of the bill by a vote of 31 to 7, with Macon voting with the majority. And the Senate rejected any restriction of slavery in Missouri by a vote of 22 to 16, with Macon again in the majority. The Senate then passed the bill stripped of these clauses.[11]

In the second Missouri debate in the 1819–1820 session of Congress, Macon and the Old Republicans took the leadership of the defense of the South and slaveholding. Risjord argues that the Missouri Controversy was the climax of the conservative reaction against the nationalists. The Old Republicans not only denied the power of Congress to legislate on slavery where the institution already existed (as was the case in Missouri), but they also doubted Congress's ability to regulate slavery *anywhere*. As with the tariff and internal improvements, they feared concessions to federal power implied in the Tallmadge amendment and were uncomfortable with a solution arranged by Congress. They would have preferred no discussion at all. Old Republican fears of Congressional action on slavery fueled opposition to internal improvements in the South.[12]

When Congress met in December 1819, Speaker of the House Henry Clay appointed a Southern-dominated special committee to consider memorials from the Missouri Territory for statehood. The committee reported a bill for the admission of Missouri to the Union with no restrictions on slavery. When the full house began debate on the Missouri bill, Northerners backed an amendment excluding slavery from the state, and the division in the debate once again fell along sectional lines. The Old Republicans led the Southern defense in the House.[13] In the Senate, an amendment restricting slavery was also added to the Missouri bill, coupled with a bill to admit the Maine District as a state. Macon took a significant part in the Senate debate and spoke against the attachment of any conditions to the admission of Missouri.

In his speeches on Missouri, Macon set out all the tenets of his Old Republicanism. Two of the staunchest of the Old Republicans, Macon and Senator William Smith of South Carolina, made the first defense of slavery as a positive good during the debate.[14] Macon put forth this argument in the context of Southern fears over the encroachment of federal power on the states—the prime doctrine of the states' rights men. Yet whatever the reason for the argument, defense of slavery as a positive good had become a part of the national political discourse, and it created further rifts in the Republican party.

In preliminary remarks before delivering his main speech on the Missouri question, Macon complained of the "noise out of doors" that had arisen during the summer and confessed that he had felt more anxiety on the Missouri question than any other recently before the Senate because it touched directly on Southern society: "It may be a matter of philosophy and abstraction with the gentlemen of the East, but it is a different thing with us. They may philosphize and hold town meetings about it as much as they please; but, with great submission, sir, they know nothing about the question."[15] In a speech, Macon called the admission of Missouri "the greatest question ever debated in the Senate." Macon opened with an appeal for Congress to stand by the Constitution and the Union; he then moved to a discussion of the equality of the states and a defense of slavery as a moral and beneficial institution, and he concluded by returning to the defense of the Constitution.

Macon began by praising the Constitution and the Union and denouncing division and agitation. Unsettled by discussions of disunion raised in the debate, Macon declared that he himself attached great blessings to the Union and the Constitution. "Get clear of this Union and this Constitution, and it will be found vastly more difficult to unite again and form another, than it was to form this." Disunion was too much bandied about. "Let us not speak of disunion as an easy thing." If it should come "it will bring evils enough for the best men to encounter" and all would lament it. For thirty years, the Constitution had stood the trial of trouble and war. "Destroy it, and what may be the condition of the country, no man, not the most sagacious, can even imagine."

Macon viewed the Republican party as a unifying organization—he desired a *national* party. His idea of the Republican party was linked to his concept of the Union. The Missouri question threatened to disrupt the national unity the Republicans had achieved. Macon asserted that the amendment to restrict slavery in Missouri was "calculated to produce geographical parties." He complained of the meetings that had been held to protest the admission of Missouri as a slave state: "Town meetings and resolutions to inflame one part of the nation against another can never benefit the people," he insisted. Macon declared that merely local parties had no place in Congress: "Let not parties, formed at home for State purposes, be brought into Congress, to disturb and distract the Union. The General Government hitherto has been productive [of] enough of them, to satisfy those who most delight in them, that they are not likely to be long wanted in it." Macon also believed that the spirit of opposition to the South in the meetings and arguments of northern congressmen showed ingratitude for the leadership that southern legislators had shown in the Revolution of 1800. He called the spirit of agitation reflected in the meetings dangerous: "It is more easy to influence the public mind, than to quiet it when inflamed." Macon wanted a national party, but one in which state equality and state sovereignty were respected. (Later, Mangum would hold a similar view of the Whig Party.) This idea of the Republican party was fundamental to Macon's concept of the Union. Missouri's entry with any provisos violated that concept.

Macon then turned to the question at hand, Missouri, and argued that all states must be equal in the Union. For Macon, state equality was tied to the Union, the Constitution, and state sovereignty. In his brand of Old Republicanism, they were all interconnected and they were all essential. "All the States now have equal rights, and all are content. Deprive one of the least right which it now enjoys in common with the others, and it will no longer be content." After this opening declaration, Macon made four points. All the country west of the Mississippi was acquired by the same treaty and on the same terms, "and the people in every part have the same rights." No conditions had been placed on the admission of Louisiana. Louisiana was a "full sister" but Missouri, if admitted with conditions, would be a "stepdaughter." Second, the Tallmadge amendment was "unjust" as it related to the slaveholders of Missouri and the South in general.[16] No one had ever before mentioned possible slavery restrictions in that territory. Missouri slave owners had carried with them the slaves they had held in the states they left "secured to them by the Constitution and the laws of the United States." Macon also thought an object of the amendment was to "pen up the slaves and their owners, and not permit them to cross the Mississippi, to better their condition." Third, the Tallmadge amendment violated "the great American principle, that the people are able to govern themselves" and form their own state governments. Finally, Macon asked the proponents of the amendment what they intended to do if Missouri refused to yield to restriction, formed a state government without the consent of Congress, and then applied for admission to the Union, as Tennessee had done. If Congress then refused admission and Missouri refused to give up her state government, would Congress then declare the people of Missouri rebels and order them to be conquered? "Will you for this order the father to march against the son, and brother against brother? God forbid! It would be a terrible sight to behold these near relations plunging the bayonet into each other, for no other reason than because the people of Missouri wish to be on an equal footing with the people of Louisiana."

Macon ended his argument for state equality by returning to his appeal for calm. His was a conservative argument against innovation and for the status quo. The Senate was intended by the long terms of its members "to check every improper direction of the public mind. It is its duty to do so," Macon insisted. He considered slavery restriction a new doctrine that would upset the Union: "But why depart from the good old way, which has kept us in quiet, peace, and harmony—every one living under his own vine and fig tree, and none to make him afraid? Why leave the road of experience, which has satisfied all, and made all happy, to take this new way, of which we have no experience?"

To counter Northerners' charges that slavery had to be restricted because it was a moral evil, Macon next turned to his most powerful and innovative argument—a defense of slavery as a moral, beneficial institution. Several other Southern senators also utilized this proslavery, positive-good argument. Macon's argument contained every element utilized by proslavery theorists of later decades.[17] He declared that Congress should not look to the philosophy of the founder of the Republican party for guidance on making policy for the admission of new states to the Union. "A clause in the Declaration of Independence has been read declaring 'that all men are created equal'; follow that sentiment, and does it not lead to universal emancipation?" he asked the Senate, "If it will justify putting an end to slavery in Missouri, will it not justify it in the old States?" He thus asserted that the language of the Declaration of Independence gave no mandate for Congress's policy on Missouri. He insisted that Congress should look only to the Constitution, not to the Declaration of Independence, whose words formed "no part" of the Constitution. After thus denying that blacks had a natural right to liberty, Macon professed the proslavery argument that blacks were better off enslaved than free. Insisting that any freed slaves "would be as much or more degraded, than in their present condition," he refused to acknowledge that freedom was a desirable state for blacks. He asked the senators from the free states if blacks were not "degraded" there, and then he answered his own question: "It may be stated, without fear of contradiction, that there is no place for the blacks in the United States—no place where they are not degraded." Macon, with little experience of free blacks, could only imagine them as "degraded." He painted a rosy picture of life in bondage and the relationship between master and slave:

> The old [slaves] are better taken care of than any poor in the world, and treated with decent respect by all their white acquaintances. I sincerely wish that [northern senators] would go home with me, or some other Southern member, and witness the meeting between slaves and the owner, and see the glad faces and the hearty shaking of hands.

Of course, Macon or any other proslavery senator did not care to explain why so many runaway advertisements filled the newspapers of their states. Macon preferred the subordination and hierarchy of slavery to the expectations of equality seen in "the white hireling" of rich Northerners. Even if a planter freely conversed with his slave, the Southern master had no expectation "that the slave will, for that free and easy conversation, expect to call him fellow-citizen, or act improperly." Macon concluded his defense of slavery by making a final point to counter the insistence by Northerners than slavery was immoral. "Nor are the owners of slaves less moral or less religious than those who hold none."

To end his speech, Macon returned to his first argument that the Constitution and the concept of state equality forbade Congress from restricting slavery in the territory of the Louisiana Purchase. Macon emphasized that the Constitution gave "no power in the General Government to touch [slavery] in any way." His solution was: "Why not leave the people of Missouri exactly as the other Territories have been left, free to do as they pleased?" Were the Tallmadge amendment adopted, Missouri would have fewer rights as a state than as a territory. Under the Constitution new states were to be admitted "on an equal footing with the original States." Both the Constitution and the treaty by which the Louisiana Territory was acquired protected people in their property. The power to touch property in Missouri was claimed "by a stretching implication." It was to be found "in no part of the Constitution or the treaty." Only by giving "a stretching construction to the Constitution" could the power to restrict slavery in Missouri be found. Macon ended his speech with a question and a declaration that summed up his arguments. He asked the senators of the Northern states, "What have the people of the Southern States done, that such a strong desire should be manifested to pen them up?" Macon declared that whatever the decision of the Senate about Missouri, he wished it to be one that "may benefit the nation and promote the happiness of the people, and that the union of these States, and the Constitution, may be as lasting as the Alleghany."[18]

The speech thus reflected the pillars of Macon's Old Republicanism: strict construction, states' rights, state equality were all tied together. Conditions on states violated his concept of the Union. The Constitution and the Union required sovereign and equal states. Macon argued that strict adherence to the Constitution prevented restriction of slavery in Missouri, guaranteed the equality of the states, and made secure the planters of Missouri in their slave property. State equality and state sovereignty demanded that Missourians were entitled to form their own state government. The Old Republican insistence on strict construction of the Constitution and state equality and state sovereignty thus became ideally suited to lead the Southern opposition to the Tallmadge amendment.

Macon set out every argument used by both Southern Whigs and Democrats for the next thirty years to defend slavery in the territories. In particular, the Constitution and the Union would form the cornerstones of Southern Whig ideology. His speech vividly illustrates the impact that Old Republicanism would have on both Southern Whig and Southern Democratic ideology. And Macon would soon pass this brand of Old Republicanism to the young Old Republicans of North Carolina—Mangum in particular.

The Old Republicans were not alone in their call for equality for Missouri. They were joined by Henry Clay, who reminded the House that he was a Southerner and a Westerner. In a speech of December 1819 on the admission of Maine into the Union, Clay made clear his concern that the West be treated equally with the other sections of the country. Clay would not consent to the admission of Maine as long as Congress placed conditions on the admission of Western states. "Equality," Clay declared in late 1819, "…is equity. If we have no right to impose conditions on [Maine], we have none to impose them of the state of Missouri." The doctrine, Clay said, that Congress had a right to affix conditions to Missouri's entry because she was part of territory acquired by purchase was "an alarming one, and I protest against it now, and whenever or wherever it may be asserted, that there are any rights attaching in the one case which do not in the other; or that any line of distinction is to be drawn between the Eastern and the Western States. It is a distinction which neither exists in reason, nor can you carry it into effect in practice."[19] Clay also took a dim view of any attempt of Congressmen to use the crisis to increase sectional power through the creation of sectional parties. He viewed such a design as "sinister."[20] The open discussion of disunion also alarmed Clay.[21]

In the Senate, Jesse Thomas of Illinois introduced a compromise amendment prohibiting slavery in the territory north of the line thirty-six degrees thirty minutes north latitude that was attached to the Maine-Missouri bill admitting Missouri without restriction on slavery. Thomas's amendment was the critical concession by the Southerners that enabled Northern support of the compromise bill. The Senate passed the Thomas amendment 34–10 and the entire compromise bill 24–20. Along with seven other Southern senators, Macon opposed not only Thomas's amendment but also the entire compromise bill.[22] In the House, Clay submitted the Senate compromise bill to the House in sections to prevent its defeat by a combination of Northerners and Old Republicans adamantly opposed to any compromise. His tactics were successful, and the several portions of the compromise bill were passed by the House.

Congress enacted the Missouri Compromise on March 3, 1820. Yet the vote on the compromise bill was almost wholly along sectional lines. In the Senate, the 24–20 vote followed sectional divisions except for four free-state senators voting for and two Old Republicans voting against the bill. In the House, the two measures requiring compromise—the striking out of the anti-slavery clause and the thirty-six-thirty Thomas proviso—drew an overwhelming majority of Northern congressmen to vote against the former and only a small majority of Southern congressmen to support the latter. As Glover Moore's analysis has shown, the vote in the Congress indicates that the Missouri Compromise was "merely an agreement between a small majority of the Southern members of Congress and a small minority of the Northern ones."[23] Almost all of the Southern votes in the House against the thirty-six-thirty Thomas proviso came from Old Republicans.[24]

Macon associated the politics of antislavery with corruption, an increasingly important theme for him. Like other Southerners in Congress, he interpreted the Tallmadge amendment as a Federalist maneuver to divide the country on sectional lines and regain the power of their party. "The feds, I fear are not done with the Missouri question," he told Bartlett Yancey, "they will, no doubt, push it with a view to form new parties on the principle of slave or no slave. It is the only hope left them by which to get power; and power gives offices which are much in demand, and which members of Congress now ask the President for, at least so I am told, and so I believe."[25] He was convinced that party maneuvering for power, not principle, lay behind the controversy and even the compromise. As he was not one to "shyhog," as he called it, Macon insisted that he only knew of the maneuvering second hand, but, he informed a young friend, "much was done and more openly about the Missouri compromise than I ever witnessed before."[26]

As Macon feared, the Missouri controversy did not end with the Compromise of 1820. In July 1820 Missouri adopted a constitution which established slavery but it also contained a clause which authorized the state legislature to pass laws to prevent the immigration of free blacks into the state. Because free blacks were citizens in some states and the United States Constitution stated that "the citizens of each state shall be entitled to all the privileges and immunities of citizens of the several states," any law passed by the Missouri legislature under the provision of the state constitution would directly conflict with the United States Constitution. When Congress met and took the Missouri constitution under consideration, the black exclusion clause became a new point of contention. The Congress passed a resolution to admit Missouri into the Union with a proviso attached that Congress did not consent to any provision in the state's constitution that contravened the United States Constitution's privileges and immunities clause.

Every Southern senator but one voted for the resolution with the proviso. Macon remained true to his arguments in the previous session that no conditions should be attached to the admission of a state and voted against the resolution because it contained the proviso. In the House, the Old Republicans led the Southern members in opposition to attaching conditions on Missouri's admission. They argued that Missouri, having been authorized by Congress to form a state government and write a state constitution, was already an equal and sovereign state; Congress could therefore attach no provisions to the resolution declaring Missouri's admission to the Union. Along sectional lines, the House rejected a resolution based on the Old Republican arguments.

In an effort to resolve the impasse that threatened to wreck the compromise worked out in the previous session, Henry Clay assembled a special joint House-Senate committee that prepared a compromise resolution. The resolution admitted Missouri "on an equal footing" with the other states provided that the state legislature never pass a law implementing the offending clause in the state's constitution and that "by a solemn public act" it make a declaration to that effect. Largely on the votes of Northerners who objected that the compromise failed to require Missouri to remove the disputed clause, the House rejected Clay's compromise resolution 83 to 80. The deciding votes against were cast by Old Republicans, including John Randolph. They remained opposed to Congress placing any conditions on the admission of a state. Clay did not give up, however, and he formed a second special House-Senate select committee that reported a new compromise resolution that was essentially the same as the first committee's resolution. Clay was able to convince all the senators and nearly all of the congressmen on the committee to approve the resolution, and this large majority on the committee for the resolution seems to have decisively altered the alignment in the House, which approved the resolution 87 to 81 on February 26, 1821. Two days later the Senate approved it by a vote of 28 to 14. The only Southerners to vote against the resolution were Randolph in the House, and William Smith of South Carolina and Macon in the Senate. All insisted on the unconditional admission of a sovereign and equal state.[27]

Though in the end many Old Republicans voted for the Missouri Compromise, their leadership of a sectional opposition was a severe blow to the unity of the Republican party.[28] The Old Republicans had defended the South, but they could not resolve the controversy. On the other hand, Clay's influence in the House was critical to the passage of the Compromise of 1820.[29] And it was Clay, one of the "new" Republicans so hated by the Old Republicans, who finally resolved the crisis with his leadership in the 1820–1821 session that worked out the final compromise resolution. The Old Republican ideology was suited to oppose and warn, but it was Clay who held the Union together.

Macon and the Old Republicans could not solve Missouri controversy; they even worsened it while the new Republicans compromised it. The Old Republicans could only warn and oppose; they did nothing to solve the crisis. Clay and the nationalists arranged the compromise. Macon's intransient opposition to compromise on Missouri showed how his Old Republicans had made pure Republicanism—Old Republicanism—an ideology of opposition. Republicans adhering to the doctrines of Old Republicanism could not govern in the post-war age of nationalism; they could only oppose government.

The Old Republicans had combined their anti-federal states' rights ideology with the defense of the South. As a study of Macon's ideology shows, in the course of opposing the Republican nationalists the Old Republicans emphasized even more strongly the anti-federal and states' rights parts of their ideology. The Old Republicans opposed every aspect of the new Republican nationalism. They despised the systems of John C. Calhoun and Clay; they deeply distrusted both and questioned their commitment to true Republicanism. The staunch Old Republicans had proven during the Missouri Compromise what had been evident as early as 1807: Old Republicanism was an ideology suitable only for opposition.

Macon's Old Republicanism had taken on its ultimate form—Constitution, Union, strict construction, state equality, and state sovereignty. In the Missouri debate, he set out every argument used by both Southern Whigs and Democrats for the next thirty years to defend slavery in the territories. The doctrines of Macon and the Old Republicans, now united to the defense of the South, were still the foundation of political success in the old North State.

Macon had defined the brand of Old Republicanism that would be adopted by the new generation of Old Republicans in North Carolina.

"The Old Republican School in Politics"

"While such men as yourself and your worthy colleagues of the legislature, and such characters as compose the Executive administration, are watching for us all, I slumber without fear, and review in my dreams the visions of antiquity." So wrote Thomas Jefferson to Nathaniel Macon early in 1819.[30] In his retirement, Jefferson clearly had come to believe that the Republic relied on the staunchest adherents to the Principles of '98.

Jefferson was more satisfied than Macon in 1819 with the state of Republican governance, but Jefferson, like Macon, believed the country should be governed by the old republican doctrines—they just differed on the degree to which the Monroe administration was following those doctrines. But by the 1820s, when Mangum entered Congress, both the old Republicans were dissatisfied with the course of government.

Macon and Jefferson exchanged letters in the early 1820s that show their dissatisfaction with the state of their party and its new leaders. The two leaders of the first Republican government who had set out to implement a government on Republican principles now believed that government threatened those principles. They saw the national Republicans as dominant in Monroe's government. Macon in particular believed that the Republican party had been betrayed by apostates. While his views contrasted starkly with those that Jefferson held even as late as 1819, Missouri and the factional divisions of 1820–1824 seem to have sapped the latter's confidence in Monroe's government (Macon had never thought that the government under Monroe was truly Republican.) They spoke in terms of shared reverence for "the old and safe principles" and reminisced about being members of "the old republican school in politics."[31] They believed that the party of the Revolution of 1800 and its principles had evaporated.

Both Macon and Jefferson asserted that the new national Republican doctrines violated the Old Republican tenet of strict adherence to the Constitution. Both also believed that strict division of power was required to check the danger of loose construction. But they differed as to which branch most threatened the Constitution. Jefferson was most concerned with the federal judiciary; Macon with Congress. Jefferson thought that Congress should declare "a strong protestation" of "unconstitutional invasions of state rights" by the Supreme Court. He declared that consolidation and corruption were the two parts of a road by which the government would "pass to destruction." The "engine of consolidation" was the federal judiciary, the "corrupting" instrument was the executive, and the "corrupted" branch was the legislature. Macon on the other hand wanted the other two branches to check Congress: "As Congress attempts to get power by stretching the Constitution to fit its views, it is to be expected, if the other departments do not check them, that each of them will use the same means to obtain power and thus destroy any check that was intended by the division of power into three distinct and separate bodies," he told Jefferson. Yet, Macon also found fault with the judiciary: he thought that tenure during good behavior violated "the great principle of the American governments" of short periods of service, and he argued that judges should hold their office for a fixed term. Macon thought that the future did not offer a pleasing prospect "especially to those who have been opposed to constructive & implied powers in the federal government."[32]

Both Jefferson and Macon complained of the corrupting dangers of the national debt. Jefferson declared: "There does not exist an engine so corruptive of the government ... as a public debt." Jefferson would rather put the navy's ships out of commission and haul them up "high and dry" and reduce the army "to the lowest point at which it was ever established" than have the government continue to borrow money and fail to pay off the debt. Macon thought that so many persons had "lived so long so well on the public debt" that it would be "almost impossible" for the nation to get clear of the debt.[33]

Placing an emphasis on Old Republicanism being out of style with the Republicans in Washington, Macon put the blame for the decline of the Old Republican doctrines on the nationalist "new men" of the party. Macon told Jefferson that "the principles which turned the federalists out of power" were "not fashionable" in Washington. He declared to Jefferson that "the acts for the banks of the United States, the tariff and internal improvements seem to have put an end to the legislating on the old republican principles." Those who did not hold the old Republican doctrines were not true Republicans, Macon insisted: "Under any party name, unconstitutional measures may be adopted, names may please, but without the principles which ought to attach to them, they are useless or worse." Looking back from the 1820s, Macon placed the blame for the eclipse of Old Republican doctrines squarely on Madison's shoulders:

> After it was known that President Madison, one of our best and most worthy men, would sign the act to establish the expensive bank of the U.S., all who were tired of the principles which put them into power immediately laid them aside and went further into constructive and implied powers than had been done at any time before.

In Macon's opinion, the "new men" among the Republicans were worse than the Federalists. "New converts," Macon pointed out, "always go beyond those who held the opinions before them." He reassured Jefferson of his respect for the old president's close friend, but commented: "the errors of a great and good man often do much mischief." In the next to last letter that he ever wrote to Macon, Jefferson agreed with Macon that the new party members were Republicans in name only. He praised Macon for his defense of "our good old principle" of strengthening the authority of the people "in opposition to those who fear them, who wish to take all power from them" and transfer it to Washington. "The latter may call themselves republicans if they please" but to Jefferson all men of such principles were "tories."[34] The prophets of Old Republicanism did not view the new Republican nationalists as true Republicans.

Jefferson's assessment of Macon and his Old Republican colleagues in Congress quoted above accurately expressed a faith in their adherence to the Principles of '98, but James Monroe gave a contrasting, and perhaps more apt, view of the Old Republicans after retiring from the presidency. Reportedly reluctant to offer his opinions on the political figures of the time, the former president made one exception: John Randolph of Roanoke. When asked for his assessment of his one-time ally, Monroe allegedly replied, "Well, Mr. Randolph is, I think, a capital hand to pull down, but I am not aware that he has ever exhibited much skill as a builder."[35] After the events of 1819 and 1820, many of those outside the South viewing the Old Republicans would most likely have shared Monroe's view rather than Jefferson's. But in the South and particularly in North Carolina Macon's Old Republican doctrines were popular, and he passed these ideas of true Republicanism to the young Republican from Orange County who joined him in Congress in 1824.

Macon and Mangum

Between 1825 and 1827, Nathaniel Macon sought to pass the torch of Old Republicanism by imparting his political philosophy to two of North Carolina's most talented young politicians, Willie Mangum and Bartlett Yancey. As we have seen, Mangum already had joined the Old Republicans in support of Crawford and already begun to imbibe their doctrines. Mangum boarded with Macon in the 1825 to 1826 session of Congress.[36] In these middle years of the decade, Mangum embraced the doctrines of the Old Republicans; to the extent that they represented a party in North Carolina, Mangum joined that party. By 1828, Mangum was a new Old Republican. After Mangum left Congress, Macon sent him "documents," printed speeches and government reports.[37] Friends in North Carolina addressed Mangum as Macon's protégé in politics and political philosophy. Thomas H. Hall requested that Mangum speak to Macon about procuring the "text book" of Madison's Report of 1800. "Mr. Macon will know at once what Document I mean."[38] Macon sent several letters to Yancey and Mangum in this period expounding Old Republican doctrines, and Mangum's own letters and his speeches in Congress unmistakably reflected an attachment to the Principles of '98. Mangum thought that Macon's spirits were depressed in this period by ill health and the shock of the death of his daughter Seigniora in August 1825.[39] Asserting that he was "growing older faster than is wished," Macon seems to have desired to impart Old Republican wisdom to his protégés.[40]

His advice centered on Old Republicanism as a doctrine, states' rights and strict adherence to the Constitution as the only protection for the South. Macon told Yancey that Republicanism had to be preserved in the states or it could not prevail in the federal government.[41] Macon insisted that Old Republicanism had become "too old fashioned for the present time"; it was "out of fashion and called, the old school."[42] He emphasized strict adherence to the Constitution and limitation of powers as the means of protecting the rights of the minority. If the federal government undertook whatever it deemed expedient under the general welfare clause, the rights of the minority would only be held at the will of the majority. The majority, he pointed out, needed "no law or rule, both are made to secure the minority."[43] Macon tied Old Republican principles to strict construction and the defense of the South against interference with slavery:

> The republican party and their principles are I fear out of fashion, though something like a revival seems to be taking place in South Carolina, at least in their Legislature. If Congress can make banks, roads, and canals under the constitution, they can free any slave in the United States.... The spirit of emancipating with those who have no slaves, never dies, it may sleep now and then ... only [to] awake more vigorous ... to free [the slaves] in the south, would be the means of destroying either the blacks or whites, as at San Domingo.[44]

He asked Yancey, "What benefit [are] written constitutions if they be departed from." Macon cited the book of Judges as evidence of the "terrible effect" on the Israelites for "departing from the laws, which was their constitution," and he warned that the young men that "the rising generation forget the principles and maxims of their forefathers, hence the destruction of free governments in every age."[45]

As early as December 1825, Mangum was acting in accord with the spirit of Old Republicanism. In late December 1825, Mangum opposed Congress granting $30,000 to Monroe, to settle the former president's accounts. Many in Congress declared that Monroe's claim was a matter of national importance and wanted it submitted to a friendly special committee assembled especially to examine the former president's claim, but Mangum disagreed. Insisting that "the same justice ought to be awarded to all," Mangum argued that the House should refer Monroe's request to the Committee of Claims as they would with any other such request. In very Macon-like language, Mangum asked, "Why shall we award to this individual, because he has lately been the President of the United States, a courtesy which we refuse to the poor soldier who has fought our battles, and who pleads his wants or his wounds before us?"[46]

Mangum's reaction to the administration of John Quincy Adams and his secretary of state Henry Clay shows the extent to which he had accepted the Old Republican creed as true Republicanism. Early on Mangum took the position that he would support Adams when he thought him right and oppose him when he thought he was wrong.[47] But after hearing Adams' first message to Congress, Mangum immediately declared that his principles were opposed to those of the president. "The administration opens upon principles that I cannot approve," he told his wife Charity.[48]

Mangum was one of the first House members to declare his opposition to the administration. In January, he used his speech against an administration bill expanding the Supreme Court to ten justices and increasing the number of federal circuit courts put forward by Daniel Webster of Massachusetts to attack the principles of the Adams administration. Mangum explained to his wife: "I gave the administration a rap over the knuckles."[49] Webster's bill increased federal jurisdiction at the expense of the state courts. Mangum told the House that he "opposed to all great and sudden innovations upon any of the principal departments of our Government, as unwise and dangerous." As had the Judiciary Act of 1801,

As Macon had in 1802, Mangum opposed expansion of the federal judiciary and along the same line: the state courts were adequate to the people's needs. He declared that Adams' election had brought on a state of "anxiety and discontent in the public mind." At such a time, experiments with the Supreme Court risked too much. He asserted that an expansion of the court's membership would invite the spirit of faction into the Supreme Court. The bill was an "assault" on the Court—the "great rampart of liberty" and the "last citadel of the Constitution." He accused the administration of using the judiciary bill to court "popular favor" in the West (where new circuits were to be added). The administration was raising up a new set of judges, not to "shelter their retirement" as had the Federalists in 1801, "but that patronage might sprinkle its delicious manna in the West" to help secure a "doubtful" administration. Mangum had been one of the first to speak against the administration; he told Charity that his speech had opened a "beehive" over his head.[50] But, he explained to Yancey, "I felt so indignant at the miserably corrupted policy as I believed it of the yankee nation, that I could not refrain from giving them a touch."[51] The sheriff of Wake County told Mangum that though some of the latter's friends thought he was too "harsh" with the administration, the county "generally approved" his course.[52] Mangum's brother informed him that his speech had brought him "considerable accession of reputation."[53]

Mangum was adamantly in opposition, but like the other Crawford men from North Carolina, he was not ready to commit to the support of any other presidential contender, and by 1826 that meant Jackson. Though the Jackson men were also in opposition, the Old Republicans were not yet prepared to join them. Mangum had hoped to support the administration but that was now impossible, he explained to Yancey: "Sir, this administration I verily believe will be conducted upon as corrupt principles indeed more corrupt, than any that has preceded it. Bargaining & compromise will be the order of the day." He referred to Adams as "John II." The Crawford party would have to "stand aloof" because they could not support the administration and the alternative (joining the Jackson men) was "as yet ... still more objectionable." He was determined to remain independent: "I mean to stand aloof from all political connection having relation to the next presidency—and support or oppose, according as my best Judgment may dictate in each particular case."[54] Yancey thought that neither the Adams-Clay party nor the Jackson party were truly concerned with "the great & national interests of the South," and he agreed with Mangum that the Crawford part should attach itself to neither and "stand aloof" for the present.[55]

Mangum's view of the Republican party factions in January 1826 showed that he had fully embraced the Old Republican opposition to the principles of the administration of Adams and Clay. Mangum had a decidedly negative view of Clay. Congress was then discussing a proposed amendment to the Constitution brought forward by Jackson men to elect the president by popular vote in state districts rather than by electors. (Jackson had won the popular vote in the 1824 presidential election, but he achieved only a plurality in the electoral college and the election had been thrown into the House of Representatives where Jackson lost to Adams.[56]) The administration opposed the amendment. If the Jackson men pressed ahead with debate on their amendment, the Adams-Clay men in the Ohio delegation were prepared to bring forward a proposed amendment repealing the clause granting 3/5 representation of Southern slaves. Mangum believed that Clay was "at the bottom of it" because he was the only man in that party "of boldness enough to go that length & touch that delicate subject." He argued that Clay, "with but little to expect from the South," was seeking to secure Northern votes by such a course. He told Bartlett Yancey that his "confidence" in Clay had been "a good deal impaired" by his complicity in the Ohioans' plan. He accused Clay of disloyalty to the South: "Now Sir, any southern man, who is capable of touching that subject in that manner & at a moment when there is so much feeling upon the subject to the North ... is reckless of everything to gratify a bad ambition." Mangum also deemed Calhoun ambitious for the presidency and thought he was courting the favor of the North Carolina delegation.[57] In January, Mangum declared that Jackson had "made his best race" and that his party was on the decline.[58] But by April the Carolina representative had changed his mind: "The Administration are both weak & wicked I fear, and the present prospect is that the Members of Congress from the south of Washington will unite to put down Adams & if they can get no better, they will take up Gen. Jackson for that purpose."[59]

Macon had thus been quite successful in imparting his views to the young Congressman. Mangum, by January 1826 was an Old Republican. He was gaining in favor with the Old Republicans and popular among his constituents in North Carolina, and his career in Congress had every prospect of success. But in 1826 Mangum committed one of the greatest mistakes of his political career.

By the late spring of that year Mangum was frustrated with the state of politics in Washington and was not enjoying his life there: "I am becoming ... very tired of the place," he told Charity, "& feel but little pleasure in any of my employments, every thing here goes on against my judgment."[60] During the summer a vacancy occurred on the superior court, and Mangum put his name forward to the governor's council as a candidate for appointment as judge of the superior court even though he had one year left on his term in Congress. The governor backed his candidacy and the council made the appointment on August 18, 1826.[61] The duties of the office began immediately as a temporary appointment subject to confirmation by the legislature. His brother and several friends advised him that a faction opposed to him was likely to form in the legislature if he did not immediately resign his seat in Congress. Priestly emphasized, "an *early* resignation is *important*." Mangum delayed his decision and was accused of seeking power and gain through holding multiple offices.[62] He eventually resigned, but did so too late to prevent the predicted opposition to confirmation of his appointment. Mangum reported to Bartlett Yancey that he was "astonished" at the "virulence" of public opinion about his hesitation to resign from Congress. He complained that he had been treated with unjustifiable "rudeness and indecorum." Mangum was bitter about the opposition that had formed to his confirmation: "A part of the opposition to me savours so strongly of deep political malignity or personal hatred; that my resistance as far as it depends upon me, shall at least be manly, tho unavailing."[63] His resistance was unavailing: the legislature refused to confirm Mangum's appointment to the superior court. By providing a pretext to his enemies to place their own favorites on the bench, he had suffered his first political defeat and raised doubts about the motives of his political career.

When he learned of the legislature's refusal to confirm Mangum's appointment, Macon conveyed the regret of "every member of the mess." He informed Mangum that "Mr. Randolph stated his in a manner, that would have made a strong & lasting impression on you could you have heard them." Mangum had clearly impressed these Old Republicans: "every member of the mess desired to be remembered to you," Macon told him. The old senator took the occasion to provide Mangum with some points of Old Republican political philosophy. Macon offered the rising young politician a series of cautions and warnings: on government spending: "those in power, unless more economy be used in public expenditure, may find an empty treasury, before the election"; on the danger of the tariff and internal improvements: the Constitution "provides for an equality of taxation, but taxes may be perfectly equal, and ruinous to our [the South's] plans & beneficial to another ... if all the expenditures be at one place & none at the other"; and finally on the cause of the destruction of "all the free governments of old times": "Debt & extravagance."[64] As Macon had imparted his views to Mangum, it is worth taking a closer look at Macon's political philosophy at the end of his career in Congress.

"The old fashioned republicans are very scarce in the Senate ... their principles are gone, never to return I fear," Nathaniel Macon lamented to Warren planter Weldon Edwards on 5 April 1828.[65] Between December 1827 and May 1828 Macon sent a series of letters to his trusted friend and fellow planter from Warren County, North Carolina Weldon N. Edwards. These letters were written during Macon's last year in Congress while he was president pro tem of the Senate.[66] In these weekly letters, Macon discussed a wide variety of topics. These letters, never meant for publication, are the closest thing to a journal Nathaniel Macon ever kept. He told Edwards, "My letters to you, must have convinced you that I consider trifling doings here, worth communicating ... & they prove also, that trifles to a friend are in my Judgment better than nothing. I have several times been astonished, at the length of my letters to you, knowing that when I begun I had not thought of what was to be contents, but the stating of one fact or circumstance brought to my recollection another, & so I went on."[67] The letters set out Macon's political philosophy at the end of his political career. Emphasizing that Old Republican doctrines had gone out of style, Macon revealed his conviction that nationalism increasingly dominated in Washington and that more corruption was certain to follow in its wake. Mangum provided a snapshot of his "friend" Macon at this period: "Mr. Macon is in extremely bad health, his spirits are occasionally deeply depressed, and he thinks frequently not only of closing his political but his mortal career. He never complains however & in that respect is one of the most remarkable men that I ever saw, at this time of life."[68]

Several letters in particular from this "journal" synopsize Macon's ideology at the end of his political career. He dealt with many topics in these letters, but all those regarding politics expressed his belief that Old Republicanism was a dying creed. In December 1827, Macon lamented the loss of republican virtue. No doubt with the factional struggle of 1820–1824 in mind, he commented that too many "great men" in a party was apt to produce rivalry and would certainly destroy "that unity of action which is generally necessary to ensure victory, & to do the most good, after the victory shall be obtained." Macon explained that this observation applied only "to the great, who are improperly ambitious" and who preferred "their own advancement, to the happiness of the people." In Macon's view

> there never can be too many men, truly great & truly good in any country, to promote its happiness & welfare. 20 such men as Cincinatus would not have injured Rome as much as Ceasar & Pompey or Marius & Sulla; no, not half as much, the 20 would not have injured it, but done it good. But ... how are the good to be known, only by strict watching, & rigid examination. The upright cannot fear investigation.[69]

In three letters written in February of 1828, Macon discussed the lack of economy in government expenditures and his concern that the new Republicans had set the Constitution aside in their pursuit of government projects. On February 17 he wrote, "Almost every bill reported is to take money out of Treasury or land from the U-S. It must be thought by some, I wish not too many, that a public debt is a public blessing & all who live on the public, no doubt think, the more taxes the better ... from such I wish to be delivered and hope the country may be free from them." Likewise on February 22 he complained: "I consider this Congress the most easy, ready & willing to appropriate the people['s] money for any purpose whatever ... a stranger would think no doubt, that the object of the contending parties was to elect their favorite candidate the president by the [size?] of the appropriations." And in the same letter he again stressed that Old Republican doctrines were out of fashion among the new Republicans; all this free spending flowed from failure to adhere to strict construction of the Constitution: "The constitution is out of fashion you know it was buried, but the funeral discourse was never published, so that its death, was not generally heard of, before fashion laid it by." As he had complained at the time of the Missouri controversy debates, he thus charged that the Republicans in Congress had in reality changed their principles, though they never admitted any deviation from the Republican doctrines of '98. In late February, Macon told Edwards that he believed the "new men" produced nothing of worth: "Congress has been in session nearly three months, & it would puzzle a wise man to find out, any good which had been done for the people."[70]

On March 22 Macon offered a devastating critique of Washington's new Republicans in terms of government spending and debt. He told Edwards that many congressmen now considered "a public debt a public blessing ... you can have no idea of the readiness, with which appropriations of money or land are made for any purpose." Macon explained that Congress was unlikely to adjourn before the tariff bill (the hated Tariff of 1828) was decided. "The fleece must be divided before a separation [of Congress]," Macon commented. Congress might go home on account of warm weather in May or June, Macon explained to Edwards, but could also find reasons to stay in Washington until its term was up "unless some violent catching complaint, was to appear in the city, & then we might hurry home, as fast as possible, as fast as troops did, when the capitol etc., etc., were burnt."⁷¹ When read with his statements about tariff men, Macon, despite his jovial tone, argued no patriots could be found in Congress: they want to rob the citizens with the tariff and appropriations but as soon as their lives were placed at risk, they would be gone. They appeared men on the make, not patriots.

In letters written in late March and early April, Macon presented some of his most bitter comments on the state of political affairs in Washington. Though he offered a critique of National Republicanism and lamented the lack of true Old Republicans in Congress, Macon's main concern was the corruption of federal patronage. Implying that Jackson and his partisans did not follow the Old Republican principles, Macon informed Edwards on March 28 that "In the Senate there is not more than seven old fashioned republicans, perhaps a few more might be found if they did not represent new states." The "money of the people" and their land, Macon complained, was given away by Congress "with as much ease, readiness & willingness as a chew of tobacco or a pinch of snuff is given away." Macon also complained that more than ever the "shy hogging" he had observed during the Missouri debates dominated Congress: "the presidential election, tariff, internal improvements, old claims for the revolution, & the public land are productive sources of it."⁷²

In his epistle of April 5, Macon used nearly the entire letter to offer a wide-ranging critique of the entire political culture of National Republicanism: government corruption and misuse of patronage, lack of economy, banks, manufacturers, and internal improvement projects. After criticizing the newspapers at Washington for injuring the "public character" and attacking both "the just and the unjust," Macon turned to his main subject: the corruption of National Republicanism. He told Edwards that he had seen men hired as laborers by the government "instead of being at work, as they ought to be, two of them standing & holding their tools in their hands, in high conservation ... now & then but slowly giving a stroke or two, & occasionally stop to join the conversation & laugh, & these men have high wages & want more; & would no doubt be willing to be put on the pension list, & some of them may probably get there." After this picture of the waste of funds by government employees, Macon described a government project to pave Pennsylvania Avenue as mere scheme to use up money and maintain the public debt "which is considered a public blessing." He mocked manufacturers as benefiting from the waste: "it may indirectly assist the manufacturers, by enabling them to furnish cloathing [sic] to the workmen employed. Thus matters go on, one [schemer?] playing into the hand of another & all cheating the people." Such were the practices of "this government of the U.S. called national instead of federal." Macon ended his critique with a comment on those who profited from the new government: The people were governed by "Jobbers in the funds, in the banks, internal improvement, public land & manufactures, all which ought to be considered the worst kind of governing." He compared these "jobbers" who "ruin the whole country" with the "common gamesters" who ruin "only a few individuals," pointing out that many considered the politicians "high quality" and everyone considered gamesters "no quality." Yet, "the last judging by the evil done, ought to be taken as the more worthy of the two, one ruins millions, the other a few individual[s]."⁷³

In his letter of April 12, 1828, Macon vividly depicted the waste of the public money on patronage projects and added a bitter critique of the goal of political patronage that summed up his view of the National Republicans' corruption. He described to Edwards a scene of workmen planting trees around the Capitol grounds:

> This morning I saw some hearty looking men, all I expect receiving wages, sent I suppose to roll a stone roller from the west end of the yard in front of the capitol to [the] east and, if a yard it may be called, four only could ... get at it to assist in the rolling, the other three walked with them, when the four stopped to rest as they often did, the three done the same, no doubt for the purpose of talking; and they go on planting trees or rather bushes round the yard, three together one slowly digging a hole, to put the bush in, one holding it, the other looking at them; I one morning asked them, why they planted the trees so thick, for it is really a thicket, was answered to take them hereafter & plant them in their proper place: other people would not be at the expense & risk of planting twice; but like master like man, all try to get from the U.S. all they can, & for as little as possible, the Tariff men, Claims men, & Laborers all alike, & all seem to act on the advice of the priest I think it was to his son, Get money honestly if you can, but get money at all events.[74]

This bitter comment on government patronage showed that Macon had soured on the new Republican politics; he believed corruption was everywhere. He lumped the abuse of patronage with the robbery of the "tariff men." In his view money had become all; principles were dead. The Old Republican at the sunset of his career thought the ideal of 1801 to be long gone. Mangum did not adopt this pessimistic aspect of Macon's political philosophy. The younger Old Republican thought that the ideal of 1801 could be reclaimed and Old Republicanism restored by a party adhering to the Principles of '98, and he remained pragmatic in regard to party building through patronage (as Macon himself had been in 1801).

Claiming that "age and infirmity" required his retirement from public service, Macon submitted his resignation as senator to the North Carolina General Assembly on November 14, 1828.[75] These letters show that Macon, like the Jackson men, fully believed that reform of the government was the chief need in Washington. Yet, in the letters Macon offers no solutions, other than a return to pure Republicanism. Macon's final political act was thus merely complaint: he returned over and over again to the same themes of lament. The Old Republican opposition ideology could offer nothing to the general government in terms of solving problems for an expanding country. Since the Missouri crisis, Macon spoke far less of the Union and far more of the South, far different from the Macon of 1801. He saw the fall of Old Republicanism as affecting only the South. In almost the last words of his political career, Macon complained that "Such a Legislature was never seen in my opinion, a contest for voting away the public money & public land, without claim or the shadow of a claim in my opinion." He told Edwards that if Congress continued its course, "The Southern states must if they are not now ruined, be shortly ruined."[76]

In the 1820s, Macon seems to have made a deliberate effort to impress Old Republican principles on his young protégés Willie Mangum and Bartlett Yancey. In Mangum's case he was highly successful. Although he did not absorb Macon's pessimism and his total opposition to nationalism, Mangum would take many of Macon's ideas forward into his political career; they would thus have a large impact on the course of politics in North Carolina in the decades to come.

The Crawford Men: Mangum and the Election of 1825

Mangum's course in the presidential election of 1825 in the U.S. House of Representatives provides an excellent snapshot of his political philosophy at the beginning of his political career in national politics. In the presidential election of 1824 in North Carolina the Old Republicans opposed the "People's ticket" of electors that united the supporters of Jackson, Calhoun, and Adams.[77] Even though the Adams men supported the ticket, it was primarily composed of Jackson-Calhoun men, and was set up to oppose the Crawford party. Like the Old Republicans in general, Mangum backed Crawford.[78] Some Raleigh Old Republicans, though, apparently questioned Mangum's commitment to Crawford. Mangum's brother, Priestly, informed Mangum that he should be on his guard because "some of Calhoun's friends about Raleigh" were proclaiming that Mangum was deserting Crawford and "fleeing to the banners of Mr. Calhoun."[79] A political friend in Raleigh, Seth Jones, likewise advised Mangum of reports that he had changed his opinion on Crawford. Mangum replied that the rumor circulating in Raleigh that he no longer supported Crawford was "wholly without foundation." On the contrary, he had become "more and more convinced" that the best interests of the country required Crawford's elevation to the presidency. "Permit me to request you to contradict that report whenever you may hear it."[80]

In the election, the People's Ticket carried the state, and this was considered a victory for Jackson and Calhoun. Nationally, Jackson won the most popular votes, but only a plurality of the Electoral College. Crawford and Adams received enough electoral votes to throw the election into the House of Representatives with an election there among Jackson, Adams, and Crawford. Yet, the Old Republicans remained the most powerful group of Republicans in the state. Bartlett Yancey was unanimously reelected speaker of the state senate, and Joseph and Weston Gales, editors of the pro–Crawford *Raleigh Register* were reelected as state printers. Macon was reelected to the U.S. Senate by unanimous vote. The legislature also chose the Old Republicans' preferred candidate for governor. In a special election for Congress in the Halifax district, Willis Alston, pledged to support Jackson in the House of Representatives's upcoming selection of the president, was defeated by George Outlaw, pledged to Crawford. The Old Republicans held nine of the states' thirteen congressional districts. Mangum and Romulus M. Saunders led the Crawford men in the House delegation.[81]

Mangum's election to the House of Representatives placed the young Old Republican at the center of the presidential election in the House in 1825. Mangum's political friends pressed him for information on his course and his assessment of the situation. At the beginning of the session, Mangum expressed a belief that Jackson would "in all probability be the president," but he insisted that "Crawford's friends" in the Virginia, North Carolina, Georgia, and Delaware delegations would "stand upon their arms" against his enemies.[82] When rumors began to circulate that Mangum might desert the Old Republicans and vote for Jackson, Mangum sought to counteract the false reports. When Bartlett Yancey wrote him about the reports, Mangum was indignant and told Yancey that he was "astonished" to hear that anybody could "form the slightest pretence or indulge the remotest expectation" that he would vote for anyone other than Crawford. Mangum also indicated that the North Carolina delegation had not considered any other course than voting for Crawford. He authorized Yancey to make clear his "determination not to give up the ship." The delegation agreed that their support for Crawford would not be "surrendered." Mangum reassured Yancey that the delegation would act together: "None of Crawford's friends from No. Ca. will move unless all move. They will act with perfect harmony, & en masse."[83]

Mangum correctly assessed that Clay's influence would be the deciding factor in the election, and, like his mentor Macon, he did not take a very favorable view of Clay's machinations.

"The election I think will depend upon the course that Mr. Clay may take," he explained to Duncan Cameron, "Of this I entertain scarcely any doubt." Though Clay and his friends were maintaining "the utmost reserve," Mangum was sure they would not "stand still"; when Clay moved, his first object would be "success." "Our notions of patriotism become quite low," he commented, "when we see a gentleman occupying so much space in the public mind as Mr. Clay regulated by no higher considerations." Clay's maneuverings somewhat disillusioned the first-term congressman: the intrigues in the House, he lamented to Cameron, exhibited "an afflicting spectacle to those that have been in the habit of considering ours the purest government that ever existed on the face of the earth."[84]

Mangum best summarized his own intentions and motivations in early January. He again stated his belief that "the best interests of our country" required Crawford's election. "I know full well that these sentiments do not suit the county of Wake," he acknowledged, "But I cannot bring myself for mere purposes of popularity, to abandon what in my heart I believe to be those principles that make for the welfare of our common country." Anticipating a negative reaction to his continued support for Crawford despite the vote of North Carolina for Jackson, Mangum insisted that his first responsibility as a congressman was to act as he thought best for the country: "It will be objected to me that I set up my opinions against the will of the State." Satisfying his constituents was secondary, he explained, to his "duty to myself & my country in all public trusts." He would not be swayed by public criticism or popular sentiment: "My great object has been to *find out the true course*, & to pursue it steadily & firmly, & leave the consequences to God, & my countrymen." As long as Crawford had "the remotest prospect of success" Mangum felt that it was his duty to vote for him. If no such chance existed, Mangum hoped that the North Carolina delegation would be among the last "to give way."[85] Mangum received at least one letter informing him that his political friends (and fellow supporters of Crawford) expected Mangum and the friends of Crawford in the delegation to hold to their course "tho' you should suffer like the martyrs of old in defence of the truth"; their friends, his correspondent assured him, would reward their firmness and his opponents would "observe your consistancy [sic]."[86] Mangum believed that the issues at stake serious enough to warrant an extended speech in the House the week before the election clarifying his position for his constituents. Mangum's defense of his course followed the outline he provided to Robertson, but the speech also encapsulates his ideology during his first year in Congress.

Mangum delivered his speech in the House of Representatives over the course of two days, February 3 and 7, 1825. In part, he was replying to a speech by Jackson supporter George McDuffie of South Carolina asserting that the state delegations were more or less obligated to vote as their state's people had voted in the recent election. Mangum focused on three topics related to the election: the assertions of some Jackson supporters that the House should abide by the plurality of the vote for Jackson, the related argument against absolute adherence to "the will of the people," and the importance of the independent judgment of congressmen. His broad themes were states' rights, strict construction, the independence of Congress, and the dangers of populism. Throughout his speech, Mangum, as an Old Republican and Crawford man, played on the People's Ticket: the name adopted by Crawford's opposition in North Carolina. The speech, which clearly reflected Mangum's Old Republican philosophy, is also important because it indicated political ideas that influenced his decisions for the remainder of his political career.

Mangum argued that the House members were not bound by any obligation to elect the candidate who happened to win the plurality of votes in the Electoral College, as some supporters of Andrew Jackson were insisting. Neither were the congressmen bound by the votes of their respective states nor even their districts, the latter "the doctrine of the *people's men*." Voting by the results of national, state, or district election, he asserted, was "a mere question of *expediency*" not a "principle," as some Jackson supporters were arguing, because the Constitution did not specify it. Voting in accordance with state results, adhered to as a principle, would actually overthrow the most fundamental rule of democratic government, Mangum argued. Electoral votes were awarded to the states based on population, but in a House presidential election each of the twenty-six states received one vote—all were equal. Abiding by the principle of voting in accordance with the results of state elections could actually enforce the "odious doctrine that the minority shall prevail over the majority": if thirteen or more small states had voted for one candidate in the Electoral College "without effect," they could come into the House and do the same "with complete effect." Mangum could not follow such a doctrine: "Sir, if these are *people's principles*, I, for one, beg to be delivered from them."

He then turned to the related argument made by some Jackson men that the results of the election in congressmen's districts were effectively instructions by the people of the district that the congressman was bound to follow. Mangum did not agree, and he criticized the doctrine of instruction of members of Congress. He set out to show that "the *people's doctrines* of instructions" was a "fallacy" when applied to the House's election of a president. In matters of legislation, it was debatable whether the representative was bound to obey the will of his constituents, though "many great and wise men" held that doctrine (including Nathaniel Macon). Mangum conceded the doctrine as "a mere theory," though he did not "give a button" for the doctrine one way or the other as regarded its "*practical* utility." The Jackson men, though, were insisting that the doctrine undoubtedly applied to the election in the House. "I argue directly the reverse," Mangum declared. In formulating legislation, the people could not act in primary assemblies, and it was therefore important in a representative government that the legislature should respond to "the voice of the people" and it should reflect "the true image of the people's wishes." In a presidential election, on the other hand, "the people *can* act in primary assemblies." But when the people had failed to elect a president, the Constitution placed the election in the House; the House was "the *umpire*, the judge on whom devolves the settlement of that momentous question which the people have been unable to settle themselves." Mangum asserted that it was the duty of the congressmen "to do what is right, according to the best dictates of our own understandings, and leave the consequences to God, and to our country.... It is we who must elect."

His assertion against applying the doctrine of instruction to the election opened his argument for the independence of Congress, and he expanded the argument to include opposition to popular appeals, a position that he tied to states' rights and the doctrine of strict construction of the Constitution. This was the central theme of his speech. In Mangum's view the independence of Congress was critical to states' rights and strict construction of the Constitution. Early in his speech, he insisted that the states were twenty-four equal and "distinct and independent sovereigns." After his critique of the doctrine of instruction, he turned to popular appeals. He recognized, he said, the "immense advantages" of those in Congress who appealed to "the prejudices and passions of the people" rather than to "the understanding and the judgment" of the people. "The people's rights, and the sovereignty of the people!—the very finest and the most popular themes for declamation!" he found great difficulty in being heard "coolly and dispassionately, at the bar of reason" when such appeals were made. McDuffie had declared that "all sovereign power resides in the people" and that "every agent in authority must act in obedience to the will." Mangum granted that as an "abstract proposition" that doctrine was true, but he questioned how the will of the people was to be ascertained. A large majority had voted *against* each of the candidates. "We are told we must bow to the will of the people. I grant it. But I shall look for the indications of that will to a source which is unerring—to the constitutional indication of it." Mangum identified what was, in his view, the "true conception" of the framers:

> That the representatives in this House would come immediately from the people—they are part of the people—presumed to be men of some character, connected with the community from which they emanate by a thousand ties; character, respect, family, children, a common interest, a common destiny. In a word, identified with that community in habits, feelings, sentiments, etc.; and, that when the result, so much to be deprecated, of the Presidential election being cast upon this House, shall happen, that all these ties and considerations form a sufficient guarantee that a wise, honest, and judicious selection will be made.

This was, Mangum believed, "conformable with the theory of the constitution." He pronounced those who insisted that the "will of the people" could be carried out by selecting a man who had not won election by the requirements of the Constitution "deluded and bewildered" by "an overweening attachment to their new-born theories"—theories brought into life by brains "highly excited by political contests." Some insisted that, though such a doctrine could not be found in the letter of the Constitution, it resulted from the "*philosophy* of the constitution." Mangum deprecated such an assumption as one deriving from the same source as Republican nationalist assaults on state sovereignty, a broad construction of constitutional powers:

> Yes, sir, the *philosophy* of the constitution! That philosophy which, I fear, is to arm this great Government with that stupendous power which is to sink our state sovereignties into mere corporations—That power which has prostrated some of these barriers that wise men of both the old parties recognized—That power which is incessantly, most fearfully, and alarmingly increasing. Yes, sir, the philosophy of the constitution! That philosophy which has [been] reserved for the ingenuity and astuteness of modern times to discover.

It was, Mangum asserted, "by courting these sovereign people sedulously and arduously, that all jacobins begin their career." Mangum viewed Congress as the regent of the sovereign people: The people were indeed sovereigns, "but they are sovereigns in minority; they never have, nor will they ever come to the *crown*" despite "the flattery of their courtiers." The House should not look to "the shouts of the multitude for the opinions of the people" but to "their opinion as fairly and constitutionally expressed."[87]

Thus, in Mangum's view, the doctrine of absolute obedience to some notion of "the will of the people" when not determined by the majority in an election was an argument of radicals—demagogues courting the people for the aggrandizement of their own power. Any belief that the people had indicated their will in the presidential election was a "fallacy." Congress had to be guided by the strict letter of the Constitution and that document made the people's representatives in the House the judges to settle the election—guided solely by "the best dictates of our understandings." His opposition to Jackson and the political philosophy of Jackson's supporters is clear. He had denounced the Jacksonian doctrine of absolute obedience to the will of the people that later became a cardinal principle of the Democratic Party.

He argued that it was the tool of "jacobins," a radical doctrine at odds with limited government under the letter of the Constitution. Mangum opposed it during his first major speech in Congress, and he was to be at war with the doctrine for the rest of his political career.

As most expected, Clay swung his support in the House to Adams. When Adams appointed Clay secretary of state, Jackson's supporters issued charges of "bargain and corruption" and refused to accept the legitimacy of the House election. Arguing that Clay and Adams were thwarting the will of the people, the Jacksonians set themselves in opposition to the Adams administration. In the August 1825 congressional elections, North Carolinians gave evidence of both Jackson's popularity and the continued strength of the Old Republicans. Demonstrating the popular displeasure that Mangum and the other Crawford men in the delegation risked by remaining loyal to Crawford, Carolinians did not return six of the congressmen who voted against Jackson to Congress (of course, this includes those who had always supported Adams). But five Crawford men won reelection.[88]

Mangum, though, won in a very close election. Nevertheless, the elections warned Old Republicans about the possible effects of Jackson's popularity. State legislator David Caldwell of Salisbury, a Jackson supporter who had been a fellow student with Mangum at the University of North Carolina, praised the latter's stand in support of Crawford: "Much to your credit, you hazarded your popularity & ran the risk of being swept out of view by public indignation. I know of no event in your public career, which has elevated you so much with the reflecting men of No Carolina."[89] Mangum's star continued to rise among the Old Republicans. Early in his Congressional career he had already established himself as opposed to the "people's doctrines" of absolute adherence to the majority will.

"Had it been contented to have traveled a plain and known road": Old Republican Opposition to the Adams Administration

Within a year and half of Adams' inauguration the Old Republicans were firmly in opposition to his administration. Many, including Macon, shared the Jackson men's characterization of Adams' appointment of Clay as Secretary of State as a "corrupt bargain." Old Republicans were so likely to accept this characterization that Clay spent the rest of his political career trying to overcome it in the South. As soon as Adams confirmed that his administration would reflect the nationalism that he, Clay, and Calhoun had championed in the Monroe administration, the Old Republicans moved into opposition (where they were always most comfortable). From the start of his administration, Adams made his course clear. The Old Republicans, almost to a man, placed themselves in opposition to the administration as soon as Adams laid out his goals in his first annual message. As historian William Hoffman notes: "Political considerations and southern interests dictated that the Crawford men should oppose John Quincy Adams."[90]

President Adams' first annual message of December 6, 1825, presenting an ambitious National Republican vision, did more to move the Old Republicans to opposition than any other action of his presidency. Adams recommended a national program of internal improvements, a national university, the financing of scientific explorations, the building of an astronomical observatory (which he called a "lighthouse of the sky"), and the creation of the Department of the Interior.[91] An enlightened plan, the National Republican agenda of 1825 embodied all the doctrines of nationalism its officers had envisioned during the Monroe administration. When presented to Congress, it raised a conservative firestorm and it went nowhere. The Old Republicans in particular were taken aback by the expansiveness of Adams' nationalist vision in this message. Macon responded negatively by declaring that Adams' "first message was enough to change the opinions of most people."[92] Macon thought that Adams had made too broad a claim for executive power in the message: "The message of the President seems to claim all the powers of the federal Government which have heretofore produced so much debate and which the election of Mr. Jefferson was supposed to have settled."[93]

Macon believed that in Monroe's second term the executive branch had attempted to reach for powers beyond the grants of the Constitution, and he perceived a dangerous union between executive power and Republican nationalism. The Senate provided the only opposition to these presidential ambitions. "The Senate of late years has been the check on executive power," he told a Carolina friend in 1825.[94] The Senate, of course, is where the sovereign states were represented. Macon thought Monroe's administration "went far towards establishing the construction & to extend the executive power."[95] Now, the charge that Adams was seeking executive power was Macon's chief complaint against the new administration. And executive power also figured into the Old Republicans' objections to the president's acceptance, without the consent of the Senate, of an invitation to send delegates to the Congress of American Republics in Panama.[96] Macon argued that Adams was following Monroe in grasping for executive powers not granted by the Constitution, and he included corruption and patronage in the charge. In a general complaint against the direction of both the Monroe and Adams administrations, Macon declared, "The bank of the U.S. and internal improvement have changed the constitution or rather made a new one containing the old form."[97]

Macon was most concerned about the corrupting power of its patronage if the administration refused to recognize the limited powers of the Constitution. He warned Bartlett Yancey that "a Government which has complete power over the purse and sword, with a patronage of millions of dollars, cannot easily be kept in check, by a constitution which by construction or implication can be made to mean whatever a majority may deem expedient or convenient." Macon thought that Adams's internal improvement plans were only attempts to increase presidential power:

> Of all schemes ever devised to increase the power of the executive, that of internal improvement is by far the most tremendous, because, it operates on all; both the rich & the poor consider it a power exercised for their benefit, and all expect an improvement near their land, by which they are to add greatly to their property and all who are in debt, expect a good contract, by which they are to pay their debts & make a fortune.[98]

Macon concisely stated the Old Republican doctrine that aid to economic development lay outside the realm of the federal government. Such aid was corrupting, and corruption meant loss of republican independence. In Macon's doctrine, then, the Senate, where the sovereign and equal states were represented, was the only check on the dangerous, corrupting and unrepublican ambitions of presidents. In short, the Constitution would be defended by the Senate.

By mid–1826 the Old Republicans had hardened in opposition to the Adams administration, which they viewed as a national Republican administration opposed to the true principles of Republicanism. In April 1826, Macon gave his assessment of the Adams administration to Bartlett Yancey. It lacked the proper conservatism for a Republican administration:

> The administration might have got along probably tolerably well, had it been contented to have traveled a plain and known road. But the Panama trip, & the visit to the sky, & the attempt to make the constitutional way as wide as the world, has and will embarrass it. The men in it are not equal to the task of doing these things. Adams is learned and Clay has genius, but prudence and discretion are wanted.[99]

Though he recognized the talents of Adams and Clay, Macon still could not accept the "new men" as the equals of the Old Republicans. Mangum absorbed these views and heartily opposed the administration.

Jackson's Revolution: The Old Republicans and Andrew Jackson

By the election of 1824, the unity of the Jeffersonian party was gone, replaced by several different factions all claiming the Republican mantra. With Calhoun in the vice-presidency and Clay as Secretary of State, Republican nationalism was now represented by the administration (by 1828 the administration party would identify itself as the National Republicans). Opposition to the administration was almost bound to be anti-national in character and thus provided a rationale for the Jackson men to unite with the Crawford men under the banner of Old Republican ideology. This union was the essence of Jackson's political revolution, but the Crawford men's suspicions of Jackson made it a difficult undertaking. Continued dissatisfaction with the nationalist course of the Adams-Calhoun-Clay administration moved the Old Republicans to the Jackson Republican coalition.

Martin Van Buren allied his New York party with Jackson and sought to attract the Old Republicans of Virginia and North Carolina to his Jackson coalition. Van Buren's highly-disciplined New York party represented a new form in American politics, and he sought to transfer that organization to his new Jackson Republican coalition. Van Buren's new style of party organization had significant implications for basing politics on an ideology of nationalism. The new form of party developed by Van Buren did not rely on ideology as its unifying premise. He and the leaders of New York's Republican liberals, or "Bucktails," ran their party with what one historian has described as "a new level of political organization, skill, and professional elan." They preferred their leaders to be "careful technicians of party consensus and loyal servants of party interests." Breaking party ranks was intolerable.[100] From Jefferson's opposition to the Federalists in 1798–1799 to 1820, ideology had been the most important factor in party politics. With Van Buren's new organization, party itself became more important than support of an ideology. "The Little Magician," notes historian Merrill Peterson, "contrived to make party itself the dominant interest."[101]

Andrew Jackson, attributed to Thomas Sully (1783–1872), oil on canvas, mounted on board, ca. 1857 (U.S. Senate).

Having strenuously opposed Jackson in

1824, the Old Republicans were initially cool towards joining his coalition and were unsure of his principles. After the election of 1824, Macon predicted the formation of new parties, but he feared the new partisans would be "rather the followers of men than principles." Though principles might mix "with the admiration of the men," he thought patronage would control such parties.[102] In early 1826 Macon doubted that a unified opposition could be formed because the anti-administration factions disagreed too much about principles and measures.[103] In March Macon opposed both Adams and Jackson and found little difference between their political principles. He disapproved of Adams' measures and thought that he had "made a bad beginning." Of Jackson, he would say only that he did not wish to see him president. He refused to decide between the two until the election approached.[104]

Yet, the Old Republicans of North Carolina entered into the Jackson coalition because it, rather than holding out for a solely Old Republican candidate, seemed to best serve their interests. In Congress, Van Buren consulted with the North Carolina Old Republicans in regard to joining the Crawford, Jackson, and Calhoun men into a united opposition to the Adams administration.[105] Van Buren made a southern tour in the spring of 1827 and visited Raleigh.[106] Some North Carolina Old Republicans, Bartlett Yancey in particular, originally leaned to DeWitt Clinton of New York as an Old Republican candidate.[107]

Calhoun made a separate bid to win North Carolina to the support of his own presidential ambitions, and he gained a large following in the western part of the state. Calhoun tried to win over the North Carolina delegation in Congress, and in particular attempted to gain Mangum's friendship.[108] Calhoun visited Bartlett Yancey in March of 1827 and may have been courting the Old Republicans of the state to support him.[109] Calhoun's main supporters in North Carolina were a group of Republicans in western North Carolina based in Salisbury led by Charles Fisher. The organ of these Calhoun "Western Republicans" was the Salisbury *Western Carolinian*. Their party was second only to the Old Republicans in political strength.[110] They strongly supported the Jackson-Calhoun ticket for 1828 (Jackson had promised to serve only a single term). The Old Republicans opposed Calhoun on the ticket, and many held out for DeWitt Clinton as vice-president. After Clinton died, the Old Republicans reluctantly accepted Calhoun.[111]

The elections of 1827 in North Carolina provided a final push for the Old Republicans to join the Jackson Republicans, mainly as a means of overcoming the combined opposition of other Republican factions in the state. In the congressional elections seven Jackson men won. But in the gubernatorial election the Fisher group of pro–Calhoun Western Republicans united with the former Federalists in the East to elect James Iredell (an ex–Federalist) governor. William Polk, the candidate of the 1824 Jackson men, withdrew his name in favor of Iredell, so the election was also partially an alliance with the original Jackson men. As Hoffman notes: "The alliance of former Federalists with the western Republicans and original Jackson men was too great for Old Republicans to overcome."[112]

By 1828, the Old Republicans of Virginia and North Carolina supported Jackson as the candidate who united their opposition to Adams, the alleged corruption and illegitimacy of his presidency, and the National Republican measures. Macon was representative of the shift. In November 1827, Macon stated that he "greatly" preferred Jackson to Adams.[113] But by the following February he had soured on the whole election: "The constitution of the U.S. I have long considered dead & gone; and the present scuffle for the presidency I consider rather a scuffle for men than principle; but this ought not to prevent trying to get one that we prefer, hence I go for Jackson," he told Yancey.[114] John Randolph reflected the Old Republicans' view of Jackson's candidacy as the remedy for Adams's departures from true Republicanism when he declared in the Senate: "Sir, if we succeed [in electing Jackson], we shall restore the Constitution—we shall redress the injury done to the people—we shall regenerate the country."[115]

Despite Randolph's seemingly greater enthusiasm for Jackson, Macon typified the attitude of the North Carolina Old Republicans more than the Virginian. In spite of Macon's protestations of having no influence, the Old Republicans would not have backed Jackson without his blessing. Macon believed Jackson better than Adams if he could not have Crawford. Republican principles were safer with Jackson than with Adams. Randolph's declaration that Jackson was the solution to the country's dangers represented more of an attack on Adams and Clay than total support for Jackson. The Old Republicans of North Carolina were not enthusiastic Jackson supporters until after 1828, and some remained lukewarm even after that.

The new Jackson–Old Republican coalition claimed the mantra of the Republican party, and it adopted the Old Republican charge that the National Republicans were apostates from true Republicanism who did not deserve the name of Republicans—many in the new coalition called the National Republicans "Federalists."

Jackson's revolution in North Carolina culminated with the election of 1828. Mangum's campaign efforts as an elector for the Jackson ticket repaired his standing with the General Assembly. The Jackson party's campaign charges against the administration party touched a chord with the Old Republicans: that the administration had come to power through "a corrupt bargain," that Adams had abused the patronage, and that he was grossly extravagant. They demanded "reform."[116] The united Jackson coalition organized "Democratic Jackson Meetings" in counties across the state and published the reports and resolutions of the meetings in the newspapers.[117] In particular a Jackson meeting of Wake County Republicans held in Raleigh on December 24, 1827, issued a lengthy report praising Jackson and indicting Adams.[118] Adams men held their own meetings, and an Adams state convention met in Raleigh on December 20, 1827.[119]

Clearly perceived as an Old Republican committed to support Jackson, Willie Mangum was chosen as a Jackson elector for the 8th electoral district (Person, Orange, and Granville counties).[120] In North Carolina, Jackson's popular vote exceeded his total of 1824. Jackson electors received 37,857 votes; Adams electors, 13,918. Adams carried only five eastern and three piedmont counties.[121] What most indicated the Old Republicans' embrace of Jackson was that the five strongest Old Republican counties in 1824 (Caswell, Person, Granville, Warren, and Bladen) gave Jackson large majorities in 1828.[122] Old Republicans had become Jackson men by 1828.

After the presidential election, Mangum was elected by joint ballot of the state legislature to the superior court.[123] The Old Republicans thus rewarded him by returning him to the superior court, and he was clearly considered one of their leading men. After Bartlett Yancey's death in September 1828 and Macon's retirement from active politics, leadership of the Old Republicans in North Carolina devolved on Richard Dobbs Spaight, Romulus M. Saunders, and Mangum. The move to Jackson allowed the Old Republicans to maintain their predominance in North Carolina politics, and they became the strongest faction in the Jackson party. As Hoffman points out: "Although the members of the Old Republican faction were late to espouse the cause of the hero, they became the strongest wing within the party."[124]

"Both Sides Claim You": Mangum's Election to the Senate

After the election of 1828, a new temporary factional political alignment emerged in the North Carolina legislature. The various Republican factions in the legislature divided into two parties. As supporters of Jackson and Calhoun, the Old Republicans joined with the "Western Republicans." Both groups shared opposition to the tariff and strict constructionist, states' rights views, and the ideological outlook of this party was Old Republicanism. Its leaders were Charles Fisher and Old Republicans Spaight, Saunders, and Mangum. This coalition was usually termed the "the Spaight faction" or simply "the party." The other Republican faction identified itself as an opponent of "the party" and might thus be called "the opposition." This opposition party included National Republicans, eastern Jackson men favorable to internal improvements, and western opponents of Fisher's faction. Prominent members of the opposition were William J. Alexander of Charlotte and David Caldwell of Salisbury, Fisher's chief opponents in the west; John Owen, a wealthy Bladen planter and Jackson man; and James Iredell and William Gaston, who were National Republicans. When the 1829 legislature selected a replacement for John Branch, newly appointed to Jackson's cabinet, the Western-Old Republican faction elected their candidate, Bedford Brown.[125] In the legislature of 1830, the two parties divided the leadership of the state legislature. Charles Fisher was elected speaker of the House and David Caldwell was elected speaker of the Senate, but the opposition believed "the party" could command a majority of the joint vote of both houses and thus elect their favored candidates for governor and the U.S. Senate.[126]

In 1830, when Iredell retired from the U.S. Senate and the legislature again had to choose a senator, Mangum became embroiled in a complicated struggle between the two legislative parties. John Owen was the opposition's preferred candidate while most of the Spaight faction favored John R. Donnell, a superior court judge. Though as an Old Republican he was in the Spaight faction, Mangum had friends in both of the parties and was seen by his friends in the opposition as a compromise candidate. Some of Mangum's friends in the opposition, though friendly to Owen, believed that neither Owen nor Donnell were "fit in point of Talent for the Station" and that Mangum was "a man of more talent." Additionally, Mangum's opposition friends believed that his support among some prominent members of the Spaight faction would allow the opposition to divide that party, elect a more suitable man to the Senate, and prevent the Spaight faction from electing their favored candidate. Opposition leader William Alexander approved of Mangum's nomination, as did Fisher. Mangum's friends in the Spaight faction also viewed him as a compromise candidate. "Both sides claim you," one of Mangum's opposition friends, Charles L. Hinton of Wake County, explained. The members from the Roanoke River counties (Warren, Halifax, and Northampton) were particularly anxious for Mangum to run. Mangum was assured by his friends in the opposition faction that Owen would not oppose him. Mangum did not refuse the overtures; he allowed his brother Priestly to authorize Hinton to inform Mangum's friends that if they thought "the emergency of the times" required it, they were at liberty to nominate him.[127] Many in the Spaight faction accepted Mangum as an alternative to Donnell.[128]

Mangum's friends wanted to delay his nomination until they were sure of a majority, but two members of the Spaight faction nominated Mangum, apparently in order to deny the opposition members the prestige of being first to name him. Mangum's nomination by "the party," created rancor in the opposition ranks that threatened to upset the strategy of his friends. One of them told Mangum that Alexander wished him to confer with him and he urged Mangum to come to Raleigh to help "assuage the acrimony of party spirit."[129] Many of Mangum's friends firmly supported him regardless which legislative party nominated him. While the opposition had largely favored him, his adoption by the Spaight faction had changed everything. As Hinton explained to Mangum, "Had you been nominated by Owens' friends they would have gone generally for you, and the same opposition would have shewn [sic] itself on the other side."[130] Owen allowed his name to be brought before the legislature and received a large block of votes, though neither candidate received a majority. Feeling betrayed by Owen, Mangum wrote Owen an angry public letter in which he advised Owen, "I have implicated your political principles in the strongest & most unequivocal manner."[131]

The letter apparently angered some in the Owen faction, but it may have helped Mangum's cause. Owen's vote total subsequently increased, but the letter apparently convinced Spaight that Mangum was not Owen's friend. Spaight began to vote for Mangum after the letter was made known in the legislature.[132] On the fifth ballot, Owen received 97 votes, one short of a majority; Mangum had 86 votes. With the Spaight faction now almost wholly backing Mangum and Owen himself in the field, the situation had now reversed from the original strategy of Mangum's friends in the opposition: to compensate for the number of holdouts among them who refused to vote for Mangum, "the party" was now trying to get enough of the opposition to abandon Owen and elect Mangum.[133]

Mangum wrote a letter to his friends withdrawing his name, but Saunders and others in the Spaight faction thought they could still elect him if they obtained a temporary postponement of the balloting and kept his name in nomination. They succeeded in the postponement, and Saunders urged Mangum to come to Raleigh as "a friend to the *cause.*" Warning Mangum that "your sayings & yr. letters have been grossly misrepresented," Saunders explained that those in the opposition hostile to Mangum were using his letter to Owen as a "menace" and were doing everything in their power to defeat him. "You have met with *traitors* when [you] had a right to expect friends," Saunders told him, indicating the unexpected nature of the opposition to Mangum. Leaders of the Spaight faction feared defeat by the opposition, partly as a result of their inability to keep some of their own members from opposing Mangum. Yet, Saunders felt sure that Mangum, if he came to Raleigh, could allay some of the opposition to his election and gain enough votes for a majority. Mangum, Saunders insisted, should come to Raleigh for "your friends & the *cause*—unless you come we are beaten—if you come we will succeed."[134]

Mangum followed Saunders' advice and came to Raleigh. He persuaded enough members to support him to win a solid majority when balloting resumed. He received 103 votes to Owen's 84 (with eight votes for various others).[135] In the end, he was elected with some support from both factions, but the original plan of Mangum's friends in the opposition to split the Spaight faction and elect a senator largely on opposition votes failed. Mangum was elected with solid support in the Spaight faction and the support of all of its leaders. He was thus placed in the Senate by Old Republicans and Western Republicans and, as his letter attacking Owen's political views shows, this was largely in accordance with his own ideological preferences.

Mangum, the ideological heir to Nathaniel Macon, would now return the political ideas of the arch Old Republican to the United States Senate. But he would soon come to oppose the party of Jackson and Van Buren that had helped to elect him.

3

The Beginning of Opposition: States' Rights and the Anti–Van Buren Party

Newly elected North Carolina senator Willie Mangum supported president Andrew Jackson, New York senator Martin Van Buren, and their party on his arrival in Washington, D.C., to take up his seat. But Mangum became increasingly disenchanted with the New Yorker. When Van Buren betrayed him over revisions to the Tariff of 1828, Mangum broke with the Old Republicans and joined the party in North Carolina opposed to Van Buren. That shift had a profound impact on the course of North Carolina politics.

"A Positive Evil upon the Whole Region of the South"

Early in 1828 Van Buren worried that the popularity of Clay's American System with its protective tariffs might jeopardize support for Andrew Jackson in the critical Middle Atlantic region states where the tariff was popular. With the Old Republicans of the South now fully supporting Jackson, Van Buren ignored Southern interests and took over the administration's tariff bill in Congress, shaping it to add benefits for the Middle Atlantic states. A combination of Van Buren supporters and administration men passed the tariff. Jackson supporters in the South felt betrayed by the Tariff of 1828, and Southerners called it "The Tariff of Abominations."[1]

Macon bitterly opposed the tariff as a device that taxed the South and transferred the wealth to the manufacturers of the Northeast states. "The tariff men, under the present law, take all the south can make, & ought to be content," he told Weldon Edwards, "but they like all other [shavers?] want, a little more [than?] all…. The labor of the slaves go to enrich those, who pretend to be, against this condition, & who know that they are better of [sic] than the poor in their own country." Macon was convinced that the "tariff has ruined the South & will continue [to] oppress it and make it poorer & poorer."[2] These were the views of the Old Republicans, and as a new senator Mangum made opposition to the Tariff of Abominations his chief issue.

In his first year in the Senate, Mangum's first policy priority was adjustment of the Tariff of 1828 and his first major speech in the Senate opposed it. The Tariff of 1828 had become the bane of all Old Republicans because of its supposedly pernicious effects on the South and its associations with Henry Clay's "American System."[3] This speech completely stated Mangum's ideology at this point in his career and was influential among North Carolina's Republicans.[4] He was responding to Clay's resolutions that would have reduced rates but maintained protection. Mangum based his argument against the protective tariff on the Old Republican belief that the Constitution's grant of power to Congress "to regulate commerce" did not entail a power to protect domestic manufactures. But the speech contained much more; the ideas Mangum explained in later shaped his future political course. His main themes were moderation, sectional equality, opposition to Clay's American System, and a defense of the Southern political economy that also was a proslavery critique of Northern manufacturing.

Mangum insisted that any revision to the tariff reestablish equality among the states. Yet, he took a moderate stance. The question of the Tariff, Mangum explained, was both "difficult and delicate." Acknowledging that a sudden shock to the manufacturers was not in the country's interest, Mangum declared that "Wisdom, prudence and justice require that [the reduction of the tariff] shall be effected with as little injury as possible to the manufacturing establishments, built up in a different state of things." But legislation on the tariff must achieve equality: all adjustments to the tariff must be done "with a due regard to all the great interests of the country," Mangum insisted, and that included the agrarian interest as well as the manufacturing interest. "[T]he great object of those I represent, and with whom I associate," Mangum declared, "is to adjust this system so as to approximate, as near as may be, an equal participation in the burdens and benefits of the Government."

Mangum then launched an attack on the "unjust exactions" of Clay's "selfish and remorseless American system." Clay's resolutions did not achieve equality; they were, Mangum claimed, "subversive of every maxim of an enlightened political economy" and were "utterly regardless of that confidence and affection cemented by mutual interest, which constitute the broad basis—and the only basis—upon which rests the noble structure of our free institutions." He accused Clay's system of burdening and depressing the navigating interest. Departing temporarily from his own call for moderation, he followed this attack with a harsh Old Republican critique of the northern and eastern "monopolists and capitalists" ("all those who consume more of the fruits of the earth than they produce by the sweat of their brow"[5]) who were in league with "bandit interests" and "adventuring politicians." Together they perpetuated the "protective system" of "inequality, rapacity, and oppression" that was "built up by selfish interests, associated together for selfish purposes; with no principle of cohesion, but a mean, base passion for money, unredeemed by any great public, and patriotic fruits."

Mangum then presented an extended defense of the South's economy compared to the New England manufacturing economy. Using one of Nathaniel Macon's favorite expressions, Mangum highlighted the regional differences in the tariff's effects by declaring that the idea that "a national debt is a public blessing" would be only the case for the Northeastern states and "a positive evil upon the whole region of the South." Mangum declared the belief that the South could ever be a manufacturing region was a "delusion." Contrasting the economies of the two regions, he exposed elements of the pro-slavery argument in his rhetoric, revealing his absolute commitment to the slave society and his failure to realize, or at least his unwillingness to acknowledge, the harshness and violence involved in the very nature of the slavery regime. Mangum believed that the conditions in the new factories of the northeastern manufacturing states were already approaching those in England's mills which used "the cheap labor of a half-starved, beggared and dependent population." The "miserable, slavish existence" of these working people did not favor liberty or morality. Jeffersonian agrarian society was far more conducive to republican liberty: "Is there not an immeasurable difference in the scale of being, between him who plants his on his own soil, feeling a high and manly sense of his personal independence—the master of his own little domain—surrounded by a happy, industrious, and virtuous family; and the day-laborer, with a scattered family, toiling from sun to sun, in crowed factories, breathing its noxious and foetid [sic] air; dependent for his daily bread upon the master of the establishment; and cringing to his testy humors, or losing his place?" The workers' dependence was so complete that "the will of the master is the law of the dependents." Ignoring the slaveholders' own violence to mothers and their children, Mangum criticized northern manufacturers' use of "delicate young females" who had been "torn from a mother's love and a mother's care" as labor in some of these factories (which Clay had praised in his speech). In Mangum's view, the paternalism of the slave labor system made it superior. In the factory system there were no "obligations on the part of the master to feed or clothe the laborer, and without sympathy for his distresses, we must be convinced that it is the *most refined slavery*, and is infinitely more grievous and oppressive than the very worst condition of negro slavery in this country. I never saw a negro pauper without shelter, clothing and bread."

Returning to more moderate rhetoric, Mangum concluded his speech with a summary of his argument for state equality, a defense of President Jackson, and a return to his call for compromise. Mangum insisted that the tariff system levied taxes of "ruinous inequality" on the South. The system was an "unequal operation" because three-fourths of the revenue was disbursed in "in the non-exporting States." The tariff was "advantageous to the Tariff States" and "disastrous to the planting states." Mangum also denied that the tariff in any way augmented "national wealth and the national prosperity." Against Clay's claims that Jackson had misled Southerners on the tariff, Mangum asserted that Southerners always understood him to favor of the protective tariff, but trusted his moderation.

> Loving him as we did, admiring him as we must, revering him as we ought, and confiding in him as we still delight to do, we, nevertheless, always remembered his opinions on this subject, with deep regret.... But *we believed he preferred his country to himself*—that he would urge this policy no farther, than he believed the great interests of the country required, and that he was wholly incapable of abusing it either to *acquire* or to *retain* power. In a word, all believed him to be an honest man—firm—patriotic and fearless. This is the fortress of his strength—The hearts of the people is the citadel of his power.

Mangum ended the speech by appealing to a "spirit of conciliation and kindness" as the policy was considered by the Senate, but also demanding recognition that the tariff in its current form was intolerable to the States' Rights men of the South. "Sir, I feel a deep conviction, that this system, and this Union cannot exist permanently together—who can be insensible to the wisdom, the patriotism of mutual consession?"

This speech shows that Mangum fully identified with the Old Republican states' rights ideology. The portions of the speech decrying the manufacturing interest, the harshness of factory labor, and the dependent factory hand as a poor republican citizen and praising the good republican yeoman farmer of the South and the mild paternalism of slavery demonstrate the Old Republicanism of Mangum's thought and specifically the influence of Nathaniel Macon. His rhetoric contrasting the economies of the Northeast with that of the South also revealed a new element in the pro-slavery argument in the 1830s: the denial that slavery could ever be as harsh to the enslaved as the factory system was to the laborer. And the speech demonstrates Mangum's paternalistic view of the slave society. Additionally, Mangum showed that he held Macon's view of the Republican party as the party binding equal states together. The tariff failed to meet Macon's (and now Mangum's) test of regional equality. The South derived no benefit from the tariff—there was no regional equality of benefit versus loss; therefore, there was no *national* benefit, no increase to *national* prosperity. Policy should be made considering *all* regional interests. But Mangum's reference that tariff policy should be made in a spirit of "mutual concession" shows his openness to compromise. Finally, the speech indicates that in early 1832 Mangum still trusted Jackson's moderation regarding policy on the South.

As a summary of his states' rights views, Mangum thought the ideas in this speech were important, and he wanted political men throughout the state to read them. Mangum modestly told Charity that though not his best, the speech would, he thought, have a good political effect: "I was not exactly pleased with my effort—Yet I have reason to believe, that the almost universal opinion of the Senate is that it was eloquent & powerful."[6] Old Republicans were pleased with his speech. Fellow Old Republican leader Romulus Saunders wrote to Mangum, "Your speech is read with approbation."[7] John Bragg, a Warrenton lawyer and state legislator, congratulated Mangum in early March on his "late stand against the Tariff" and urged him to have his speech printed and "extensively distributed" throughout North Carolina.[8] Mangum followed his advice and distributed the speech widely in pamphlet form to men he knew were active participants in politics.[9] One of the recipients, Francis Jones, a justice of the peace in Warren County, praised the speech as "a bold and manly defence [sic] of Southern interests." Robert B. Gilliam, an Oxford (Granville County) attorney, likewise approved "not with satisfaction merely, but with pride, & ever with exultation." John Long, a former state legislator from Randolph County (in the Piedmont region), however, took a different view of the speech. "I can assure you," he wrote, "as far as my knowledge extends you are quite mistaken in supposing the people of No. Ca. are so hostile to the Tariff. I have not conversed with a single individual on the subject who is opposed to it."[10] Mangum's ardent hostility to the protective tariff soon attracted him to a new party in North Carolina formed to oppose the ambitions of the man who had organized President Jackson's victory, but who many Carolina Republicans came to believe stood in favor of the tariff and against the South—Martin Van Buren.

Anti–Van Buren–States' Rights Republicans

When John Henry Eaton, Andrew Jackson's confidante and Secretary of War-designate, wed Margaret O'Neale Timberlake, widow of a naval officer and daughter of an Irish-immigrant tavern keeper, they unwittingly began the prelude to a political revolution in North Carolina. The marriage produced tensions among Jackson's cabinet officers, and John Branch of Halifax, North Carolina was the chief opponent of the Eatons in the cabinet. An important leader in North Carolina state politics, Branch was a former governor and, since 1828, the senior senator from North Carolina. He was one of the original Jackson men of 1824 and the foremost advocate of the Hero of New Orleans in the state. Appreciating Branch's ardent championship of the cause and his political influence in North Carolina, Jackson selected him to be Secretary of the Navy. Branch was the first cabinet officer ever appointed from North Carolina, and the appointment was praised in the state's newspapers. Branch, however, opposed Eaton's appointment as Secretary of War, thinking that it would endanger the administration, but Jackson appointed his friend Eaton to the office.[11]

After John Eaton and Margaret Timberlake were married, the wives of some cabinet officers and other prominent women in Washington tried to drive Margaret Eaton out of Washington society. Vice-president Calhoun's wife Floride was the chief opponent of Mrs. Eaton but Branch's family also marked Mrs. Eaton as unfit for Washington society.[12] Calhoun did not restrain Floride's opposition to Margaret Eaton, and Jackson blamed Calhoun for the Eaton affair. Calhoun became estranged from Jackson.[13] Martin Van Buren's championship of Mrs. Eaton and Jackson's resulting preference for him created a personal rivalry with Branch.

The social spat over Mrs. Eaton became entangled with Calhoun and Branch's resentment of Van Buren's rise as Jackson's chief counselor. Jackson also believed Calhoun was maneuvering to succeed him. Furthermore, Jackson regarded Branch as an ally of Calhoun. By early 1831 the Branches' social snubs to Mrs. Eaton had reinforced Jackson's belief that Branch was seeking to oust Eaton from his cabinet and raise John C. Calhoun to the presidency as Jackson's successor (Jackson had promised to serve only one term). Jackson could not remove Calhoun as vice-president, but he could change his cabinet.

In April 1831, Jackson asked for Branch's resignation as part of a general cabinet reorganization suggested by Van Buren as a way to move both Eaton and Branch out of the way without risking the wrath of North Carolinians.[14] Branch wrote letters explaining that his "dismissal" from the cabinet was the result of a "malign influence" on the president.[15] Calhoun published letters complaining of intriguers who caused the break between him and Jackson. The press recognized Van Buren as the arch-conspirator in Calhoun's letters. The Salisbury *Western Carolinian*, the principal Calhoun organ in North Carolina, blamed the "disturbance in the administration" on "the intriguing spirit of Mr. Van Buren."[16] After his dismissal, Branch returned to North Carolina determined to build his popularity in the state to thwart the influence of Martin Van Buren. He succeeded in forming a formidable opposition coalition.

The formation of a party by Branch and his allies composed of all men and factions opposed to Martin Van Buren and in favor of John C. Calhoun was a pivotal event in North Carolina politics that altered all previous factional alignments among Republicans. Branch organized his election to Congress from the Second (Halifax) District and then used his position as a platform to build an opposition party.[17] In addition to his political friends, Branch succeeded in gaining the cooperation of William Polk and other original Jackson men who opposed the rise of Van Buren, and many of the Independents, including former governor James Iredell, Samuel Carson, and John Owen. Charles Fisher and other Western Republican supporters of John C. Calhoun broke their alliance with the Old Republicans and allied with the new party. And some Old Republicans began leaning towards the new group.[18] John Martin from Wilkes County told Mangum in March 1832, "The Jackson party are getting into Confusion in this part on the subject of the Vice Presidency."[19] Such indeed was the case. The Jackson coalition of 1828 had split. As the new group's unifying element was opposition to Van Buren, this party is best termed the "Anti–Van Buren" party. (Some of its meetings were described in the press as "Jackson Anti–Van Buren" meetings.[20]) In the campaign of 1832, the Anti–Van Buren party adopted a strong anti-tariff stance and campaigned to defeat Van Buren as a vice-presidential nominee and nominate the strongly anti-tariff Philip Pendleton Barbour of Virginia instead on a Jackson-Barbour ticket.[21]

The newspapers of the Anti–Van Buren party touted Calhoun's loyalty to the Old Republican doctrines (and by implication, Van Buren's disloyalty to them). Under the heading "North Carolina is true to the doctrines of Republicanism," the Salisbury *Western Carolinian* drew attention to extracts from various opposition newspapers praising Calhoun's loyalty to Old Republican principles. The *Western Carolinian* described the state as "old Republican North Carolina" and declared that the state's people were "Republicans of the old school and not of Van Buren's or Henry Clay's." The extract from the Raleigh *Star* declared that Calhoun's ideology was founded on the "Virginia Resolutions of 1799" and the "Kentucky Resolutions of 1799" (mistaking the year)[22] And the paper noted under the title "The Jeffersonian Doctrines of '98" that a printer was offering for sale a pamphlet containing "The Virginian and Kentucky Resolutions of 1798-'9, with Madison's Report"; the paper described it as a "valuable and useful political compilation ... that every American citizen should treasure up for reference and illustration."[23]

Opposition to Van Buren emerged in the pro–Branch press and in Jackson meetings held in the counties in early 1832. Some Jackson meetings which declared a preference for Barbour but pledged themselves to support the nominee of the Baltimore convention were reported in the anti–Van Buren press.[24] The main movement for Barbour occurred in the Roanoke River counties. A group of Halifax Republicans led by John Nicholson and Willis Alston met on March 17 to select a Jackson elector for the district. The meeting declared the "necessity" of nominating an elector who would oppose a vice-president candidate who aspired to the office of president. It recommended Philip Barbour for vice president because of his opposition to the Tariff of 1828 and "the soundness of his political creed."[25]

When the Halifax Republicans met at the county courthouse on April 22 to consider sending delegates to the national convention in Baltimore, a bitter division arose between the Van Buren and anti–Van Buren men. After a "long and heated debate" over the convention and Van Buren, a "personal fracas" arose between several members that resulted in a "pretty general row" among the members. The meeting was adjourned, and the next day the Anti–Van Buren party, some 136 in number, held their own meeting. Chaired by Willis Alston, the meeting declared that Jackson's administration was "strictly republican" and in "perfect unison" with the "principles which actuated Jefferson and Madison." It then recommended his reelection and declared its disapproval of the Baltimore convention as "instituted by the partisans of Mr. Van Buren and composed chiefly of his adherents, for his special support." Those at the meeting could not support Van Buren because he voted for federal internal improvements and because he was "the effective author of the tariff of 1828." They recommended Barbour as "a fit person to be voted for as Vice President of the United States," and they suggested a state convention in Raleigh on June 18 to nominate him for the vice presidency on the Jackson ticket. The Halifax *Advocate* hailed the meeting as "a great triumph of the friends of Free Trade and State Rights."[26] Anti–Van Buren partisans held county meetings to select delegates to their state convention in Raleigh. Many meetings specifically endorsed Barbour for the vice-presidency; others simply approved the convention and voted delegates.[27]

The Anti–Van Buren convention that met in Raleigh on June 18, 1832, united anti–Van Buren sentiment with opposition to the tariff. In fact, the convention directly linked Van Buren with the tariff. An eastern affair, the convention assembled representatives of the Anti–Van Buren Republicans from most counties of the east. Eighteen eastern, Roanoke River, and capitol-region counties were represented at the convention by thirty-seven delegates. (A letter of support from three Anti–Van Buren leaders in Wilkes county declaring that people in the western counties also favored Barbour was received and read at the convention.[28]) James Iredell of Raleigh chaired the convention; Willis Allston (Halifax), Edward B. Dudley (New Hanover), and William Blount (Beaufort) were vice presidents; Charles Manly (Wake), Kenneth Rayner (Hertford), and Warren Winslow (Cumberland) were appointed secretaries. This was a roll-call of future Whig leaders. Alston, Iredell, and Dudley were on the committee appointed to draft resolutions and an address. After indicating Jackson as their choice for president, the convention declared the tariff "destructive," "odious," and "subversive" of the principles of the Constitution and the "fundamental question" in selecting a vice-presidential candidate. Van Buren, they declared, decidedly favored continuing the "odious system of taxation." The Southern states could expect only that he would attempt to "fix it upon us forever as the settled policy of the country." Expressing their belief in his "uniform and efficient" support of the principles advocated by the convention, the delegates nominated Barbour to North Carolinians as the vice president for the Jackson ticket and approved the address drafted by the committee. The convention approved Jackson-Barbour electors for the eight districts represented at the convention and recommended that meetings be held in the districts not represented to select Jackson-Barbour electors. They also established a central "Jackson and Barbour" committee at Raleigh to coordinate with the electors and publish 5,000 copies of the convention's address.[29]

The address of the Anti–Van Buren/Jackson and Barbour convention shows just how much the Anti–Van Buren party *was* an *anti–Van Buren* party. In opposing the rise of Van Buren, they were defending the South, states' rights, and slavery. The convention projected Van Buren as the enemy of the South, the opponent of the principles of Southern Republicans, and the choice of party men, not the true body of Republicans. The selection of a vice-presidential candidate involved "fundamental principles of our government," the convention asserted. The convention declared the issue to be "a question vitally affecting a great principle of civil liberty, of constitutional law, and of true devotion to the Union." Van Buren, they declared, favored the protective tariff: he had helped author the Tariff of Abominations. The convention at Baltimore was a "convention of Mr. Van Buren's friends" only. The Raleigh convention stated that the five North Carolina delegates at Baltimore, representing only five districts, could not and did not represent the state. Insisting that Jackson stood on his own merits, the convention denied that the nomination of Barbour threatened Jackson's reelection. They declared that Van Buren's political principles were "obnoxious to the South" and drew up a list of charges against Van Buren: he opposed Madison in 1812; he opposed the South on the Missouri question by favoring the right of Congress to restrict slavery in the territories; he opposed the South on "the great Tariff question" in 1828; and he went against "a large majority of the South" in preferring Crawford to Jackson in 1824 (a charge reflective of the large number of original Jackson men in the Anti–Van Buren party). They countered the suggestions of the Van Buren party that Jackson preferred Van Buren and Republicans should be guided by his wishes by charging that such implicit obedience to the "Executive will" was un-republican.

Couching their appeal in religious imagery, the convention delegates stated their reasons for preferring Barbour for the vice presidency. "We ask you to support him because he is a candidate of the true political faith," the address stated. The Raleigh delegates belonged to "a political church which holds fast to that faith" and thus would not recommend to North

Carolinians the "heretic minister" Van Buren; they would offer instead the "true believer" Barbour. Barbour had been "an able defender of our rights" and "a faithful coadjutor in our cause." He was with North Carolina "in opinion, in interest, and in feeling."

Insisting that a crisis of government was at hand, the delegates declared that the choice was between "a consolidated General Government" on the one hand and a Union of "sovereign States" bound together by a strictly limited Constitution on the other. The tariff, part of Clay's hated "American System," was an unconstitutional tax on the South. Declaring their "deep attachment to the Union of these States," they insisted it was their duty to oppose the tariff's "encroachment on our rights" and men such as Van Buren who had authored it. Barbour's principles, on the other hand, were "our principles." Reflecting Macon's insistence that granting the power of internal improvements granted the power to free slaves, the Anti–Van Buren party declared that the tariff—and the "American System"—represented an "unlimited power of taxation" by the general government. Failure to oppose this legislation would grant the principle "that the minority hold their property at [the] will of the majority." "Can it be possible," they asked, "that such a principle is to be found in our Constitution!" If such a construction of the Constitution was sanctioned by the North Carolina voters, then the government would have, they insisted, "all the power which the most despotic government could wish." Barbour stood for "the great principles ... at the foundation of all free government," which were: "equality of political rights—equality of benefits and burthens—that every citizen shall be *protected* in the enjoyment of his property, and of the fruits of his labor." The safety and permanence of the Union and the preservation of Carolinians' liberty depended upon "firm and united resistance" to the tariff system by "every constitutional means."[30] The Anti–Van Buren Party was thus an opposition party and a party professing an ideology fully in accord with the Old Republican doctrines: professing loyalty to the "true political faith," in favor of strict construction and states' rights, and anti-tariff, anti–American system, and of course, anti–Van Buren. The states' rights tone of this address also accorded with the views of the Western Republican anti–Van Buren men.

Though not present at the Raleigh Anti–Van Buren party convention, the western opponents of Van Buren held their own meetings. In line with the Western Republicans' support for Calhoun and South Carolina, they called their meetings "state rights and anti-tariff meetings." Westerners had already held "anti-tariff meetings" in support of the Philadelphia anti-tariff convention,[31] and the new party combined this sentiment with opposition to Van Buren. Charles Fisher's newspaper, the *Western Carolinian* in Salisbury, was already denouncing Van Buren and Fisher's Rowan Republicans took the lead.[32] The paper had praised the Jackson meeting in Halifax in March that had recommended Barbour and approved of the call for the Anti–Van Buren convention in Raleigh.[33] The paper had already associated Barbour with the defense of Old Republican principles. "Jackson Republicans" should oppose Van Buren because his politics were not "Southern." Southerners advocating the "great principles which the *old* republican party once contended for" should only support a vice president who would "strictly maintain them."[34]

Western Anti–Van Buren men held a "State Right and Anti-Tariff Meeting" in Rowan County. They assembled at the Salisbury courthouse on July 4, 1832, under the leadership of Charles Fisher, who chaired the meeting, and adopted a set of resolutions. They supported the reelection of Jackson and declared Barbour their preferred candidate for the vice presidency, as a man of "talents and of patriotism—a true Republican of the old school of '98—

a friend to State-Right and to *equal* rights—opposed to the Tariff and in favor of the principles of Free-Trade." The resolutions of the meeting condemned the Tariff of 1828 as "unequal" and "unjust." Denying the right of the delegates at the Baltimore convention to speak for all of North Carolina, they decried the convention as "a piece of party machinery" designed to accomplish the "ambitious views" of the "aspiring politician" Martin Van Buren. They would not support him for the vice presidency because Van Buren possessed "no feeling or principles in common with the people of North Carolina, or the other Southern States." No true Republican, he had actively worked to defeat Madison in 1812 and his support for Jackson was motivated solely by desire for office. They cited his vote in the New York legislature during the Missouri crisis for resolutions that had seemed to oppose the admission of Missouri as a slave state as evidence that his opinions differed from southerners on this question of "vital importance to the South" that aimed a "fatal blow at the rights of all the States."[35] Furthermore, Van Buren had been a "fire brand" among Republicans sowing dissension, "generating bad feelings among old and long tried friends," and almost breaking up the party. They denounced Van Buren as an "avowed friend" of the tariff who was "highly instrumental" in "imposing" it on the South. Resolutions called for the formation of a "State-Rights and Anti-Tariff association" in Rowan County. Three delegates were appointed to meet with delegates from Davidson and Montgomery counties to nominate an elector on the "State rights ticket."[36]

Though the Anti–Van Buren party in the west stressed its opposition to the tariff, both the eastern wing and the western wing strongly opposed Van Buren and proclaimed their defense of the rights of the states against federal "consolidation." They shared a common opposition to Van Buren and gave an almost identical critique of his course. Thus, the opposition to Van Buren in the east joined the pro–Calhoun Western Republicans on a platform of adamant opposition to the Tariff of 1828. Though the large body of Old Republicans continued to remain loyal to Van Buren, Mangum's commitment to states' rights and opposition to the tariff began to move him to the new Anti–Van Buren / Anti-Tariff party.

"I quit V. B. ... in accordance with my principles": Mangum joins the Anti–Van Buren Party

At the same time that the Anti–Van Buren Party movement was taking shape, Mangum was growing disenchanted with Van Buren. Through early 1832, Mangum remained with the Old Republicans and the alliance with Van Buren. In opposition to Calhoun and the anti–Van Buren party in the Senate, Mangum voted to confirm Jackson's appointment of Van Buren as ambassador to Great Britain. His vote pleased the Jackson–Van Buren party in North Carolina. Mangum received many letters in praise of his vote. John Bragg, a state legislator from Warrenton, told Mangum that his vote for Van Buren reflected the sentiments of the whole of the "Roanoke Country" (the counties along the Roanoke River). "We remember not to forget those who ... so truly reflected our wishes by their votes on the Nomination."[37] Mangum also wrote a friendly letter to William S. Ransom, editor of the Raleigh *Constitutionalist*, who opposed the coalition then forming in opposition to Van Buren—a coalition Ransom called "the Iredell-Calhoun junto."[38] The paper was considered the organ of the Van Buren party in Raleigh.[39]

Yet Mangum was being courted by the Anti–Van Buren party. The anti-tariff, pro–Calhoun western wing of the Anti–Van Buren party already favored Mangum as a result of his well-received speech against the Tariff of 1828. The Western Republicans praised the speech. In two successive issues, the *Western Carolinian* printed the speech in its entirety. Calling it an "excellent" speech, the paper noted that the speech was "highly spoken of" in the Washington papers. It was, the paper said, a speech with "an able straight forward argument which must carry conviction to every mind." It declared the speech "replete with sound argument and true southern feeling." And Mangum favored the Western Republicans: at the time they were praising his speech, he sent a packet of "documents" (speeches and reports) to the editors of the *Western Carolinian*.[40]

In February, Iredell wrote Mangum a letter that seems designed to influence Mangum against Van Buren. Mangum may have already been leaning against Van Buren because Iredell mentioned a recent exchange of political ideas with Mangum that apparently left him with the idea that Mangum shared political sentiments similar to his own. But the main thrust of Iredell's letter was opposition to Van Buren. "Towards Mr. V.B. *personally*.... I have never had any but the kindest feelings," Iredell informed Mangum, "But I have never admired his political *management*—I have always detested 'New York politics' in which he has borne so conspicuous a share." Alluding to the so-called Albany Regency in New York, Iredell accused the Republican party in New York of being an oligarchy. "Is this *republicanism* to be engrafted into our United States' administration," he asked Mangum, "I cannot trust the man who has always been endeavoring to flatter & fawn upon the *People*, professing his *democracy* while in fact he has continued to fasten upon them a machinery (pardon *me* if I allude to the *caucus* system) by which two or three men (it may be *one* man) govern them, not under the name of *Kings*, but of *republicans*." Iredell believed Van Buren did not share Southern principles: "Is it not of the utmost importance to the South that we should have a Vice-President of our principles?—I have never yet seen an election of President in which I thought the choice of a Vice-President so important."[41]

Even as Mangum was being courted by the Anti–Van Buren party, Romulus Saunders, fellow leader of the Old Republicans, continued to remain loyal to Jackson's favorite for the vice-presidential nomination. Saunders and Mangum personify the division of the Old Republicans over loyalty to Van Buren as Jackson's successor. Saunders and Mangum had been political allies since 1824 when they had led the Old Republican's Crawford campaign in North Carolina.[42] In January, Saunders and Mangum agreed that Van Buren should not be brought forward as the vice-presidential candidate, but Saunders wrote that in his view the only man who should be nominated for the vice-presidency was one "who will give General Jackson a bona fide cooperation in his administration."[43] Though Saunders clearly believed that Mangum sided with him in support for the administration and Van Buren, he also knew that Mangum maintained ties to the Branch-Iredell party.[44] Unlike Mangum, Saunders completely opposed the Anti–Van Buren party. In March, Saunders thought that support for Van Buren was strong in the state, despite a "strong opposition" party.[45] In sentiments that completely departed from Mangum's, Saunders reported that he would put a "damper" on Willis Alston's attempt to form an Anti–Van Buren party.[46] Mangum then had not firmly committed to either side in the emerging contest between pro- and anti–Van Buren factions. Before the 1832 Democratic Party convention, held at Baltimore on May 21, 1832, Mangum had made no decision to move to the new Anti–Van Buren coalition.

Van Buren's course on the revision of the Tariff of 1828 turned Mangum decisively to the Anti–Van Buren party. As Mangum's selection of the tariff for the subject of his first major speech in the Senate indicated, he considered the tariff the most important issue for the Southern states. In Congress in March 1832, Henry Clay had proposed revisions to the tariff that would have increased rates on many items. The anti-tariff men in the Senate, Mangum among them, hoped the administration would aid them in fighting Clay's measures and getting the tariff rates revised significantly downward from those in the 1828 "Tariff of Abominations." Mangum later claimed that Van Buren had promised Southern congressmen that he would work to adjust the Tariff of Abominations. Van Buren's friends, Mangum told a fellow Whig in 1834, "held out the fairest promises to Southern men" on tariff revision.[47] Even before the convention, though, doubts arose among the Carolina Old Republicans regarding Van Buren's intentions. In late March, Saunders informed Mangum of his shock over the movement of the New York senators to the support of Clay's tariff; he told other Jackson supporters that he would abandon Van Buren if his course was to ally with Clay. But he reported to Mangum that he was "certain" that Van Buren's "feelings were with the South" and he assured Mangum that despite the action of the New York senators Van Buren would "go as far as practicable in relieving our just grounds of complaint." Saunders remained loyal to Van Buren. He told Mangum he was likely to attend as a delegate the Baltimore convention that was expected to nominate Van Buren as vice president in accordance with Jackson's wishes.[48] Mangum did not attend the convention, but he supported Van Buren for the vice-presidential nomination because he believed Van Buren would work to craft an adjustment of the tariff that would be satisfactory to the South.[49]

Soon after the Baltimore convention, however, Mangum informed Graham, "it was perceived that the Van Buren party were playing falsely with us."[50] Despite Mangum's efforts to exert political pressure on Van Buren's party in Congress through articles in a pro–Jackson paper in Raleigh, the Van Buren men in Congress refused to back a significant reduction of the tariff rates and continued to favor a compromise with Clay. The Jackson administration proposed a compromise bill that left most of Clay's high rates intact. The bill passed Congress and Jackson signed the Tariff of 1832 into law on July 14. Mangum and the anti-tariff senators—in particular the South Carolinians—were infuriated.[51] Mangum believed that Van Buren betrayed the North Carolina Republicans on his promise to work to adjust the Tariff of 1828.

Mangum broke with the Old Republicans over loyalty to Van Buren. Though Mangum strongly opposed the tariff, his rift with Saunders and the Old Republicans was more about opposition to Van Buren than simply anger over the administration's failure to support tariff reduction. As Mangum explained in 1834, the Old Republicans divided over loyalty or opposition to Van Buren:

> The party continued to play falsely [on the tariff]. & the only difference between those Gentlemen & myself, is that I quit V. B. then in accordance with my principles on that *leading* subject—& they (it being the safer course) more wisely perhaps as they think, stuck to him through thick & thin.[52]

Mangum's primary opposition was to Van Buren. He viewed Van Buren as false in his supposed alliance with Southern Republicans; Van Buren appeared to be in accord with states' rights and Southern interests, but he was insincere in his promises to Southern men. Mangum would not support an opponent of states' rights and one who refused to support the South on the tariff. Mangum had become convinced that Van Buren was no friend of the South.

Mangum's opposition to Van Buren put him into the North Carolina Anti–Van Buren party by the time Jackson signed the Tariff of 1832 into law. By August, Mangum had openly broken with the Van Buren Republicans and was an anti–Van Buren partisan. That month, Charles Fisher reported to Mangum about an "anti–Tariff meeting" held at Salisbury. Firmly believing Mangum was with him, Fisher wanted Mangum's help in rallying the anti-tariff/anti–Van Buren party in the western counties. Fisher asked him to come to Salisbury in support of the Anti–Van Buren party. Stating that it would be "most desirable," Fisher asked Mangum to make a public address in Salisbury. In his letter Fisher combined opposition to the tariff with opposition to Van Buren. "We have now *rallyed* [sic] against us all the *Clay-men, Tariff-men,* and *consolidationists,* and the few *Van-Buren* men have joined them." He described his party as opposed to the "Van Buren ticket" and told Mangum that "the whole clan" of Clay men and Van Buren supporters advocated "the broad doctrine of *consolidation*."[53] By the fall of 1832 Mangum's opposition to Van Buren and the tariff had put him firmly in the Anti–Van Buren Party and in support of Fisher's Western Republicans.

The close alliance between the Western Republicans and the Anti–Van Buren Party no doubt made Mangum's decision easier. In that coalition he could oppose both the tariff and Van Buren. The two groups differed only in their emphasis; both opposed the tariff and Van Buren. For Mangum, though, his move to the Anti–Van Buren Party was more about his opposition to Van Buren than the tariff. He was thus closer to the Anti–Van Buren men who met at the June 18 convention in Raleigh than to the pro–Calhoun Western Republicans of Charles Fisher. The Anti–Van Buren convention was formed by Republicans from the counties of the Roanoke River and Wake-Orange regions. Mangum was naturally at home with such a regional movement. Nevertheless, his alliance with Fisher's pro–Calhoun Western Republicans and his own strong opposition to the Tariff of 1832 placed him in sympathy with Calhoun and the South Carolinians who would soon seek a drastic remedy to the tariff.

Jackson, Nullification and the Bank

Jackson's actions in 1832 and 1833 severely weakened his support in North Carolina among the Anti–Van Buren Party men. Jackson had never been a friend of the Bank of the United States (BUS) and in 1832 became convinced that the president of the BUS, Nicholas Biddle, was actively working with the National Republicans to defeat his reelection. When Clay and other friends of the BUS pressed for an early re-charter of the bank, Jackson determined to veto it.[54] Many of Mangum's political friends in the Anti–Van Buren–States' Rights coalition supported the Bank of the United States. Iredell told Mangum in August 1832 that he supported the Bank: "whether right or wrong, that Bank is at this time very popular in our State—I believe, indeed I know, it has done us vast good and as yet we have felt no evils from it—where is the check upon State Banks, if not to be found here!"[55] Mangum himself believed that the BUS was an "almost indispensable necessity," but held that seeking its re-charter before the election in 1832 was unwise because Jackson would view it as a challenge. If Congress deferred re-charter until 1833, Mangum thought Jackson would be more receptive to compromise and negotiating the terms of a revised charter. "By deferring its application to next Session I have no doubt, with but slight modification (to save appearances) it would have met with Executive favor," he explained to a friend, "It is *now* more than doubtful whether it will. And the whole may ultimately take the appearance of a trial of strength between Gen. Jackson & the Bank. In that case the Bank will go down—for Gen J's popularity is of *a sort* not to slaken [sic] at present."⁵⁶ Mangum correctly gauged that Jackson would view an extension bill in the current session as a trial of strength between his popularity and that of the Bank. Mangum predicted in a letter to William Polk, an original 1824 Jackson man who had joined the Anti–Van Buren party, that any challenge to Jackson would be fatal to the BUS: "[H]e will not shrink from the Contest," he predicted to Polk, "and in that Contest the fate of the Bank will certainly be sealed for the *present*, & possibly *forever*."⁵⁷

By late May, Mangum was convinced that a veto would jeopardize any chance of getting a revised charter after the election. He thought that pushing the re-charter in 1832 as a political tactic was unwise. He explained to Duncan Cameron: "I think it to be regretted that it is now pressed—Political considerations will urge it—& the danger lies, in the effect the veto may have, backed by the popularity of Gen. J. upon the passage of the Bill hereafter."⁵⁸ Cameron preferred the early re-charter of the bank, but most of Mangum's correspondents in early 1832 opposed the extension of the BUS charter in its current form. They favored either its continuation or the creation of a similar institution with modifications and restrictions.⁵⁹ In June, despite his favorable opinion of the BUS, Mangum voted with the South against re-charter. Mangum's vote against re-charter should thus be understood as a compromise measure: With his fears for the fate of the institution if Jackson were presented with a re-charter bill and his belief that a Bank was vital to the nation, it is likely that Mangum cast his vote against the re-charter bill to preserve the fading opportunity to obtain a modified charter for the Bank in 1833. Most of the Anti–Van Buren party in North Carolina opposed re-charter so Mangum's vote did not affect his political friendship with that faction. In June the Senate passed the re-charter bill 28 to 20, and in July the House passed it 107 to 85. The North Carolina congressional delegation split on the vote between the anti–Jackson men who voted for re-charter and Branch men and Jackson Republicans who voted against.⁶⁰

As Mangum expected, Jackson vetoed the bill. He based his veto on countering the influence of the Money Power and defending both states' rights and the powers of the executive branch. The Money Power argument appears throughout the document, and Jackson strongly appealed to states' rights sentiment, declaring that the government was not "to be maintained or our Union preserved by invasions of the rights and powers of the several states." He argued that the General Government must not bind the states "more closely to the center" but instead should leave "each to move unobstructed in its proper orbit."⁶¹ Such arguments appealed to all Republican factions in the state except the Nationalists, but Jackson made new claims for executive power that did not comport with Old Republican ideology. As Robert Remini has pointed out, the veto changed the relationship between the legislative and executive branches.⁶² Previous presidents had depended on their friends in Congress to guide legislation, but Jackson demanded to be consulted on legislation: "Neither upon the propriety of present action nor upon the provisions of this act was the Executive consulted." And in making his determination that the Bank of the United States was "dangerous to the Government and the country" Jackson showed his conception of his new role as the Tribune of the People. These claims, which Jackson further developed after his reelection, were to figure significantly in the future political struggles in North Carolina.

In North Carolina the pro–Jackson Old Republicans, like most other Jackson loyalists, praised the veto. But the Anti–Van Buren party was divided. Former National Republicans and anti–Jackson men condemned the veto, but the former Jackson supporters favorable to states' rights, the Old Republicans and the Western Republicans, supported the veto. Given this division and his expectation of the veto, Mangum did not turn against the administration. As long as Jackson continued a states' rights stance, Mangum would be inclined to support him.

The action of Jackson that moved the Anti–Van Buren men to oppose him was his reaction to South Carolina's nullification of the Tariff of 1832. South Carolina's call in late 1832 for a convention to nullify the Tariff of 1832 did not create any new divisions in North Carolina. The issue of nullification had arisen in the state as part of the debate over the tariff and the rift over the vice-presidential nominee in the 1832 election campaign.[63] Given the states' rights ideas in his speech against the Tariff, Mangum certainly sympathized with the South Carolina nullifiers, and though the members of the Anti–Van Buren party refused to make any public declaration in support of South Carolina's nullification ordnance they openly sympathized with nullification and many, especially Fisher's Western Republicans, were partisans of Calhoun.

Jackson reacted strongly to South Carolina's nullification ordinance. His annual message to Congress on December 4, 1832, was ardently states' rights in tone, but in a special Proclamation of December 10 Jackson declared uncompromising opposition to nullification. He declared nullification "incompatible with the existence of the Union," denied the right of a state to secede, and denied the theory of the Constitution as a compact between the sovereign states that was a key tenet of Old Republican ideology. The Proclamation pleased National Republicans, but many Democratic-Republicans in the South, even those supporting Jackson and Van Buren, expressed shock and dismay. And in January of 1833 Jackson sent to Congress what became known as the "Force Bill Message." It asked for measures to allow federal officers to collect the customs in South Carolina at the federal fortresses in Charleston harbor and requested Congress to update laws empowering the president to use the militia and the army and navy to enforce the laws of the federal government.[64]

Macon, in retirement, reacted negatively to the doctrines of the Proclamation, and the unintended publication of a letter he wrote on the Proclamation touched off a war of words between Jackson and the Old Republican sage. Macon, in a letter to former North Carolina Senator Samuel P. Carson that Carson published in *Niles Register* against Macon's wishes, stated his opinion that no state could nullify a federal law and remain in the Union. But he held that a state could secede whenever it wished as long as it paid its share of the public debt. Insisting that the Constitution had been "buried in the Senate in 1824, Macon declared that Jackson's Proclamation contained "principles as contrary to what was the constitution as nullification." He described it as "the great error" of an administration that had otherwise been satisfactory "in a high degree." "A government of opinion established by sovereign states, for special purposes," he told Carson, "cannot be maintained by force."[65]

Jackson disliked the letter, and in the summer of 1833 sought an acknowledgement from Macon that the latter's own effort to enforce federal law—the Embargo Act—in 1808 and 1809 against the will of the states of New England was the same in principle as his Proclamation. Macon claimed "no recollection" of his support for calling out the militia in that case, but acknowledged that he might have "done wrong" in "hot times." Macon also continued to insist on the right of secession. Jackson sent Macon a long letter stating his reasons for holding secession to be "a virtual dissolution of the union" and declaring the doctrines contained in his Proclamation in accordance with the principles proclaimed by Jefferson, Macon, and the "other fathers of the school of '98." In reply to Jackson's last letter, Macon refused to change his opinion on the right of a state to secede and declared that the Union would not be weakened by it. He suggested that "the proclamation and nullification ought to be laid by as unfit for use in the United States. To nullify and be in the Union and to be conquered and be in the union, seem to be impossible." Macon had refused to give Jackson the sanction he wanted, and Jackson, mocking his states' rights opponents' name for the Force Bill and applying it to the Republicans' enforcement of the Embargo Act, ended the discussion with the following note written on the back of Macon's final letter:

> Mr. Macon—on the subject of the proclamation. To be filed carefully. A.J.
> It is evidence of weakness—his votes and speech in 1808 and 9, in support of the laws to enforce the embargo. He voted for the bloody bill then—it was treason to resist the laws by force—it was treason to secede. Preserve this for history. A.J.[66]

Thus, even after the crisis had been resolved, Jackson sought a statement from Macon declaring that the president had acted in accord with the Principles of '98; when he was unable to elicit it, he reacted angrily and declared Macon's refusal to acknowledge suppression of secession as within the Jeffersonian doctrines evidence of "weakness." Jackson's mistake was arguing that enforcement of the embargo was in accord with Republican principles; he rightly identified the "fathers of the school of '98" as the enforcers of the embargo, but he failed to realize that their passage of the embargo and their efforts to enforce it were two of the greatest violations of their own doctrines.[67]

Like his old political mentor, Mangum reacted strongly against the Proclamation and the Force Bill. Mangum expected Jackson to defend Southern liberties and abide by a strict construction of the Constitution.[68] So Jackson's Proclamation came as a shock, and Mangum told Charity: "His proclamation is violent & dangers [sic] in its principles."[69] He declared to his brother that he would rather resign than give sanction to Jackson's Proclamation.[70] On Christmas Eve, Mangum gave a speech in the Senate against the Proclamation and appealed for a resolution to the crisis that would preserve the Union. "It is action—action, we want.... The republic is in danger. It is upon the verge of a precipice. The republic must be saved, liberty must be preserved. The Union must be saved." Congress should act to resolve the crisis "in a spirit of kindness and conciliation, with a determination to save the republic." But, declared Mangum in a reference to the Proclamation, the country "cannot be saved by force." "A Government based upon the stable foundations of opinion, and the affections of the people, can be saved only by the public opinion and the affections of the people."

> It is as much as I can do at this perilous crisis—a crisis of universal alarm, and one signally marked with the most flagrant dereliction of principle, to walk forward and steadily upon my own principles—principles which I believe to be conservative of liberty, of the Union, and of harmony and brotherly love throughout our extended and once happy borders. At this perilous crisis I know no man, and will support no man, further than I may believe he may be instrumental in saving the republic, and preserving the liberties of the people. I go for my country, my whole country, and, first of all, for the liberties of the people.[71]

Mangum also adamantly opposed the "Force Bill" which he believed Federalist in its principles and in conflict with Old Republicanism: "No one could look at this bill without discovering that it revived all the distinguishing characteristics of the old parties." Much in the bill was "odious." "It carried out to their full extent the principles of one of those parties with alarming and startling *addenda*, and came in conflict against all the principles of the other. It touched the fundamental character of our institutions...."[72]

The nullification crisis ended when Henry Clay proposed a compromise tariff that did not repudiate protection but provided for a gradual reduction of duties over a period of nine years, at which time all duties would be reduced to a uniform rate of twenty percent. Most anti-tariff men in the South accepted the compromise as offering legislative stability on the tariff and reducing rates to a level more acceptable to the South. Though it did not give the nullifiers all they wanted, Calhoun accepted the compromise tariff as the best the South Carolinians could achieve without risking civil war.[73] The hopes of the Anti–Van Buren Party in North Carolina had already been dashed when Barbour issued a letter in the fall of 1832 that withdrew his name from consideration on an alternative Jackson-Barbour ticket.[74] Mangum and many Anti–Van Buren Party men reluctantly voted for the Jackson–Van Buren ticket. Jackson overwhelmingly defeated Clay who ran at the top of a National Republican ticket.

In the decade of the 1820s, Macon viewed himself as one of the few remaining champions of the Principles of '98 and the Revolution of 1800. He completely opposed almost every aspect of the National Republican Adams administration. Old Republicanism was defined as an ideology opposed to a "federal" political economy. Mangum also embraced that opposition ideology. In his speech on the election of 1825 Mangum had exhibited a resistance to the emerging doctrine of Van Buren's party that touted the "the people's doctrines" of the will of the majority as the overriding concern of the Republican party. The courting of the Old Republicans by the Jackson–Van Buren party showed the continuing ideological (though not political) power of Southern conservatism. Mangum's quick conversion to Old Republicanism upon his joining Macon in Congress also showed the attraction of Old Republicanism for a new, younger group of North Carolina Republicans. By the time of his entry into the Senate in 1830, Mangum was a new Old Republican. Van Buren embraced the doctrines of Old Republicanism to win Virginia and North Carolina to the cause of Andrew Jackson, and the Old Republicans of North Carolina eventually embraced Jackson as the best candidate for Southern interests.

Yet, the political crises of the early 1830s threatened to undo the Old Republicans as a power in North Carolina. Jackson's anti–South policies (the Tariff of 1828, his Proclamation against nullification, and even to some extent, his Bank veto) and the rise of Van Buren in the administration, created divisions in the North Carolina Republican party between administration loyalists, Calhoun states' rights men, and those opposed to Martin Van Buren. Van Buren's political maneuvering, in particular, generated criticism of the administration in North Carolina, though no Republican was prepared to oppose Jackson. The Anti–Van Buren Party, formed specifically to oppose Van Buren, while still supporting Jackson, showed the high degree of opposition to Van Buren among North Carolina's Old Republicans and Jackson men opposed to Van Buren. It was tantamount to an opposition party. Van Buren was especially unpopular with the Old Republicans and Jackson men in the eastern part of the state. Mangum's preference for this party showed that his strong embrace of Old Republicanism (and loathing for Van Buren) made him truly comfortable only in opposition. He was an administration man for less than four years. The end of Old Republicanism as a political power in North Carolina (but not as an idea) only awaited the formation of an opposition party that could unite the factions uncomfortable with Jackson's course. Mangum, and men like him, were a minority. Jackson remained popular as his reelection had shown. Even states' rights men like Mangum who utterly opposed Jackson's course on nullification were not yet prepared to openly oppose the popular president. In the coming decade, Jackson's revolution of executive government would finally split the Jackson Republicans and create a more successful opposition party. And Mangum, as a Jackson- Republican Senator turned opposition man, was at the center of the struggle.

4

The Whig Opposition: States' Rights and the Senate

By 1833, Andrew Jackson's revolution had run its course in North Carolina. Jackson's revolution of 1825–1828 had united all the Republican factions loyal to Jeffersonian first principles and brought the state's strongest political faction, the Old Republicans, to the support of his election in 1828, which he claimed would vindicate the will of the people after Adams' un-democratic election by the House of Representatives. Yet soon after the election of Bedford Brown and Willie P. Mangum to the U.S. Senate in 1829 and 1830, the coalition in the legislature had begun to unravel. In 1832, this alliance between the Jackson men, the western Calhoun states-rights men, and the Old Republicans evaporated. The old general still commanded sufficient popularity in the state to win its presidential election in 1832, but his insistence on the New Yorker Martin Van Buren as his vice-presidential candidate had resulted in the formation of the short-lived Anti–Van Buren party in North Carolina. Although most states' rights men, including Mangum, voted for the Jackson–Van Buren ticket after the opposition party collapsed, they were not comfortable with the vice president and the spirit of opposition remained.

The Jackson administration's failure to fulfill its pledge to adjust the Tariff of 1828 to accommodate Southern interests and its forceful response to South Carolina's ordinance nullifying the Tariff of 1832 in that state separated many states' rights men, including Mangum, from the president and his Democratic-Republican Party, which they usually referred to simply as "the party." Mangum believed that Van Buren betrayed the Southern congressmen on the tariff, and he had broken with Van Buren and "the party" over the issue. Yet, early in 1833 Mangum preferred to maintain an independent rather than opposition stance towards the administration. Jackson's actions in 1833 soon changed Mangum's position. The Whig opposition in North Carolina resulted from Jackson's failure to adhere to the doctrines of Old Republicanism.

The Whig Party in North Carolina formed as a coalition between States' Rights Republicans adhering to Old Republican doctrines—the Western Republican Calhoun party and many "original" Jackson men and Old Republicans—and National Republicans united by opposition to the course of President Andrew Jackson and the rise of Martin Van Buren. The protective Tariff of 1832 and South Carolina's reaction which resulted in the Nullification Crisis of 1832–1833 had strained the loyalty of the states' rights men to the Jackson administration. The Compromise Tariff of 1833, arranged by Senator Henry Clay of Kentucky with

Mangum's support, ended the crisis, but the nationalism of President Jackson's "Proclamation" against the South Carolina nullifiers nearly drove Mangum to opposition. Mangum believed it a complete betrayal of the South and states' rights.

More important in creating an opposition among the president's former political friends in North Carolina than the bank veto and his response to nullification were his actions after the Compromise of 1833. Specifically, United States senators and congressmen opposed Jackson's claims for executive power, his reliance on unofficial advisors, his selection of the New-Yorker Martin Van Buren as his Vice-President, his removal of the deposits from the Bank of the United States, and his proscription of his opposition in the Senate—the last a virtual war on the Senate. In North Carolina, the opposition interpreted this war on the Senate, where the state legislatures were represented, as an attack on the rights of the states. And the opposition party also sprang from antagonism to what they called "the party"—the methods of Jackson's political organization, specifically its use of federal patronage. Thus, Jackson's methods of executive government, radically different from those of past Republican presidents, and dissatisfaction with Van Buren united Old Republicans and National Republicans in opposition. This opposition coalition, which took upon itself the name of Whig, built an anti-party party for a counter-revolution of conservatism against Jackson's radical revolution of executive power and patronage. Between 1833 and 1836 Mangum separated from Jackson, helped build the opposition Whig coalition, and lead its counter-revolution in North Carolina against Jackson and his party.

Mangum had believed that the Union was seriously endangered during the Nullification Crisis, and he praised the settlement embodied in the Compromise Tariff of 1833 as a "glorious consummation." Expressing his "deep gratitude to those who had come to our deliverance, in the hour of our deepest gloom," he at the same time lambasted the "Force Bill" as part of the administration's misdeeds. "With a zeal which could not be exceeded," Mangum asserted, the Jackson administration had supported a measure of "abominations." "The last argument of kings they chose as the first argument of a republic. They sent out the sword, the bayonet, and the banner, but no olive branch." Mangum believed that the compromise would "tranquilize the agitations which threatened to produce a desperate result," and he hoped that "those who had come forward to save our Government, and restore peace and harmony to the country would … receive the deep and lasting gratitude of their fellow citizens."[1]

Andrew Jackson's next act, though, once again threatened the harmony of the country and convinced many in Congress and in the country that Jackson not only was a nationalist who threatened the rights of the states but also was a president who threatened republican government. Jackson's first official act in his second administration was the removal of the government's deposits from the Bank of the United States. Jackson considered his victory over the National Republicans as "a decision of the people against the bank."[2] Believing the bank too powerful for the safety of republican government, Jackson, ever since his veto in 1832, was determined to break it. When he asked his cabinet officers for their opinions on removal of the deposits, only Postmaster General Amos Kendall and Attorney General Roger Taney fully favored it, though Vice-President Van Buren also pledged his full support. Treasury Secretary Louis McLane opposed removal. The law establishing the bank specified that the deposits could only be removed if the Treasury Secretary determined the bank was unsafe and required him to report his determination to Congress. Recent investigations by the Treasury and Congress had found the bank solvent and safe, and McLane refused to carry out Jackson's removal policy. Jackson transferred McLane to the State Department and appointed William J. Duane, who opposed renewal of the bank's charter, in his place. But Duane also concluded that the government's deposits were safe. He refused to admit Jackson's assertion that he was merely an executive agent of the president and not responsible for the act. Duane insisted that under the law Congress held the Treasury Secretary responsible. Jackson then dismissed Duane and appointed Roger Taney, already pledged to support Jackson, to the Treasury. Taney immediately ordered deposits to the bank to cease while continuing to draw drafts on the bank for payment of government debts. Daniel Walker Howe calls the process "a fig leaf" to legitimate removal. Taney shifted the government deposits to selected state "pet banks," whose selection was a form of political patronage; the pet banks were chosen "more for their political friendship to the administration than for their financial soundness," Howe notes.[3]

As Howe indicated, Jackson's removal of the deposits was a political act. "The reasons for removal submitted by Taney to Congress related more to the Bank's anti-administration activities than to its financial condition."[4] The removal of the deposits was an assertion of executive power that violated the provisions that Congress had enacted into law. Jackson was determined to interpret the law in his favor and insisted that his reelection gave him a mandate from the people to crush the bank. When Congress returned in December, the Senate, with a majority of senators opposed to the administration, refused to confirm Taney and began debating a resolution declaring his reasons for removal insufficient as well as another resolution, put forward by Clay, of censure on the president.

More than just Jackson's high-handed removal of the deposits was at work though. Past Republican presidents had governed through their cabinet officers who had maintained good relations with Congress. Jackson chose to break with this tradition, and resentment against Jackson's corps of unofficial advisors was building. Madison's administration, those who had even briefly tolerated unofficial advisors, had created opposition among Old Republican purists. Early in the session in December, Mangum wrote a long letter to Governor David L. Swain marked "confidential" in which he complained that any middle ground between the Jackson administration and complete opposition was rapidly disappearing. "All opposition here to bad influences, is attributed to *enmity to the hero*, to National republicanism & to nullification," he explained. "In these bad times, no man can be honest without being denounced with the sins of hatred of Jackson, nullification, &c &c." Mangum disliked the influence of Van Buren and the so-called Kitchen Cabinet in Jackson's councils: "He is not suffered to be friendly to Jackson unless he be likewise friendly to Amos Kendal, Martin Van Buren & all the others & their views." Those who were not would be "denounced as the enemies of the President, & as Nullifiers." Expressing concern for the "rights of the States" and opposition to the consolidation of "this Central Machine," Mangum wanted to continue to steer his independent course but he was already feeling the "powerful pressure" Jackson was applying to the Senate. Despite this pressure and the "most unsparing vituperation of the [administration] press," Mangum intended to adhere to his independence: "I shall," he explained to Swain, "give cordial support, where I can to the administration. But I shall also give what aid I can to the exposure of abuses." Mangum was convinced that the Senate was vital to the maintenance of political independence from the administration:

> The only check to as absolute power, as that in Russia is found in the Senate. The policy of men in power is to destroy that body in public opinion. Every other branch of the Government is unquestionably & almost unqualifiedly subservient to the will & passions of One Man—or to speak more truly, to the will & passions of a Cabal that gives a decided direction to the Executive.

And the obstacle to the ambitions of that Cabal, Mangum informed Swain, was "found in the obstinacy of the South."[5]

Other Whigs also found the Kitchen Cabinet threatening. The Washington *United States Telegraph* declared that the Union "now more in danger from the triumph of the Kitchen Cabinet, than any other circumstance."[6] The nationalism of Jackson's Proclamation and Van Buren's betrayal on the tariff moved Mangum to independence from "the party." The lawlessness of removal convinced him that Jackson and Van Buren and their "party" threatened republican government, not just the South. Now Mangum was convinced that the Senate was the only remaining power that could check the Executive and only the Southern senators could hold the Senate against the menacing influence of the Cabal.[7]

Mangum in Opposition

Mangum found that the consequences of separation from Jackson were felt in North Carolina as well as in Washington. Because he was elected to the Senate as an Old Republican and Jackson supporter, Mangum's course of independence from Jackson and "the party" in Washington was already separating him from his Old Republican friends, some of whom believed that by failing to support Jackson, Mangum was betraying the Old Republicans. At the end of December William Montgomery, one of Mangum's old political friends, apprised him that some of his old associates were "mortifyed" at the course he was taking in the Senate. "Many severe anathemas are Made against you," Montgomery explained, "they all say you were Elected by the Administration Men and to support the Administration, and that you Have gone over to our Enimies [sic]."[8]

Despite such gathering disapproval of his political course, on February 5, 1834, Mangum decisively declared his opposition to the removal of the deposits. Like the other Senators attacking the removal, he declared the issue one of constitutionality and legislative supremacy rather than a question of the constitutionality of the Bank of the United States. The Jackson party was trying to change the issue, but Mangum declared that he "would not suffer such a change to be made. The question is not, nor ever was, 'bank or no bank.' The question was, emphatically, 'law or no law—constitution or no constitution.'" Those senators calling for an inquiry into the action of the administration were asking "whether or not the Executive had declared war on the bank, without law or constitutional right—and were the reasons assigned by the Secretary of the Treasury sustained by law, and was his conduct to be upheld." If it were true, as Jackson claimed, that the BUS was a "monster" and ought to be crushed "then, … it deserved that fate." But Mangum did not advocate "disregarding all law on the subject"; he was willing to give the bank "fair play."[9] By thus implying that the legality of Jackson's actions could be questioned and examined by the Senate, Mangum placed himself in the opposition, certainly so in the eyes of Jackson.

Mangum's response reflected his Old Republicanism. Mangum's belief that removal of the deposits was an unconstitutional usurpation of power by Jackson combined with his loyalty to the Principles of '98 and his anti-party sentiment. He believed that Van Buren would use removal to build "the party." Mangum thought that Van Buren represented a corrupting, centralizing policy and resented the administration influence being brought to bear in state politics. In Mangum's mind, Jackson's destruction of the BUS and the administration's decision to place the deposits in selected "pet" banks in the states were directly linked to Martin Van Buren's drive for the presidency. Mangum explained to his friend and political confidante Duncan Cameron that he regarded it as certain that "the affiliated Banks will be used in this Presidential campaign; and that ultimately if Van Buren shall succeed a district Bank will be established controlled by a control regency and by combination with the power and patronage of the government, controlling and corrupting every thing." Executive power was at work in the state legislatures. Pennsylvania's legislature, which had supported re-charter before Jackson's war on the Monster Bank, changed their policy "at Executive Command, and now lies at the foot of power, hopeless and helpless." Like Pennsylvania, Maine, New Hampshire, New York, and Ohio were held in chains by the "discipline of the Albany school." Mangum believed that failure of the South to oppose Jackson's course on nullification had emboldened his assertions of executive power, "Jacksonism" as Mangum termed it. "The events of the last winter have given boldness and insolence to power unknown to us in our former history."[10] Mangum's fears were not unwarranted. Howe points out: "Pet banks became an additional form of Democratic Party patronage," and their number eventually rose to over ninety.[11] Mangum thus believed that Jackson and Van Buren had to be opposed; the South and the Senate must be the bastion against these unconstitutional assertions of executive authority.

By the end of February 1834 Mangum had decided that opposition was the only course possible for a States' Rights Republican. He was ready to break publicly with Jackson and join the opposition. In the Senate on the 25 February Mangum made the most important speech of his political career. His friends aptly called it his "Philippic." He denounced the administration, its acts, and its principles. Mangum irrevocably left the Jackson Democratic-Republican party and declared himself part of the opposition party in the Senate. Mangum first explained his reasons for joining the opposition. "My object," he declared to the Senators, "is to check, if possible, bold and lawless usurpation...." He realized it was no light matter to take a position against the acts of the administration; only "stern necessity" made him place himself in opposition. Yet, Mangum declared, too often "over-prudence or timidity of public servants ... permits the outrages of power to pass without rebuke, rather than incur the known penalties of resisting them." Mangum's denunciation of Jackson's government was twofold: he denounced both the administration and the party that sustained it.

Mangum excoriated Jackson's administration of the government as corrupt, lawless, and lacking in principles. Except for the corrupt, party-building largesse of "its favors and its patronage," Mangum declared that the public was ignorant of the "enormous, the monstrous abuses and corruptions of this Government." It was Mangum's "solemn conviction" that the members of the administration held the "great interests of the country" subordinate to the elevation of the favorite [Van Buren] to the Presidency" and placed the "gratification of the ambition of one man" above questions of the public interest. Mangum had supposed Jackson's principles conservative, but the latter had failed to fulfill the promises of 1828 and 1832. In 1832, the South believed that Jackson was with them "in feeling and principle," but the nullification crisis exhibited "the deep and deliberate betrayal of the trusting South." Mangum accused Jackson of failing to redeem a single pledge made during his revolution against the

National Republicans. The administration held only two principles: "the principles of elections and of office." Its highest policy was "to have no settled policy."

Then he turned to Jackson's latest offense. The administration's "reckless" and "violent" removal of the deposits was a miscalculation.

> It never occurred to them that the country could doubt their wisdom, or that the country would feel the slightest shock in public confidence.... It never occurred to them that a people who had done so much for them, could feel the slightest unwillingness to entrust the whole currency of the country, in all its commercial and financial aspects, to Executive or Treasury regulation. But, sir, a people deeply imbued with veneration for the law, could not but feel a deep shock in the public confidence, when they witnessed a bold and high-handed violation of law.

Opposition in North Carolina did not arise from the resulting economic distress but from the act itself; "it rested upon a deeper sense of violated law, the startling pretensions of power, and the manifest tendency to the isolation of all power in the hands of one man."

Mangum attacked the group that sustained and enabled these corrupt and lawless acts. In North Carolina, the party zealously supported the whole course of the administration. It was an organization "unknown to the constitution" that was "animated by a principle of ambition … with its eye steadily fixed upon the elevation of the Executive favorite, and its heart upon the loaves and fishes … and all those good things, that come in the train of power. That party defends the violent and lawless seizure of the deposits, as it will continue to defend every act of the administration."

Removal was tied to the party, Mangum claimed. The deposit "pet" banks would be "more or less controlled by a political party" and would use the money "to refresh the whole party and sustain it." The goal of such a policy could only be "the ultimate establishment of a money domination, contrived by the use of the banking system." In Mangum's view such a scheme was "the refined and ingenious conception of the Albany school, and requiring, for its successful administration, the adroitness, tack, and delicacy of Albany managers." Mangum warned that the country would not be satisfied with such a course.

> The country will not long bear it. But all this violence on the part of power, and this distress on the country, are to be borne, to put down the "monster." As if the Executive power, armed with a patronage of twenty millions, with forty thousand office-holders and retainers in the field, sustained by a devoted, and, in many instances profligate press, is not incomparably more dangerous to liberty, and all the valuable institutions of the country, when it shall be wielded to gratify vindictive passions, and to advance mere personal ambition.

In Mangum's view, then, the threat to republican government was a monster patronage, not a monster bank; an executive Power, not a money power; and the Albany School, not the Aristocracy. But more than the Senate was necessary to stop the lawless course of the Jackson administration. Mangum believed that a political revolution was required. Several weeks earlier he had argued to Cameron that only "a powerful uprising of the people" could prevent such disastrous results.[12]

The administration's actions set off rounds of political meetings in North Carolina both for and against the administration. Between February and May of 1834, what might be best described as a war of memorials took place in the Senate between Mangum and his fellow Carolinian senator Bedford Brown, who remained loyal to Jackson and Van Buren. Mangum presented memorials from these political meetings that attested to the distressed state of the economy, protested the removal of the deposits, and requested their restoration. For his part, Brown offered memorials and resolutions from pro-administration meetings. The memorial war shows the interaction between local partisans and the states' highest representatives in Washington.

Resolutions from Burke County touched off the war. In January, citizens of Burke County in western North Carolina assembled and passed resolutions critical of removal and asking for the restoration of the deposits. Reading these Burke County Resolutions in the Senate on 11 February 1834, Mangum pointed out that the people of Burke up to that time had been friendly to Jackson, but that now they were "universal in condemnation" of the removal of the deposits from the BUS. "Sir, these resolutions speak the grave, calm, and deliberate tone of the best friends of the Executive, who emphatically say that they cannot submit to be ruined, to gratify the whims or caprices of any man." Mangum complained that too many people "instead of listening to the humble petitions of their fellow-citizens, were looking at the will of one man. In other words, the destinies of the country are held by one man, sustained by an organized party." In response to Mangum's presentation, Brown declared that the Burke county resolutions "came to the Senate in a very questionable shape." He asserted that though some of the signers had indeed once been friendly to the president, many of them had been his opponents. Brown denied that the opinions of the petitioners were in fact the sense of the people of North Carolina. Unconvinced that public opinion in the state ran against the president, Brown accused Mangum of denouncing executive usurpations of power while himself acting in opposition to the expressed opinion of his own constituents "thus violating the great principles of republican government."[13]

Brown's speech launched a storm of protest from political leaders in Burke County. Having just received a copy of the senator's remarks in the Senate, Isaac T. Avery, lawyer, planter, and prominent citizen (from one of the wealthiest families in the county), wrote Mangum to contest Brown's characterization of the meeting. After assuring Mangum that "your course meets the approbation of this Community," Avery described the meeting as having been called by the friends of district's representative, James Graham, and "the original friends of Genl. Jackson" (supporters of Jackson in 1824); the meeting, the largest political meeting he had ever witnessed save one, was "composed of men of all parties." Avery also told Mangum that Brown should be more careful in gauging political sentiment in the state, especially in the West. "I can find one hundred Men, who would sighn [sic] an address, requesting him to resighn [sic], for every one he could get who approbates his course," Avery assured Mangum and continued, "he must look to the Kitchen Cabinet, and not to the freemen of No. Ca. either for support or reward."[14] Colonel Samuel Hillman, who had introduced the resolutions at the meeting, also denied that the meeting had been held for political purposes and assured Mangum that his course "meets with the most cordial approbation of all parties."[15]

The Burke citizens countered Brown's assertions with a formal protest. As the final act in this battle of the memorials war, the leaders of Burke (including Avery) reassembled in late March and passed a second set of resolutions defending their right to present their grievances by "petition or remonstrance," which they sent on to Mangum. Their resolutions, they declared, were "entitled to a respectful consideration and should not be treated as coming 'in a questionable shape' without investigation and proof." They reaffirmed their conviction that Jackson's removal of the deposits had been an "unauthorized illegal and unconstitutional act" and thanked Mangum for his exposure of "the encroachments of executive power." They approved of Congressional opposition to removal, called for re-charter of the Bank, and pronounced their judgment on Brown:

> Resolved, That the Honorable Bedford Brown by representing the proceedings of the meeting in January last as coming before Congress "in a questionable shape" has manifested a dereliction towards and a want of respect for his immediate constituents and by trying to thwart instead of seconding the efforts of the meeting he has shown a much greater devotion to "the powers that be" than to the interests of those whom it is his [torn] to represent.[16]

The Whigs of Burke thus engaged directly with their senators in defense of their political rights and held one of them accountable for his aspersions.

The battle of Burke County was just the beginning of the war of memorials between Mangum and Brown. On the 25th of March, Mangum presented memorials from the citizens of Wilkesboro and Halifax who complained of the "the violation of law and assumption of power by the Executive." Six days later Mangum presented memorials and resolutions from three more counties asking for the restoration of the deposits, another memorial from Wilkesboro, a preamble and resolutions from the citizens of Mountsville in Rowan County, and resolutions and a memorial signed by 500 citizens from Beaufort County.[17] On the April 7, Brown presented the proceedings and resolutions of a public meeting in Tarboro, Edgecombe County, approving of Jackson's removal of the deposits. Mangum responded by declaring his "profound respect" for the opinions of the memorialists and predicted that Edgecombe would soon shake off loyalty to Jackson and join the "large majority" in the state who were now in opposition "combating the unwarrantable encroachments of Executive power."[18]

On May 20, Brown presented the resolutions of a public meeting in Wake County, led by men, "of the first respectability" and by a chairman who had been a long-time member of "the republican party" (probably R.M. Saunders). The resolutions approved removal "as a measure judicious and indispensable." Mangum countered that the petition was the work of "a meeting of eighteen gentlemen" whose chairman was a partisan agitator. Mangum then presented a memorial from Raleigh signed by "four-fifths of the voters of the town" which opposed the removal of the deposits and requested that Congress re-charter the BUS. Remarking that he had "met with no man of intelligence from the South, who did not say that there was a necessity for an establishment which should regulate the currency," Mangum declared that the people "are rising *en masse*: and I do think, that in Virginia and North Carolina, the people feel a deep conviction that something is to be done." In rebuttal, Brown asserted that continuation of the Bank would threaten "the liberties of the country." The people of North Carolina, he believed, saw the Bank as "an attack upon the constitution of the United States."[19] Even as the session was drawing to a close, Mangum continued to receive resolutions and memorials against Jackson's actions and in favor of his opposition.[20] This "memorial war" demonstrates the interaction between debate in the Senate and local political activity in North Carolina: what was said in the Senate mattered to the political leaders in the state's counties.

After lengthy debates on the removal of the deposits and Clay's resolutions of censure that lasted nearly the entire course of its session, on March 28, 1834, the Senate passed by a vote of 28 to 18 the resolution declaring that the Treasury Secretary's reasons for removal of the government deposits from the BUS and its branches to be "unsatisfactory and insufficient." The same day the Senate passed by a vote of 26–20 Clay's resolution of censure against the president:

> *Resolved*, That the President, in the late executive proceedings in relation to the public revenue, has assumed upon himself authority and power not conferred by the constitution and laws, but in derogation of both.[21]

By their vote on the latter resolution, these twenty-six senators became the leading opponents of Andrew Jackson and "the party." They also became the chief objects of Jackson's wrath. Yet far from restraining Jackson, the censure resolution would lead to Jackson's greatest claims yet for executive power and, in North Carolina, a contest both to unseat Mangum from the U.S. Senate and to claim the mantra of the people's will.

"So Vindictive a Power": War on the Senate

Andrew Jackson viewed the Senate as the only rival to his executive authority. Mangum had arrayed himself with the opposition senators and publicly questioned Jackson's principles. Macon and the old Republicans had long ago looked to the Senate as the counter to presidential ambitions. Mangum defended the Senate as the bastion of states' rights and the only remaining barrier to Jackson's ambitions. Mangum and the opposition senators, who refused to acquiesce to Jackson's claims for new presidential powers, thus became, in Jackson's view, his personal enemies. He sought to purge those senators whose state legislatures were majority Jacksonian and change the Senate from a rival to a body controlled by his partisans.

In his 1834 reply to the Senate's resolution of censure, Jackson proclaimed a new conception of presidential power. In reaction to the Senate's censure resolution, Jackson sent a "Protest" message to the Senate,[22] which presented his claims for executive power to the Senate and informed the senators that they had no right, short of trial for impeachment, to judge his actions. He also declared that the Senate lacked "competent authority" to censure the executive branch and called their resolutions "the illegal censures of the Senate." A single branch of the legislative department, Jackson insisted, had no right to consider or "decide upon the official acts of the Executive." Jackson told the Senate that he could not submit to be censured because if he did so "the confidence of the people in his ability and virtue and the character and usefulness of his Administration will soon be at an end." (Why the people's confidence in the ability and virtue of the president was more critical to government than the people's confidence in the ability and virtue of the Senate, Jackson did not address.)

Even before his answer to the censure, Jackson had made this new concept of the presidency clear in a message to his cabinet (which later became public) explaining his decision to remove the deposits. Jackson claimed a mandate to act against the BUS, independent of Congress. Jackson explained that "Whatever may be the opinions of others, the President considers his reelection as a decision of the people against the bank." Jackson asserted that the power of the Treasury Secretary over the government's deposits was "unqualified" and that the provision in the law that the Secretary report his reasons for removal to Congress was "no limitation." The judgment of the executive alone was sufficient to determine if a change was warranted (a recent investigation by the Democratic-controlled House had determined the deposits to be safe). Congress had no power over the current financial arrangements of the government; its only role was to make a future law for the deposit of the public revenue.

Jackson thus took it upon himself to judge whether Congress had properly disposed of the public money. Jackson claimed that Congress in its law chartering the bank, surrendered control of the public money "exclusively" to the Executive. "It is useless now to inquire why this high and important power was surrendered by those who are peculiarly and appropriately the guardians of the public money," Jackson informed the cabinet, "Perhaps it was an oversight." Congress not only gave up its power to control the public revenue, it also surrendered its power to legislate on the arrangements for winding up the affairs of the BUS. The executive branch of the government alone now assumed that responsibility. Jackson concluded the document by asserting that he assumed these responsibilities to protect the people.[23] Claiming the mantra of the people's tribune, Jackson thus asserted that the president, not Congress, would make national financial policy.

In his "Protest" Jackson further explained his new conception of the presidency. He informed the Senate that only the president was "the direct representative of the American people" and thus only he was directly responsible to the people. Jackson denied that the Senate had authority over cabinet officers; the "whole executive power" was vested in the president. And Jackson claimed that all public property, including the government revenue, was exclusively in the charge of executive officers "appointed by the President, responsible to him, and removable at his will." And he repeated his assertions made in the cabinet message that Congress had surrendered control of the public monies to executive discretion.[24] The "Protest" was notice to the Senate's opposition majority that Jackson refused to defer to Congress. By claiming an unqualified power over the deposits, Jackson was declaring that his judgment alone was sufficient to determine the suitability of the place of deposit, but the "Protest" (and Jackson's message to his cabinet) went beyond this; it restricted legislative power to narrow limits while making broad claims for executive power.

In the view of Mangum and the opposition senators these claims were radical; they challenged the Jeffersonian concept of the supremacy of the legislature in government. Calling Jackson's "Protest" message "a bold and vigorous statement of presidential prerogatives and independence," Robert Remini holds that it "constituted a most dangerous challenge to the Whig theory of legislative government."[25] Harry Watson points out in his history of the era that Jackson's assertions of independent presidential power broke with the tradition of previous presidents: "No previous President had ever described his election as a popular plebiscite on a matter of policy, or asserted such an unlimited power to act in the name of the whole people, independently of their elected representative in Congress."[26] In short, in Jackson's new conception of the presidency, the president would no longer defer to Congress. Instead, in the name of the People, the president would set government policy; Congress would ratify policies publicly emanating from the president's office: the government would be an executive government.

Jackson's "Protest" was a declaration of war on the legislative-primacy concept of government, and the opposition senators, now beginning to call themselves Whigs, saw it as such. Henry Clay denied Jackson's claims for sole executive authority, and insisted that the officers of the executive branch were not solely responsible to the president. "All are responsible to the law," he declared. Daniel Webster criticized Jackson's policy as executive usurpation; citing the mode of election of the president by the Electoral College, he pointed out that the Constitution nowhere called the president the direct representative of the people. He also argued that Jackson's assertions ran counter to the nature of a republican government with "written laws and limited powers." Calhoun agreed with Webster that Jackson was no closer to the people than the senators elected by the state legislatures. Why did Jackson make such claims to be the sole representative of the people, Calhoun asked the Senate. "The object cannot be mistaken," Calhoun explained. "It is preparatory to further hostilities—to an appeal to the people ... to enlist them as his allies in the war which he contemplates against this branch of the government."[27]

Ideologically, Jackson's "Protest" declared war on the concept of the supremacy of the legislative branch in government; operationally, the "Protest" declared war on the Senate of the United States. By proscribing the opposition senators, Jackson made it clear that he considered the Senate to be defying the will of the people. The "Protest" called for Democratic state legislatures to replace senators who were thwarting their will. Jackson quoted the resolutions of four state legislatures and noted that the vote for censure by the senators from these states conflicted with the will of their legislatures. He pointed out that had those senators had followed the resolutions of their legislatures, no opposition majority for censure would have existed in the Senate. Jackson claimed that he was not attempting to intervene in the relations between legislatures and senators. Yet why give these resolutions such a prominent place in the Protest if he did not want action by the state legislatures? When Jackson declared that the Whig senators from states with Democratic-majority legislatures were defying the people's will, North Carolina and Virginia became important battlegrounds.

Jackson sought to purge the opposition senators from the Senate. Resolutions of instruction from the state legislatures were his chosen weapon. As one historian of Southern politics has pointed out, "The practice of instructions in the 1830s constituted a standing invitation to the President to intervene in state politics and purge his opponents."[28] Jackson, in a letter to his son in which he mentioned the "usurpations of the senate," hoped that his protest message would encourage the state legislatures to exercise their "power to recall [the senators] by a majority at pleasure." Jackson anticipated the action of the state legislatures against the opposition senators. He told his secretary of state, Edward Livingston in June 1834, "The third of March terminates the term of seven members of the Senate who have violated their pledges, and are acting in open violation of the instructions of their constituents—the 4th of March gives us a new Senate and I trust a virtuous majority."[29] Jackson essentially was trying to create a new majority (replace the opposition senators with Jackson loyalists) in the Senate before the constitutional term of those senators was completed.

As Jackson viewed Mangum as one of the senators who had "violated their pledges" and Jackson's party controlled the state's legislature, North Carolina became a prime battleground in Jackson's war on the Senate. As early as December 1833 Mangum had suspected the administration of making "prodigious efforts" to manipulate the North Carolina legislature. Asking Governor Swain to help counter the meddling, Mangum informed him, "Certain leaders & through them, the Legislature are constantly plied with the correspondence of the Kitchen—Gen. Saunders goes home charged with plenepotentiary [sic] powers.... Their object is [to] get an expression of the Legislature favorable to Gen. Jackson."[30]

Shortly after Clay introduced his resolution of censure, Jackson loyalist and Missouri senator Thomas Hart Benton introduced resolutions to expunge the censure resolutions from the Senate journal. Instructions to Mangum were soon presented in the North Carolina legislature. On 28 November 1834, Dr. John W. Potts of Edgecombe County introduced two resolutions in the North Carolina House of Commons—one asserting the right of instruction, the other instructing Mangum to vote for Benton's expunging resolution.[31] Opposition leader William A. Graham, who represented the Hillsborough district in the House of Commons, informed Mangum that the opposition men in the Legislature were "undisciplined." Although

Graham doubted the resolutions could be defeated in the debate, he was firm in his belief that expunging the journal was unconstitutional: "I deny the right of the Senate to expunge any thing from its Journals after they have been published—Or if they had the constitutional right to do so, they could do it only by motion or resolution which they would have to record—and thereby perpetuate the thing expunged." Graham avowed that he would not relax his efforts in Mangum's defense, "since it is demanded of me not merely by the obligations of a friendship which I value, but by my regard for the constitution and the Laws." Graham called the proceedings of the Legislature "disgraceful."[32] Later, after the Whigs had gained control of the legislature, William Graham, speaker of the House of Commons, drew up an "Address of the Republican Whig members of the General Assembly"[33] in which he condemned the Senate Democrats' expunging resolution. Graham defended the Whig Senate's 1834 censure of Jackson and concisely stated the Whig position supporting legislative supremacy. The Address was a "solemn protest of the Sovereign State of North Carolina" against the "dim eclipse" into which the Senate had been cast by "the devotion of party to an Executive magistrate." In 1837, when the Democratic Senate "did violence" to its Journal of 1834, it had acted "without the warrant of the Constitution." Graham and the Whigs viewed the expunging resolution as a part of the Executive's war on legislative power. It was, they asserted, an act "avowedly designed to humble and degrade that body" for daring to censure the president. Contrary to Jackson's assertions in his "Protest" message, the Senate, representing the sovereign states, had a right to censure the conduct of the president, "declare its opinions" about his conduct, and examine the execution of the laws. As the representatives of the states, the Senators were charged "with the care of their interests" and the defense of "the peculiar rights of the States committed to their charge"; they could not allow those rights to be "trampled under foot with impunity," by the doctrine of executive supremacy implied in the expunging act.

With the instructions under debate in the legislature, Mangum was convinced that the opposition to Jackson and the defense of the Senate had become part of a political cause—a cause for "the Constitution and the laws." Mangum was certain that Jackson and the administration were aiming to break the Senate. And he was sure that the Jacksonian majority in the Carolina legislature had framed the instruction resolutions to help destroy the Senate as a bastion of opposition to the Jackson administration. Mangum believed that Jackson's popularity had intoxicated him; for Mangum, Jackson's popularity represented "a complete national prostration to the will of one man." The Senate, he told Graham, would be "subjugated by the seduction of Executive favor" or it would be "over awed by popular violence" because it presented "the only barrier to an *absolute power practically* on the part of the Executive.... Hence every effort is made to remove that barrier." Mangum questioned whether any senator could resign under such circumstances "without giving countenance to a gross perversion of the spirit of the Constitution." If Jackson succeeded, the Senate, designed to be the most stable element in the federal government, would be made "a mere tenancy at will."[34]

At this period Mangum also considered the implications of his resignation both on the state legislature and the Senate. Two thoughts dominated his mind: the power such a resignation would confer on the Jackson majority in the state legislature and the effect it would have on the Whig opposition in the Senate. Despite his expressed desire to not hold a political appointment "an instant beyond the moment that the power which conferred should express a wish to disrobe me of the trust," Mangum believed that "the Constitution and the State of the Country" would not allow him to follow such a course.[35] If only personal considerations mattered, Mangum explained that he would be content to resign if he could do so with honor and respect. "But the Cause is far above all personal considerations—The unit is & ought to be regarded as nothing viewed in Connexion [sic] with the unexampled & alarming pretensions on the part of the Executive," he told Graham. And Mangum did not want his resignation to embolden the Democrats. "I have no idea of resigning to the present legislature.... If I shall resign *at all*, my present impression is, that it will be only, when the trust can be surrendered to the *people*."[36]

Mangum was thus convinced that the current majority in the legislature did not truly reflect the will of the people. He explained to newspaper editor John Beard that if the majority of the state proved to be against the opposition that "without recognizing the principle [of instruction], I have said that I will not remain an instant against the public will—This I must comply with."[37] Mangum also believed that his outright resignation would affect other senators. Two other Opposition senators who were also facing instructions to vote to expunge the censure had assured Mangum that his course would determine theirs. "They both say that if I resign, it will be impossible for them to stand up against the storm that will blow upon them." In short, he explained, "If I resign Jackson will be able to command the Senate in the *next* Congress.—If I stand firmly, the opposition will continue in the ascendancy in the *next Congress*."[38] By the end of December 1834 Mangum had decided that the Executive's bid to control the Senate was a kind of political revolution that he had to oppose: "If there shall be a general yielding, it will settle practically, the Constitution in the South; and in my judg't will be deeply and fatally revolutionary."[39]

No doubt can be entertained that the Democrats intended to use instructions to obtain Mangum's resignation from the Senate. Late in 1834, during the session that passed the instructing resolutions, the editor of the *North Carolina Standard*, the leading Jackson press in the state, called for the use of instructions to remove Mangum, implied that a campaign existed to instruct other senators, and explained the reason why the legislature must do so. The opposition Senators must be removed, the paper proclaimed, because it could not be expected that "the views of the Executive will be fairly expressed, or the measures he recommends justly expounded" when the Senate's committees were chaired by the opposition and the committees "packed" with those "who are his active political enemies" and "unfriendly and hostile to the Executive Departments of the Government." But this situation would soon change, the *Standard* asserted.

> These partizan Senators seem resolved to make the most of their short-lived ascendancy. Let them do their worst, however: The fourth of March next will terminate their factious reign. Ere then, the People, through their constitutional organs the Legislatures, will in a good degree have pacified that body of aristocratic character.... No period in the political history of our country, has more emphatically shown the importance and necessity of not only asserting, but of *exercising* the legislative right of instruction.[40]

The opposition Senators, then, must be removed and replaced with friendly senators so Jackson's measures would not be impeded or modified. To oppose Jackson's measures, the paper claimed, was unjust. This Senate-packing would remove an obstacle, *the* obstacle, to Jackson's political course. The *Standard* asserted that there must be no check to the executive as the representative of the popular will. This desire to remove checks to the president's ability to implement the people's will was in line with Democrats' ideology. As Daniel Walker Howe notes, "Where Whigs voiced reverence for the supremacy of the law, Democrats more typically celebrated the autonomy of the sovereign people."[41]

Most of the letters that Mangum received from his personal and political friends approved of his course and confirmed him in his resolve to defy the instructions. From Fayetteville, federal judge and state bank director Henry Potter told Mangum that the instructions were "but empty recommendations" and that "all your political friends in this section of the State ... expect you to remain at your post 'unmoved by party rage.'" William Albright, farmer and merchant from Sandy Grove in Orange County, reminded Mangum that he was elected for six years and was "not accountable to any set of Political Demagogs [sic] you are only accountable to your God and to the honest yeoman [sic] of the Country, and I do believe they will Sustain you in the Course you are pursuing." Likewise, Dr. James S. Smith, former U.S. Representative and N.C. legislator, informed Mangum that only "*Collor* men" (Whig rhetoric for slavish Democratic party-men) thought he should resign. "The intelligent part of the people think you should pay not [sic] respect to the instructions ... because the opinion is that the majority of the people are on your side ... [and] because the legislature requires of you to do that which you cannot do without violating your oath."[42]

Western legislator Thomas Clingman reported that his information suggested the people were "very generally dissatisfied with the conduct of the General Assembly" and doubted both "the propriety of their instructions to you, and the right of the body to pass them."[43] Jackson Republican Robert H. Jones of Warren County, former legislator and attorney general of North Carolina and one of Mangum's long-time friends and advisors, told the senator that he was "much pleased not to hear of your resignation." Even while believing the Senate had no right to censure the president and that Jackson had the power to remove the deposits, Jones counseled Mangum that though "the electors have a right to offer instructions and advice to their representative" he was not bound to follow that advice or to resign if he disagreed with it. Binding a representative to conform to instructions was in Jones' view "not a representative Government, but to all practical purposes a pure democracy."[44] Mangum's brother Priestly wrote that "your personal and political friends are all ... well pleased with your determination. It is believed that those resolutions, were not, by any means, a fair or just expression of the will of the state."[45]

Another letter showed that Mangum received support of a different, but perhaps useful, sort from some of his friends in the opposition. Fellow Whig Sam P. Carson wrote Mangum in January 1835 at the height of the instruction controversy:

> I received a letter this morning from My Brother Chas Carson dated at Salisbury. He requested me to write to you & say that the Resolutions had been the subject of conversation from the time of their introduction & every intelligent man that he had seen (including Jackson men) deprecated them & also the idea of your being at all influenced by their passage. He says *Stand* to your *Post* & do the *talking* & if *necessary* send for him & he will go & do the *fighting* for he is confident he says, that he can whip a Score of the d—d collaer dogs.[46]

Despite the efforts of Graham and other opposition legislators, the General Assembly, passed the instruction resolutions on December 27, 1834, and Governor Swain transmitted them to Mangum just after the New Year.[47]

Mangum dutifully presented the resolutions in the Senate, but he declared that he would "not conform to them" and that he intended to vote against the expunging resolution. The Legislature, he explained, had no right to require him to become the instrument of his own personal degradation. Mangum "repelled the exercise of so vindictive a power" with "scorn and indignation." Both the honor of the state and his own personal honor required him to disregard the instructions.[48] One historian of North Carolina politics has accused Mangum of inconsistency for refusing to obey the instructions, since in 1833 he had asked in a letter to Governor Swain to be instructed by the legislature to support Clay's distribution bill.[49] But this interpretation disregards the distinction Mangum made between policy measures and constitutional judgments. Mangum, like many of his fellow opposition leaders, had never denied the right of instruction on policy measures; what he denied was the legitimacy and constitutionality of instruction regarding constitutional matters—in this case, censure and altering the journal of the Senate. In weighing constitutionality, senators were judges not representatives, and judges could not be instructed. Here, Mangum acted on the same grounds as he had in the House's election of 1825: then he argued that the representatives were acting as constitutionally independent *judges* of the best person to be president, not as representatives of their constituents. The General Assembly demanded that Mangum vote for what he considered an unconstitutional act to obliterate from the journal of the Senate a censure that he believed warranted, or that, alternatively, Mangum resign and thus aid Jackson in bending the Senate to his will. Such instructions Mangum would not follow.

"Mere Conservative Powers": The Defense of the Senate

Almost as soon as the legislature enacted the instruction resolutions, opposition meetings were organized in the counties to protest them, register support for Mangum in resisting them, and condemn Jackson's usurpation of power. At a public meeting held in Fayetteville to protest the instructions, the "assemblage of the Free People of Fayetteville" declared that they could not "sanction any act or admit the policy of any measure ... originating in violation of Law, and having a direct tendency to subvert the Constitution." The meeting condemned Senator Brown because "in his hands, the great interests of the country have been sacrificed to those of mere *party* consideration" and praised Mangum, "the able defender of constitutional liberty," for "manfully and boldly contending against the usurpation of power by the Executive, and resisting the principle that the will of one man, in this Republican Government shall be the supreme law of the land."[50] A meeting in Chowan County, in addition to criticizing the instructions and praising Mangum's resistance, specifically requested him "to pay no regard to the directions given by the late General Assembly of the State of N. Carolina relative to the [instruction resolution] vote."[51] A meeting of "the citizens of Beaufort County" declared their great alarm at "the usurpations" of the "chief magistrate of the United States" in his effort to "subvert the rights of the States," seize the public monies, "overawe and control a coordinate branch of government," and influence the right of suffrage by patronizing his partisans and proscribing those whose political views honestly differed with his own. They praised Mangum's conduct "in ably and fearlessly opposing the corrupt course of the present administration" and expressed their indignation at "the attempt made by our Legislature, at its late session, to embarras [sic] his political course." Pledging Mangum their support "so long as you continue the able champion of the rights of the States and the fearless denouncer of federal usurpation," the committee of invitation forwarded the meeting's resolutions and invited Mangum to a public dinner.[52] Opposition meetings in Chowan and Tyrrell counties passed resolutions censuring the legislature and approving Mangum's course in voting for the censure and defying the instructing resolutions. The Tyrrell Whigs declared that in instructing the senators the Legislature was "guilty of usurpation and a glaring violation of the rights of the people." Because the Senators were not the representatives of the Legislature "but the representatives of the sovereignty of the State of North Carolina," the meeting held that "consequently, the Legislature have neither the inherent, constituent, nor constitutional right to instruct our Senators."[53] These resolutions summed up the opposition view of Jackson's offenses of the last two years. They contain all the key tenets of Southern Whig ideology: states' rights, anti-executive power, and anti-party/anti-corruption. And they recognized that instructions to Mangum were part of Jackson's campaign to control the Senate.

The defense of the Senate was the perfect issue to energize the opposition in North Carolina. The States' Rights men in the opposition—mainly the Western Republican Calhoun party and the Old Republicans—were convinced that only their doctrines could check Jackson. Calhoun insisted, "That it is only on the elevation and commanding position of state rights, that the contest against executive usurpation can be permanently maintained."[54] And the popularity of states' rights in North Carolina added strength to the opposition when the States' Rights faction joined the National Republicans in the Whig cause. The Whigs argued that an attack on the Senate was an attack on the rights of the states. Mangum, as one of the proscribed senators, symbolized that attack. Additionally, both wings of the Whig coalition could agree on the defense of the "Constitution and the Laws."

The North Carolina opposition's position on the instructions, the censure, and the "Protest" was ably stated in the General Assembly's House of Commons by William A. Graham, Mangum's friend and political ally from Orange County. The defense of the Senate offered the opposition legislators the chance to defend states' rights at the same time as they opposed Jackson's usurpations of executive authority. True to his correspondence with Mangum, Graham delivered a speech against the resolutions of instruction that defended the rights of the United States Senate. Graham's speech is noteworthy because in 1835 he would be the Whigs' candidate for speaker of the House of Commons. Thus his speech on what would become a leading issue of the 1835–1836 campaigns must have reflected the sentiments of a great many Whigs in the legislature. And it was meant as a party statement in the battle for public opinion.

The speech was well publicized, appearing in full in the *Raleigh Register* and the *Hillsborough Recorder*. Graham thought that the debate in the House of Commons had not presented the arguments that the opposition party needed to put before the people: "I don't think the questions involved in the resolutions have been elucidated at all," he explained to Mangum, "It has been mere wandering in the fields of party politics. I think I am prepared to present some views not yet mentioned in the house."[55] Graham defended Mangum and the Senate's right to censure, set forth Jackson's errors, and explained why expunging the censure was unconstitutional.

In his speech Graham asserted that Jackson's claim in the "Protest" to have exclusive control of the public funds was a "bold usurpation." Congress had surrendered none of its authority over the public funds to the executive branch—in the members' view (and that of Duane) the Secretary of the Treasury was responsible to Congress for the disposition of the public funds—that was the spirit if not the exact language of the charter act. Graham refuted Jackson's claim that Congress had somehow surrendered its power to determine where or when to direct other arrangements for the deposit of the public money.

The Constitution expressly granted Congress control of public funds and public property and the power to make laws for their regulation. Moreover, Graham asserted, the Congress was the superior branch of government. Other than the president and vice-president, executive officers were the creations of Congress, their duties were prescribed by the laws of Congress, and they served Congress in the performance of their duties. Jackson could not construe the right to remove from office into a power to arrest all laws, to substitute "the President's will as a rule of conduct for all officers." The Constitution, Graham insisted, conferred no such power on the president:

> The executive department in every government of laws is merely ministerial to the legislative, and is but the executor of its will.... [The President] has no executive powers properly so called which are not dependent on the Legislature for their exercise.... Except so far as Congress wills, he has no military force, either land or naval, to command, no culprits to pardon, no treaties which he can fulfill, no officers to commission, and of course none to remove, no laws "to faithfully execute," no money to deposit or remove, not even a salary of a single dollar, to purchase his food or habitation.

In regard to the specific right of the Senate to censure the executive that Jackson denied in his "Protest," Graham argued that the U.S. Senate had the right to defend all its powers against infringement. He also asserted that the right of the Senate to examine and, if called for, to censure the conduct of any executive officer was a "right of all legislative bodies as one of the elementary principles of freedom." Such rights were fundamental to the Senate's ability to perform its constitutional duties. Graham noted that a "head of a department" had recently declared that "the Senate has no right to investigate its affairs," but Graham pointed out that were this the case, "then is the Senate deprived of half its efficiency in the enactment of laws; for how are they qualified to pass new laws, unless they can ascertain not merely how the old laws are written, but how they operate practically?" The Senate, then, must watch the executive branch and "examine the administration of the laws." Moreover, Graham reminded the House, the state legislatures should be the last body to seek to restrain the Senate, "the great palladium of the rights of the states." Destroy the independence of the Senate "and you rear over our heads one consolidated government."

Finally, Graham addressed the resolutions of instruction. Mangum had voted for the censure as part of his legislative duty to observe the administration of the laws and to declare when the laws were misinterpreted or the Constitution violated by an executive officer.

> Yet we are about to command him, to aver that this resolution is not merely untrue, but unworthy to remain among the records of the things that once were done.... [The instruction resolutions] would ask him to declare the non-existence of a fact, which all the world knows to exist.... Is it expected or desired, that he shall obey this mandate? Can he do it, without the lowest humiliation and infamy?

This being the case, the resolutions could only be designed for one purpose: removal—that "a place may thereby be vacated."[56]

That it was printed in full in the *Raleigh Register* indicated the importance attached to Graham's speech by the opposition party. The speech powerfully upheld the opposition position, and it completely denied Jackson's claims for executive supremacy. Graham's conception of government sharply conflicted with Jackson's assertions in the "Protest" of absolute presidential authority over the executive branch. Instead, Graham defended the theory of legislative government as the only theory of government that a strict-constructionist states' rights man could find in the Constitution. Moreover, Graham linked the defense of the Senate to the defense of states' rights. Graham did not address the legitimacy of the right of instruction, which few states' rights Whigs denied, but he questioned its use to undermine the Senate, the bastion of states' rights in the federal government.

The instructions to Mangum spurred a debate in the press. An exchange between two opposing newspapers offered a Whig opposition perspective on instructions versus a Democratic one. "Vindex" appeared in the *Raleigh Register*; "Civis" replied in the *North Carolina Standard*.[57] Vindex denied the power of the legislature to instruct United States senators. State legislatures were given power in the U.S. Constitution only to elect senators, not to direct and control them. According to Vindex, the idea that a representative, sworn to uphold a constitution, should obey the instructions of his constituents on constitutional question was "preposterous." The General Assembly was not elected to instruct Mangum; it held no mandate from the people to do so because the campaign was not contested on the issue; therefore, Vindex insisted, the instructions did not represent the voice of the people. Moreover, Vindex argued, the right of instruction "must involve the right of *thinking* and *judging* for the Senator instructed"; but Constitutional questions "must be decided according to the understanding and conscience of the Senator."

The attempt by the legislature to force a resignation and deny the senator his constitutional term was an "outrage" against the Constitution of the United States. "Civis" replied that the right of instruction was "a great popular right" connected directly to the will of the people. Civis insisted that "[T]he people have the right of making known their will, and of requiring obedience upon all subjects in which they feel a particular interest." Civis asserted that the General Assembly was "merely executing the public will" when it instructed Mangum because "the matter was fully discussed and explained before the people" and the people's sentiments on the issue were "made known, or in some way ascertained by their members in the State Legislature."

Thus, like Jackson, "Civis" argued that Congress did not represent the people—only the president and the state legislatures were the agents of the people. Though "Civis" claimed that instructions did not destroy agency, he failed to address the question of the *moral* agency of senators raised by "Vindex"—what if their conscience or judgment of a constitutional question did not allow them to obey? "Civis" implied that no Senatorial judicial function existed for constitutional matters; only the people could judge and only their agents—the president and the state legislatures—could act on such questions. "Civis" also implied that a legislature could shorten the constitutional term of a senator through instruction. The legislature represented the will of the people as embodied in the state legislators. And, in effect, "Civis" was asserting that the will of the people trumped the Constitution.[58]

In addition to Mangum, other opposition senators—several of them from southern states—were resisting similar instructions from their legislatures. The defiance of the instructed senators raised Jackson's anger and increased his determination to purge them from the Senate. The opposition party, now calling itself the Whig Party, was putting forward regional candidates for the presidency in an effort to block Van Buren's election. In the South their candidate was Senator Hugh Lawson White of Tennessee, one of Jackson's oldest associates who had gone into opposition primarily from resentment about the rise of Van Buren. Jackson now connected White's presidential campaign as a Whig to the party's determination to defend the Senate. In the spring of 1835 Jackson complained to a Tennessee friend that "the men who at this moment defy the positive Instructions of their immediate constituents in various states of the union" were the same men who were making war "against the cause of the people" and calling on "Judge Whites [sic] sectional popularity in aid of their object," which was the "subversion of Republican principles."

Jackson proposed to James K. Polk that he prepare resolutions of instruction and bring them before the Tennessee legislature to pass before the election of a senator. Such instructions could block the possible nomination of his opponents, White, known to be opposed to the expunging resolution, and Bell, who refused to be committed on the issue, by insisting on a pledge by any candidate to comply with the instructions if elected. Jackson gave Polk a list of opposition senators who were acting in disregard of "all instructions from their constituents" and "violating all pledges" that included Southern Whigs Mangum, George Poindexter and John Black of Mississippi, Gabriel Moore of Alabama, and Benjamin Watkins Leigh and John Tyler of Virginia. The opposition senators, Jackson informed Polk, had "entered into a League to maintain a majority in the senate, regardless of instructions."[59] Jackson was thus fully prepared to intervene in state politics as part of his effort to bring the Senate under his control.

Three of the "instructed" Southern Whig senators made public declarations that received much attention in the North Carolina Whig press. Mangum gave a speech in the Senate that defended his course in resisting the instructions and detailed almost the entire ideology of the Whigs' new opposition party. Virginia's opposition senators Benjamin Watkins Leigh and John Tyler of Virginia sent letters to the Virginia legislature setting out their response to the instruction resolutions of the Virginia legislature. Together these statements sketched the basic beliefs of the Whigs of North Carolina and Virginia in the defense of the Senate. The contrasts in their statements are also important for understanding differences in Southern Whig ideology.

The Virginia senators adhered to Old Republican doctrine. In letters published in March 1836, Leigh and Tyler accepted the doctrine of instruction as a republican principle, but both concluded that they could not obey the instructions to vote to alter the Senate's journal.[60] Tyler emphasized that expunging the journal of the Senate was unconstitutional: "I dare not touch the Journal of the Senate. The Constitution forbids it." He admonished the legislators who claimed to be States' Rights men that they were placing loyalty to Jackson above the Constitution and defiantly argued: "The only object of my political worship shall be the Constitution of my country." Tyler also reminded the Virginia legislature that the Senate's passage of resolutions expressing its judgment on the actions of the president was vital to its independence. "If [the president] adopt a course which he may believe to be correct, but which the Senate thinks unconstitutional—may it not say so?" he asked. Leigh emphasized that Jackson's war on the Senate threatened the security of the states. The legislature of Virginia, he warned, was taking action in support of the federal executive that it had never taken in the defense of states' rights: "I see the General Assembly of Virginia coming forward to vindicate *the rights and powers claimed by the President*, by this process of expunction, which it has never thought of resorting to, for the vindication either of *the rights of the people*, or *the rights of the States*." Leigh also claimed that the rights of the states were also threatened by the act of removing senators by instruction. The Senate, he reminded the legislators, represented the states in the national government. "And whatever tends to diminish the weight of the Senate in the system, must tend to impair ... the State sovereignties themselves." Moreover, Leigh argued, the only purpose of the expunging resolution was to "signalize the triumph of the Executive power over a department of the Legislative that has had the firmness to oppose its measures." It would "set a mark of disgrace and humiliation upon the Senate."

But Leigh and Tyler differed on their reaction to the instructions and their loyalty to the opposition. Leigh explained why he would not resign. "[T]he real and only purpose of the instructions was to compel me to resign," he admonished the legislators. If the senators were bound to yield obedience or resign, they were no longer moral agents; they would be the mere agents of the legislatures. And such a situation would tempt future presidents to do just as Jackson was now doing: "Whenever the President shall feel the check of senatorial opposition ... the President will be placed under the strongest temptations to have recourse to the State Legislatures, in order to disembarrass himself of the opposition." Thus Leigh averred that "resignation would inflict a more vital blow on the Constitution, because it would be followed by far more serious and mischievous consequences to both the Federal and the State Government, than a literal obedience to the instructions." Therefore, Leigh firmly explained, "I have ... come to a resolution, that I cannot, ought not, and will not resign."

In contrast, Tyler placed the republican doctrine of legislative instruction and his deference to the Virginia legislature above all other considerations. He would resign, he told the legislature, because he did not believe that he should stand between the legislature and the accomplishment of their object in the Senate. "I am bound to consider you, as in this, fairly representing the sentiments of our common constituents, the People of Virginia," he continued. "[N]ot a day or an hour could I desire to remain in the Senate beyond that hour wherein I came to be informed that it was the settled wish of the people of Virginia that I should retire from their service." Unlike Leigh, Tyler saw himself as part of no Whig cause, no greater morality. "What would it profit the country or myself, for me to remain in the Senate against [the General Assembly's] wishes? By retaining my place in opposition to their fixed, declared, and settled will, I should aid no cause—advance no great purpose," he declared. Thus, for Leigh the Whigs' Cause—the defense of the Senate, the defense of states' rights, and the resistance to the power of the Executive—was greater than the principle of instruction. Tyler clearly placed republican principles above any loyalty to the Whigs' fight against Executive "tyranny."

On February 3, 1836, Mangum provided his own defense of his course and the Whigs' cause in a Senate speech on national defense.[61] Mangum ably articulated the Southern Whig opposition ideology. To summarize his view of Jackson's war on the Senate, Mangum drew a powerful contrast between a centralizing, corrupting executive and a conservative Senate.

> The Executive, in its very unity, possesses a great element of strength. As an emanation from the popular will, it possesses great power, because of its popularity.... These great and various powers, centered in a single individual, upheld and controlled by a single will, capable of indefinite expansion and the minutest contraction, like the proboscis of an elephant, now tearing up an oak by the roots, and now picking up a pin; now overawing and subjugating a State Legislature, and now subsidizing a political hack; and all this re-enforced and sustained by an unscrupulous press.... The Senate, on the contrary, is merely passive; it has no patronage or gold to tempt the ambitious or mercenary. It possesses none but mere conservative powers. It is a mere staying power—a sort of political breakwater—resisting on the one side the excessive ebullitions of executive ambition, and the waves of a temporary popular fury on the other.[62]

Mangum explained that he and the Whigs had to fight for the Senate because the rights of the states were directly at stake: "If the Senate shall be permanently broken, either by direct action upon it, or indirectly, through the State Legislatures, one of the great safeguards of liberty will have fallen. The direct and inevitable tendency will be to the centralization of all political power." Essentially Mangum was declaring that the defense of the Senate and the defense of the rights of the states were one and the same.

Leigh and Mangum thus agreed on almost every point—the instructions were a war on the Senate and must be resisted if the opposition party were to continue and the rights of the states were to be safeguarded. North Carolina opposition leaders lauded Mangum's speech and thought it would aid the Cause in the 1836 campaign and the Whigs in Raleigh saw that it was printed in full in the *Register*.[63]

The Constitution and the Laws

Historians have passed too lightly over Jackson's new vision of executive government; it deserves a re-examination in the context of the war on the Senate.[64] Southern conservatives such as Mangum and Leigh were certain to oppose Jackson's radical new conceptions. The Senate was the conservative element of the government; Jackson sought to subjugate it to his will in his radical quest for executive power. In the view of these southern conservatives, the Whig cause was the defense of true conservatism: it alone sought to defend the rights of the states against the consolidating national government. Yet the Southern Whigs advocated democracy—the competition to capture the "popular will"—as much as the Democrats, as long as the primacy of the legislative branch of government remained intact. Mangum's use of memorials and his speeches in the Senate show that he thought public opinion was important and he was willing to contend for it.

The Whigs believed that Jackson and his party allies were seeking to undermine the Senate and the Constitution to aggrandize executive power. Whigs viewed the Constitution as the country's fundamental law while Jacksonians tended to associate the law with the will of the popular majority. Jackson's claims to executive power were based on his notion of the president as the embodiment of the popular majority. Lawrence Kohl, a historian of Whig ideology, points out: "Whigs deplored the way in which Jackson's vetoes and his theories of the Constitution had unsettled America's fundamental law."[65] This difference may be the reason why some Old Republicans, like Mangum, broke with Jackson and others remained with him. The Senate, in the view of Southern Whigs, was the conservative body in the government serving to check popular fury and defend the rights of the states. As Kohl notes, in the Jacksonian conception of government the popular will needed no check.[66]

Moreover, Jackson held the Senate's powers to an exact and absolutely narrow reading of the Constitution while, as the people's tribune—their representative, defender, and advocate, he interpreted *executive* power very broadly. Strict construction now only applied to Congress. Southern Whigs asked why Jackson and his partisans desired to break the independence of the Senate, "the great palladium of the rights of the states," as Graham called it. Yet the arguments of the Whigs also raise the question: why were supposedly strict-constructionist Southern Democratic-Republicans willing to give such broad constructive powers to the Executive? The Democrats' answer, of course, was that they now believed that the president, not the Senate, was the defender of states' rights. To the Southern Whigs the Senate was the bastion of states' rights; to the Southern Democrats, the president was the guarantor of states' rights. Mangum's speech expressed the Whigs' view of the Senate as a conservative power resisting executive ambition, but Jackson and the Democrats viewed the president as the people's tribune. What need then for a Senate to defend the rights of the states and check presidential ambitions?

Jackson's claims went beyond states' rights though; he placed the president beyond the control of Congress. Jackson claimed that the Senate had no right to issue independent resolutions and held no power short of an impeachment trial to examine the affairs of the executive branch. Jackson also argued that Congress surrendered all control of the public property once it was placed under executive charge. Jackson interpreted the law to give him the power to place the deposits where he willed. Although Democrats believed that Jackson was using his power to break corrupt institutions, the Whigs thought that Jackson's claims placed the president above the law. It is important to keep in mind that the Whigs' conservatism applied mainly to their resistance to Jackson's assertions of presidential authority, rather than to economic policy. As Lawrence Kohl notes, "Whigs were conservative only in the sense that they accepted the current constitutional and legal system as a sufficient framework for American development."[67] Jackson insisted that his actions defended Republican principles,[68] but during the war on the Senate it was the Whigs' principle of the Senate as a conservative power defending the people from executive ambition that was derived from the traditional Jeffersonian/Old Republican conceptions.

Although scholars have tended to overlook the war on the Senate, they have noted that Jackson's radical break with Republican tradition unified Whigs in opposition to him. "Insofar as traditional republican thinking vaunted legislatures over executives as more directly beholden to the voters, Jackson's assertions did mark a great departure," Sean Wilentz points out. "Jackson sought to sustain and enlarge the American presidency as an independent instrument of the popular will...."[69] Historian of North Carolina party politics Thomas Jeffrey points out that all Whigs were "genuinely alarmed" by Jackson's claim of authority to shift the deposits to the state banks. They agreed that the chief executive had become too powerful and that "this accretion of power threatened the very existence of republican government."[70] And Michael O'Brien has noted that Jackson's invocation of the popular will was the source for his claims to broad executive powers: "For Jackson ... the sovereignty of the people was an executive force, not a resistance to power; through him, it made things happen.... Andrew Jackson himself was but the people's servant, the instrument of what they would master." Majority rule conferred sovereign power. Under Jackson's conception, checks and balances were thus rendered moot "for no check was legitimate if it checked the popular will.[71] And Jackson's association of the popular will with *his* will, which he placed beyond challenge with his refusal to admit the power of the Senate to examine his actions, conflicted with Whigs' reverence for the supremacy of law. "In the Whig mind the man of great ambition, the man of indomitable will, represented a powerful challenge to the rule of law.... It was this fear of the personal will of one man which lay behind the violent Whig reaction to Jackson's use of presidential power."[72]

Thus, Jackson's concept of executive power combined with his attack on the Senate moved his claims to act as the direct representative of the people to a formulation that was radical and one that Whig conservatives were sure to resist: The will of the people trumped the Constitution. Although radical, this view derived directly from Jackson's "Protest" and thus from his conception of executive government. Its antecedents can be traced to Jefferson's concept that the president, in exceptional circumstances, was empowered to exceed the Constitution.[73] Jefferson's approach, however, preserved legislative supremacy since he believed the president's actions would and should be judged by Congress. Jackson gave Congress no role. To act in the name of the will of the people left no place for Congress.

1836: States' Rights Whigs

As the symbol of opposition to Andrew Jackson, Mangum increasingly came under severe attack in the Democratic press.[74] Nevertheless, the instruction controversy spurred the growth of the Whig Party. As historian Clement Eaton pointed out: "The fight of the anti–Jackson senators against legislative instruction to expunge the censure of the president was a powerful force in the growth of the Whig Party in the South."[75] John C. Calhoun was convinced that the combination of the National Republicans and the states' rights men in the great Whig coalition against Jackson's usurpations was part of a "great political revolution." Like Mangum, he thought the opposition in other sections was now looking to the South for protection against the ambitions of the Executive.[76]

A political revolution in North Carolina could put an end to "Jacksonism" in the state. Mangum knew the only hope of retaining his Senate seat after 1836 was Whig control of the legislature. If Mangum and the other Whig leaders could bring about a Whig revolution in the state and capture the government, they would not only demonstrate the superiority of Whig principles among the people of North Carolina (thus vindicating Mangum's stance), Mangum would also not need to resign. The Whigs of North Carolina could set the example for the South, and a blow would be struck against Van Buren. Moreover, if the opposition could capture the government of North Carolina, it would not only stop the pernicious effects of "Jacksonism" (also increasingly termed "Van Burenism") in the state, they could also deliver a blow to Executive ambitions and check the Executive bid to control the Senate. The political contest of 1835–1836 was a campaign to prove that the president did not represent the people's will in North Carolina. The campaign would center on Jackson's principles versus Whig principles.

The Whigs of the South were moving to support Hugh Lawson White of Tennessee as their candidate for president, but he was not Mangum's preferred candidate. Though he eventually backed White, Mangum's first choice, as a States' Rights Whig, was Calhoun. Pressed by the States' Rights Whigs to declare for Calhoun, Mangum explained to John Beard, editor of the Salisbury *Carolina Watchman* that he preferred Calhoun "to any man in the country" and was reluctant to oppose the "States Rights party ... the party to which I belong & which has all my sympathies." Calhoun, though, could not win a majority, and Mangum thought a Calhoun candidacy would simply drive North Carolina and Virginia into the arms of Van Buren. Mangum had reservations about other candidates: Clay had exhibited insufficient attachment to states' rights; John McLean lacked principles, and it was "next to impossible" for Mangum to endorse Van Buren. Mangum stated his position:

> You perceive that I am a *Non-Content*—And though I will go for no man who does not either *profess* my principles—or place himself in a position not to trample on them—yet I will not aid a scheme wholly impracticable [Calhoun's candidacy], & which, in my judgment, inevitably leads to the result, above all others, by me deprecated....[77]

Thus to Mangum and the other Southern Whigs of North Carolina, the campaign's most important aspect was the defense of states' rights.

After the reforms of the constitution in the summer of 1835 making the office of governor an elective office, that struggle could not be won without winning public opinion. As Daniel Walker Howe points out, "The history of the young American republic is above all a history of battles over public opinion."[78] The campaign of 1835–1836 was the first organized state-wide campaign for public opinion waged between two political parties in North Carolina. And the parties began to consider the popular elections for governor and president the truest test of the state's political character.

The work of local party organizers and Whig newspaper editors was critical to this campaign. The Whig editors explained partisan positions and gave prominent coverage to Whig campaign events. Though the editors aimed their pieces on party policies for the most part at the educated reader, they also wrote campaign appeals targeted to less well-educated Whig partisans. The political events that local organizers sponsored stimulated party enthusiasm. "Whether these leaders were moved by ideological conviction, or the hope of patronage, or a combination of the two, they strove increasingly to persuade their neighbors to join the party bandwagons," Harry Watson notes in his study of the second party system in Cumberland County. "Above all, the most active leaders went to great lengths to involve large numbers of voters in organized party activities." Watson also points out that these leaders were able to find linkages between local and national events that made the Whigs' party ideology credible to voters.[79] With more experienced and talented editors, the Whig opposition proved better at the mobilization of public opinion in these early years of the party than the Democrats.[80]

Two components of this Whig organization to capture public opinion were particularly important: public celebratory events, mainly dinners of honor and public celebrations, and political meetings of Whig partisans in a county. Published lists of toasts at the dinners were used to make a statement of ideology, as were the printed resolutions of county political meetings. Dinners of honor and public celebrations had their toasts prominently recorded in the opposition newspapers. Political dinners in tribute to Mangum were a prominent feature of the campaign. The instruction fight made Mangum the symbol of the Whig cause, and the party used honorary dinners to celebrate him. The dinners of honor also counteracted the negative portrayal of Mangum in the Democratic press. While allowing the Whigs to celebrate Mangum and his resistance to Jackson, these dinners also honored other prominent Whig invitees. Additionally, the dinners (often called "barbecues") and celebrations gave guests of honor the opportunity to speak to like-minded persons in the county. In 1836, the campaign ideology of the Whigs reflected the issues of the instruction controversy and the dominance of the state-rights/Calhoun wing in the Whig coalition. Whig ideology was states' rights, pro–Southern (defense of slavery was a prominent theme), anti–Van Buren, and anti-executive power (defense of the "Constitution and the Laws"). Such a focus also fit with the rhetoric of defending the Senate as the "the great palladium of the rights of the states" and the negative program of protecting North Carolina from the corruption of "the party." Positive government measures were not prominent.

Three celebratory events formed the centerpieces of the Whigs' campaign and were heavily publicized in their press. They were styled as the "Great Dinner" at Raleigh, the Mecklenburg "Grand Celebration," and the "Tribute to Worth" held in Southside Virginia. All these honorary dinners and grand celebrations took a distinct states' rights thrust in addition to their rhetoric against Van Buren and executive power. The Whigs launched their public opinion campaign with a celebratory dinner ("public entertainment") given to Mangum in Raleigh by his "personal and political friends" in Wake County. Taking advantage of Mangum's presence in their town on his way from Washington to Raleigh, the "Whig citizens" of Halifax invited Mangum to an honorary dinner on March 10, 1835. The speakers at this assembly of the county's "thoroughgoing State Rights men" addressed the central themes of the opposition's forthcoming campaign: opposition to executive encroachment, corruption in office, executive patronage, and Martin Van Buren; they also praised the U.S. Senate and Hugh L. White.[81] William Long, the president of the dinner, declared the central focus of the campaign: "Let the people then be awakened to a true sense of the calamity with which they are threatened."[82]

The dinner in Halifax was merely preparatory though. The Whigs intended Raleigh to be the scene of the great tribute dinner marking the start of the campaign to awaken the people to the danger of "Van Burenism." Attended by more than 150 Whigs, the dinner at Raleigh was presided over by Governor Swain assisted by the Intendant of Raleigh and editor of the *Raleigh Standard*, Weston R. Gales.[83] Gales published a list of the toasts given which included all the themes the Whigs wished to emphasize: "Agriculture, Commerce and Manufactures"; "Our honored guest, Willie P. Mangum ... true to his country's best interest, the Constitution and the laws"; "Constitutional liberty"; "the Whig cause—now as in the days of the Revolution—resistance of the people against arbitrary power"; "Executive patronage—a good man will not desire it—a bad one ought not to possess it"; and "the security, and the only security of a Republican Government—the virtue and intelligence of the people."[84]

The Mecklenburg County "Grand Celebration"—the second of the great Whig celebratory events—commemorated the Mecklenburg Declaration of Independence signed in Charlotte on 20 May 1775. Ostensibly a non-partisan celebration, it had been taken over by the Whigs,[85] and they made it a vehicle for the themes they planned to emphasize in the coming contest: Mangum as symbol of the Whig cause, Mangum's principled resistance to the resolutions of instruction, the defense of the Senate, and resistance to executive usurpation. Whigs from North Carolina, South Carolina, and Virginia were present, and women were prominently involved. The description of the beginning of the Mecklenburg Celebration noted that "[t]he day was ushered in by the firing of cannon, and at an early hour the streets of our flourishing village were thronged by a well-dressed and orderly population of both sexes, mingled with the glitter of the beautiful and appropriate uniforms worn by the regiments of Cavalry and Volunteers, called out on the occasion." The celebration itself prominently featured women:

> On the right and immediately over the revolutionary soldiers, waived a beautiful flag, presented on the occasion to the Lafayette Artillery, by the ladies of Charlotte, bearing the inscription "Mecklenburg Declaration of Independence, 20th May, 1775," while the ladies themselves, with hundreds of their fair companions from this and the adjoining counties, filled row after row of the benches immediately in rear of the revolutionary soldiers....[86]

After a reading of the Mecklenburg Convention's Declaration of Independence and an oration, the company (the account numbered them at 500–600) sat down to an "elegant and sumptuous" dinner.

Mangum delivered a two-hour speech defending his political course in resisting the "expunging resolutions" of the Legislature, which he characterized as an attempt to make him the instrument of his own dishonor.[87] Showing that the celebration was a states' rights event, letters read to the assemblage from those political leaders who had been unable to attend—a muster roll of the States' Rights Whigs from three states that included Senators John C. Calhoun and William C. Preston from South Carolina, Gov. McDuffie of South Carolina, Senators John Tyler and Benjamin W. Leigh of Virginia, and Opposition presidential candidate Hugh L. White of Tennessee.

The main political messages of the celebration, however, came in the after-dinner "volunteer toasts" that were printed in the newspapers.[88] The celebrants praised the Senate as a Whig bastion against Jackson's presidential ambitions. "The Whig Senate of the United States" was toasted as "a wall of defence for the rights and liberties of the People against the encroachments of Executive ambition" and as a body Whigs desired to "ever stand inflexible against Executive usurpation." And the Whigs disparaged Martin Van Buren as anti–Republican and anti–Southern: "Martin Van Buren: Opposed to the last war, opposed to James Madison, opposed to Southern interest; can the Southern people go for such a man?" Showing that the national wing of the party was not entirely unrepresented at the celebration, several toasts praised Henry Clay.

Featured in twelve toasts, Mangum was associated with all the main tenets of the Whig cause: he was "the able and fearless champion of Southern principles" and "the firm and intrepid defender of our constitution and laws." He had "planted himself upon the ramparts of the Constitution and boldly defended it against the assaults of a servile majority of the State Legislature." He was "the servant of the people and not of the Legislature" and "the eloquent and consistent advocate of the honor and interests of the South." For the Whigs at the Mecklenburg celebration, the instruction controversy was a critical part of the political contest underway in the state; their toasts united praise of Mangum, states' rights, defense of the Senate against executive usurpation, and defense of the Constitution.

The third of the great Whig celebrations demonstrated the dominance of the states' rights wing in the Whig parties of North Carolina and Virginia in the 1835–1836 campaign. A public honorary dinner was given to Senators B.W. Leigh of Virginia and Mangum by the citizens of Mecklenburg County, Virginia at Buffaloe Springs on August 13, 1835. States' rights and the defense of the Senate were the themes of this "Tribute to Worth" as the editor of the *Western Carolinian* chose to describe the meeting. Both men had been proscribed by Democratic legislatures, so the presence of Leigh and Mangum together at the meeting made it a celebration of the Whig cause in the two states and clearly emphasized opposition to instructions as a central theme of the meeting.[89] Prominent Whigs unable to attend included former governor Branch of North Carolina, Gov. Tazwell of Virginia, Senator Tyler of Virginia, and Judge Upshur of Virginia. Mangum and Leigh spoke to the assemblage after the dinner.

In addition to toasts emphasizing the themes that had been presented in the "Great Dinner" and the "Grand Celebration," this dinner's toasts were "of the real genuine State Rights stamp" and emphasized the states' rights component of the opposition ideology, the ties of that ideology to the Old Republican Principles of '98, and the Senate as the bastion of states' rights. The Whigs praised the Federal Constitution as "a *compact* between *Sovereign* confederated States" and states' rights as "our '*Sine Quanon*' in the compact of confederation." They called on the Senators of the United States to "stand to your posts and save your country." They gave a toast to the Whig members of Congress "who have been placed under the hand of Executive proscription." They lauded Mangum as "a fearless defender of State Rights as expounded in the Virginia Resolutions of '98 and '99." The celebrants associated the two guests of honor as the representatives of the Whigs of the two states: "Virginia and North Carolina: Leigh and Mangum; patriots and Statesmen: The advocates of State Rights and State Remedies who have dared to resist the mad career of Andrew Jackson." They decried "the Proclamation, the Force Bill, and the seizure of the Public Money" and castigated Jackson for seeking to turn the government into "a Government of *Force*." And reflecting the Old

Republican concern that had arisen during the Missouri Controversy about radicalism in the North, the Whigs complained of "the ignorance and Fanaticism of the North" that by goading the slaves "into desperation" would "diminish their comforts and rivit their chains." And reflecting worries about the antislavery agitation of the Liberty Party and other abolitionists in the Northern states, they questioned Northerners attachment to the Union because of their failure to "halter" such "fanatical incendiaries" as "Tappan, Garrison & Co."[90] Such toasts leave no doubt that this was an assemblage of States-Rights Whigs.

And the report of "The Tribute to Worth" provides further evidence about women's participation in "the Cause." The paper recorded two toasts "By a Lady":

> Benjamin Watkins Leigh: His puny revilers imitate the impotency of the snail; which endeavored to deface the faultless symmetry of the Statue of Venus by trailing its dirty slime over every part....
>
> Col. J.H. Gholson: His enemies have consigned him to a private life; the greatest honor they could have conferred upon him.[91]

Such partisan after-dinner toasts were normally the province of men, but women were apparently welcomed as participants at these politically-oriented toasts, evidence that Whigs, even in the years of party formation, desired women's participation in their political events. The North Carolina—Virginia "Tribute to Worth" shows the dominance of Old Republicanism in the Southern Whig opposition parties as they conducted their first presidential campaign: the toasts emphasized the Principles of '98, "state remedies," and state sovereignty. The Old Republican, states' rights emphasis in these toasts and their prominent publication in the Whig press fit the White candidacy: *Southern* Whig.

These events illuminate the ideology of the Carolina Whigs and reveal their strategies for winning the people's will for the Whig Party. The emphasis on Old Republican themes and states' rights in the ideology the Whigs expressed at these dinners and celebrations shows them to be a party coalition dominated by the states' rights men: the Old Republicans, "original" Jackson men, and pro–Calhoun Western Republicans, who together had become a "States Rights party," as Mangum called them, inside the lager Whig coalition. The majority of Carolina Whigs were States' Rights Whigs. Also, these three events illustrate how the Whigs used celebrations to rally party spirits and promote their ideology in the Whig press through speeches and toasts. Additionally, these celebratory and festive political events show the Whigs accepting and perhaps even courting the participation of women. The prominent participation of women in the "Grand Celebration" and the "Tribute to Worth" suggests that they were involved in Whig campaigns from the outset of party formation in North Carolina. The Whigs wanted all of society engaged in their cause to overturn Jacksonism.[92] Their ideology was pro-state sovereignty, pro–states' rights and emphasized Old Republican themes. This reflected the strength of the States' Rights wing in the state coalition. And the impact of Jackson's war on the Senate is also apparent: The Carolina and Virginia Southern Whigs associated states' rights with the defense of the Senate. Mangum was thus the perfect symbol for the Carolina Whigs' cause: Leading senator, proscribed by Jackson, Old Republican, anti–Van Buren, and now a States' Rights Whig.

Other, smaller county dinners and barbecues reflected the same themes, but usually by printing of letters of invitation that included resolutions passed by the Whig county committee. Mangum received numerous invitations to these public dinners and "barbeques." Such "barbecues" and "festivals" were also county political meetings.[93] Resolutions of the county committees show that the ideology articulated by the opposition leaders was present at the county level as well. "The Whigs of Lenoir County" invited Mangum to a public dinner for their Whig legislator. (The writer, Isaac Croom, explained to Mangum that he had been "laboring for years against the 'Slippery Elm, the wiley [sic] little Dutchman" Van Buren.) Viewing themselves as part of "the Cause," these Whigs focused on their attacks on Van Buren. The enclosure from the committee members praised Mangum's "noble stand" in the "great and sacred cause" in the Senate. In "one of the gloomiest periods of our Republic" he had acted "in vindication of a violated & bleeding Constitution." The committee disparaged "the monstrous claims to Executive power" put forth in Jackson's name by Van Buren ("the Candidate of Baltimore Humbug") and decried the Democrats as a "Pretorian [sic] Band of office holders & office hunters."[94]

Similarly, the committee of invitation to a meeting in Northampton County declared the Senate "the principal practical barrier to Executive encroachment." The Northampton Whigs praised Mangum for "battling in the course of law and liberty against Executive supremacy." And the committee appointed to invite Mangum to a "Barbicue" in Wake County approved of Mangum's "Strenious [sic] & able exertions to check Executive encroachments & usurpation upon the rights of the states & the people" and his efforts "to restore the Good-old, republican doctrine of a strict adherence."[95] These Whigs held the same view as the Whig senators: executive power menaced states' rights and the Constitution. The Senate, not Jackson, was upholding Old Republican principles.

Whigs also resorted to yet another method, the county meeting, which they used to perfect local organization, draft and pass resolutions, and elect delegates to district conventions. (Unlike the political dinners and barbecues used in the 1801–1808 period, county meetings were a relatively new form in state politics: they had been introduced during the 1824 Jackson campaign.[96]) Also these meetings—used to pass resolutions and elect delegates—were more strictly political or electoral rather than celebratory or festive; thus no women participated. In his history of the North Carolina Whig Party, Herbert Dale Pegg notes, "The county meeting ... was the most important wheel in the machinery of the Whig party."[97] Local opposition newspapers published the resolutions in support of "the Cause" passed by county meetings which were numerous and well publicized. And Harry Watson notes, "The most popular organizational measure ... continued to be a general meeting of the party membership in the courthouse to listen to speeches and pass resolutions."[98] Like the celebrations and county barbecues, the county resolutions focused on state-rights themes and opposition to executive power.

Setting the pattern for such county meetings was the Whig meeting at Salisbury on May 18, 1835, organized by the opposition leaders of Rowan County. The meeting was held several days before the Democrats were to gather in Baltimore to nominate Van Buren as Jackson's successor.[99] By 1835, when it was clear that Jackson intended to have Van Buren nominated as president, the Whigs' redoubled their attacks on Van Buren as the symbol of party corruption.[100] Charles Fisher invited Mangum to attend the Salisbury meeting and deliver an address. The meeting would be a large one, Fisher explained, "as we do not do things by halves here." Governor Swain was also expected at the meeting.[101] Styled as a "Great Meeting of the People" by the Salisbury *Western Carolinian* (a Calhoun newspaper), the meeting issued a set of declarations that stated almost completely the ideology of the North Carolina Whigs:

> That in our opinion, the rapid *progress* which the Federal Government, within a few years past has made, and is still making in the usurpation of power not granted by the Constitution—in the abuse of powers

that are granted—in the extravagance of public expenditures, and in the corruption of republican principles—is such as ought to alarm all patriotic and thinking men, not only for the safety of our Republican Institutions, but even for Liberty itself.

Reflecting the Whigs' anti-party ideology and their association of Van Buren with "the party," the Whigs declared that the Democratic convention, held for "the purpose of nominating MARTIN VAN BUREN," was "another attempt to subvert the Constitution of the country" because it would transfer the people's right of election "to an irresponsible CAUCUS, composed of interested Office-holders, and Office-seekers."

The assembly's longest resolution was a lengthy indictment of Van Buren emphasizing his hostility to Southern interests; it also accused him of being "chiefly instrumental in introducing into the practice of the Federal Government that system of proscription, and party discipline, which is so rapidly destroying the freedom of opinion, corrupting the morals of the country, and making government itself a distinct interest from that of the people." The election of Van Buren to the Presidency, the Whigs argued, would thus be "fatal to the welfare of the Union, if not to Liberty itself." Following a declaration of support for White, the assembly stated its approval of Mangum's course in the Senate, particularly, "the firm and manly stand which he has taken against all Executive encroachments on the Constitution, or on the Legislative Department of the Government." The meeting strongly condemned the conduct of the Legislature as "instructing our Senators to do an unconstitutional act" and as an "outrage on the Constitution" and a "disgrace" to the measure's authors. Finally, the meeting issued a call for the Opposition men to organize "for active and open operations" across the state "for the purpose of arousing the people of North Carolina to a just sense of their danger."

Nearly all the resolutions of the committees of the county meetings of 1836 followed the lead of the Salisbury mass meeting. They took an anti-party, anti-executive stance and focused their resolutions on Van Buren. The report of a county meeting held at Hillsborough in Orange County, drafted by Mangum's friend William Graham, indicted Van Buren as a false Republican and an enemy of the South: in 1812 he supported De Witt Clinton not Madison; he favored internal improvements funded by the general government; against the interests of the South, he actively supported the Tariff Acts of 1828 and 1832; in the New York legislature he voted for a resolution of instruction opposing the admission of Missouri as a slave state; on the "great question" of the preservation of "the Institution of Slavery" he was unreliable; and while the expansion of executive power and patronage threatened to overwhelm "the liberties of the country" Van Buren had remained silent.[102] Resolutions from a meeting in Halifax declared Van Buren "utterly incapable" of "enlarged, just and wise views of public policy" and declared he sought "by intrigue and cunning to promote the selfish designs and purposes of party, wholly regardless of the country." A Whig meeting in Warren County, a Jackson stronghold, called Van Buren "the determined and deadly enemy of Southern rights and interests." A meeting in Stokes County proclaimed him "the head of a party of office holders and office seekers" and hostile to republican sentiments. The citizens of Granville County decried the "alarming assumption of power" by the Executive "subversive of the rights of the people and destructive of the *blessings of liberty*." And a meeting in Hertford County accused Van Buren of being "a supple courtier and political changeling" who would prove dangerous to "our free institutions."[103]

The consistent condemnation of Van Buren is evidence of the central role that criticism of Van Buren and the "Van Buren system" occupied in the opposition ideology. (Though the

Democratic newspapers criticized White's Republican credentials, Mangum bore the brunt of the attacks from Democrats, because he was their version of Van Buren.) Clarence Clifford Norton, historian of the Democratic party in North Carolina points out that "no presidential candidate ever caused more personal hostility, or called for more labored support from his partisans in North Carolina than Martin Van Buren."[104] As the resolutions on Van Buren as the enemy of Southern interests and his unreliability on slavery attest, the "politics of slavery," as William Cooper has called it, played a prominent role in the Whigs' campaign against the Democrats.[105] But in 1836 the anti–Van Buren and anti-"Van Burenism"/anti-party ideas were equally important and they were firmly established as part of the Whigs' rhetoric and ideology. Opposition to Van Buren allowed National Republicans to join the States' Rights men in condemnation of the administration. Over the course of the entire 1835–1836 campaign the ideology put forward by the Whigs in their public dinners, celebratory "festivals," barbecues, and county meetings was an Old Republican ideology of states' rights and anti-executive power combined with a thorough opposition to Martin Van Buren and "the party."

The Whigs' efforts to move public opinion to Whig principles succeeded in the August elections for the state government. A Whig governor was elected on Whig principles. In the legislature, the Whigs gained a majority of one in the senate and nearly captured a majority in the commons (the Democrats won a majority of one). Mangum looked to Edward Dudley's triumph as proof that Carolinians had been won away from "the party" to Whig principles and approved of his course in defending the Senate against presidential ambitions.[106] Whigs shared his view.

The Whigs, of course, trumpeted Dudley's great victory rather than the divided legislature. The editor of the *Carolina Watchman*, in a celebratory mood, prematurely claimed that with Dudley's election by decisive majority of over 4,000 votes, North Carolina had been, "REDEEMED!! REGENERATED!! AND DISINTHRALLED!!" and that she had "renounced Van Burenism." Looking ahead to the November presidential election, the editor found it difficult to believe that Van Buren "with his abolition, his high-tariff notions, his aristocratic manners, his deceitful courses and abject servility" could receive more votes than had Governor Spaight. "We repeat that North Carolina is purged from Van Burenism."[107] Gales's *Raleigh Register* declared, "PATRIOTISM TRIUMPHANT!" and "Honest North Carolina is Free! Free from Jacksonism, free from Van Burenism." Gales predicted that "the White Revolution" would achieve a "signal defeat" of Van Buren in the presidential election.[108] In their invitation to Mangum to attend a "Barbicue" in celebration of the "Glorious triumph" of the Whigs, the Whigs of Wake County proclaimed the election as "the complete triumph of Whig principals [sic]" and predicted the "certain rescue" of "the Good old, North State" in the coming presidential election "from the aims, and support, of the arch Majician [sic] abolitionist and political intriger [sic] Martin Vanburan [sic], & thereby the complete triumph of Republican principals [sic]."[109]

Elections in the fall, however, proved that Mangum and the other Whig leaders had not fully purged the state in their campaign as the *Watchman* claimed. Whig principles were clearly on the rise and receiving a favorable reception among the electors, but "The Cause" had not yet completely triumphed in the Old North State. Special elections in two counties gave the Democrats a narrow majority in the legislature on joint ballot of the houses. In the November presidential election, the Whigs failed to generate the votes for White that they had for Dudley. Whig voters did not come out in the presidential election in the numbers they had for the gubernatorial election in August. White, with no hope of winning outright, failed to generate Whig enthusiasm in North Carolina. Van Buren won a sizable majority, and North Carolina remained a Van Buren state.

Even before the results of the presidential election were known, Mangum considered resigning. Apparently concerned that he might be considered by some a burden to the party and that in an evenly divided legislature a few Whig "delinquents" might be able to exact favors from him as the price of reelection, Mangum wished to withdraw his name. Graham was worried about the effects of a withdrawal before the meeting of the legislature would have on the still-fragile party coalition, and he urged Mangum to reconsider. "Your withdrawal would exert a pernicious influence on our cause," Graham warned him. Some "timid" Whigs might interpret it as the result of "a conviction that Van Burenism was irresistible," and Graham cautioned that "'The Party' would shout it, as the striking of our flag." He remained convinced that "the great body of our party" desired Mangum's reelection and would not consider their triumph complete until that was achieved.[110]

Indeed, the Whigs of Wake County had recently praised Mangum's "strenious [sic] & able exertions to check Executive encroachments & usurpation upon the rights of the states & the people" and approved of his "Great and Manly course" in defending "the Good-old, republican doctrine" of strict construction of government powers.[111] When it became apparent after the special elections in the fall that the Democrats would command an outright majority in the legislature, Mangum resigned on 24 November 1836. The Democratic legislature then re-elected Bedford Brown and elected Robert Strange to the Senate.

The Governor's House had been won, but the war for the Senate was lost. Nationally, the Whigs lost their majority in the Senate. Whigs were concerned that the Senate, no longer a barrier to "Jacksonism," was becoming the tool of the administration. In their view, Whigs who had upheld true Republican principles were giving way to the unprincipled men of "the party." After Mangum's resignation from the Senate, James Graham, brother of William Graham and Whig representative from the Mountain district, wrote upon his arrival in Washington in December 1836: "The Senate is undergoing a rapid and unfortunate change. Talents of the highest rank are giving way and exchanged for third and fourth rate men who have Indian Rubber principles."[112]

In the first popular election for governor, the new Whig Party had proved the resonance of its message by electing Dudley, and they had nearly overturned the Jackson majority in the state legislature. But their revolution against "Jacksonism," Van Buren, and "the party" was far from complete. After a two-year struggle, Mangum had been forced to resign from the Senate and the Whigs had been defeated by the Van Buren men in the presidential election in North Carolina and the Union. The Whigs had demonstrated the strength of their ideology and the people's lack of support for "the party." But they did so with an Old Republican ideology that emphasized states' rights, opposition to executive power, and anti-party/anti-corruption ideas—an ideology akin to Jackson's own rhetoric in the revolution against the National Republicans.

The rhetorical campaign against Van Buren like the White candidacy stood chiefly on the Old Republican states' rights opposition ideology and advocated no positive measures. Its failure to appeal to former National Republicans may have contributed to the lack of turnout in the presidential election. States' rights and Old Republicanism were still the dominant ideologies and the States' Rights party the preeminent group in the Whig coalition.

Mangum's removal was a sore spot for the party and for Mangum himself. To complete their revolution against "Van Burenism" and "the party," the Whigs' would have to capture the legislature, re-elect their Whig senator, and elect a Whig president. The failure of the Whigs' regional campaign for Hugh Lawson White showed that they could not achieve the latter goal with a regional Southern Whig candidate. The North Carolina Whigs, like their counterparts in the other Southern states, would need to move closer to a national Whig coalition if the Whig Party were to win a presidential election.

Because North Carolina had always been strongly Anti-Federalist and Old Republican in its sentiments, the States' Rights wing with its Old Republican doctrines, of which Mangum was the most notable member, was able to energize the Whig opposition in North Carolina with doctrines of strict construction and states' rights long popular in the state. With its popular doctrines, the States' Rights wing moved the Whig Party to a position where ascendancy over the Jackson–Van Buren Republicans seemed possible—an ascendancy the National Republicans could never have gained on their own.

In March 1834, John Beard, the editor of the Salisbury *Western Carolinian*, had called for a political "counter-revolution" by "the friends of Constitutional Liberty" against the "corruption and usurpation" of the Jackson administration's revolution, a revolution "gradually accomplished by the Federal authorities, more extensive and radical than any heretofore witnessed in our country since the adoption of the Constitution." Beard pointed out that the people had achieved such a counter-revolution against the broad-construction principles of the Federalists in 1801. At that time, aroused to the danger by the "celebrated Resolutions of Virginia and Kentucky," the citizenry had elected Thomas Jefferson, "who restored the Government to its true principles."[113] That counter-revolution had now begun in North Carolina.

5

The Revolution of 1840: From States' Rights Whigs to Clay Whigs

The Whig opposition had been successful in loosening the grip of the Jackson–Van Buren Democratic Party on the state of North Carolina. By electing a Whig governor, these opposition members had shown that the principles of "the party," as they called their Democratic Party rivals, did not hold sway in North Carolina. Opposition on Old Republican principles, though, had not been enough to win in the presidential contest. The Whigs needed to find a means to wage a political revolution against the party of Jackson and Van Buren as the Democrats had waged a political revolution against the supporters of Adams and Clay. After the failure of White's South-only campaign in 1836, the North Carolina Whigs rapidly moved to backing a unifying national candidate. Old Republicanism, especially opposition to executive power and corruption, continued as the core component of the North Carolina Whigs' ideology, and the focus on executive power enabled the coalition party of diverse factions—Calhoun states' rights men, like Mangum, national Republicans, and eastern Independents—to hold together while the party was in transition. The search to find a balance between Old Republican principles and a unifying national candidate would result in a "revolution" in state politics that would allow the Whigs of North Carolina to establish a political ascendancy that would last a decade. In 1837, though, this evolution was just beginning; and many North Carolina Whigs, including Willie P. Mangum, remained very much *Southern* Whigs who were uncomfortable with their northern opposition allies and were still committed to Calhoun's states' rights doctrines.

"The Real Conservators of Our Political System"

In the midst of the war between the Senate of the United States and Andrew Jackson in 1834, the Senate gave its Finance Committee the task of investigating the affairs of the Bank of the United States. The investigation was undertaken at the request of bank president Nicholas Biddle to counter one launched by the Democratic-controlled House that was certain to be unfavorable. The Finance Committee's report was delivered too late to help the bank,[1] but Mangum's diary-like account of his participation in the five-member investigating team's travels in New England, given in a series of letters to his wife Charity, reveals the strangeness of New England society for the Southern senator and his discomfort with its ways. A letter written to a political friend reporting on the impression of his trip reveals his distrust of his new political allies. Though written two years before the 1836 election, together the letters provide a window into the difficult politics of maintaining the new Whig coalition between the opposition States' Rights men of the South and the National Republicans of New England.

The investigating committee was to commence its work in Boston. On August 16th, at the close of the congressional session of 1834, Mangum traveled from Washington to Baltimore where he met Whig senator and former governor of Virginia John Tyler, another member of the committee. In company with Tyler and his family, Mangum went by steamboat to Philadelphia and then on to New York, where Mangum braved the cholera reportedly raging in the city to make a brief tour of the city's sites. New York, with "its bay, its rivers, its city & its heights about it," he found "the most picturesque & delightful spot I ever saw—except some scenes of the mountains; which I admire above all things."² Mangum returned to his steamboat in the evening for the trip up Long Island Sound to Newport, Rhode Island. With a little bravado he described his passage through Hell Gate to Charity:

> These waters are the terror of mariners and many vessels have been lost there.—Cooper the novelist describes them in his "Water Witch"—and as you have the book let me ask you to turn to the novel, and read the account of these dangerous narrows—The tide happened to be full, and I saw none of the dangerous & peculiar features of this pass—I regretted it, and had much rather the tide had been ebb or ebbing, so that I might have formed a juster idea of those dangers that have so often appalled the heart of the sailors.

Daniel Webster attributed to Richard Francis Nagle (ca. 1835–1891), oil on canvas, ca. 1849 (U.S. Senate)

The party arrived at Newport on 19 August, but due to his poor accommodations Mangum refused to stay in the town more than a single night despite the pleading of Gov. Tyler and his family, who wanted to spend more time in Newport. He quit the town the next morning ("though not until I walked over the island") and traveled by coach and sail boat through "flourishing" towns and cities to Providence where he found City Hotel, "a splendid establishment." Departing the city on the morning of the 21st, Mangum traveled fifty miles to Boston, where, finding the hotels full, he lodged at a "respectable boarding house." The next day he called on Whig senator Daniel Webster, chairman of the investigating committee, who received him "with great cordiality" and insisted that Mangum change his lodging to the fashionable Tremont House hotel, where he had arranged for the committee to stay. Mangum yielded to Boston "fashion" and shifted to the hotel, giving up "comfort for show."³

The trip to Boston took Mangum the farthest he had ever been from home. To him New England was a "strange and distant land." Though he found New England "a wonderful Country" and New Englanders "a wonderful people," Mangum told his wife he felt constantly "amongst strangers."[4] In his trip from Providence to Boston, Mangum passed "through a succession of towns & villages, & through the most highly cultivated country that I ever saw." The beauty of the countryside, he told his wife, "far surpasses my former conception of it." New England seemed to him "the land of churches." At Boston Mangum spent three days touring the city and its environs with Webster as his guide. He described the country about Boston as "absolutely enchanting" and Boston itself as "not only beautiful, but grand." Yet, true to the South and his Jefferson Republicanism he held that "all Cities are rather vulgar things." "When you see one great city," he told Charity, "you have nearly seen all." He was more impressed by the country views. The view from Milton Hill near Boston offered "the finest combination possible of Bays, arms of the sea, heights—islands—ships, bridges, marsh meadow ... speckled with villages & sprinkled with pretty dwellings—every thing painted, pretty, neat, white, & lovely—Altogether, the country about Boston, is the finest in America in the summer..."

The investigating committee began its work on 25 August, working each day for the next five days, but the committeemen found time to make several excursions, including one to attend the Harvard commencement ceremonies as guest of honor and one, on Mangum's suggestion, "to the Town of Quincy to pay a visit of *respect* to Mr. [John Quincy] Adams & his lady." The many social events in the evenings gave Mangum an opportunity to report his observations on Boston society. Fashion, he reported, was their "tyrant," a much greater tyrant, he felt than among his own society in Carolina and even a greater tyrant "than Gen Jackson himself." At a party at Webster's townhouse on the 25th Mangum noted the presence of "many Gentlemen and ladies from the South." The Bostonians "seem to be the most civil people in the world & the kindest—They only differ from the South, in this, they are always attentive to persons of distinction." Despite the flood of invitations the committee received from Boston's society, Mangum noted, "These invitations were to *Senator Mangum*—poor Willie P. Mangum might have been here years, & not seen so many. ...If the world were to desert me, in this City I should be a Cypher." The Bostonians were "especially proud of their city" and were surprised by Mangum's opinion of cities as "vulgar things"; "When they talk of Cities—I talk of the magnificent scenery of our mountains."[5] Mangum found the society of Boston "gay, polished & refined," but, he told Charity, "the ladies generally are not pretty— far from it—much less so than at the South."[6]

In his third and final "diary" letter, Mangum reported on his tour of the mills at Lowell, "the great manufacturing town," west of Boston with senators Ewing and Wilde, guided by Nathan Appleton, "one of the wealthiest proprietors at Lowell." His reflections indicate Mangum's Old Republican anti-manufacturing bias at conflict with his Whiggish admiration of technology and enterprise:

> We arrived before 10 oclock, & for 6 (Six) hours, we were constantly engaged in examining the machinery, etc. The Capital invested here is prodigious & the ingenuity & enterprize [sic] are truly admirable. Everything indicated a prosperity leading rapidly to wealth & was every way agreeable except the thousands of Girls from 12 to 18 years of age, that labor here. They look unhealthy & unhappy & altogether, presented to my mind a melancholy & painful spectacle. I had rather my daughters should go into the cornfield with their hoes, incomparably rather than they should go into a factory.[7]

Mangum's last comment hints at the proslavery argument then gaining prevalence among some Southern thinkers and politicians (especially in Calhoun's South Carolina). Mangum asserted that these young white women would be better off doing the work of slaves in his corn fields than laboring in these Boston factories. Such an assertion was not far from the proslavery argument that Southern slaves were better treated than Northern factory workers.

The committee had completed its work in Boston by 8 September and on the next day the committeemen, without Webster, who remained in the city, left for Providence to examine the banks there, which they did on the 10th. The committee spent the rest of September and early October examining the banks in Philadelphia and New York. By December Mangum was back in Washington working with Tyler and Webster to prepare the committee's report.[8]

In his trip with the committee Mangum clearly tried to observe as much of New England and its people as possible, apparently, in part, assessing his new Whig allies in New England. A letter to John Beard, editor of the Salisbury *Western Carolinian* and a political friend, written while the committee was working in Philadelphia, confirms that this was one of Mangum's goals. Mangum wrote to share "some views I have been compelled to take during my sojourn in the Eastern & Middle States." The letter served as Mangum's report on the Southern opposition's new Whig allies in New England.

Despite his warm reception in Boston, Mangum remained wary of the New England Whigs. "In a word," Mangum wrote, "the prospect before us is any thing but encouraging." Mangum found the opposition coalition "discordant" and "opposite upon great elementary and vital principles" because the "conservative principles" that Beard and Mangum shared had not taken root among the opposition men of the middle and northeastern states. Mangum declared such principles to be "scarcely comprehended by the most intelligent of the National republicans.... The basis of all party organization in the North & East is *naked interest*."

Moreover, Mangum was sure that almost all he had heard from the New Englanders in favor of the views of the South had been put forth only to secure the support of the states' rights men to "to views & opinions alien to the true interest of the South." Though he found the New Englanders "highly intelligent, industrious & moral & *patriotic*," he pronounced their views of national policy to be "selfish" and "destructive of the whole system." As with all allies united only by a common enemy, Mangum found vigilance to be necessary; indeed, the New Englanders almost seemed worse than Jackson men: "We have nothing for the present to hope from New England. And deeply as I abhor the treachery & the usurpations of the present administration, I fear their weak & rash excesses, much less than I do the settled, steady & preservering [sic] policy of New England." Struggling with the problem of the popular majority of the northern states that had led Calhoun to nullification in defense of states' rights, Mangum contemplated the "interested majority" of the North with "a species of suffocation—remorseless, heartless and persevering." Nothing could resist them "but the highest spirit of Liberty." "What," he asked the editor, "with false opinions, interested purposes & weakness & vacillation, & ignorance & immobility—the last worst of all—have we to hope, in future efforts, against this majority?"

Describing his discussions with the Bostonians on specific issues of politics and political economy, Mangum showed himself a solid Calhoun man. As to abolition, he reported that "*Nothing on the Slave question is to be found*. All looks well in this respect." On the crucial issue of the tariff, Mangum feared that the New Englanders would not allow the tariff compromise of 1833 to remain a settled policy. "New England looks to interest," he reported, but would not fight for the higher tariff. "But she will push it—without a fight." Mangum, the Old Republican and States' Rights man, still exhibited the spirit of nullification: "Our only safety is in a prompt & high & determined defiance—& resistance at all hazards." Any attempt by New England's Whigs to re-enact the Tariff of 1828 "would be the signal for universal resistance throughout the South." "The Union," Mangum had told his startled Boston hosts, "could not endure under the application of *force* to the *States*." The only papers from the South that Mangum could find in New England, he told Beard, were the "base" South Carolina "*Union papers*," and Mangum held "that party in So. Ca. as the most atrocious that this Country has produced." Mangum was even reluctant to embrace the party name of Whig which the New Englanders were beginning to use: "I appeared in the character of *one of the Whigs of the Senate*," he reported. "Whigs!!!—now My Dear Sir, suffer me to say that no man has more respect, than I, for the Whigs of the *revolution*—But as to our modern Whigs tho, I quarrel with no man for calling me Whig—yet I feel it no compliment."

Concluding his report about their new allies against Jackson, Mangum made it clear that he considered the Southern States' Rights men, not the New England National Republicans, as the hope for the Whigs to defeat the administration and its party. In Mangum's view absolute fidelity to states' rights principles would be required for Southern statesmen to preserve the states' liberty against those dedicated only to self-serving interest:

> The south has before her a high & glorious destiny, if our people have the virtue to achieve it.—It is a high destiny—& more than all, it is a virtuous one.—*Forbearance and self-denial* are our lot.—If we have virtue enough for this high destiny, we may be happy.—We are, in truth, the real conservators of our political system.—If we shall love Liberty enough to seek & defend her; regardless of the usual *official* bounties & honors; Liberty may be preserved.... "Off with the heads" of *all* who seek office by the slightest sacrifice of their own, or their country's principles—The press of the South, should lose no occasion to impress this opinion on the public mind.[9]

Despite the cordiality of Webster and the warmth of his reception in New England, Mangum was convinced that the New England Whigs would be difficult partners in the opposition coalition. He looked to the Southern Whigs as the true defenders of Republican principles, rather than the nascent national Whig Party. At the time of the first opposition campaign, Mangum was wary of the Whigs of New England. His letter suggests the impact that the Whig defeat in 1836 would have: before the presidential election, when Mangum gave these views, the North Carolina opposition, like the Whigs in other Southern states, looked to the Tennessee State-Rights Whig Hugh Lawson White as their presidential candidate. The failure of that campaign proved that allegiance to a merely regional Whig party could not defeat the Van Buren men in a presidential contest. To complete their revolution against "the party," the Southern Whigs of North Carolina would have to rally to the standard of a national Whig. Despite his staunch Calhounist states' rights ideology, Senator Willie P. Mangum would make that critical evolution and that change would set the course of his political future.

The Apostasy of John C. Calhoun and the Rise of Henry Clay

In early 1837 Mangum considered himself more an Old Republican and States-Rights party opposition man than a Whig just as he did when he wrote Beard in 1834, and he still viewed Calhoun as the national opposition leader with whom he was politically most comfortable. On pure principles Mangum had preferred Calhoun as a presidential candidate in 1836 but realized Nullification disbarred him.[10] Yet in Calhoun the States' Rights wing of the North Carolina Whig coalition had a leader with commensurate national stature to the National Republicans' Henry Clay. Not only was Calhoun important as a counterweight to Clay, Calhoun symbolized states' rights principles.

And Mangum was Calhoun's ally in North Carolina for the States' Rights party. In February 1837 Calhoun wrote to Mangum, "As to the opposition ... it stands firm." Calhoun was sure that their States' Rights Party was "the true opposition ground." While Calhoun expected the opposition would be "more abundant than ever" in the coming session, he also thought "they will all be such as belongs to us, and not the national branch." Calhoun urged Mangum to stand for election to the House: "Let nothing dissuade you."[11] Duff Green, Calhoun stalwart, editor, and political organizer, seconded Calhoun's urgings and saw Mangum as a key ally: "We want you as a leader for the House—You in the House and Calhoun in the Senate the South may yet be saved." Green's reports from opposition men around the country assured him that there would be a "general rally" of the Whigs, but that only Calhoun could lead it: "Webster goes out of Congress. Clay surrenders and Calhoun will give Van a hard fight in a clear field, for such a crisis your place in Congress cannot be supplied by any one else."[12]

In North Carolina, Whig activist and Mangum's political associate C.P. Green shared this view. The states' rights men wanted to unify the Whigs around Calhoun. "The Administration is going down very fast," he wrote. "If the Presidential election took place today Van could be beaten in this State. The only difficulty is in what manner to get *clear* of Clay and Webster."[13] Yet, a Whig victory in 1837 revealed that the States' Rights men were wrong in one aspect of their calculations: Clay and the National Republican Whigs were not as weak as they believed.

The Whigs scored an impressive victory for their cause in the district elections for Congress in August 1837. The panic of 1837 helped Whigs throughout the country, and North Carolina was no exception.[14] The Whig candidates for the House of Representatives blamed the economic crisis on Jackson's financial policies of the past four years—the destruction of the BUS, the pet banks, and the Specie Circular. Whig candidates touted Whig policies and principles: a safe currency, distribution, opposition to Van Buren's independent treasury, opposition to executive usurpations and Van Buren's "extravagance." Many called for a national bank.[15] The Whigs won a majority of the Congressional districts, taking eight of the thirteen districts. The Democrats did not even contest the two western-most districts (the Twelfth and Thirteenth). Whig editors lauded the victories as evidence that the state was thoroughly Whig in sentiment and opposed to the administration.[16] Gales claimed in his *Raleigh Register* that the Whig victories represented "an immense accession to the Whig strength."[17] The triumphs were indeed important as a Whig delegation would now represent North Carolina in Congress.

Though some Whigs felt that the Democrats' extended campaign against Mangum had prejudiced some voters, especially in Wake County, against him, leading Whigs in the Eighth District (Orange, Person, and Wake counties) were confident in Mangum's campaign skills and popularity with Whigs. They urged him to become a candidate for Congress, but Mangum decided against entering the contest.[18] Though Mangum claimed "private affairs" kept him from running,[19] his reluctance to "take the field" most likely stemmed from a fear that seeking a seat in the House of Representatives instead of the Senate might appear as an admission of defeat. Party leaders in Raleigh persuaded William A. Graham, a rising star of the Whig Party and member of the House of Commons from Hillsborough, to stand for the seat in Mangum's place.[20] Graham ran as a National-Republican Whig, issuing a campaign circular asserting the constitutional power of Congress to charter a national bank and declaring it had proved "highly beneficial."[21] Though Graham did not prevail in the Eighth District, the Whigs' success state wide in the 1837 elections largely on issues of political economy must have signaled to Mangum and other States' Rights men that the National Republicans' program was popular in the state. The Whig Party could win without states' rights at the head of their platform. The Whig victory in the congressional elections and Graham's national Whig, pro-bank stance in his contest suggested that the States' Rights wing was no longer the strongest part of the Whig coalition, especially during hard economic times. National Republicanism now at least rivaled Old Republicanism in the Carolina Whig Party.

Shortly after the elections of 1837, the Carolina States' Rights Whigs encountered an even greater shock. John C. Calhoun abandoned the opposition. He decided that the true home of the States' Rights party was with the Democrats and that Van Buren's Independent Treasury plan was the best economic measure in the face of the Panic of 1837.[22] Southern Whigs were dismayed by Calhoun's apostasy. In 1834 when the Bank War was at its height, Mangum had believed that Calhoun was "unquestionably the ablest man here upon questions of this character."[23] However, he was not willing to move with Calhoun to the arch-enemy Van Buren merely for the sake of banking policy (or for the sake of Calhoun's ambitions.) When Mangum learned of Calhoun's shift to Van Buren, he wrote to his Southern Whig friends in the Senate to learn their views. William Preston, Calhoun's South Carolina colleague in the Senate and an original nullifier[24] explained that Calhoun had broken with him "without warning." Mangum shared Preston's disappointment with Calhoun's leap to the administration. Preston told Mangum that he rejoiced "to see how exactly coincident your opinions are with my own" and that he was glad to have "the advantage of having the authority of your concurrence." Preston added that no opposition senators were following Calhoun's support of the Independent Treasury. He believed that Calhoun had calculated that the current crisis was "a favourable *financial* and *political* conjuncture" to assert his long-held principles against the banking system. According to Preston, Calhoun thought that the entire country now harbored a "deadly hostility" to the banks.

Other motives had also been at work. Preston believed Calhoun had made a "political calculation" that as a result of the financial crisis Van Buren was "defunct." And Calhoun's friends had persuaded him that he "could mount upon the vacant shoulders." Preston, however, was convinced that such notions were "vain delusions" and that Calhoun's move to the administration actually had resuscitated Van Buren's political standing. Preston averred that "a majority of the South Carolina delegation is with me," as well as all but one of the North Carolina delegation. And Preston told Mangum early the next year that Calhoun had "bamboozled him self" into thinking that "the hard money project was a State rights measure and for the benefit of the South."[25]

Mangum expressed to Kentucky Whig senator John Crittenden his amazement at Calhoun's betrayal and his disapproval of the Sub-Treasury. He informed Crittenden that hardly any of the state-rights Whigs in North Carolina would follow Calhoun to the Van Buren Democrats. Crittenden replied that Calhoun's "strange and eccentric movement" was "a mystery &

a wonder—I can find no sufficient *reason* for his conduct." Crittenden expressed shock at how easily the States' Rights leader had abandoned the Opposition and "gone over" to Van Buren: "I have been chagrined at the *facility* with which he appeared to me to quit old friends, and the *amiable associations* so readily formed with *new ones*." Like Preston, Crittenden was convinced that few Southerners were inclined to abandon the Whigs and follow Calhoun to the Democrats. "He carries scarcely any body with him," Crittenden assured Mangum.[26] Regardless of these assurances of Calhoun's miscalculations and the loyalty of state-rights opposition men to the Whigs, Calhoun's apostasy left the States' Rights wing of the Whig Party without a national leader in Congress. Calhoun's betrayal cast Mangum in "deepest gloom."[27] Without Calhoun, Mangum, like the other States' Rights men in North Carolina, had to look for a new national leader.

In the winter of 1838, Willie P. Mangum became a Clay Whig. Three years earlier, as Mangum was looking for a leader of the opposition and a presidential candidate for 1836, he had distrusted Clay's nationalism and wanted him to move closer to state-rights principles. "I *cannot now* vote for Mr. Clay under *present* circumstances," Mangum had declared to a pro–Calhoun editor in Salisbury, "He must first come to the grounds that I can support him."[28] In 1837 Clay remained true to the Whigs, and that fall Mangum began to recognize Clay as the leader of the Southern Whigs. Mangum's friend and opposition Senator from South Carolina William Preston believed that though some Whigs favored "the hero of Tippecanoe" (William Harrison) or Daniel Webster, Clay was the only opposition man who could find favor from Whigs in all the sections. "The only opposition man who has the slightest chance for the next Presidency is Mr. Clay—who is really a noble creature," Preston advised Mangum.[29] Preston's support of Clay undoubtedly carried great weight with Mangum since Preston was both a close personal friend and a States' Rights man of the first order.[30] Mangum sent Clay a friendly letter with a newspaper clipping showing increasing support for the latter in North Carolina.[31]

Mangum also must have been influenced by the move of all the state's leading Whig newspapers to Clay as the preferred Whig presidential candidate. In November, Hamilton Jones, editor of the Salisbury *Carolina Watchman*, declared for Clay[32]; shortly thereafter Mangum told Jones that he was sure that only the Kentucky senator could lead the Whigs.[33] A month after endorsing Clay, Jones informed Mangum that "Since I have hoisted the flag I have received the *all hail* of every prominent Whig I have met with." Jones had even received letters from "distinguished gentlemen in the West" who previously had opposed Clay.[34] The opinion of the most influential newspaper editor among western Whigs no doubt carried great weight with Mangum. By March of 1838 almost all the major Whig newspapers backed Clay: the *Raleigh Register*, the Salisbury *Carolina Watchman*, the *Fayetteville Observer*, the *Newbern Spectator*, and the *Wilmington Advertiser* declared for him. In March, as evidence "of the strength of the popular current in this State, in favor of Mr. Clay," Gales published in the *Raleigh Register* a collection of articles from other Whig newspapers in the state favorable to Clay. The *Fayetteville Observer* declared: "Mr. Clay's course for several years has been such as to efface the recollection of his connection with the Administration of Mr. Adams, and his high Tariff opinions.... The people look upon him as the fast friend of the Union, as the patriot who has repeatedly reconciled conflicting interests when that Union seemed to be endangered by the violence of the struggle, and as the able and uncompromising opponent of Executive usurpation." The *Wilmington Advertiser* announced that "Mr. Clay is emphatically *the* Statesman of the age." The *Newbern Spectator* argued that Clay was "the choice of a vast majority of the National Republicans of the United States as the successor of Mr. Van Buren.... North Carolina, *we know*, prefers him to *all* other candidates spoken of." And the *Carolina Watchman* declared Clay "decidedly the favorite with the Western counties."[35] These endorsements left little doubt which way public opinion among Whigs was moving.

Most likely another reason Mangum moved so quickly to Clay was a realization that the North Carolina Whig Party would succeed best with a Southern Whig at the head of the national party. By the spring of 1838 Mangum's friends were addressing him as the friend of Clay.[36] In March he wrote a long letter to Clay on Whig politics. The man who three years earlier did not want to be called a Whig now spoke of the Whigs as "our friends." Concluding that only a party headed by Clay could defeat

Henry Clay by Henry F. Darby (1829–1897), oil on canvas, ca. 1858 (U.S. Senate).

Van Buren in North Carolina, Mangum became optimistic that "the Administration may pretty certainly be displaced; & we think, we can throw the vote of this State against Mr. Van Buren." Mangum had determined that both the Whig leaders and the Whig rank and file were coalescing behind Clay. Based on his "extensive Correspondence" with Whigs in North Carolina, Mangum reported to Clay that the Whig leaders in the state strongly supported him. He believed that the Whig leaders were in agreement that "we will not *make a ticket even* for any other than yourself ... that we will make a ticket for you, & vote it, whether any other state in the Union shall join us or not." And Mangum sensed that more than just his political friends favored Clay. The Whigs of the state were beginning to move with them: "a fine spirit pervades the Whig ranks—I do not refer to the papers & leaders only, but I mean to include, the bone & sinew of our population—the substantial Country gentlemen & farmers—With that portion of our population, that think & read, I have never known so strong an interest in the success of any Presidential Candidate as in your Case, with the exception perhaps, of that of Mr. Crawford."[37] Mangum, then, moved quickly after the 1837 elections and Calhoun's apostasy to embrace Clay. Yet he moved with the assurance that important Whigs were accompanying him, and he closely monitored opinion to confirm that North Carolina Whigs were becoming Clay Whigs.

Mangum's shift from distrust to avid support for the Kentuckian is not surprising. Clay had remained loyal to the opposition when Calhoun had gone with the arch-enemy Van Buren. Opposition to "Van Burenism" (as many Whigs now styled the administration's party tactics and governmental policies in place of the old "Jacksonism" label) was more important than any loyalty to Calhoun. The States' Rights Party was dead. The apostasy of Calhoun had cleared the way for the ascendancy of the Clay-nationalist wing of the Whig coalition. Mangum placed party over principles in his move to Clay. He placed loyalty to the opposition over the primacy of Old Republican/states' rights principles, but he did not abandon those doctrines. Mangum had not yet committed himself to the national Whig program—Clay's American System. Clay was a National Republican Whig, but he was a Southern Whig as well. And no man in Congress despised Jacksonism-Van Burenism more than Henry Clay. With Calhoun's return to the Democracy, Mangum looked to Clay as the Whig leader. Mangum was a Clay Whig. For such men as Preston and Mangum, opposition to Van Burenism was more important than pursuit of pure principles. Opposition to Van Buren could rally a party; banking principles, though important, were not enough to make men vote Whig.

In the state elections of 1838 the Whigs were even more successful than in 1837. Eight of thirteen congressional districts were already Whig. Now, for the first time they brought the state government under their control, once again electing Edward B. Dudley governor, this time by an overwhelming 17,669-vote majority, and placing Whig majorities in both houses of the legislature.[38] Declaring that a "great political *Revolution*" was in progress, Gales in the *Register* jubilantly proclaimed a grand victory for "Republican Whig principles." "Yes, the Old North is now emphatically 'redeemed, regenerated and disenthralled.' ... Make way then for us, and proclaim to the utmost verge of the Union, that NORTH CAROLINA HAS ELECTED A WHIG GOVERNOR! A WHIG SENATE!! AND A WHIG HOUSE OF COMMONS!!!"[39] Paul C. Cameron excitedly wrote to Mangum to give him the "pleasing intelligence" of the Whig victories which he hoped would "spread, like a prarie [sic] fire, over the Van Buren districts—& may it have the same cleansing and purifying effect!"[40] The North Carolina Whig Party had achieved ascendancy in the state.

The triumph in 1838 showed all Whig leaders, especially the States' Rights men, that the Whigs could win in the state without Calhoun at the head of their banner as he had been for the States' Rights Whigs in 1836. Such a victory must have removed any doubts that Mangum had about shifting to Clay, but it also meant that the National Republicans in the coalition were likely to act more independently of the former Calhoun men and challenge their leadership of the Whig coalition. The Whig victory also emboldened the Whigs in the new legislature to declare Henry Clay the choice of the Whigs of North Carolina.

By early 1839 the Whig leaders of North Carolina were convinced that Clay was the candidate best able to unite the Whig coalition; they also believed that his popularity with the people of North Carolina would allow them to confirm the Whig ascendancy in the state elections with him as the party's presidential nominee. When the General Assembly met in the winter of 1839, the Whig caucus in the legislature moved to confirm their sense of growing Whig support for Clay and place the Whig Party in the state firmly behind him as the party's presidential candidate—a Southern Whig to head their ticket for the campaign of 1840. The Whigs in the legislature published resolutions at the close of the session that expressed their "decided preference" for Clay as the presidential candidate of the Whig Party and declared him to be the "unanimous choice" of the Whigs in the legislature. William Graham, speaker of the House of Commons, drafted a letter for the Whigs in the General Assembly addressed to the Whig representatives in Congress endorsing Clay as "the only Candidate of the Whigs who has the least prospect of uniting the party throughout the State."[41] Mangum's move to

Clay thus accorded with the views of the state's other Whig leaders. Publicly declaring for Clay as their presidential candidate, by early 1839 the North Carolina Whigs were firmly Henry Clay Whigs. They wanted Clay at the head of their banner in 1840.

Whig Instructions

"I hope, I believe, the senators will be driven out," Mangum announced to a close friend. "As to the successors, it would be comtenptible [sic] affectation to say, that I do not desire a *certificate* from the state, after suffering what I have—yet…. I trust you will believe me, when I say, however important that point may be regarded by me, yet it is wholly subordinate."[42] Not surprisingly, Willie Mangum desired the vindication of a return to the Senate. So did his party.[43] The Whigs, with an overall majority of 14 votes in the new legislature now had the power to elect a senator if either Brown, Strange or both resigned their seats. In 1835–1836 Mangum had come to symbolize the opposition cause and the Whig cause could not be completely triumphant until he returned to the United States Senate.

The Whig victories placed the Democrats who had accused Mangum of resisting the people's will in 1835–1836 in a difficult position. Would their senators now obey the popular will? The Whig press chastised Brown and Strange for resisting the mandate of the elections. In the *Register*, Gales pointed out the contrast with Mangum's position just two years earlier: "Only a few months ago, a party of men were loud and earnest in their denunciations of a Senator, for not resigning his post when it was *supposed* that he acted contrary to the wishes of his constituents…. But a 'change has come o'er the spirit of their dream.' The Senator, whom they sent to fill the place vacated by Mr. Mangum's resignation, now finds *himself* placed in a hostile attitude towards a large majority of his constituents." The *Petersburg Intelligencer* declared that the government should have received the letters of resignation of such "pure democrats" the week after the election results were known.[44]

Yet the Whigs had an ideological difficulty of their own. In 1835–1836, they had vehemently denied the Democratic legislature's right to instruct Mangum to vote for the Senate resolution expunging Jackson's censure. If the Democratic senators did not resign, should the Whig legislature now instruct Brown and Strange to vote for Whig measures? Before the meeting of the legislature, Whigs were calling for the legislature to instruct the senators. "LET THEM HAVE IT," the *Register* advised.[45] Denying an absolute right to instruct, the Washington (N.C.) *Whig* nevertheless recommended, "Let them be instructed: This will prevent any excuse, on their part, for continuing to misrepresent the State."[46] The *Carolina Watchman* argued that whether the communications of the legislature were called requests, exhortations, or instructions, the senators ought not to lack "*full advices* from all their constituents."[47]

By the time the General Assembly met in November the Whigs had concluded to make a legislative statement, but one that would not concede the right of instruction. Some Whigs remained hopeful that Brown and Strange would resign, given the accumulated evidence of Whig ascendancy from the elections of 1837 and 1838 (the *Register* was calling the elections themselves "instructions") and the Whig unity in the legislature demonstrated by the election of William Graham as speaker in the House and the easy victory of a Whig as speaker of the Senate as well. But if the senators held on to their seats "against the known will of the people" the *Register* reported "little variance" of opinion among the Whig legislators as to their course:

"not to instruct them, as their party instructed Mr. Mangum, to do a particular act or resign, but to give so decided and unequivocal an expression of the opinions of their constituents, that they cannot disregard it, unless they are determined to set at naught the popular will."[48] In short, the Whigs would use democracy against the Democrats' senators: the legislators would not "instruct" but would pass resolutions stating the Whig position on Whig principles and measures, send them to the senators as an expression of the will of the people, and ask them to carry out that will.

Although he was not an elected member of the legislature, Mangum took the lead in formulating these resolutions. He had been urged by Preston as early as 1838 if he should be elected to the legislature to bring resolutions in there, "resolutions against the Subtreasury & hard money as anti Southern & anti State rights."[49] Though his own campaign had failed, Mangum meant to follow Preston's advice and use the Whig majority in the legislature to aid the Whig cause in the U.S. Senate. At the November meeting of the legislature, Mangum spent two weeks in Raleigh designing and winning Whig support for a statement of Whig principles and policies for the legislature to adopt. "My object was to beat up the quarters of our derelict Senators," he explained to a friend.[50]

For Mangum the resolutions held a dual purpose. If Brown or Strange or both resigned, the Whig legislature would elect their successor(s) and Mangum would be the foremost Whig on the list of candidates. It is therefore likely that a second goal of Mangum's sojourn in Raleigh was to shore up his support among the members of the legislative Whig caucus. During his meetings with the Whig legislators, Mangum wrote a letter to reassure states-rights Whigs in a period of transition. Mangum dictated a letter to Louis D. Wilson and W. A. Blount that later caused him some political embarrassment when the North Carolina Whigs had committed to the Clay-national program. It set forth his history of loyalty to the Old Republican/ States' Rights creed:

> Willie P. Mangum says, that he never voted for a bank in his life, neither state nor federal. He further says, that he never voted to appropriate a cent in his life in favor of internal improvements by the general government, without the district of Columbia. He further says, that he never voted in favor of a tariff of protection, but did and said every thing in his power to defeat every measure of that description. He further says, that he has uniformly voted in favor in favor of economical appropriations, and has strongly disapproved of the increase of expenditures to upwards of $33,000,000 at one or two years, and the general increase at all times for the last 4 or 5 years by this general government. That he professes and hopes that he has acted uniformly upon the principles of strict construction of '98 and '99, and that he has never consented to be harnessed by any party, so as to deviate from the above principles. And he defies any documentary proof in contradiction of any of the essential principles contained in the above. Mr. Mangum further says, that he is decidedly opposed to the present administration, believing that the head of the government and many of his friends, have violated the most, if not all of the essential principles contained in the above.
> In the presence of [signed]
>   Louis D. Wilson
>   W. A. Blount[51]

Although the statement in the letter was technically accurate as to Mangum's votes on the Bank and the Tariff and accurately reflected his ideological preferences, Mangum had never absolutely opposed the Bank or the Tariff. He voted against the Bank re-charter on tactical grounds and claimed he would have voted for it in 1833[52]; and he voted for the Compromise Tariff in 1833. The letter was probably meant to reassure his fellow state-rights Whigs (and maintain their support for his election) at time when the party was in the midst of a shift to Clay and the state-rights wing was losing ground in the coalition. And Mangum, ever cautious, certainly did not want to burn his bridges to the states' rights wing before the relative strength of the two wings had been finally decided. Wilson's later statement that he preserved the letter "as conclusive evidence that Mr. Mangum had not departed from his old political creed" lends further weight to this view of the letter. One must keep in mind that at this period of 1838–1839 the party was seeking unity and the ground was shifting; if Mangum wanted to be reelected, and he very much did, he needed to be sure where the majority of the Whig caucus stood before committing himself to particular measures. In December 1838 the Whig caucus had not declared for Clay or national Whig measures.

Mangum's resolutions, introduced by Kenneth Rayner in the House on December 4, 1838,[53] condemned the expunging of Jackson's censure as an unconstitutional act "calculated to degrade the character of the Senate" and called on that body to condemn and rescind the expunging act. They also declared the Independent Treasury plan one of the "fatal experiments" of the Jackson–Van Buren administrations tending to "augment Executive power." Highlighting Whig policies and anti-executive, anti-party ideology, the statement called for distribution of the proceeds of the public land sales, protested against "the wasteful extravagance" of the Administration, and expressing alarm at the increase in "the power and patronage of the Executive Department." Finally, the Whigs called on the Democratic senators to "represent the wishes of a majority of the people of this State" by voting to carry out the resolutions, something they knew Brown and Strange could not do if they wanted to remain Democrats.[54] The implication of the Mangum-Rayner resolutions was that Brown and Strange should represent the majority will or resign. Mangum called the resolutions "*arsenic* to unfaithful public servants" and was convinced that the senators would resign.[55]

But Mangum was overoptimistic. Undoubtedly believing that the Whig ascendancy would be transitory, Brown and Strange held their seats. James Graham thought that the senators' refusal to resign was helping the Whigs more than the Democrats. "It is much better for the Whig cause they should not resign," he explained to his brother. "And our Editors should open their batteries forthwith *upon them* and *their party* for violating their own doctrines."[56] In the *Register* Gales again accused the Democratic senators of ignoring the will of the majority and of failing to follow their own professed principles. They had refused to follow the direction of the legislature because the resolutions were not specifically worded as *instructions*. "After having solemnly pledged themselves, over and over again, to conform to the will of their constituents.... Messrs. Brown and Strange now violate those pledges on a mere *quibble*. The fact is, that our Senators must know that these Resolutions express the deliberate judgment of a large majority of the freemen of North Carolina.... If the principles proclaimed to the world, and acted on by the Van Buren party, when they were endeavoring to put down Mangum, Leigh, Tyler, &c, were orthodox, what has occurred to alter their correctness? If the rule was a correct one then, it is equally so now."[57] After the legislature adjourned, the *Standard* announced that Brown and Strange intended to remain in the Senate until the next session of the legislature in 1840–1841; if the elections for that legislature went against the Democrats, they would then resign.[58]

The Whigs began to look to the campaign of 1840 as the decisive event—an election for the legislature, governor, and a president—that would prove the state was Whig. Mangum and the Whig leaders and legislators preferred Henry Clay as the representative and embodiment of national Whig principles and measures—a national Whig, but a Southern Whig slaveholder who did not threaten North Carolina's slave society. Yet to unseat Brown and Strange, the Whigs realized that they would have to prove that their ascendancy was not transitory—they would have to repeat their success of 1838—and elect a President.

The Revolution of 1840: "The Great & Good Cause"[59]

The leading Whigs viewed the campaign of 1840 as revolutionary—a campaign for Whig reforms to counter Jackson's 1828 revolution. They believed that it would determine the political alignment of the state for years to come.[60] And they believed that a victory for the Whigs in their state would the cause of the Whigs in Washington. At stake was the party's ability to implement Whig measures, not just block the Van Buren program. Two years earlier William Preston had told Mangum, "As to our political condition here it is just this—*we* have the power to prevent evil and wicked measures, but not the power to do any positive act for the good of the Country."[61] The Whigs' outlook was not only revolutionary but far more national than in 1836; yet "Van Burenism" remained the enemy. "Every mail brings intelligence of some new Whig victory," William Battle wrote to Graham in April, "May the good cause speed until every nook and corner of our wide spread country is freed from the devastating influence of Van Burenism, which is but double distilled Jacksonism, and is the very worst ism with which any Country pretending to be free, was ever afflicted."[62] Mangum himself saw the election as determinative of the political character of the state. At a meeting of the Whigs of Orange County at the courthouse in Hillsborough early in the campaign, Mangum presented several resolutions, the last of which framed the spirit and goals of the campaign:

> *Resolved*, That in these times of pecuniary distress and general calamity in all the business concerns of the country—the result ... of a deeply disordered and deranged state of public affairs,—it is the duty of every good citizen to take that position the public will may assign to him, and to struggle with a true Whig spirit, for the ascendancy of genuine Republican Whig principles and Whig practices.[63]

The Whig Central Committee hoped to make Graham's "Address of the Republican Whig members of the General Assembly of 1838," intended as a defense of the Mangum-Rayner resolutions, a campaign document. Gales urged Graham to complete it so he could get it in print.[64] The committee's eagerness to publish the address shows that they intended for the Whigs to contest the 1839–1840 campaign on the issues in the resolutions. The heavy emphasis on states' rights in the Address shows that that wing of the party still carried much weight in the legislature, and it also indicates that defense of legislative supremacy in government remained central to the North Carolina Whigs' ideology in 1838. Recently elected Whigs in Congress shared the legislature's view. Kenneth Rayner (who had introduced the resolutions) believed there had been "an alarming increase of executive power" and that Congress had sunk to a "depth of degradation." "The Senate has long since, surrendered its high character for independence and character," he lamented, and now a "want of independence" prevailed in the House as well. The "practical despotism" of the executive "represses all the talent and energies in our house, and weighs down the prosperity and commerce of this *once* free people."[65]

The elections of the Revolution of 1840 began with a Whig setback. The cause suffered a defeat in the district elections for Congress in August 1839 when the Whigs lost three districts. The Democrats won eight districts and the Whigs five, but all the votes were close in contested districts. The Whig press called for stronger exertions to prevent further erosion of the newly-won Whig ascendancy.[66] Though the Whig caucus had endorsed Clay, the Whigs had not yet officially nominated Clay to head their party's banner in the state, and the blow of the 1839 losses lent urgency to holding a state convention.

The Whig caucus in the legislature of 1838–1839 had called for a Whig state convention. Despite the efforts of some of the Raleigh Whigs to convince the Whig caucus to declare itself a convention and nominate Clay immediately, the majority of the caucus voted for a state convention of delegates to meet in November 1839, one month before the national Whig convention. They requested a convention in Raleigh on the second Monday of November to propose candidates for president, vice-president, and governor. And showing that the Whigs were looking to the organization and coordination of their campaigns against the Democrats, the Whig caucus named a state central committee "to disseminate such intelligence among the several Counties as they shall deem calculated to advance the Whig cause in this state."[67]

The Whigs' call for a state convention was part of their effort to achieve greater party organization. Once permanently established, the Whig central committee in Raleigh took on the vital coordinating role in party operations—disseminating "documents"; publishing party announcements, addresses, and resolutions from Whig meetings; coordinating campaign events and county and district "mass meetings." And the *Raleigh Register* essentially became the organ of the central committee. In 1833 Joseph Gales, Sr., editor of the *Register* since 1799, had turned the newspaper over to his son Weston Gales. The *Raleigh Register* had a close connection to the Washington *National Intelligencer*, "the central organ of whiggery." Joseph Gales, Sr., was the father of Joseph Gales, Jr., and father-in-law of William Winston Seaton of the *National Intelligencer*. Both Joseph Gales, Jr., and Seaton had worked with the senior Gales on the *Raleigh Register*.[68] Despite these concessions for more effective organization they remained the anti-party party. As Daniel Walker Howe notes, Whigs always held the view that partisanship had been forced on them by the Democrats. Howe points out: "Fundamentally ... the Whigs saw their party not as an end in itself but as a means to set policy. When they deplored what they called 'the spirit of party,' it was not because they themselves had no party but because they resented a partisanship that substituted for policy."[69]

The Whigs held their first state convention in November 1839. Mangum and some other Whig leaders so zealously supported Clay that they opposed sending a North Carolina delegation to the national Whig convention scheduled to meet in Harrisburg, Pennsylvania in December that would likely choose William Henry Harrison of Ohio. Mangum reported to Clay that "a fine spirit pervades the Whig ranks" and he thought that any other name than Clay at the top of the Whig ticket would depress the Whig enthusiasm and harm the ability of the Whigs to carry the state.[70] William Graham agreed with Mangum that Clay was the ideal Whig candidate for North Carolina, but he thought they should be represented at the convention and that the North Carolinians should yield to the nomination of Harrison for the sake of Whig unity, if the latter proved more popular in the other state delegations. The convention should pledge the delegates to assent to the nomination of Harrison only for "the sake of success" nationally. Harrison, though "highly respectable in qualifications," was "not the man, for whom we should consent to suffer defeat in our own State, except for the strongest probability of carrying the general election," Graham advised.[71] The assembled Whigs at the North Carolina convention chose Graham's course. They expressed their strong preference for Henry Clay, but they pledged themselves to support the nominee of the national party convention. The North Carolina Whigs wanted no more Hugh Lawson White regional candidacies. They also nominated Morehead as their candidate for governor and elected twelve delegates to represent the state at the national Whig convention.[72] The North Carolina Whigs thus formally recognized Clay as the representative of their Whig principles.

At the Whig national convention in December, John Owen, of the North Carolina delegation, was chosen as a vice-president of the convention and chairman of the nominating committee. In accordance with the direction of their state convention, the delegation supported Clay's nomination; but when Harrison won the nomination, it loyally shifted to Harrison. The party soon rallied behind Harrison. The Raleigh *Star* immediately supported the nomination of Harrison and the *Register* soon shifted its support to him, as did the *Fayetteville Observer*.[73]

Although North Carolina's Whigs preferred Clay as their presidential candidate, they reluctantly accepted Harrison for the sake of unity with the other state parties and the hope of achieving what had been unobtainable in 1836 with regional candidates—electing a Whig to head the national administration, thus ending "Van Burenism." Yet, by the contingency of having to rally to the nominee of the national Whig convention, the Carolina Whigs were able to run a candidate at the top of their ticket who, as an old Republican stalwart who had served as a territorial governor under Jefferson and Madison, embodied Old Republican principles, but one also who would accept the National Republican program. In the Carolina Whigs' campaign for "Harrison and reform," "Harrison" represented Old Republicanism, and "reform" stood for Clay nationalism.

With Harrison as their presidential candidate and the National Republican program of Clay, the Whigs opened the campaigns of 1840, the campaigns that they hoped would prove their ascendancy in the state and nail the lid on the coffin of "Jacksonism." Though the Whigs' campaign of 1840 has often been described by historians as lacking substance or solely focused on the politics of slavery, such was not the case in North Carolina.[74] The Whigs certainly made the log cabin a central motif of the campaign and organized themselves into "Tippecanoe Clubs," but Whig principles and measures were emphasized as much, if not more, and were constantly contrasted to the administration's measures. Evidence throughout the campaign showed that the focus on executive tyranny and states' rights of 1836 was broadening to include national Whig measures as the North Carolina Whigs moved closer to the national party. Though the Whigs were not shy of referring to Harrison as the "hard cider and log cabin candidate," the Whigs' central campaign theme was "the Cause of Harrison and Reform" for both the state and presidential elections.[75]

The Whigs contested the campaigns of 1839–1840 on the issues embodied in the Mangum-Rayner resolutions. The resolutions were more than just a Whig counter-attack in the instruction-expunging controversy; they set out the main elements of Southern Whig ideology and the preferred Whig policy measures. Together they formed a coherent Whig campaign document. "They are well drawn and will make an impression before the People," Congressman James Graham wrote to his brother, William Graham. He thought the speeches made in the legislature defending the resolutions should be printed as pamphlets for the legislators to "scatter among their constituents. The speeches will be commentaries on the propositions contained in the Resolutions, and explain the doctrines and principles of the *Republican Whig party*."[76]

Harkening back to the Old Republican "Principles of '98," the Whigs contested their most important campaign yet on the issues of executive power, corruption, and the failure of the Democrats' financial and economic measures. They emphasized their plans for instituting a stable currency and their intention of distributing the proceeds of federal land sales to the states for internal improvements and education. Old Republican doctrines were thus proclaimed in conjunction with Clay's National Republican economic measures. These issues grew out of the 1834–1835 instruction controversy, but the states' rights rhetoric had been toned down to reflect Harrison's national campaign. The degree of ideological unity achieved on these issues is impressive. The legislature, Whig meetings in the counties, the Central Committee, and the Whigs in convention all addressed these themes in their statements. Whigs in the state could agree on these issues; so such a focus allowed the Central Committee to bridge both regional and ideological divides in the party. The unity achieved with the focus on these Whig principles was a major reason for the Whigs' success in 1840.

As in the 1836 campaign, Whig meetings in the counties across the state passed resolutions setting out their views of political affairs. One early scholar of the North Carolina Whigs has pointed out that the "Whigs always considered the mass meeting, whether precinct, county, or district, a potent campaign agency."[77] The meetings were fully reported in the Whig newspapers, ensuring that party members not only were informed of the activities of their fellow Whigs across the state but also were fully indoctrinated in the party's campaign ideology. Some county meetings simply elected delegates to district conventions to nominate presidential electors but most Whig meetings also passed resolutions in which they praised Harrison as a friend of the South and true Republican, condemned Van Buren and the measures of his administration, called for government reform, and declared for Whig policies and measures. In an attempt to counter the Democrats' charges that the Whigs were Federalists and not true Republicans, the Whigs at many of the meetings often styled themselves "Republican Whigs."

The Whigs' county mass meetings highlighted both Old Republican ideas and Clay's Whig measures. The *Raleigh Register* reported the resolutions of the meetings over a wide range of eastern and piedmont counties.[78] The Whigs of Davie and Iredell, from the Whig heartland of the western Piedmont region, drafted resolutions typical of these county meetings that illustrate contrasting emphases. The Whigs of Iredell County viewed with "the deepest alarm, the unauthorized and illegal encroachment of the Executive upon the Legislative and Judicial departments" that was tending to "concentrate in the Chief Magistrate of the Union all the powers of the other co-ordinate branches of the Government" and make "the President a King in all but name." They declared that Van Buren's "mal-administration" of the government was evident in "the deranged condition of the currency, the reduced prices of produce, and the most cringing and sycophantic servility to the President by men in office or expecting office." A change of rulers was, they insisted, "indispensably necessary" to return the government to "its original purity." Harrison's election would "arrest the tide of Executive usurpation and corruption." They praised his "devotion to pure Republican principles" and pointed out Tyler's "unwavering Republican principles."[79] The Whigs of Iredell thus chose to emphasize Old Republican ideas: Harrison's devotion to "pure Republican principles" and his opposition to "Executive usurpation and corruption."

The Whigs of neighboring Davie, on the other hand, chose to emphasize issues of political economy and Clay's Whig measures. They resolved: "That we believe the measures of the present Administration are hostile and destructive to the best interests of the country: that their pernicious effects are seen in a deranged country, a general scarcity of money, [and] a ruinous depreciation in the prices of every thing which the farmer or planter has to sell; and in a degrading servility" among office holders unknown "in the pure days of the Republic." A change of governors was essential "to restore confidence and prosperity to the Country, and purity to the government." Davie politicos made a point of stating that their support for Henry Clay: "That our confidence in the talents, integrity and patriotism of Henry Clay, is not only undiminished, but strengthened, by his magnanimous and patriotic course in the present crisis; but that this is no time for a contest about *men*, our warfare is for *principles*." They followed this declaration, though, with resolutions approving the nominations of Harrison, Tyler, and John M. Morehead. On Whig measures, they resolved: "That the proceeds of the Public Lands rightfully belong to all the States," and they condemned the Democrats' plan for ceding the revenue of the land sales to the Western states. The Davie Whigs denied Democratic charges that distribution was an assumption of state debts by the federal government and declared that "distribution would greatly promote the general welfare, and therefore ought to be made."[80] The resolutions of the Whigs of Davie and Iredell encapsulated the two ideological sides of the Whigs' appeal to the electorate in 1840.

In the election of 1840, the Whigs used district mass meetings for the first time.[81] Sixty-three delegates from the five counties of the Seventh electoral district (Anson, Cumberland, Moore, Richmond, and Robeson counties) set out a complete indictment of the Van Buren administration and passed resolutions condemning Van Buren's policies and approving the nominations of Harrison and Tyler. Their resolutions indicate a combination of Old Republican and National Republican ideas. The Whigs declared their conviction that "our Government has been grossly mismanaged by those intrusted [sic] with its administration." They condemned the "selfish" policy of the Van Buren administration "the effect of which is to break down the barriers with which the Executive department of the Federal Government has been guarded by the wisdom of our forefathers, and to vest in the Executive, powers not delegated by the Constitution…." They condemned the Sub-Treasury. They adamantly opposed Van Buren's financial policies as "at war" with both commerce and "agricultural interests." His policy on the public lands was "a species of legalized bribery" of the western states. His militia reorganization plan was an attempt to impose a "standing army" on the country. They heartily approved the nominations of Harrison and Tyler and resolved that the executive branch had "usurped the exercise of important powers which do not constitutionally belong to it." And they declared their belief that "it is the duty of enlightened patriots to expose the usurpations and abuses of power, and to oppose, by all constitutional means, any measures by which the Executive department may be unduly strengthened."[82] Thus, Whigs in meetings across the state focused their political statements on opposition to executive power, corruption, and Van Buren's maladministration of government, but they also passed resolutions reflecting distribution, education, and a more reliable currency—a fusion of Old Republican opposition principles and positive-government National Republican ideas.

In the August state elections the Whigs once again won a majority in the Legislature 104–66 (gaining 17 seats and losing only 5), which gave them a commanding 38 votes on joint ballot (a majority of four in the Senate and 34 in the House). Mangum and Graham had been unanimously nominated by the Orange County Whigs in May-Mangum for the state senate and Graham for the house[83] and both were elected. Morehead was elected governor by a margin of over 8,500 votes over Saunders.[84] This was final confirmation that the Democratic former Old Republicans (who were led by Saunders) had lost their grip on North Carolina. North Carolina was now clearly one of the strongest Whig states, and the Whig editors loudly proclaimed the party's success. The *Register* trumpeted "North Carolina right side up! GLORIOUS WHIG TRIUMPH" and in the following edition, "VICTORY ! VICTORY !! VICTORY !!!"[85] The editor of the *Raleigh Register* summed up the import of the victory: "We regard this triumph as more important in its consequences, as doing more towards the effective prostration of this odious Administration, than any event which has occurred since Gen. Harrison's nomination. Yes, Indiana, Kentucky, Rhode Island, Connecticut, Virginia and Alabama have all done well; but WELL and GLORIOUSLY as all have done, the OLD NORTH STATE has eclipsed them all—*all*—ALL."[86]

After the August elections, Congressman James Graham offered his brother William advice on strategy for the presidential election. His plan was an all-out assault on Van Buren. "Make *no issues* with Jackson, let him alone; give his letters the go-bye," he advised. "*Hold Van up*, on the Sub Treasury the *Militia Army*, the negro [sic] testimony, the Expenditures, the Defaulters, the want of Capacity to manage the Florida War, which has now lost 25 millions." Whig victory in November was also critical to exposing the administration's corruption: "A change of men is necessary to investigate frauds. Power will never condemn itself." And to show that the Democrats had no monopoly on republicanism, he also offered advice on rhetorical strategy: "Let the Whigs hold on to the word & name *Republican* on all occasions and put it on their Ticket."

Despite their party's victories in the state elections, Whig leaders feared a slackening of Whig enthusiasm as had occurred in 1836 and wanted to ensure that the Cause would prevail completely this time. "For no matter how high may be the spirit of our friends in August, it will cool off before Nov. unless means are used to keep it up," Rayner warned William Graham before the summer campaign.[87] And in June Rayner wrote Mangum, "I very much fear, we shall relax our exertions after the August elections. If we do, we lose the State."[88] To prevent such a slackening of ardor as Rayner feared, the Central Committee called a state convention to meet in Raleigh on the 5th of October, the anniversary of Harrison's victory at the Battle of the Thames in 1813.[89]

The party rally in Raleigh was the centerpiece of the presidential campaign. True to Rayner's call for ardor and enthusiasm, the "Great Whig Convention" featured a procession of the county delegations from the "Whig encampment" to Capitol Square replete with campaign banners, log cabins, and canoes and a "plain Republican dinner" for the delegates. Women again figured prominently in a Whig rally, as they had at the Mecklenburg Celebration in 1835. As the county delegates began their procession, Whig women "from every section of the state" stood at doors, windows, and porticos to give "every demonstration of approbation" to the marchers. The delegation from Wake County marched with a "magnificent banner" presented by the "Ladies of Raleigh."[90] In line with Graham's advice to attack Van Burenism, the central committee made certain that the slate of speakers, including George Badger, Rayner, Edward Stanly, C.P. Green, and James Bryan, addressed "the great political topics of the day" and that the assembled Whigs adopted resolutions that could be published as the statement of the entire party. Badger presented the convention with a declaration (which he most likely drafted) and the delegates accepted it "in the affirmative by a deafening shout."[91] As an "essential aid in keeping the minds of the people intent on the abuses of the administration," William Graham had earlier recommended that the Whigs put the resolutions of their 1839 state convention in the form of a pamphlet or handbill for circulation.[92] The Whigs now adopted such a course with the resolutions of this party convention. The statement of the convention was probably the key document circulated by the Whigs before the November election. Gales thought it should be "circulated by thousands throughout the State."[93] Undoubtedly the Central Committee made sure that it was.

"The Unanimous Declaration of the Whigs of North Carolina in Convention Assembled, 5th October, 1840," set out all the Whigs' charges against Van Buren and lauded the Republicanism of Harrison. The "leaders of the Party in Power," the Whig delegates declared, were unworthy of "the confidence of a free People" because they had violated all their pledges to the nation. They promised a sound currency but their policies had led to economic crisis; they professed horror at the idea of government patronage interfering with free elections but they "converted the whole body of office-holders into mere dependants upon Executive favor," bound to "maintain a party" instead of serve the country. The Whigs charged that the Democrats had destroyed the Bank of the United States, which had safely kept and disbursed the government revenue for nearly as long as the government had existed and substituted for it Van Buren's dangerous Independent Treasury which placed the revenue under the control of executive officers and subjected the revenue and the currency to "Executive control and misapplication." The Whigs asserted that Van Buren had swelled the number of office holders beyond the demands of the public service, increased their salaries, purchased the support of "the venal and ambitious," and had "sought by every art of corruption to secure themselves the possession of power." They claimed that the administration's recommendation to Congress to reform and reorganize the militia was in reality an attempt to impose a 200,000-man standing army on the states. Their last reasons concisely indicted Van Buren's administration of the government and summed up all their charges:

> BECAUSE, by seizing on the custody and control of the Public Treasure—by attempting to surprise the Nation into the establishment of a vast Standing Army, and by converting the Office-holders into a corps of Spies and Electioneerers, they have manifested a settled purpose to erect a Throne in the midst of our Republican Institutions, to concentrate in the hands of the Executive all the powers of Government, and thus to convert a free People into the slaves of a Despot.
>
> BECAUSE, they found the Country prosperous and happy and by unwise and wicked experiments upon its trade and currency, its industry and property, have brought it to the verge of ruin.
>
> WHEREFORE, we declare it to be our full and settled conviction, that a change in the administration of public affairs is indispensably necessary for restoring prosperity, preserving the Constitution, and securing the freedom of the People.

Finally, the Whigs contrasted the corrupt and dangerous Van Buren with their candidate declaring that "WILLIAM HENRY HARRISON, of Ohio, is the very opposite in principles and purposes, of the present head of the Party in power":

> BECAUSE, he is *in truth* a Republican, who desires the freedom and happiness of his Country, and the equal protection of all in their rights and property:
>
> BECAUSE, he is against any Chief Magistrate holding Office for more than one Presidential term; against Executive encroachments upon the powers of the Representatives of the People; against the abuse of the Veto Power; against Extravagance and Corruption in administering the Government; against removing Officers without cause, and against employing them as Electioneering Agents of the President....

For those reasons the Whigs' declaration concluded, "WE, the Whigs of North Carolina, declare that WILLIAM HENRY HARRISON, ought to be elected President of the United States."[94]

If log cabins and hard cider were the central motifs of the Carolina Whigs' campaign, opposition—both to executive power and Van Buren's administration of the government—was certainly its central idea. Such opposition principles reflected the Old Republican ideology of the States' Rights wing. Yet, the Whigs also loudly proclaimed the measures of political economy favored by the National Republicans. The "Unanimous Declaration of the Whigs" shows how the Whigs were fusing Old Republican opposition principles with the National Republican measures that had been so effective in 1838. This marriage had not been by design, though. The Whig leaders had only reluctantly embraced Harrison for the sake of unity. Yet Harrison was an old Jeffersonian Republican who had loyally served Jefferson and Madison as governor of the Indiana Territory. Though his military service had given him a national outlook, he was not averse to the Old Republican creed. And Tyler's addition to the ticket allowed the Old Republicans among the Whigs to feel that Old Republicanism would help shape the policies of a Whig administration. Support for Harrison and Tyler, while not undermining enthusiasm for Clay, allowed the Whigs to unite their party and appeal to a broad coalition of the electorate with both Old Republican and National Republican ideas. The combination was formidable.

The Harrison campaign also meant that defense of slavery and accusations of Van Buren's alliance with the abolitionists would not be at the forefront of the campaign as it had been in 1836. This also reflected the receding of the States' Rights wing in the coalition and the increased importance of the National Republican measures. Though Harrison was often described by Whig county meetings as "the unwavering friend of the South,"[95] the "Unanimous Declaration of the Whigs" does not mention defense of slavery or the abolitionists. Anti-abolition was not absent from the campaign and some campaigners chose to emphasize it, but it was not prominent in 1840.[96]

After Harrison triumphed in North Carolina and nationally (Harrison carried nineteen of twenty-six states winning 234 electoral votes to Van Buren's 60) the Whig press was jubilant. The *Hillsborough Recorder* proclaimed, "GLORIOUS NEWS!!! The People Triumphant!!!—and Harrison elected!!!" and pronounced "North Carolina 'wide awake.'" The *Raleigh Register* declared, "*Vanburenism Prostrate!* Loco Focoism Annihilated!!!" The *Recorder* announced to all Whigs: "Rejoice—your country is saved—your liberties are secured—and each one of you may with pride say, 'I did my part in the glorious and patriotic work.'"[97]

The Carolina Whigs were certain that Harrison's victory meant that they had achieved their political revolution. The rhetoric of "revolution" was wide-spread in the Whig press after their election triumph. The *Raleigh Register* considered the election of Harrison the result of the most a "remarkable political revolution" and the *Hillsborough Recorder* declared to Whigs, "your country is saved—your liberties are secured."[98] Robert G. Moore, editor of the *Newbern Spectator* exclaimed:

> *The Country is redeemed! The Spoils Party is defeated, prostrated, annihilated! Corruption is driven from office! Harrison, the incorruptible Patriot, the wise Statesman and gallant Soldier is elected President!!* Most devoutly do I thank HEAVEN that the virtue of the American People has enabled me to make this announcement![99]

The Revolution Completed: Mangum's Return to the Senate

Since Brown and Strange had resigned before the August 1840 elections and the Whigs were again in a majority in legislature, one of the first actions of the Whig Legislature was to elect new senators. Mangum was chosen for the full term of six years and William Graham was elected to fill the remaining two years of Strange's term.[100] Mangum's election was not automatic, showing that the state party's realignment from states' rights to the ascendancy of the national wing had weakened his standing in the party. The Whigs in the legislature divided between the nationalistic and states' rights wings in their preferences to fill the senate seats. The National Republican wing of the party favored William Gaston, George E. Badger, Lewis Williams, David L. Swain, Joseph Caldwell, and William A. Graham. The States' Rights men preferred Mangum, William B. Shepard, John Owen, and Governor Dudley as candidates.[101] Thus, in addition to being a vindication for Mangum and the party, the election of Mangum and Graham seems to have been a compromise between the two wings.

Despite the division, a majority of Whig legislators remained friendly and confident in Mangum's ability to represent the party in the Senate. As early as late August and September, after the August Whig victory and Mangum's election to the N.C. Senate, his political confidantes were discussing his return to the U.S. Senate. Charles P. Green wrote from White Sulpher [sic] Springs in Virginia, "*You* must be elected for many good reasons.... Your own standing (I mean popular) requires that you should by all means go again to the Senate from which you were forced out."[102] Though the Whigs of Wake and Orange, including the Central Committee, seemed comfortable with Mangum's election to the Senate, some opposition to him in the Whig Party existed. In the Raleigh area Mangum's friends detected a "general disposition" among the Whigs to return him to the Senate, but some "prominent" western Whigs opposed Mangum. At least one prominent Whig (Lewis Williams from Surrey County) came to Raleigh "prepared to make war on Mangum," William Graham reported.[103] William Gaston, Owen, Badger, and William Graham received consideration for Senate seats.[104]

Additionally, some Whigs were unsure of Mangum's ideology. When the legislature met in November, Mangum had to affirm his support of the Clay Whig program before the Whig caucus would agree to his election. As a former Old Republican and Calhoun Republican, Mangum had to prove his loyalty to the newly ascendant Clay-nationalist wing of the Whig party. The Whigs who opposed Mangum's election could not command the majority of the Whig caucus, but were they to hold out, the Democratic caucus could intervene in the election. To quell the Whig minority and assure a united vote of the Whigs in the legislature, the caucus agreed to a minority "proviso" to the resolution pledging all the Whigs to abide by the decision of the caucus in the vote in the legislature. The proviso stated that the party would nominate only Whigs who favored a United States Bank and the distribution of the proceeds of the sales of the public lands in the West.[105] Mangum was nominated for the longer term, and according to William Graham, was "called out on the questions" and avowed his consent to both. There were no other nominees.[106]

With his pledge to support the nationalist program, Mangum's caucus majority seems to have been sufficiently commanding to deter rivals, although Graham reported that some die hard opponents planned to renew the "war" on Mangum by attempting to show that "he has given written pledges against a Bank."[107] Most likely this referred to the Wilson-Blount letter of 1838. Earlier during the campaign some questions arose about Mangum's stance on the Bank, and his friend in Raleigh, C.L. Hinton then questioned him about his position: "By the bye, it is said by some that in your public addresses in Orange you stand pledged to oppose a U.S. Bank." Wishing Mangum to clarify his position, Hinton revealed how far the state's Whigs thinking had changed on such national measures since the states' rights Opposition days of 1834–1836: "Should you have feelings adverse to the constitutionality of an institution of the kind it would bring many of your strong supporters to a halt...."[108]

Despite Mangum's pledge, some former National Republicans in the Whig coalition remained torn between their loyalty to Mangum as the symbol of the party's cause and their doubts about his conversion to Clay's nationalist economic program. James Bryan told Graham that "Your appointment seems to have given very general satisfaction but I find that Mr. Mangum is the cause of much heartburning among some of the Whigs."[109] Bryan's comment indicates that some Whigs from the east, the bastion of national Whiggery in the state, remained uncomfortable with a former state-rights Whig representing the party in Washington. The newly dominant National Republicans in the N.C. Whig Party wanted guarantees that a former Calhoun States' Rights man would back their program of measures (Mangum had only been a Clay Whig since 1838). But Mangum recognized the power of the national wing of the party and accepted the pledge to support the bank and distribution in the Senate, even though he personally was not fond of the concept of a national Bank. Mangum thus put Whig Party measures above his own personal principles.

Though more candidates vied for the other senatorial seat, this appointment seems to have given the Whigs less trouble. Williams, Badger, William Gaston, David Swain, William B. Shepard, and William Graham were considered by the caucus for the seat. The same meeting that decided on Mangum for the long term nominated Shepard and Graham for the two-year term. Both were queried regarding their opinions of a national bank and distribution as Mangum had been, and both pledged to support the Whig measures. In the caucus vote, Graham received the majority.[110] With the election of Mangum and Graham to the Senate, the Whig victory in 1840 was total: they controlled the legislature and the governor's office, held the majority in the Congressional delegation, and now held both United States Senate seats.

The North Carolina Whigs thus achieved their political revolution. Between 1837 and the end of 1840, the North Carolina Whigs attained ascendancy over the Democrats. As the party moved toward unified support of Henry Clay as its preferred presidential candidate, it began to feature national Whig measures more prominently in its political campaigns: a national bank, the need for a national currency, and distribution of the proceeds of the public land sales to the states. Clay represented Republicanism as it had been in 1816: still anti-executive emphasizing Congress as supreme, but with nationalism derived from the lessons of the War of 1812 and from Clay's views of Madison's political philosophy and Jefferson and Madison's mode of governing. As we have seen, Clay always held the key tenets of the Principles of '98, but his political economy was more nationalist. In this period, the Carolina Whigs accepted and embraced Clay as their party's national leader—they became "Clay Whigs."[111] With that move the national wing of the state party became dominant over the states' rights wing that had led the party in 1835–1836. National Whig measures were featured more prominently in party resolutions, and as the party evolved to a Clay Whig party, the "politics of slavery" that the Whigs had used to attack Van Buren in the 1836 campaign ceased to be a central component of its campaigns. Moreover, to attain their ascendancy in the state the Whigs had to surrender some of their anti-party ideology. The constant theme of the Whig Party in these years was greater organization.

The state party shifted to Clay, but it was the unexpected need to support a national Whig Party candidate that allowed the Carolina Whigs to find a way to firmly join the National Republicans with the States' Rights men/Old Republicans. The combination was critical to

Whig success in the state. They were able to marry the two aspects of their ideology—Old Republican and National Republican—into an ideology of "Whig principles" that, along with organization, became the foundation of their ascendancy over the Democrats for a decade. Many Carolina Whigs viewed such a turn in the state's political alignment as a revolution akin to Jefferson's Revolution of 1800. And during this period they moved from the sectional outlook of *Southern* Whigs to Whigs of the Union.

The 1840 elections ended with two Whigs in the United States Senate and the Whig Party firmly in control of the state government. In the crucible of the instruction controversy the North Carolina Whig Party's principles had been established. And during the contest over instructions and the independence of the Senate, the Whigs had made the state-wide gubernatorial and presidential *elections* the test of whose *principles* would triumph in the state. But the Whigs only attained their victory over "the party" by making a revolution in the state in the name of Whig principles. Sean Wilentz's characterization of the rise of the Whigs between 1835 and 1840 as "a revolution of American conservatism" is on the mark.[112] Mangum and the Whigs of North Carolina used democracy, Old Republicanism, Whig measures, party organization, and anti-party and anti–Van Buren sentiment to take the state from the Jackson–Van Buren Democrats. The Whigs had won majorities in two legislative elections, elected three governors, and elected a Whig president. North Carolina was now beyond doubt a Whig state.

The Whigs of North Carolina were Clay Whigs. They embraced Harrison after the national convention but Henry Clay had been their first choice. Considering Clay's unpopularity in the 1832 election, this was a considerable achievement for the state's Whig leadership. Carolina Whigs became convinced that Clay was the best candidate for the state and the South, but Whig unity had been aided by Calhoun's apostasy in returning to the support of the arch-enemy Van Buren. A majority of North Carolinians clearly favored Whig principles and Whig measures. The slogan "Harrison and reform" embodied the idea of reform on Whig principles; it also indicated measures to counter the reform that supposedly had been brought in during Jackson's revolution of 1828. Thus the Whigs' revolution had countered the "party" and "Jacksonism."

The Whigs' rise to ascendancy was founded on Whig principles that owed much to Old Republicanism: opposition to executive power and opposition to party—the central themes of Whig principles. Added during the battles with Jackson was the key *Southern* Whig principle: the Senate as the defender of states' rights. The North Carolinians shared with all Whigs the principles of the rule of law, supremacy of Congress over the executive branch, and party as a means to measures, not an end in itself. Sharing these principles, some Southerners such as Mangum could make an ideologically comfortable move to the opposition as Southern Whigs. By 1840 Mangum and the North Carolina Whigs also accepted the *national* Whig political economy and its measures.

In their ideas about political economy Southern Whigs such as Mangum had changed most in becoming Clay Whigs between 1837 and 1840. Whig principles derived from Nathaniel Macon's Old Republicanism remained at the center of their Southern Whig ideology. Their ideas on political economy had had to evolve. By November 1840 when he was elected to the Senate, Mangum was a Clay Whig fully committed to a political party; his pledge to the Whig caucus is the best evidence of his evolution: it was a pledge to a party and a pledge to work for the national Clay Whig measures. Party loyalty now took precedence over absolute adherence to principles. The evolution to a Clay Whig state allowed North Carolina to become a vital bastion of national Whig power in the 1840s. Not coincidentally, Mangum became a national Whig leader in the early 1840s. Mangum's reelection gave him the opportunity to reestablish his leadership in the North Carolina Whig Party.

The marriage of Clay's American System with Harrison's Old Republicanism lay at the foundation of the success of the North Carolina Whigs. The resolutions of the county meetings of Whigs in the 1840 campaign show that party activists and committed Whig partisans expected a government on Whig principles. They wanted Whig measures implemented by a Whig government. The election of Harrison in 1840 committed the North Carolina Whigs to national measures and confirmed the dominance of the national wing in the party. Placing a Whig in the White House meant the Whigs would have to govern. The people of North Carolina had catapulted the Whig leaders to power and would expect them to deliver a return on the Whig principles, as Jefferson had delivered on his revolution. Harrison appeared ready to cooperate with Clay's Whig Senate. But could Whig principles govern? When Harrison died suddenly only one month after assuming the chief magistracy, the Whigs suddenly found themselves with President Tyler, a man who had put principles before "the Cause."

6

The Whig Ascendancy: Whig Principles and Clay Whigs

"I arrived here last night, late in the night ... after a most dangerous passage over, sleet, ice, and snow," Mangum reported to Charity the morning after his arrival in Washington, "I am well, and barely escaped with my life at Petersburg—Gen. Waddy Thompson was run over by the cars, and I barely escaped.—In a thousand cases, not more than five would probably escape. He is much bruised, and is now at Richmond.—Gov. [Clement C.] Clay of Alabama and myself were near being run over." At the end of his letter Mangum noted that "The Whigs meet & rejoice more than I ever witnessed before."[1] After arriving in Washington, Mangum took up quarters with William Graham in Mrs. Preuss's boarding house on Missouri avenue, which offered "fine large rooms and a very neat parlour, & tolerable accommodations in the eating line." The two expected James Graham and Kenneth Rayner to join them.[2] Yet, despite the rejoicings of the Whigs, their party was soon to suffer difficulties that would make the train accident seem a mild upset.

The apostasy of John Tyler from the Whig Party that had placed him in power was the central event of the first half of the Whig ascendancy in North Carolina. Tyler's defection renewed the ideological and political struggle between legislative and executive supremacy in the federal government that had given birth to the Whig Party in 1833–1834. In Washington, the struggle with Tyler became a battle between Tyler's Virginia Republican principles and Whig principles—symbolized by Mangum's strong opposition to Tyler. In the 1840s politics were personal and in North Carolina the battle with Tyler involved not just an ideological contest but a contest over political patronage as well. Federal patronage was the point at which the struggle over executive power reached the individual.

In this period the Whig party in North Carolina continued the ascendancy won in 1838–1840. The Whigs' strength in North Carolina meant the state was viewed by national Whig leaders as vital to the national coalition. And Mangum was its foremost representative in this period of ascendancy, chairing the Senate Whig caucus and then elected president pro tem of the Senate (and acting Vice-President). In Congress, Mangum led the Whigs in separating from Tyler. Mangum's close association with Clay and his leadership position in the Senate tied the North Carolina party closer to the national Whig Party.

Mangum's leadership position in the national coalition reinforced his commitment to Whig principles and moved him further away from his states' rights, Old Republican ideological roots. Under the leadership of their state's senior senator, North Carolina Whigs reacted to Tyler's apostasy by completing their movement to becoming ardent and enthusiastic Clay Whigs.

On their arrival in Washington for the 1840–1841 short session of Congress, the Clay Whig senators hoped to persuade Harrison to call a special session to pass the party's measures of reform. In January the Whig senators allied with Clay, including Mangum and Graham, met in caucus at a Washington restaurant to map out their legislative agenda.[3] After persuading president-elect Harrison to call a special session of Congress, the senators saw the president's selection of his cabinet as the other business of prime importance during the short session. Because the Whigs had campaigned against the supposed incompetence and corruption of Van Buren's administration, they wanted the first Whig cabinet to embody Whig administrative competence: men who would ensure that Whig principles were implemented by the administration. The party expected the president to treat the cabinet as a board of advisors, "coequal with the president."[4] As this would be the first Whig cabinet, the North Carolina senators believed that the importance of their state party to the national coalition should be recognized by the inclusion of one of their own in the cabinet. Graham feared that North Carolina would, "as usual," be overlooked in the selection of the cabinet officers,[5] but the North Carolina congressional delegation was intent on gaining a cabinet position. "We have been determined that No Carolina should not be neglected," Mangum explained to his wife.[6] Early in the session the delegation resolved to press Harrison for the appointment of a North Carolinian.[7] Graham reported "a pretty severe struggle with our Southern neighbors" for a cabinet appointment, but the delegation won the appointment of George Badger as Secretary of the Navy despite the combined opposition of Virginia, South Carolina, and Georgia. Graham proudly stated, "So highly however is the devotion of N.C. to true Whig principles valued, that we succeeded against them all."[8] Harrison's cabinet appointments of Badger, John Crittenden, John Bell, and Thomas Ewing, all Clay allies or friendly to Clay, were balanced by Daniel Webster and Francis Granger. The Whigs viewed the short session as merely a prelude for a special session they wished Harrison to call (where they would have the majority.)

Harrison's administration endured for only a single month, cut short by his death in April 1841. Virtually his only acts after the selection of his cabinet were his inaugural address and his reluctant decision to call the special session because of the economic crisis.[9] In his inaugural speech Harrison expressed his intent to govern in accordance with Whig principles. He pledged to serve only one term, decried the use of the veto to "control Congress ... in its ordinary legislation," promised deference to Congress on arranging financial matters, acknowledged the Whig position that the Secretary of the Treasury was not solely an executive agent, and promised to fully explain his reasons to Congress in the event that he must remove his Treasury Secretary.[10] The death of the elected President raised questions for the Whigs. Who was the leader of the Whig party? No vice-president had ever before assumed office in such circumstance; should the "acting President" defer to Congress? At his ascension to the presidency, Tyler chose to take the oath of the president.[11]

In lieu of an inaugural address, Tyler issued a letter to the country. He declared that a "complete separation" should take place between the purse and the sword, expressed the need for a "rigid economy" in government, declared against the sub-treasury, and pledged to consider currency measures formulated by Congress. Tyler's rhetoric accorded with Whig opposition to executive power and preservation of the union (cardinal Whig principles), but far more reflected his Old Republican states' rights principles. Nowhere did he indicate acceptance of the nationalist-Clay Whig measures. He committed himself to no specific measures except on patronage and removals from office. Most notably, he made no such statement as had Harrison deferring completely to Congress on the bank and currency reform.[12]

Most Whigs chose to ignore the lack of such deference to Congress and instead focused on his endorsement of conservative principles. The Whig press was generally pleased with the letter. The *National Intelligencer* pronounced that "President Tyler is a Whig—a true Whig" who would "prove himself a true exponent of those great principles for which they have so long struggled, and struggled at last successfully."[13] The *Hillsborough Recorder* declared: "The last doubt is now dispelled: Mr. Tyler will pursue the policy marked out by Gen. Harrison."[14] Shortly after his arrival in Washington to take up his Cabinet post, Badger wrote to Graham, "I am decidedly of opinion that as far as depends on the new President the cause of the Country is safe."[15] Yet, it would soon become clear to the Whigs that, unlike Mangum, Tyler had not come to accept the measures of the national party.

During the special session the Whigs succeeded in repealing Van Buren's Independent Treasury, passing a temporary revenue measure, and a tariff revision-distribution measure, all of which President Tyler signed into law. A new bank, though, was the signature Whig measure of the special session. Although the congressional Whigs had difficulty passing the distribution and tariff measures, the Bank proved the most difficult issue and, because of Tyler's vetoes, created the greatest conflict over Whig principles regarding executive power.

"The Betrayer of the Great and Victorious Party"

In his message to Congress for the special session, Tyler had indicated he would be receptive to Congress enacting a "suitable fiscal agent," but he made no specific proposal. He reserved the right to reject any measure that in his view might "conflict with the Constitution."[16] Clay asked Treasury Secretary Ewing to submit a plan for a bank that would meet with Tyler's approval. With the endorsement of the cabinet, Ewing sent the administration's plan for a "Fiscal Bank of the United States" to the Senate on June 12, 1844. Reflecting Tyler's concern for states' rights, the Treasury Secretary's proposed bank was a bank of the District of Columbia, not a national bank. It would have no power to establish branches in the states without the approval of their legislatures.[17] Clay and his Whig allies in the Senate, including Mangum, were not pleased with the Treasury plan. While Clay set up a special Senate committee to examine the Treasury plan and report, the Whig caucus, chaired by Mangum, set out to formulate a Bank bill more in line with Whig principles around which they hoped to rally the congressional Whigs. The Senate Whigs wanted a *national* bank with *national* powers, and they considered the power to create branches vital. They would not concede to Tyler's limited Bank.

Mangum was at the center of these events. In seeking to unite the party on a Whig bank bill, Mangum redeemed his pledge to the North Carolina Whig legislative caucus, but he was also responding to the party's call for a bank. Mangum was no bank man and insisted that the bank be "well regulated and well guarded,"[18] but as chairman of the Senate Whig caucus he supported it as a national Whig measure. Arguing that the power to set up branches was vital to a national bank, Mangum informed his friends in New York that he would rather give up the bill than pass a bank bill without that power.[19] By leading the Whigs on this bank issue,

Mangum showed how far he had moved toward the support of the National Republican Whig program and away from strict adherence to his States' Rights Whig doctrines of just three years ago.

Mangum's Whig principles no longer accorded with Tyler's Old Republican principles. Pledged to support a national bank and with a strong National Republican wing in his state party, Mangum could no longer insist on pure Old Republicanism; Tyler did. As a Clay Whig, Mangum took a position in the Senate that encompassed the interests of the national party. Tyler resisted the National Republicans and insisted on Old Republican orthodoxy.

Mangum's insistence on a national bank also stemmed from his knowledge of his own Whig constituents. He explained in the Senate debate that in North Carolina, as long as the bank was "well regulated and well guarded," the Whig party "with a near approach to unanimity" desired a national bank. Graham seconded Mangum's statements.[20] North Carolina's Senators felt under great pressure from their state's Whigs to deliver a Bank. Raleigh lawyer and active Whig Henry Miller reminded Graham: "I do hope we shall have a Bank & that too at once."[21] Former Whig governor Edward Dudley informed Graham, "Congress is looked to anxiously for relief, & if something is not done, the execrations of the people will be deep & wide."[22] Richard Smith, a wealthy Raleigh merchant often active in Whig politics, told Mangum, that he and others feared for the fate of the Bank Bill, "as we consider it one of the principal measures of carrying the Government on upon that open fair and just plan so ably advocated by Mr. Clay, yourself & all the whole congress...." All the Whig measures, Smith added, were "vitally necessary."[23] Such letters constantly reminded the Whig legislators of their pledge to work for enactment of a national bank.

On June 23 Clay reported to the Senate the Whig caucus's bill for a truly national bank with power to open branches.[24] Historians have often interpreted the bill as Clay's effort to "dictate" to Tyler on the bank.[25] It was not. The bill was intended to bring the Cabinet to a compromise on the bank and thus present Tyler with a bill backed by a unified Whig Party. Mangum believed the Senate Whigs' plan was best, but he sought a compromise for the sake of Whig unity and the future of the Whig Party.

The Senate Whigs' bill was the *national* bank plan that Mangum and the Clay wing in the Senate thought was the best for the country and the party; they believed that a large majority of Whigs agreed. The Senate Whigs met for five days on the Bank. In this caucus, as Mangum explained it

> the whole measure was canvassed in its principles & its details, with the minutest care, & the most *signal moderations & deference*. The whole subject was discussed & considered maturely in regard to its intrinsic merits & demerits; and all the consequences of disunion & discord, were fully considered & painfully canvassed, as they would affect the party; & more especially, as they would affect the great interests of the Country, Commercial & political.... Upon each & every point we *gave instructions* to the special committee & upon the point of greatest difficulty, the *Branching power*, we thought it due to our own characters & position to assert & maintain our own principles, & the principles of 95 in every 100 of our Whig friends throughout the Country, & if evil came of it, let the responsibility rest upon those, who by endeavoring to wrench us from our natural position, were about to launch us on a troubles sea of new experiments.[26]

Mangum reported that the senators received reports from Whigs in the major cities that they considered the power to create branches to be "vital" and approved of the Clay bill."[27] North Carolina Whigs agreed. Richard Smith told Mangum, "Mr. Clay is right about the establishment of the U.S. Bank, without the consent of the States...."[28] Mordecai M. Noah reported to Mangum that "not one in a hundred" of the Whigs in New York City approved of Ewing's bank plan.²⁹ They agreed that without the branching power and without protection from state taxation, the bank would not be a national bank and investors would not buy the bank's stock.³⁰ The bill was meant to push the Cabinet to seek a compromise along lines close to the Senate bill. Mangum reported that a short adjournment of the Senate in late June was intended "to give the Physic time to do its office."

Mangum and the Senate Whigs were convinced that the Treasury plan would be "entire failure" and would risk "dissolution of the party." They preferred to "go to the Country and take all the consequences" rather than agree to the Treasury plan. "They now know that failure is *inevitable* on their plan," Mangum reported. The Cabinet now realized that the Clay bill "contains what the Country needs and what the Whigs ought to require," Mangum explained to his friend and confidant, Duncan Cameron, "*If it can be got.*" Efforts were afoot by Webster and Ewing and their friends in Congress to arrange a compromise on "some safe & practicable ground." Mangum feared the "appalling" consequences of failure. "Our first duty is to put the Vessel of State on a right tack," Mangum explained. If the Whigs in Congress failed they would be "swept by the board, with a fury nearly resembling that of last year."³¹ Such a compromise would show the country that the Whigs could govern while failure would threaten the party. Thus, any compromise would have to be one that the party could defend— a compromise that would preserve Whig principles—and that meant a *national* bank.

Mangum realized that Tyler, with his veto power, was the ultimate problem for the Whig Party. Tyler's principles had become a threat to its dearly won ascendancy; their own President's principles stood in the way of Whig government. "The Whig party is in a most woful [sic] plight," he lamented. The first "great error" of the session was made by the Cabinet in yielding to Tyler's principles. At the outset they should have "brought the President to the broad Whig platform, or to have handed in the seals of office." Willie Mangum had already made his own assessment of Tyler as but an "impersonation" of a Whig president who would work to achieve "the fruits of the gallant struggle of this great and victorious Whig party." At the moment of victory, when Whigs at last had the chance to implement Whig principles, Tyler's dogmatic adherence to Old Republicanism was betraying the Whig party. Mangum bitterly summed up Tyler's rigidity:

> If now he shall throw himself in the fact of this great & gallant party, after an accession by a contingency, dash all the hopes of a seven years unexampled perseverance & struggle, & bind this great & victorious party in the net work of Virginia abstractions & lay it at his feet the contempt & scorn of the world, that he will be regarded by his contemporaries & by posterity as having successfully perpetrated the most stupendous fraud that in modern times, has been played upon any great people or party.

In essence the conflict was ideological, and it threatened the future of the Whig Party. In Mangum's view, Tyler had only two choices: "The alternative put to him is, that as a man of Honor he ought to resign or accede to Whig principles."³²

On July 23, Clay presented a compromise amendment that would preserve the national power of the bank, and allow a limited role for states' rights. State legislatures would be able to refuse a bank branch at their first session after passage of the bank law, but if they failed to act, their consent for a branch would be presumed. If Congress determined a branch was vital to the national interest, it could establish a bank branch in a state despite the legislature's refusal. Earlier, Mangum reported to Graham that he had been involved in discussions to arrange a compromise bill that had the cabinet's sanction "& it is supposed of course of the President," he explained.³³ Graham and Mangum had received assurances, probably from

Badger, that the Cabinet would support the compromise bill and would try to persuade Tyler to sign it. Graham reported, "The Cabinet will approve the compromise, and will exert their influence with the President to secure his approval."[34] The compromise amendment passed the Senate 25 to 24. On July 25th the amended bill passed the Senate 26–23, with the Virginia Whigs in opposition. The House passed the compromise bill 128 to 98.[35] Mangum had achieved his Whig unity and passed a Whig measure.

Tyler informed the cabinet on 11 August 1841 that he intended to veto the bank bill, but he discussed neither his message nor his particular objections to the bill.[36] When the cabinet members learned of Tyler's intentions, the North Carolina senators expected a separation between Tyler and the Whigs, with potentially dire effects. Graham predicted "injurious" consequences for the Whig party and the resignation of the Cabinet.[37] Mangum thought the veto would bring an "explosion." "The most, if not all the Cabinet, will retire from office, & none, in my judgment, can stay with honor." Tyler had failed the Whig Party, and Mangum thought the Whigs would do best in opposition if the president was not with them. "Tyler has sadly disappointed all our expectations.... In twelve months he will be in the arms of the Locos—the best result, if he will not carry out the Whig measures.... The Veto & the loss of our other measures, will place a gulf between him & nearly the whole whig party in Congress—and a reunion is impossible.—We have sacrificed every thing to his vanity & inflation—all to no purpose." "Sick in body and at heart," Mangum reported an excursion of cabinet officers, congressmen, and dignitaries "dancing attendance on the President" during a visit the battleship *Delaware* in Annapolis and angrily remarked: "Nero Fiddled while Rome was burning—I have no heart to go.—I cannot think of an excursion of pleasure, while our Whig measures are failing, and almost the temple of liberty falling about our ears. And least of all, could I dance in the train of one likely to become the betrayer of the great and Victorious party."[38]

On August 16th Tyler sent his veto message to the Senate. He informed the senators that he could find no grant of power in the Constitution for Congress to establish a "national bank to operate *per se* over the Union." Despite the bill's compromise provision giving state legislatures a veto over the establishment of branch banks, Tyler found Congress's power to create branch banks under the bill too great. The bill gave Congress the ultimate right to establish "offices of discount and deposit" in the states, "a principle to which I have heretofore been opposed and which can never obtain my sanction."[39] It was a veto in defense of states' rights and the compact theory of the Union.

The Cabinet and the Congressional Whigs perceived, however, that Tyler might be willing to agree to a national bank dealing in bills of *exchange* (commercial notes secured by trade goods in transit) instead of bills of *discount* (loans) on promissory notes. Graham wrote to William Gaston that in his message Tyler, "insinuates, and it is said, agrees" that a bank with branches so empowered would receive his approbation.[40] At a cabinet meeting on August 18th, Tyler agreed to the outline of such a national bank; with the bank limited to dealing in bills of exchange, he made no objection to the branching power.[41] The Whigs quickly produced a bill based on that outline. As Michael Holt points out, "Far more eager to charter a bank than to break with the president, the congressional Whig caucus immediately agreed to pass such a measure under the impression that Tyler was committed to it."

In the interim, Tyler had turned against own agreement with the Cabinet. Stung by a speech Clay made on the 19th of August against the veto of the first Whig compromise, Tyler apparently hardened his position after the publication of the so-called "coffeehouse" letter of the Virginia Whig congressman John Minor Botts who claimed that the Whigs would "head" Tyler on the bank issue. Tyler told congressmen that he would veto the new compromise bill, but he did not inform the cabinet secretaries of his decision, an indication that he no longer considered them his advisors and confidants.[42]

In his second Bank Bill veto message, Tyler explained to Congress that he could not conform to "mere regard to the will of a majority." The Constitution, he asserted, must be guarded "against the will of a mere representative majority" and he had a duty to protect "the fundamental will of the people themselves." Specifically, he objected to the national character of the proposed bank. In a complete reversal from Harrison's stated policy and his own declarations in his special session message, he now proposed to send his own bank plan to Congress in the following session.[43] John Tyler now regarded himself as the guardian of the people against their own representatives.

During the special session of the summer of 1841 the North Carolina Whigs became convinced that Tyler was being influenced by the Virginians they labeled the "Virginia Cabal," an influence that was separating Tyler from the Southern Whigs. In June, as he was working to secure a compromise between the Senate bill and the Treasury plan, Mangum complained that Tyler was "a weak & vacillating President surrounded & stimulated by a cabal, contemptible in numbers, not strong in talent, but vaulting in ambition." Mangum believed that the "Cabal," which he named as Virginia congressmen Henry Wise, Thomas R. Gilmer, Robert M. T. Hunter, and Francis Mallory, was in correspondence with Calhoun's "So. Ca. Clique."[44] In Mangum's view, Tyler would have signed a national bank bill shortly after succeeding Harrison, but the cabal had worked on him through "coaxing, cajolery, intimidation, and the plying of his ambition, in connexion [sic] with a second term." The lure of a second term was thus drawing Tyler away from Whig principles; if the influence of the Virginians continued, Mangum feared Tyler would "lose all consciousness of his personal and political identity" as a Whig.[45] The Virginia Cabal could turn a Whig president into an ambitious executive.

The Clay-wing members of the cabinet had agreed with the Senate Whigs since the formulation of the first Whig compromise Bank Bill, but the North Carolina senators strongly suspected that the Cabinet secretaries were no longer Tyler's principal advisors; Tyler's reluctance to sign the second compromise bill convinced them that the Virginians of the Cabal, not the cabinet officers, had become Tyler's policy advisors. "If he shall take the counsel of his Cabinet, he will sign the Bill without hesitation," Graham wrote in regard to first compromise bill, "but there is a cabal principally of Virginians, not in political life, who have been about him of late, and will do their utmost to procure a veto."[46] Mangum shared Graham's view that the Virginians lay at the root of Tyler's opposition to the Whig measures: "The President & his Virginia cabal are against all our measures, at heart, as I believe.—Certainly it is true of [the] cabal."[47]

By late August, as the second compromise bill was moving through Congress and rumors of Tyler's change in sentiment was reaching the congressional Whigs, Graham was describing Tyler as "our Veto President." He questioned Tyler's principles and accused him of changing his position with every new consultation of "domestic advisors." Graham complained, "It is a most singular state of things now, that another set of persons know far more of the intentions of the President than the Cabinet Ministers."[48] The North Carolina Whig senators were convinced that Tyler preferred his "Virginia Cabal" to his cabinet as his advisors. Whigs viewed the cabinet as co-equal with the president and believed that the cabinet officers were his only legitimate constitutional advisors.[49] Tyler's total disregard for the opinions of his cabinet after August 18, 1841, and his preference for the extra-governmental and extra-constitutional advice of the Cabal was seen by the Whigs as dangerous to republican government, just as Jackson's Kitchen Cabinet had been in their eyes. The supreme law designated the cabinet as the president's executive councilors, and the Whigs expected that the cabinet officers would be consulted on all policy and measures. Tyler's preference for the unofficial "Cabal" was, in their view, another violation of the "Constitution and the Laws."

As the second Bank bill sat on Tyler's desk in early September, Mangum was certain of the veto and wrote, "Tyler is mad, weak, and a traitor I fear" and forecast the breakup of the Cabinet.[50] Graham predicted that a second veto would "inevitably separate him from the Whigs." The distrust of the Whigs had so increased "that there can hardly ever be a cordial reconciliation."[51] When Tyler sent back his veto message on September 11, 1841, all of the cabinet secretaries except Webster resigned.

With the resignation of the Cabinet, the pride of the Whig Party—the Harrison cabinet—was abolished. The resignation letters of Ewing, Bell, and Badger all stressed the second veto as an act of betrayal. Tyler, they proclaimed, had failed to treat them as his advisors. Ewing insisted that Tyler well knew the issues involved in the bank question and could not have been taken unprepared on the question; thus he implied that Tyler could hardly have discovered new objections since the August 18th meeting. Ewing also claimed that he had "strong ground" to believe that the Botts letter had caused Tyler's shift. Asserting that Tyler had agreed to approve the bank outlined in the August 18th cabinet meeting, Bell and Badger emphasized that Tyler had asked the cabinet to act as his agents with the Congress in moving the bill to passage. Badger had assured members of Congress that Tyler would approve the bill.[52] Not only was it Tyler's "plain duty" to have notified the cabinet of his change of opinion on the bank, Badger believed the president should have offered them "an apology" for placing them in such an uncomfortable position with Congress. "But this the President did not do." Badger declared his conviction that the president's inexcusable and unexplained conduct "constituted ... ample ground for a withdrawal from his Cabinet without delay."[53]

Mangum chose to respond to Tyler's second veto through the declarations of the united Whig caucus. Knowing the danger posed to the party by the failure of their signature economic measure, Mangum and the majority of the Whig delegation in Congress preferred to make it clear to the country that they were once again in opposition to the Executive. The North Carolinians took the lead. At a meeting of the Whig congressional caucus on the 11th of September, with Rayner acting as secretary, Mangum offered a resolution calling for the Whigs to publish an address to the country explaining their course in Congress and stating their case against Tyler. Rayner was appointed to the committee charged with drafting the address.

The Address read Tyler out of the Whig Party. After setting out the legislative goals of the session, the Whigs explained their hope that a spirit of unity and compromise would have allowed them to unite as a party to enact the measures. They emphasized their expectation that Tyler would be loyal to Whig principles as defined in the Revolution of 1840:

> We only knew him as one professing to be a member of the Whig party, and as seeking to identify himself with those great leaders of that party whose opinions and principles were deeply engraved in the most conspicuous acts of our political history, and were read and understood by every citizen in the land. In this connection, where he had sought to be prominent, we discerned what we conceived, and what doubtless

he meant, to be a pledge of faithful adherence to the cardinal doctrines for which we struggled, and with which the hopes of the country were indissolubly bound up.

They explained that the National Bank had been defeated solely by the president's exercise of the veto power, "a power which we had hoped was never to be exhibited, on this subject, by a Whig President." Moreover, the president was seeking "new political combinations." The Whigs expected that Tyler would have sought the "wise and prosperous counsels" of the distinguished and able Whig Cabinet, "the chosen vanguard of the Whig party," whose officers were "the very embodiment of the principles of the party to which they belonged." Instead he had chosen to associate with those who had the "least interest in the success of Whig measures." By all these actions the president had "voluntarily separated himself" from the Whig Party, and the Whigs in Congress could no longer "in any manner or degree" be "justly held responsible or blamed for the administration of the Executive branch of the Government."

Finally, the Whigs set out three sets of "duties" that remained for the Whig Party to perform: first, a reduction of executive power by a further limitation of the veto, the adoption of a single term for President, and the "separation of the Purse from the Sword" by giving Congress the power to appoint the Secretary of the Treasury; second, the establishment of a national bank; and third, the "introduction of economy in the administration of the Government, and the discontinuance of all sinecures and useless offices." At the end of their Address, the congressional Whigs called on the state legislatures to "express the public will in relation to these great questions."[54] Rayner signed the address as a member of the committee of the House of Representatives. The Whigs were declaring political war on Tyler.

"Virginia Abstractions"

Mangum and the Whigs in Congress expected that a Whig president would conduct his administration in accordance with the Whig principles defined in the campaign of 1840—an administration of government that would fulfill the promise of the revolution of 1840. In the conduct of government, a Whig administration promised deference to the supremacy of Congress. William Henry Harrison had pledged himself to such an administration of government, proclaiming in his inaugural: "And it is preposterous to suppose that a thought could for a moment have been entertained that the President, placed at the capital, in the center of the country, could better understand the wants and wishes of the people than their own immediate representatives." In particular, he promised deference to Congress on financial legislation. Declaring the "impropriety of Executive interference in the legislation of Congress," he stated that though it was the constitutional duty of the president to communicate information and recommend measures to Congress, he was not intended to be the source of legislation "and, in particular, … he should never be looked to for schemes of finance." Harrison insisted that "the delicate duty of devising schemes of revenue should be left where the Constitution has placed it—with the immediate representatives of the people. For similar reasons the mode of keeping the public treasure should be prescribed by them, and the further removed it may be from the control of the Executive the more wholesome the arrangement and the more in accordance with republican principle."[55] This was exactly the issue on which the Whigs had battled Jackson and Van Buren. Harrison was thus committed to govern by the cardinal principle of the Whigs. The Whigs expected that the conservative Virginia Whig John Tyler would likewise govern according to these principles.

The Clay wing of the party failed to recognize that Tyler was a state-rights Whig of 1834 who had not evolved as Mangum had to the national Whig program. Tyler's principles remained far closer to Old Republican principles of 1816–1819 than to the Whig principles of the Revolution of 1840. As noted above, Tyler promised in his inaugural letter to give his sanction "to any constitutional measure which, originating in Congress, shall have for its object the restoration of a sound circulating medium." Tyler's use of the word "constitutional" implied his intention to judge the constitutionality of any measure and that implied the possibility of a veto. Tyler followed this with an extended explanation of the principles that would guide his judgment. In judging a measure's constitutionality, he stated that he would "resort to the Fathers of the great republican school for advice and instruction." Then he presented his Old Republican vision of government:

> The spectacle is exhibited to the world of a government deriving its powers from the consent of the governed, and having imparted to it only so much power as is necessary for its successful operation. Those who are charged with its administration should carefully abstain from all attempts to enlarge the range of powers thus granted to the several departments of the Government, other than by an appeal to the People for additional grants, lest by so doing they disturb that balance which the patriots and statesmen who framed the Constitution designed to establish between the Federal Government, and the states composing the Union.[56]

Tyler thus indicated his criterion of judgment would be Old Republican, not the full body of Whig principles recently defined in Harrison's campaign. Because Southern Whig rhetoric also pledged loyalty to these principles, the Whigs were not alarmed. The rhetoric of Tyler's inaugural included opposition to executive power and preservation of the Union (cardinal Whig principles) but it emphasized his Old Republican states' rights principles. In 1830, Mangum would have agreed with Tyler's ideology, an ideology akin to Nathaniel Macon's; by 1841, Mangum's ideology was more akin to Clay's.

The Whigs further expected that Tyler would defer to Congress on the Bank because in his message to Congress for the special session Tyler left it to Congress to determine the type of "fiscal agent" the country should have. He would, he said, submit the "entire question" to Congress. Acknowledging that Congress, who had "come more directly from the body of our common constituents, was "best qualified to give a full exposition of their wishes and opinions," Tyler declared:

> I shall be ready to concur with you in the adoption of such system as you may propose, reserving to myself the ultimate power of rejecting any measure which may, in my view of it, conflict with the Constitution or otherwise jeopardize the prosperity of the country—a power which I could not part with even if I would, but which I will not believe any act of yours will call into requisition.[57]

Tyler's reservation was significant. He implied deference to Congress but reserved the veto power to reject any measure not meeting his principles. And he reserved the right to veto for constitutional or policy reasons. It was a formula for confrontation, as he surely knew that many Whigs and many Southern Whigs had campaigned on the reestablishment of a Bank of the United States. Mangum and Graham were pledged to support a Bank. Tyler refused to recognize a national bank as a Whig measure. When Tyler exercised his reserved power to veto a bank bill, he presented the Whig Party with the picture of a Whig president who was violating essential Whig principles.

The Whigs reacted so strongly to Tyler's veto messages because they expressed principles inimical to the whole Whig ideology. Tyler's vetoes implied presidential authority over the disposition of the public monies and plans for national financial measures. While the Constitution nowhere gives the president power over the disposition of the public revenue, Jackson, Van Buren, and now Tyler claimed such power. The Whigs viewed the president's encroachments on Congressional authority as nothing short of revolutionary and dangerous to republican government. Such presidential assertions of power over public finance as Jackson's and Tyler's were revolutionary at the time. The Whigs also interpreted these assertions of power as un-republican, as reflected in their constant declarations against unifying the powers of "the purse and the sword." The Whigs' proposal to bring the Secretary of the Treasury under Congressional authority was yet another facet of this interpretation of power. In his inaugural address Harrison had proclaimed that the president should have no part in proposing schemes of finance and deferred to Congress. While Tyler seemed to agree in his special session message, he proposed at the end of his second veto message to send a plan to Congress. Despite his professions of deference to Congress in his special session message, Tyler wanted to make his own policy on the federal "fiscal agent."[58] The president, not Congress, would make national financial policy.

Tyler's veto messages also raised further and deeper issues regarding the conflict of his principles with Whig principles. For the Whigs, their victory in 1840 plus the approval of one of the fathers of republicanism, James Madison, meant that the Bank could not be denied on policy or constitutional grounds. Clay and Mangum were seeking to implement the measures of their triumphant party—to ratify their political revolution, and garner its fruits. But Tyler, who had resigned his Senate seat in 1836 rather than defy the will of the Virginia legislature, refused as president to conform to will of the majority party expressed in Congress.

Henry Clay dealt with some of these issues in his August 19th speech against Tyler's first veto. Addressing the broad concerns of the Whig Party in regard to Tyler's veto,[59] Clay accused the president of disloyalty to Whig principles and to the Whig majority in the country. Clay also called for deference to the will of the majority as represented in Congress. The Whigs had contested the election of 1840 on measures of reform that included a national bank, and they had won a majority in the presidential election and in Congress. Clay pointed to "the majorities in the two houses of Congress as ... strong evidence of the opinion of the people of the United States in favor of the establishment of a Bank of the United States."

Clay was perplexed by why a man who would not interpose his opinions against the will of the Virginia legislature in 1836 could stand against a Congress that represented the whole union. "It did not enter into my imagination," Clay remarked, "to conceive that one, who had shown so much deference and respect to the presumed sentiments of a single state, should display less towards the sentiments of a whole nation." Tyler was defending the principles of a state-rights Whig minority against the national Whig majority. Arguing that the president had duties beyond guarding his own personal principles, Clay queried why Tyler felt obliged to place his principles above those of the Whigs. If Tyler had personal reservations, Clay suggested that he could have let the bill become law without his signature. "All that could have been justly said would be, that he did not choose to throw himself in the way as an obstacle to the passage of a measure indispensable to the prosperity of the nation, in the judgment of the party which brought him into power" and of the Whig Congress and the Cabinet. Clay further pointed out that in 1840 the people voted for the reform measures of the Whig Party

Henry Clay in the Senate by Phineas Staunton (1817–1867), oil on canvas, 1866 (U.S. Senate)

rather than for Tyler's principles. In his second veto message Tyler no longer pretended any deference to Congress, but instead insisted that he was the judge of the Whig majority in Congress, not its servant. Unlike Jackson, Tyler, the aristocratic Virginian, was uninterested in majority politics; he held to the anti-majoritarian views of the Old Republicans. But, Jackson-like, he wanted to appear as the people's tribune; thus he proclaimed himself the guardian of the "fundamental will of the people" against Congress.

Tyler seems to have perceived a basic difference between the majority in the Virginia legislature and the majority in Congress. Tyler's states'-rights Old Republicanism led him to distrust Congress; he and his fellow state-rights Virginia Whigs remained uncomfortable with the majority party politics of the Clay Whigs. In some respects Tyler's vetoes harkened back to Madison's veto of the Bonus Bill in 1817. Like Madison's veto, Tyler's veto blocked the action of a congressional majority in defense of states' rights and the Constitution and because of fears of "consolidation" and corruption. Madison, however, was vetoing internal improvements; he had accepted the Second Bank of the United States as "necessary" and constitutional, and signed it into law. Tyler's veto was defending *Virginia* Old Republican anti-majoritarian principles. Madison had recommended that Congress seek an amendment to the Constitution granting them the power to fund internal improvements. Madison was thus willing to defer to the judgment of the sovereign people. Tyler made no such recommendation; *he* was the guardian of the "fundamental will of the people." He used Jacksonian rhetoric but unlike Jackson did not really believe in majoritarian politics.

Nathaniel Macon's old Federalist opponent and National-Republican Whig William Gaston realized the source of Tyler's principles and saw that Tyler had not evolved with other Southern Whigs to Clay's national Whig principles. He explained both to his friend, Senator William Graham:

> It is the misfortune of Mr. Tyler and great calamity I regard it, to have imbibed in his youth certain political dogmas, not wanting in plausibility and even partially founded in truth, but as preached and expounded by political zealots, impracticable and absurd, as the revelations of perfect verity. He ought not to be severely blamed for not being able to free his mind entirely from the bondage of his early faith. It requires mighty powers to do this. Such intellects as those of James Madison and of Henry Clay, have been able to effect it—but not until such observation and long experience had demonstrated fallacies too plainly to be overlooked."[60]

Gaston's comments hinted at another, larger truth revealed in the struggle over the Bank bill. The Old Republican creed was incompatible with Whig government.

The contrast between Mangum and Tyler was striking. Tyler remained a Whig of 1835. He respected the rule of law but not the rule of a party, and he held the Old Republican's distrust of Congress and Clay nationalism. Tyler had not accompanied the North Carolina senators to the union of Old Republicanism and National Republicanism embodied in the Whig principles of 1840. Former Old-Republican Southern Whigs like Mangum had adapted to a revised conception of Whig principles that could serve as the banner of both the national and state parties in the Whig coalition; moreover, they accepted national Whig measures that served as a popular Whig program for government. Tyler had not. Both started at nearly the same ideological position in the Opposition of 1834/1835, but Mangum adapted to the political realities of North Carolina (his pledge for the Bank and distribution was only the most recent example) and the move to Clay had brought his party to ascendancy in the state. Tyler had moved along no such path and had never shown any loyalty to the Whig party (as his course in the instruction controversy had shown). In their confrontation with Jackson in the 1830s, the Whigs faced the will of one man against the rule of law. In their contest with Tyler, the Whigs faced the will of one man against the rule of a party. For Tyler, Virginia Old Republican principles remained paramount. But the Old Republican's "Principles of '98" were no longer synonymous with Southern Whig principles, as Mangum had declared them to be in 1834 when he broke with Jackson. For Clay Whigs of the South, states' rights no longer held first place—the Whig Party itself and the Union of the states essential to its maintenance now held that place.

"First Place in the Affections of the Whole Whig Party": The Clay Convention

"I was pleased to see the proceedings of *your* meeting in Orange & more so, that you have made the first move," Charles Green told Mangum regarding a Whig political meeting held in November shortly after Mangum's return from the divisive special session of Congress.[61] As Green indicated, Mangum sponsored the meeting whose purpose was nominating Henry Clay for the presidency. The Orange nomination put in motion an official end to Tyler as leader of the North Carolina Whigs and set Clay firmly in that place.

After the failed special session and the break with Tyler, Mangum returned to North Carolina, determined to put the declaration of the Whigs into practice and have North Carolina take the lead in nominating Clay (as the state party had not in the 1840 campaign). At a meeting of Orange County Whig leaders at the Masonic Hall in Hillsborough on November 23, 1841, a committee presented a set of resolutions that declared the Whigs' separation from Tyler, praised Clay, nominated him for the presidency, and called for a state-wide Whig convention in April.

The resolutions embodied the position of the Whig Party. The Whigs declared their "unabated confidence in the principles of the Whig party" upon which Harrison had won his victory. The apostasy of Tyler had reinforced the extent to which Harrison's death was "a great and grievous national calamity." Expressing a "deep and abiding disapprobation and reprobation of the principles and policy" of the Van Buren administration, the Whigs declared that the "great body of the Whig party" in Congress had "proudly and justly vindicated their claims to the respect and confidence of those who placed them in power." Confessing that "the great and glorious party" that triumphed in 1840 had been "grievously disappointed" by Tyler, the meeting declared that "we cannot and ought not to recognize him as a Whig President." Tyler was no longer their president: they demanded a Whig at the head of the party and as president who would carry out the program of the Whig party. Loyalty to the Principles of '98 alone was no longer sufficient—only a true friend to all Whig principles and measures would meet their approval as president.:

> taught by experience, we will in the future, avoid all nominations made upon the ground of "availability"; That as our principles are undisguised and open as day, so we will have none to represent them, but such as we in our hearts believe are firm, faithful, able, and willing to accede to, and vindicate them, and the whole of them.

They asserted that "as in this community, so in almost every portion of the Union, as far as we are informed, the People—the real Whig People ... approach as near unanimity in favor of one individual as has happened in our history." The Orange Whigs resolved to "hoist the flag of that illustrious citizen and nail it to the mast." Affirming their confidence that his record "affords the fullest and safest guarantees that he will be an able, faithful, and patriotic magistrate" they nominated Clay as their candidate for the next presidency. They declared their approval of the "able and patriotic" administration of Governor Morehead and nominated him for reelection. The final resolution called for a general convention of the Whigs in April "to organize our forces for the ensuing summer election—perhaps more important than any that has occurred in ten years past."

Though not members of the drafting committee, both Mangum and Graham were present and endorsed the resolutions. Following the presentation of the resolutions Mangum addressed the meeting and, according to the account in the friendly *Hillsborough Recorder*, "sustained the principles set forth in them with his accustomed force and eloquence." Following Mangum's address, Graham offered "a few impressive remarks" after which the Whigs unanimously adopted each of the resolutions.[62] Mangum and the Orange County leaders thus set the nomination of Clay in motion. The resolutions left no doubt that Mangum and Orange Whigs intended to contest the coming elections on Whig principles.

The timing of the nomination meeting was driven by more than Mangum's desire to distance himself and the state party from the failed session. It was important for the state elections of 1842. In the 1841 congressional elections (held in May before the special session) the Whigs had continued their success of 1840 and reversed the losses of 1839. Whig candidates were elected in eight out of thirteen districts, reinforcing the party's ascendancy in the state and once again securing a Whig majority in the congressional delegation.[63] The early nomination of Clay would help to sustain this momentum and ensure the party had a presidential candidate to tout in the 1842 state elections. The Orange County Whigs had vowed that the party would "rally as one man" at the 1842 elections and to use "all honorable efforts" to bring "our whole force" to the polls.[64] Clay was the foremost advocate of the Whig measures in Congress and the embodiment of Whig principles. Undoubtedly he would approve all the measures of a Whig Congress. As Mangum knew from the campaign of 1840, Clay was the favorite of the North Carolina Whigs. Because North Carolina's Whigs had already demonstrated that theirs was one of the strongest Southern Whig states, taking the lead in nominating Clay would provide a powerful impetus to his nomination by the other state parties.

With the process to place Clay at the head of the North Carolina Whig ticket started, the ground was clear for Mangum to make a personal statement denouncing Tyler. Mangum returned to the Senate in December to deliver a major speech against Tyler's "Exchequer" bank plan. The speech, while yet another demonstration of his fulfillment of Mangum's pledge to support a United States Bank, also was designed to make it clear to North Carolinians that the Whigs' break with the president was complete. It would help launch the campaign to bring down the apostate and reassert Whig supremacy in the state.

Mangum drew sharp ideological lines for the electorate of North Carolina to read in the newspapers. Excoriating Tyler and the measures of the new Cabinet, Mangum left no doubt that he was once again in Opposition. He associated the Exchequer Board with Tyler's unwarranted assumption of executive power. Tyler had ascended to the Executive chair and was now following the course of Van Buren: Mangum was "compelled to come to the conclusion that even in the worst of times this Government had ever yet seen, never had there been so bold, so reckless a push for absolute power, as was now unblushingly made in the paper before the Senate." The plan would unite the "entire money power" with the government's patronage power. "What a concentration of power did it not attempt to achieve!"

In particular, Mangum argued the incompatibility of the Exchequer Bill, with the powers it gave to the president, with the Old Republican doctrines Tyler professed to revere. The Southern Whigs had opposed both Jackson's pet banks and Van Buren's Independent Treasury because they united the "purse and the sword" under executive control. The Whigs preferred a bank under private control as less susceptible to government corruption. "One of the most striking things attending this project was that it should have originated in the Virginia school of politics; and that its supporters ... should be found in that quarter." Mangum professed his "deep veneration for the ancient dominion. No man entertained a higher respect for the principles she inscribed upon her banner in '98 and '99—a period in which she had resisted the vices of the age." Virginians then had opposed a national bank as unconstitutional. "But here there emanated from that ancient dominion a system in which all the banking faculties were fully developed; a monster, which might not merely act upon and influence the Government, but was fixed upon it as a part and parcel of the Government itself."

Asserting that the Exchequer joined financial power with the president's military power, Mangum declared that the bank in the Treasury's bill was "ultra, beyond any United States Bank that had ever been thought of." It conferred a "gigantic" power on the president. As he had done with Jackson's pet banks, Mangum associated the "money power" with presidential control of the banks. He ended his speech against the Exchequer Bill by uniting this idea with executive usurpation, corruption, and Tyler's infidelity to Old Republicanism. He declared that "next to the daring and presumptuous attempt at the subjugation of the people by the seducing influence of the money power," what most offended him in the Exchequer Bill was "the spirit of *base* and *vile* subserviency and flattery towards the President which every where marked its pages, and which presented the revolting spectacle of a gross and mercenary adulation, in the face and at the sacrifice of principle, nobly avowed and defended for twenty years!"

Mangum essentially accused Tyler of betraying his own principles. Mangum used Old Republican principles to oppose Tyler's bank; the Principles of '98 could not be used to defend a bank, but Mangum showed how they could be used to bring one down, just as Tyler used them to oppose the Whigs' bank. Tyler and Mangum were thus at odds over interpretation of Old Republican principles: Mangum was most concerned with executive power and corruption; Tyler with state sovereignty. And of course Mangum's emphasis allowed him room to accept National Republican ideas of a national bank. Mangum would use Old Republicanism to attack Tyler's plan and the popularity of the National Republican political economy to justify the Whigs' national bank. But Old Republican opposition to executive power stood as the Whigs' chief argument against Tyler. Mangum's speech settled the Carolina Whigs' rhetoric for the Clay campaign; they once again would emphasize the founding component of their ideology: opposition to executive power and corruption.

Many Whigs of North Carolina were pleased with this powerful opposition speech from their senior senator. Jeremiah Whedbee of Perquimons County pronounced his satisfaction with the speech, and Jeremiah Hatch of Granville County wrote to request a copy. S.H. Harris, a doctor from Clarksville, asked Mangum for a copy and reported, "I have heard only one opinion among those who have read it, and that is, that it was a speech of great power and brilliancy." After reading the copy of the speech Mangum sent him, Harris reported that he was "delighted" with it. "It is ornate, pungent, sarcastic, argumentative and every thing else that your friends could desire on such an occasion. Either its intrinsic merit or the occasion which called it forth has caused it to be more extensively read probably than any speech which has been delivered in Congress for some time."[65] The speech was also well received by Whigs across the country. The day after Mangum delivered it, Reverdy Johnson wrote from Baltimore, "accept my warmest thanks for your denunciation yesterday, of the vile Presidential ... plan of a fiscal agency." An attorney from Trenton, New Jersey requested a copy of the speech, as did a young army officer stationed in New York. Needless to say the *Standard* attacked the speech and Mangum's principles. But the *Hillsborough Recorder* defended and praised the speech's "perfect consistency, its sound doctrine, and its unanswerable arguments."[66] Mangum's Old Republican opposition to the bill (and Tyler) appears to have struck a chord with North Carolina Whigs.

The Whigs moved quickly to set up the convention called for by the Orange County Whigs. The convention was a pivotal moment for the North Carolina Whigs as they moved into the forefront of Whig states. The eagerness of the local party leaders to secure Clay's attendance at the convention attests to their confidence about his popularity in their counties and districts. Yet, the state's Whigs in Congress were more worried about protecting Clay's image; they counseled him to stay away lest he appear too eager for the presidency. The difference created a brief period of tension between the two groups of Whig leaders.

Leading Whigs, both in Washington and in North Carolina, agreed with the call of the Orange County Whigs for a convention. Even before the November meeting in Orange, Mangum's friend Charles P. Green was suggesting a convention in Raleigh for the spring of 1842: "My opinion is that we should hoist the Clay flag forthwith."[67] The congressional delegation wanted North Carolina to lead the nomination movement with a strong convention. Graham reported to his friend legislator James Bryan: "Our delegation here feel much anxiety that there should be a respectable turn out of our friends to the Convention at Raleigh in April. We have also suggested the propriety of at once nominating Clay for the Presidency." Reflecting the motives of the Orange County meeting Graham thought that it would be "an advantage to have a distinct flag up in the summer elections."[68] Graham wrote to Whigs in the state, particularly in the West, encouraging attendance at the state convention.[69]

Mangum agreed with his friends—the Carolina Whigs should nominate Clay in state convention and insist that Clay be the nominee of the national Whig Party. Having "thought much on the subject" and having had conversations with Whigs in Congress who concurred with his views, Mangum explained his concept of the purposes of the convention to Green: "I am clear, that the Convention ought to nominate Mr. Clay for the Presidency, *unconditionally*, & nail his flag to the mast." Mangum counseled no surrender to a Harrison-like movement as in 1840. "They ought to propose to go into a National Convention, *not to select any other Candidate*, but for the purpose of organizing to carry through his nomination, & *to select a Vice President*. We ought to go into the National Convention with *none* but our Clay friends," Mangum insisted. Mangum told Green that he had relayed these ideas to Raleigh Whig George Badger, the manager of the convention.[70]

Mangum wanted North Carolina, not New York, to be first to nominate Clay. And he wanted to ensure that Clay's nomination would emanate from local Whigs, not just Whig politicians in the state capitols. Correspondence with his political friends in New York had assured Mangum that the New York Whigs were ready to follow the North Carolina Whigs.

He relayed that impression to Green: "New York will instantly follow our lead.... I have urged, that No. Carolina ought to lead off." New Yorkers wanted to nominate Clay in Legislative caucus; Mangum wanted local Whigs to lead the movement: "I have strongly urged them to decline that," Mangum explained, "& to follow our nomination by 'Mass Meetings' as they call them, sweeping from Lake Frontier to the Atlantic border." Mangum believed that such nominations of Clay in the states "with zeal and enthusiasm" would provide the Whigs with "confidence & a resolution to triumph" in the 1842 summer elections.[71] Some Carolina Whigs in Congress still hesitated, though. Graham explained that the delegation was not unanimous: "Some of the delegation thought a nomination premature, and that it might be against us in the Summer elections, but a majority of us think differently."[72] Graham's own opinion agreed with Mangum's and reflected the sentiments of the meeting in Orange County: "My impression is, that we should at once throw [Tyler] overboard, cut loose from all responsibility for his administration and hoist the Clay flag."[73]

The locals Whigs acted on Mangum and Graham's advice for the convention but moved ahead of them in their enthusiasm for a visit from Clay. Party members in other counties followed the call of the Orange Whigs in support of the convention and called for Clay to accept his nomination in person. Green, who wanted Clay to attend the convention, seems to have authored a letter to the editor of the *Raleigh Register* proposing such a visit by Clay; he asked Mangum to pass the article to Clay.[74] A meeting of the Whigs of Wake County at Raleigh in February framed an invitation to Henry Clay to the convention. Proudly advising Clay that the Whig delegates to the convention would "assemble as the Representatives of the great Whig party of North Carolina," they also expressed their conviction that his presence at the convention would "inspire new ardour in the heart of every true Whig."[75] Meeting in early March 1842 to appoint delegates to the convention, the Whigs of Warren passed a set of declarations and resolutions criticizing the "disgraceful and reckless" course of the Van Buren administration. They called for a Bank of the United States as an "indispensable" measure and an amendment to the Constitution to remove the presidential veto power, and they pledged themselves "to spare no laudable exertions to re-establish and maintain Whig principles in the State and in the Nation." Stating their determination to rally in defense of "the great Whig party," the Warren Whigs declared for Clay and Morehead, resolving to "cheerfully raise the Flag of HENRY CLAY, of Kentucky" which they pledged to "stand by and defend it under all circumstances."[76] Their flattering letter of invitation to Clay seconded the invitation of the Whigs of Wake and expressed their "great delight" in inviting him to attend the April convention.[77]

Local Whigs urged the congressional delegation to accept their letters of invitation. Green reported on the Warren meeting to Mangum, "We had a glorious meeting yesterday & adopted the strongest kind of resolutions which you will see in the Register. A resolution passed inviting Mr. Clay to visit Raleigh on the 4th of April & [the committee] wrote him a letter today. I wish you to say to him that the letter is genuine & urge him to accept.'"[78] Shortly thereafter Green forwarded a letter from a committee of Granville County Whigs and urged the "necessity" of Clay's attendance at the state convention. The Granville committee declared that the Whigs of the state were prepared for "an enthusiastic rally" in Raleigh and that the leaders of the party would "gather there in thousands" if they could be assured of Clay's presence. Declaring that "our cause requires his presence," they entreated Mangum to "urge every consideration possible upon him. We all want him to come. The whole Whig party in this section—in all the counties around Raleigh—is looking anxiously for his response to the Committees of invitation."[79]

Although the county leaders anxiously awaited Clay's response and continued to ply the senators with queries, the delegation had decided that it would be unwise for Clay to travel to Raleigh and accept the nomination.[80] Clay had consulted the North Carolina congressional delegation as to whether he should attend the convention and they had advised against it. Though they thought it was "politic to nominate him at once for the Presidency," they believed it would be "indelicate" for him to be present at his nomination.[81] The delegation reached their decision with advice from other Whig leaders in the state. William Graham queried Whig leaders in the state about whether Clay should attend the convention. In response, Ralph Gorrell reported from Greensboro that he thought Clay should not attend and that his presence at the convention would not help the Whig cause ("in this opinion, hereabouts, our friends generally concur.") Gorrell reiterated that while all Whigs would be proud to have Clay visit North Carolina at a time when his visit would be advantageous to his candidacy and "our cause," that time was not now, but he approved of the nomination: "That he *ought* to be nominated by it I have as little doubt. Our Whig meetings throughout the State are nominating him … the party want some name to rally around."[82] Following the advice of the North Carolina delegation, Clay declined the invitations, but emphasized that his "wish, long entertained" of visiting North Carolina was only being postponed.[83]

The convention managers eventually reconsidered the wisdom of Clay's attendance and accepted as sound the reasoning of Mangum and the congressional delegation. Yet some discontent remained. Mangum expressed regret that the Raleigh Whigs felt dissatisfied with the decision of the Whig delegation advising Clay to postpone any visit to North Carolina.[84] After chairing the Granville committee that had asked Mangum to urge Clay to attend, H.W. Miller on the day before the convention apologized to Mangum for the "warmth" of his letters. "But I felt with many of our friends about here much disappointed." After seeing letters Mangum had written to George Badger about the decision, Miller became convinced that Mangum had "advised wisely" and "that we who were anxious Mr. Clay should attend the Convention were in the wrong.… We have all been convinced you were right." Miller then summarized the objectives of the Convention: to nominate Clay "with all possible éclat" ("He is our strong man here," Miller assured Mangum) and "cut loose" from Tyler, assigning his "soul, body, and principles (if he has any) to the Locofocos."[85]

"It seems to your Committee expedient, that some one should be selected as the Whig Candidate for the Presidency, who truly holds and will truly carry out, the great principles to which that Party stands pledged.… Such a man is HENRY CLAY of Kentucky," declared the published report of the Whig convention that met in Raleigh on April 4–5, 1842. It was attended by approximately 240 delegates representing the Whigs of thirty-five counties.[86] The convention offered these delegates an opportunity to make a policy statement for the party, and, most important, to declare that their party firmly backed Henry Clay. Significantly, George Badger, who felt personally betrayed by Tyler, assumed a leading role at the convention. Mangum planned to attend the Convention but his duties and press of business in the Senate prevented him being present. He wrote to Charity, "I had intended to be at the Convention at Raleigh but such has been the State of business here that it was impossible to leave."[87]

The first purpose of the convention was to indict Tyler and make clear to North Carolinians that the Whig Party had separated from the president. A report drawn up for the convention by Badger and Raleigh Whig Henry W. Miller[88] and endorsed by a select committee of thirty-five (one from each county represented at the convention) declared that Tyler's vetoes had shown that the president "if a Whig in profession, was not one in principle." It also accused him of an attempt at "absolute dictation to the Representatives of the States." In his key-note address, Badger excoriated Tyler as "faithless" to the party, possessed of "impracticable notions," and no longer a Whig "in principle, practice, or name." After praising Harrison and declaring loyalty to "the great Whig principles" of 1840, the resolutions adopted by the convention indicted John Tyler for his apostasy in failing to carry out those principles and accused him of "wooing" Democrats and adopting their measures. He was guilty of using "profligacy" in the distribution of government patronage to "buy up a party" and secure his reelection. They declared their complete separation from him:

> This Convention disavows all political connexion [sic] with and support of the said John Tyler; approves the proceedings and Address of the Whig Members of Congress at the close of the late Extra Session, and holds the Whig party discharged from all responsibility for the conduct of public affairs whilst controlled by the present Administration.

Other resolutions of the convention addressed Whig measures and called for distribution—the most popular Southern Whig measure.

The second and main purpose of the convention, of course, was to nominate Clay and the party's candidates. Declaring that Clay held "the first place in the affections of the whole Whig party of this State" the delegates nominated him to be the next President of the United States and urged "the Whig party of the Union" to unite with them in the nomination. They proclaimed their continued confidence in Morehead as governor, nominated him for reelection, and asked him to canvass the state to "promote the cause of truth and sound political principles." Morehead accepted his nomination in person.

The final aim of the convention was to organize the Whigs for the upcoming state elections for governor and the legislature. Badger called the plan for Whig organization "absolutely indispensable." The convention report recommended that the Whigs in every county hold meetings to appoint county and precinct committees "to collect and distribute information" and "visit the good people within their bounds, explain to them the nature, and enforce the truth and value of Whig principles." The report also called on the delegates to set up a Central Whig Committee "charged with the general superintendence of the Whig cause throughout the State." And the convention formally named the Central Committee "to represent the Whig Party of the state."[89]

The North Carolina Whigs thus led the way in the nomination of the man of Whig principles considered the party's favorite in their state and the nation. The convention left no doubt that the North Carolina Whig Party completely opposed Tyler and decidedly and enthusiastically favored Henry Clay for president as the candidate who would fulfill the promise of 1840 and conduct an administration on Whig principles.

If Raleigh Whig C. L. Hinton was typical of the Whig delegates in attendance, the Convention succeeded in inspiring the Whigs with enthusiasm. He delightedly reported to Mangum that, "the very mention of [Clay's] name appears to brighten the countenance of every member and inspire him with fresh and increased zeal." Hinton was convinced that the delegates would carry home "pleasing intelligence of a pleasant, harmonious meeting and *Union to a man*, having raised the Clay flag nailed it to the mast and sworn their hearts to rise of fall with it."[90]

The Whig press in North Carolina and across the country lauded the action of the convention. The *Raleigh Register* proclaimed, "It will be seen that North Carolina has led the way, and thrown the broad banner of Harry of the West to the breeze."[91] The *Richmond Whig* commented: "North Carolina has only led where the whole people will find it their true interest to follow. There is no State, which has a better right to make so important a movement … her voice will not be without its influence on her sister States." The *New York Courier* also approved, proclaiming, "The old North State has led off in a glorious cause … the cause of justice, of right, and of our country."[92] The Whigs in Congress also rejoiced over the convention's work. "The proceedings of the Raleigh Convention have been received by our friends here with great joy," Graham reported to James Bryan.[93]

All was not harmony, however. Even as C. P. Green reported Whig unity, he also pointed to some lingering resentment over Mangum's role in blocking Clay's personal acceptance of the nomination. He thought Mangum would be pleased that the convention "passed off so harmoniously.… Every Whig in the State is now convinced that it was the proper course to nominate *old Hal*," he reported, "and nearly all were glad that he did not attend, though some pretend to blame you for preventing his acceptance."[94] Governor Morehead, however, shared Mangum's view that it was important that the nomination be seen as an independent action of local Whigs. "I am extremely glad that Mr. Clay did not come," he told Graham, "that was my opinion from the first—that he should not do so. Now it is the movement of the people themselves." Morehead expressed pleasure that his campaign could now be part of Clay's campaign for the presidency: "I should like much to lead Clay triumphantly through the State, as we did Harrison.… I will do half the work this Campaign & leave the balance to my successor."[95]

Despite their optimism, the party leaders who had assembled in Raleigh for the nomination of Clay failed to inspire Whig partisans sufficiently to maintain control of the legislature in the contests of 1842. The Democrats captured the majority in the legislature, but the Whigs were successful in the state-wide election and re-elected Morehead governor. The Whig press blamed Whig apathy for the loss of the legislature.[96] With a majority in the legislature, the Democrats were positioned to elect a Democrat to replace Graham. The Democrats argued among themselves for a month before finally electing William Henry Haywood, Jr., to the Senate. The legislature also filled all state offices with Democrats. The Democrats used their majority to gerrymander the congressional districts, but otherwise passed little legislation, though a lengthy but inconclusive debate about the state banks took place. Whig editor Edward J. Hale of the *Fayetteville Observer* dubbed the legislature "The Terrapin Assembly" for passing few measures other than a prohibition on citizens from other states catching terrapins in Pamlico Sound.[97]

A Clay Whig as Vice-President: Mangum as President of the Senate

In June 1842 Mangum became Vice-President of the United States. He was elected president pro tem of the Senate and since there was no elected vice-president, Mangum's presidency of the Senate by the law then in effect made him next in line for the presidency. Letters to him often addressed him as Vice-President. Mangum's election by the Clay wing in the Senate showed that he was viewed as one of Clay's foremost allies and second only to Clay in leadership of the Senate. And not just of the Senate but the party as well. If Tyler should die in office, Mangum was the man that the Senate Whigs wished to succeed to the presidency—evidence of the trust in his leadership and confidence in his loyalty to Whig principles that his leadership in the 1841 special session had built. The post of president pro tem of the Senate made Mangum the leading Southern Whig and a national Whig leader. His election also recognized the success of the North Carolina Whigs in making their party one of the strongest in the country.

Nonetheless, this election came after considerable controversy. In June of 1842 the president pro tem of the Senate, Samuel Southard of New Jersey, had become gravely ill and was not expected to live. The Clay Whigs desired to elect one of their own in his place—a Whig president of the Senate to oppose the apostate president and further their cause against Tyler. "We resolved to press perseveringly to the end, a Clay Whig," Mangum explained to Clay. Crittenden of Kentucky and Mangum were the only candidates with sufficient support for a majority in the Whig caucus. When Crittenden declined nomination, Mangum received the nod from the Whig caucus. During the election in the Senate, some Clay Whigs were prepared to vote for Thomas Hart Benton, a Democrat who opposed Tyler, rather than see "one of the Conquered Tylerish *Clique*" elected by the Democrats and the Tyler Whigs. Richard Bayard was the preferred candidate of the Tyler men. As Mangum complained, "To elect Bayard, was to Consumate a Tyler triumph." Some senators attempted to move the question of whether the president pro tem should be from a slave holding state but the question was disallowed, a "no go" as Mangum reported. Even Mangum was concerned that his old friend Preston of South Carolina would vote along with the Tyler group and the Democrats for Bayard, but the South Carolinian along with twenty-five other Whigs present gave Mangum the majority.[98] The united votes of the Clay Whigs elected Mangum, and only the small Tyler minority joined the Democrats in opposition. Benton apparently intended to come to the aid of the Clay Whigs if it appeared Bayard might be elected. But the Clay Whigs mounted sufficient unity to make such aid unnecessary. Mangum declared himself proud to be chosen by the Whigs alone. "I very *much* desired, if elected at all, to be elected by Whig votes, exclusively," he reported to Clay.[99]

The Tyler administration reacted strongly to Mangum's election by heavily attacking him in its organ, the Washington *Madisonian*. In early June, Graham wrote to Priestly Mangum, "You have no doubt heard before this of the election of your brother as President of the Senate—It is quite galling to the occupants of the palace, and the Madisonian is out in great fury."[100] Henry Clay wrote to congratulate Mangum on his election and sarcastically noted that, "Your appointment must have given particular satisfaction at the White House."[101] Mangum replied, "The Wailing & gnashing of teeth at the White house was so ridiculous, as weak & excessive. It was an 'insult, personal insult' &C.&C.&C. The Madisonian every sunny morning, for a week, paid me especial respect."[102]

Although a few Whigs from Orange and Wake thought that Mangum's election as president pro tem drew him too far from North Carolina politics, the Carolina Whigs generally were proud of Mangum's election. The *Hillsborough Recorder* recognized the connection between Mangum's election and the strength of the state's Whig Party: "This selection may be regarded not only as a mark of the high estimation in which the talents and personal qualities of Mr. M. are held by members of the Senate, but as a tribute of respect to the firmness and fidelity of the old North State."[103] Hugh Waddell told William Graham, "I really thought the other day that we were going to be too big for our breeches when I saw yr name with a western gentleman as spoken of for the Presidency of the Senate & then saw Mangum actually receive it."[104] Charity proudly declared to Mangum, "Your Friends are all very well pleased.... I hope my husband will fill the station with honour and fidelity."[105]

With his elevation to President of the Senate and acting Vice-President, Mangum's correspondence became more national and even international. Unquestionably Whigs across the country now viewed him as a national Whig leader. He received letters from New York Whigs on tariff policy and on New York politics; he was invited to the city to consult on Whig policy. The Whigs of Petersburg, Virginia wanted Mangum to visit their city en route to Washington.[106] He received letters from persons in Europe seeking diplomatic appointments and letters of recommendation. As "President of the Senate," he received resolutions from state legislatures. During the campaign of 1844, Mangum received numerous invitations from Whigs in other states to attend party conventions and meetings. And his election as President of the Senate gave Mangum control of the patronage of that office, and he received many requests for appointments.[107]

Mangum's elevation did not free him from the Democrats' efforts to unseat him again by the use of instruction in 1842–43. That year the Democratic legislature passed resolutions of instruction in an effort once again to force his resignation. These resolutions opposed the Whig measures enacted in the 1841 and 1842 Congresses and instructed the senators to vote against them. Immediately following the adjournment of the legislature, its Whig members published an address to the people of North Carolina that set out the Whig position on all the actions of the legislature. Their position on the instructions to Mangum is of particular interest because it was their final considered position on the doctrine of legislative instruction to senators after a decade of contesting that issue with the Democrats.

The Democrats, the Whigs charged, were not "satisfied with one Senator ... the party took the only remaining means in its power to destroy the last vestige of Whig Representation in the Senate of the United States, by passing resolutions of instruction, with the sole view of driving from his seat our Whig Senator in Congress." The Whigs declared that senators were independent of the power that elected them. The senators and the legislature were coequal "servants of the people"—the senators in regard to federal powers and the legislature in regard to state powers. "The people," the Whigs asserted, "have never made the one set of servants, master of the other set; but do retain their mastery, *themselves*, unless it is expressly granted away." The senator's duty was to "conform his views, as nearly as he can, to the ... expressed views of the people." For that purpose the senator should "consult the most authentic evidences of the people's wishes." The senator should judge whether the legislature spoke for "the wishes of the people," but every legislature had "the right to express its views of federal policy, and to *advise* with, but not to *control* other servants of the people." The legislature should require obedience using instructions only when it was sure that it acted with "the will and wish of a majority of the people." Any legislature that instructed without such certainty would be "guilty of a palpable and obnoxious usurpation." The Whigs proclaimed that the Democratic legislature was guilty of acting without such sanction: "We hold, that the late Legislature possessed, from four gubernatorial elections, evidence, next to conclusive, that a majority of the people did neither will nor wish Mr. Mangum to abandon Whig principles or vacate his seat." The Whigs thus defined the state-wide gubernatorial election (and the presidential election), rather than the majority in the legislature, as the true indicator of the will of the people. Jackson used the legislatures against the Whig senators in the instruction confrontation of the 1830s citing their majorities as the will of the people, but the Whigs of North Carolina now appropriated Jackson's own definition of the will of the people in the Bank War—executive popular election. Mangum evidently concurred with the statement of his fellow Whigs; he did not resign.

As president of the Senate, Mangum was more than a North Carolina Whig senator. He was a leader of the national coalition of state Whig parties. He worked to maintain Whig unity through regional balance and a spirit of compromise. Two examples provide case studies of this leadership.

Mangum was involved in the consultations to select the vice-presidential candidate for Clay's 1844 campaign. Had Mangum not been from a slave state, he arguably might have been the vice-presidential nominee on the Whig ticket in 1844. His consultations with other national Whig leaders demonstrated that Mangum realized the need for regional balance to increase the chances for the party's success, but he also considered loyalty to Whig principles and strength in the party. Although Mangum knew that the northern state Whig parties would want to put one of their own on the ticket with Clay, he thought John M. Clayton from border slave state Delaware might be acceptable. If not Clayton, Mangum thought the nominee should come from Massachusetts, as the possible nominees from other states were either unreliable on Whig principles, weak in their own state parties, or unknown in the South and West. Of the last group, Mangum deemed Millard Fillmore from New York the strongest candidate because of his standing in New York, but feared that Fillmore lacked "firmness and decision for so high a station." Of the possible Massachusetts Whigs, Mangum was friendly to Governor John Davis, but worried that some anti-slavery remarks by Davis would make him unpopular in strong Southern Whig states such as Virginia, Georgia, and Tennessee upon which the Whigs relied and thought he was weak in the critical state of Pennsylvania. Mangum himself preferred the wealthy Boston merchant and textile manufacturer and former "Cotton-Whig" congressman, Abbott Lawrence. Mangum believed Lawrence would "run smoothly" and "by waving his Wand, the sinews of War [campaign money], would spring from the bowels of the earth. Those sinews so indispensable in the north & east." Even though Mangum doubted whether Lawrence possessed the "caliber" for the vice-presidency, he told Clayton, "in the event of the most disastrous contingency, I think the Country might expect from him a gentlemanly administration, surrounded by the talent and character of the Country—a thing so much needed for the last 10 or 15 years." In other words, Mangum was confident that Lawrence was no John Tyler.

Specific potential running mates aside, Mangum considered Clay's own strength the most important consideration: Because of Clay's popularity, the Whigs would not have to make their selection based on the weight of "slight differences" in the strengths of their possible vice-presidential nominees. They need only pick the candidate who would least hamper Clay. First and foremost the Whigs "must avoid placing unnecessary weight upon Clay." In sum, Mangum told Clayton, "It ought to be Lawrence or you, if the thing can be managed without giving sectional offence."[108] Clayton was prepared to follow Mangum's directions in the matter and stand aside if necessary.[109] For the most part, Mangum's Southern Whig correspondents shared his views about men and completely agreed with him that the vice-presidential nominee must be one who could be trusted to govern in accord with Whig principles.[110] Mangum also consulted with Whigs in New York about the best nominee.[111] Mangum's ideal vice-presidential candidate, then, was one who, like Clay, would be popular North and South and who adhered to Whig principles.

When anxieties about Southern Whig reaction to Tyler's Texas policy emerged,[112] Mangum demonstrated his concern for sectional compromise, party unity, and the Union. He then intervened to calm a possible rupture with the Whigs of the Boston area. His letter of April 1844 to William Hayden, co-publisher of the Boston *Daily Atlas*, soothed tensions with the Massachusetts Whigs and reassured them about the loyalty of the Southern Whigs to the national party. Hayden explained that Mangum's "kind, conciliatory and patriotic" letter relieved him "of a heavy pressure of anxiety" and was "entirely satisfactory, in regard to the feelings and intentions of our Southern & Western Whig friends in the Senate." Asserting that he had never doubted the Southern and Western Whigs, Hayden explained that he, prior to Mangum's reassuring letter, had had no means to satisfy Boston Whigs on the point. Indicating that the letter had helped "calm the public mind, upon the Texas and Tariff questions," Hayden reported that he had published an extract from it, and he thanked the North Carolina senator for "the kind and friendly tone of your letter—its deference to the feelings and views of the North, on these great questions—for the spirit of patriotism that pervades it." Appreciating Mangum's concern for the national Whig coalition, Hayden argued that the "acerbity" of debates on regional issues might be avoided "if leading men from the different sections would be governed by the same friendly, national feelings that are so well expressed in your letter." The other motive of Mangum's letter—to help ensure the continued loyalty of these New England Whigs to Clay—was apparently successful. Hayden reported, "The Whigs of our State are firmly attached to Mr. Clay.... I most sincerely hope, and confidently believe, that his election, and administration, will dispel many of these sectional controversies, restore the Country to its wonted state of quiet and repose, and realize all the hopes which we so confidently repose in the full prevalence of Whig principles."[113]

Mangum thus used his authority as president pro tem of the Senate and his standing among pro–Clay Whigs to calm possible divisions in the national Whig party. Mangum's election as president of the Senate thus confirmed his position as a national Whig leader and the equivalent of the Whig vice-president. Intimately involved in national party counsels, he appeared even more a party unifier than a Southern Whig.

The Tyler Party

The election for president of the Senate was one of the first clear indicators that Tyler had abandoned thoughts of wresting the Whig Party away from Clay and was instead attempting to form a third, or "Tyler," party. Aside from the conflict of such efforts with their party, the Whigs were offended by the implied goal of such a third party. Tyler's election in 1844 would violate a cardinal Whig principle: presidents should serve only a single four-year term. By forming his own third party, Tyler was seeking a "dynasty" like the Democrats Jackson and Van Buren.

As early as the battle over the bank bills in the 1841 special session, Mangum and Graham suspected Tyler of desiring a second term and using the bank issue to attract non–Clay Whigs like Webster to a Tyler Party. That June, Mangum sensed Tyler's ambition for election in his own right. "It is well understood that Mr. Tyler would have no invincible objection to an election by the People," he informed Duncan Cameron, "and it is equally well understood, that he and Mr. Webster will unite, if practicable, their fortunes for weal, or for woe."[114] By August, just before the first veto, Mangum was convinced. "[Tyler] is drunken with vanity," he declared to a Raleigh Whig, "and goes for the succession with all his heart."[115] Likewise, Graham early suspected Tyler and identified Tyler's possible political strategy. He informed an eastern Whig friend in June, "Suspicions are entertained that President Tyler designs to run for the succession and that he may break with the Whigs on [the Fiscal Bank of the United States] question, hoping to carry off a fraction of the party and unite with the Locos."[116] Graham thought that Tyler, despite his professions of no-partyism, might attempt to win the nomination of the Democratic Party. In Graham's view Tyler was still too much of a Whig for the Democrats to take him. Such a president without a party was "destined to have an irregular & hobbling administration" from which "the country will experience but little benefit."[117]

By the beginning of the 1841–1842 session, the Carolina Whigs were convinced that Tyler was using patronage appointments and nominations to build his own party—a Tyler Party. Graham complained that Tyler was refusing to remove Democrats and was nominating "personal favorites" for vacant offices, even some persons previously removed by Harrison.[118] Graham reported to James Bryan: "His nominations are made, with reference to his own popularity solely." Aided by Webster's influence with some senators, Tyler was appointing "loose Whigs … from whom he exacts fealty to him."[119] Already distrusted by Southern Whigs, especially former Calhoun states' rights men like Mangum, Webster attracted further disfavor by remaining in Tyler's cabinet and aiding the Whig apostate. The North Carolina senators thought that Webster was damaging the Whig party by working against Clay. "Tyler is more controlled by him [Webster] than by any member of his Cabinet, and will use all his official power to prevent the election of Clay," Graham observed.[120] Mangum, who never fully trusted Webster, was equally convinced of the latter's opposition to Clay. Despite united Whig support in the Senate for Webster's treaty settling the Maine boundary dispute and Webster's hope of it providing an avenue for reconciliation with the Clay Whigs, Mangum refused to be conciliated. In 1842 he was convinced that any power Webster could gain would be used "to crush or disband the Clay Whigs." Mangum fully backed Abbott Lawrence's anti–Webster seizure of the September 1842 Whig convention in Massachusetts and the nomination of Clay for the presidency and Massachusetts governor Davis for vice-president.[121] Webster's aid to Tyler convinced Mangum that Webster was an enemy to the Clay Whigs.[122]

By the summer of 1842, as Michael Holt explains, Tyler gave up on winning over moderates in the Whig Party and increasingly looked to building his own party from minority elements of both parties. His Tyler Party would be composed of state-rights Whigs, Southern Democrats, and anti–Van Buren northern Democrats. In his many cabinet reshufflings of 1842 and 1843, Tyler appointed Democrats, the only exceptions being Caleb Cushing and Thomas R. Gilmer. Federal patronage was Tyler's means to build his party. As Mangum and Graham noted, in the spring and summer of 1842 Tyler began removing Whigs from patronage posts and appointing Democrats in their place, a process that he accelerated in 1843 with his so-called "reign of terror" against Whig office holders across the country. "The loss of local appointive offices, as well as the frustration of the Whig program in Congress," Holt notes, "sapped the enthusiasm of state and local Whig organizations as they entered the campaigns of 1842 and 1843."[123] In a state so favorable to Clay as North Carolina, Tyler's attempts to build a new party were most likely to result in his loss of the state; surely Tyler was aware that his appointment policies would lose him such strong Southern Whig states as North Carolina, Louisiana, and Kentucky. To declare war on Clay Whigs was to concede North Carolina.

The Spoils of Victory

The political patronage that Tyler sought to deny the Whigs was especially important to the Whig leaders in North Carolina, where the Whig Party had become ascendant. With a Whig administration in Washington, the Whig congressional delegation had their first opportunity to dispense federal patronage to their partisans. Notwithstanding the anti-spoils rhetoric of the party, patronage posts were the expected fruits of the victory of 1840.

In the 1840s partisan politics and political patronage were linked to party operations and political loyalty; at the local level federal patronage was the measure of victory and the reward for political loyalty. The triumph of Whig principles was important to Whig leaders and Whig partisans, but victory in a presidential election was also important to local Whig partisans and congressmen because it meant the possibility of federal patronage. The comparatively high salaries of patronage posts alone accounted for the large number of office seekers for the roughly 18,000 offices in the federal government.[124]

But patronage was also immensely important to the workings of partisan politics. The Whig senators and congressmen were known to most North Carolinians only through their printed speeches or their appearances at campaign rallies. Patronage, as Michael Holt has pointed out, was the evidence of political victory. At most times it was the local federal office holders who personified the national government. "Thus it mattered greatly to Whigs that Democrats be turned out of local post offices and customs houses and good Whigs put in their place. To Whigs at the grass-roots level, only such changes proved the power of the popular will." Holt has also pointed out the importance of patronage for elected leaders and local party activists. Party leaders enhanced their prestige and secured political loyalty by securing offices for their friends. Committed Whig partisans "insisted that Democratic heads roll in order to keep up their élan, to allow them to boast and brag over their fallen foe.... What mattered to committed partisans was victory over the archrival, no matter what the context of that triumph."[125]

In the campaign of 1840, rhetoric against Van Buren's "army of office holders" was a consistent theme of Whig meetings in North Carolina. The Whigs of Davie County denounced the "degrading servility in those holding or expecting offices from the General Government unknown in the pure days of the Republic." The Whigs of Iredell County approved a resolution that mentioned "the most cringing and sycophantic servility to the President, by men in office or expecting office."[126] The "Republican Whigs" of Robeson County declared their condemnation of the Van Buren administration's supposed "avowal of the doctrine that to the victors belong the spoils of office."[127] In their "Unanimous Declaration," at the October 1840 state convention the North Carolina Whigs attacked the Democrats' "spoils" policy. The Democrats had "habitually conferred office as a reward for ... electioneering services" and they had

> converted the whole body of office-holders into mere dependants upon Executive favor; bound, not to serve the Country, but to maintain a party.... Professing boundless devotion to the will of the People ...

they have ... repeatedly rewarded with honors and emoluments, men whom the People have discarded from their service for incapacity and corruption.[128]

The anti-party/anti-spoils ideology of their party made Whigs cautious about demanding patronage as the reward for victory, and they usually placed their requests in the context of meritorious reward, an application to fill a vacant office, or the replacement for a corrupt, incompetent, or overly-partisan Democrat who had abused the office. Local Whigs nonetheless expected the spoils of victory.

Political patronage was inseparable from the operations of the North Carolina Whig Party. The large number of letters Mangum received in the early 1840s, especially before Tyler became estranged from the congressional Whigs, show that Whig politicos and partisans considered him as the senior North Carolina senator the major dispenser of federal patronage in the state. It was a key element of his political power. Party loyalists viewed patronage as a reward important to their livelihood and critical to their family fortunes and prospects: if the Whigs rose, so did their families; if the Whigs fell, so did their families. In the correspondence of Mangum and Graham during this period, applicants for federal patronage posts usually represented themselves as loyal Whig partisans seeking an office as a reward to support their families or as Whig leaders seeking to reward loyal partisans and symbolize victory over county or district foes. The position of postmaster, as the primary federal office at the county level, was the most coveted reward for political service; these were almost always political appointments. Most of the office seekers sought to remind the senators of friendship or some other personal connection. In the 1840s, politics remained personal; all the requests combined the personal with the political.

Many office seekers sought appointments to improve the circumstances of their family. The requests began even before Mangum and Graham took their seats in the Senate. Robert Ransom wrote Mangum from Warren County in December 1840 to request a West Point appointment for his son and a post for himself. "I am now forty years old," Ransom explained, "have a large family of promising children, two sons & three Daughters, the eldest son in his sixteenth year, the second in his twelfth, will be thirteen the 12th day of February, he is a fine healthy robust Boy, of *good mind*, who I wish to be Educated at West Point."[129] Ransom then informed the senator of his situation: "Some dozen years ago I went down, was stripped of my all, and left penniless & behind hand, with that burthen, and the support of my Wife & children, I have been tugging ever since to get up the Hill, and I now *advise* with *you* my *friend* in *person* & *Politicks*, if I had not better try *through you* to procure some office or appointment under the next administration, by which I shall be able to support & educate my children, and discharge the Dutys [sic] with honour to myself & family, & country." [Italics in original] Like a good Whig Ransom placed his request in terms of merit and party loyalty, in addition to the needs of his family. "If I had no Family, I would not impose myself on you, or the Departments. But as I have a promising one, and am desirous to promote them, and my only means, are my own hands. I most humbly, & respectfully, beg the favour of you to present me, in my naked garb, as you think my merits deserve. I am a true Republican of your faith, as ... my Recorded Votes for Govr. & President will shew."[130]

Reflecting Mangum's new importance in the national party, some patronage requests even crossed state boundaries. James Harvey, a mariner and shipmaster, wrote Mangum two letters from Baltimore that combined the personal with the political. Harvey explained that he had always been "faithfull to the Constitution and Laws of my country" and had "ever been devoted to the Whig cause." He had been "one of that little Band under Comodor [sic] Barney who served in the deffence [sic] of Washington and Baltimore in the United States service." Harvey explained that his family consisted of his ill wife, a son at sea, and two daughters "for whom I must provide and sorry I can not give them anything like an education[.]" Harvey desired a post as a customs house officer or a keeper of a light house. "It hase [sic] been generally acknowledged that such offices should be held by respectable ship masters," Harvey informed Mangum, "thow [sic] this has not been the practice of the present administration, but those who could make the most noise and ware [sic] very buisey [sic] at Elections generally got such appointments."[131] In his second letter Harvey again reminded Mangum of his impoverished circumstances and his deserving military service:

> I am now very poor through the failures of others and the various losses incident to a seafaring life.... If I have any claim on a free and grateful people for whom I have suffered much and served Honourabley in trying times last war.... I would humbly solicit your interest and influence to procure for me sum humble subordinate position in one of our Navy Yards the keeping a Light House or any office whare I could be useful and keep my little family from want.

Mangum endorsed the letter "Ansd. 16 June 41"[132] Politics and patronage was local: one can sense Harvey's rivalry with his Democratic competitors.

A letter Mangum received in his capacity as chairman of the Senate Naval Affairs Committee shows that the size of the government budget itself reflected Whig patronage; it also reveals the personal effect of Whig reform and economy. A "plain man" wrote to Mangum from New York under the assumed name of "Hoffman Whithouse" to urge the Whigs in Congress to reconsider their program of economy in government expenditures. Despite his "common education" that left him unaccustomed to writing letters to members of Congress, "Whithouse" assured Mangum that he was a friend of Henry Clay but thought that Whig policies overlooked the plight of the workingman. He called the Whig program of economy a "suicidal policy." He was most concerned about the policy's effect on the workers in the New York Navy Yard:

> [The Whig Congress] have reduced through professed feelings of economy the appropriations for the navy to nearly one half its actual wants. The consequence is that the Secty of the Navy has been compelled to give orders to the commanding officer on this station to discharge *all the working men* at the Brooklyn Navy Yard.... This too at a time when the labouring man with a large family depending upon him is unable to find other employment and are of consequence reduced to great misery and suffering.... I have [heard] their complaints loudly made against the present congress as taking the bread out of their mouths and in some instances compelling American born citizens to send their children to the county poor house.

Whithouse urged Mangum to increase the Navy appropriations and warned that "if something is not speedily done the friends of Henry Clay in congress will suffer by it." He appealed to Mangum to "take the matter in hand and relieve the poor." He signed the letter, "A TRUE WHIG."[133]

Many applicants sought posts for themselves or other loyal Whig partisans as a reward for political victory over local rivals or for loyalty to the Whig cause. Robert Bond, a physician and friend of Mangum's from Halifax, wrote to urge the appointment of Col. William Long as the superintendent of the U.S. Mint in Charlotte. Old political associates of Mangum, Bond and Long had been active Whigs since the first campaign. In March 1835, Long had been president and Bond vice-president of the assembly of "thoroughgoing State Rights men" that had hosted Mangum at an honorary dinner in Halifax. Long, in fact, had offered the toast that preceded Mangum's speech.[134] "The Col. Has laboured long and faithfully in the Whig cause," Bond reminded Mangum, "and more especially in the late Presidential canvass." A week later another of Long's friends from Halifax wrote to request he be appointed to a diplomatic post in Europe. "Although I do not hold the doctrine that 'to the victors belong the Spoils,'" he wrote, "Nevertheless it dose appire to me, that the Sacrificees which Col. Long has made in indevering to secure the assendancy of Whig principles, should to say nothing of his high qualifications, entiteal him to an Office of Some respectibility."[135]

Many Whigs sought to claim postmaster positions as reward for the party's victory and their own party loyalty. Addressing both Mangum and Graham, William Kerr requested from Coffeeville, Mississippi to request appointment as a postmaster: "[W]hat I would ask of you, is to get me the appointment of post-master at this place, as the present Incumbent is a strong Democrat (Mr. Rayburn) now that we whigs have come into office, I think we have Somewhat a claim to a Share of the *Spoils....*" Kerr also suspected the Democrat of tampering with the mails, and he complained that his letters were "undergoing a scrutinizing examination" before they reached him.[136] Another office-seeker, John Van Hook, an Alabama farmer and ploughmaker and "a known opposer of the Jackson & Van Buren Administrations," claimed to be "almost too old to plough" and asked Mangum for "a small office or appointment" under Harrison. Though he was no advocate of "the proscriptive policy," Van Hook expected that the Whigs would remove many officers who had opposed Harrison merely to retain their offices and "the spoils." And if the Whigs removed the deputy postmaster in Huntsville, or if he resigned, Van Hook wrote, "I would be glad to obtain the office, should you deem it honorable & proper for me to ask for it."[137] Whig ideology criticized Democrats for unrestrained use of patronage ("to the victor belong the spoils"), but this loyal Whig saw the reward of a postmaster's office as the visible evidence of Whig power. For these Whig partisans a postmaster's office was the measure of political victory.

Whig leaders in districts or counties often wrote to the Whig senators to obtain appointments for their political friends (and for themselves). Whig congressman Edward Stanly wrote Mangum from Washington, North Carolina to request an appointment in the Navy for the son of a friend, Col. Joshua Tayloe, "a whole souled, true Whig & noble hearted gentleman." Stanly wanted to help a friend, but he also wished to demonstrate to the people in his district that he could secure posts for loyal Whigs. He explained, "It would be a favor done to a most worthy gentleman, & agreeable to me, chiefly on his account, but also for the reason, that it would shew some folks, the Whigs can now & then help their friends, as bad as matters stand in Washington City."[138] John Poindexter, a Whig activist and state legislator, wrote to Graham (who apparently forwarded the letter to Mangum) on behalf of Peter Adams, who desired to be a special agent of the Post Office Department for the district encompassing North Carolina. "Until he informed me, I did not know that it was the practice of the Department to employ special agents," Poindexter explained. He praised Adams's character and business habits and noted that his appointment would gratify "the friends of Genl. Harrison" in the northern (mostly Democratic) counties. Poindexter deemed Adams "about the most suitable man for that station in my acquaintance." This was particularly the case because irregularities had occurred in the Stokes County postal service that required Adams' particular abilities. Adams was "just such a man as the department needs in our section of the State—for in Stokes County I am of opinion it is high time the conduct of some Van Buren Post masters was investigated, and I know of no man who would do it more effectually and correctly than Mr. Adams."[139]

The number of these requests was large. Mangum and Graham received many requests from North Carolina and other states for patronage posts. Graham complained of the volume and was somewhat overwhelmed. He told his wife Susan in February 1841, "I, and I suppose each member of Congress receive about two letter [sic] daily requesting, that if there be any thing agoing, in the way of office, that would suit the writer, to put in his claims." And later the same month, he noted: "The applicants for office are very numerous, and hundreds of letters daily arrive on the same subject."[140] The sheer number of requests the two senators received attests to the vital importance of political patronage to the ascendancy of the Whig Party in North Carolina (and the country).

Thus, the patronage that Tyler sought to deny the Clay Whigs was immensely important to the North Carolina party's ability to maintain its ascendancy in the state. Patronage was where the struggle over executive power reached the individual partisan, even the fortunes of his family. Not only the Whig leaders, then, but Whigs at all levels in the North Carolina party had a large interest in removing Tyler in favor of a true Whig.

The "BIG DAY": Clay's Visit to Raleigh

After the success of the 1842 Whig convention, Mangum became increasingly convinced that only Henry Clay could lead the Whig cause and told him: "You must keep yourself [well]; for everything interesting to thorough Whigs depends (an extent that I regret to see) upon your continued life and health. I regret it because a cause and the principle involved in it, ought to be able to succeed in many hands. Such I think is obviously not the Case." Mangum rightly believed that all Southern Whigs were rallying to Clay: "As far as I can judge, I think, the cause is constantly brightening: All eyes are turned in a single direction." All Whig eyes were now focused "upon the admitted head of the Whig party, with an intensity of interest, that I am very sure, has never happened before, in my time.[141] A month later, Mangum reported: "You have never seen the Whig party *so united* in firm phalanx as they are at present; and the tone is high." Since his recent election as president of the Senate had ratified his position as Clay's most important Southern Whig ally, Mangum was gushing with praise for Clay. The Carolina senator also was firmly convinced that Clay was the man around whom the party would rally as the embodiment of Whig principles. "I greatly misconceive the signs of the time," he assured Clay, "if *this day* shall not give the most unequivocal evidence of the rising, & aroused spirit of the people." Writing on the Fourth of July, he said:

> ... The spectacle of a great party Comprehending more than a moiety of our people, eminently intellectual & patriotic, bursting loose as one man from the man in power, scorning & treading upon, his patronage & bounties, & with, as it were, but one Will, & a fast fealty to their principles, rallying around the Farmer of Ashland, as the leader & best exponent of those principles, with scarce an eye in these multitudinous masses, looking towards any other, though others there be, many, eminent and patriotic![142]

Clay's April 1844 visit to Raleigh confirms that Mangum was correct about the Whigs rallying to Clay, at least in North Carolina. Whig Party leaders there were eager for Clay to visit the state as such a visit of the head of the Whig ticket would rally Whigs, provide stirring newspaper accounts, and potentially attract new voters to the Whig cause. Clay's visit to Raleigh was part of his tour of the South with the unannounced purpose of arraying Southern

Whigs behind his candidacy.[143] His visit to Raleigh was the centerpiece of the Whigs' 1844 campaign. It demonstrates the interaction of national and state politics that was so crucial to the Whig ascendancy in North Carolina.

As early as January 1843, Charles Green, who had eagerly sought a Clay visit to the 1842 convention, was asking Mangum, "What time will Mr. Clay like to visit this State?"[144] In June 1843, a committee representing the Whig caucus in the North Carolina Legislature officially invited Clay to visit North Carolina, reminding him of his promise to visit the state. The committee also emphasized that the North Carolina Whigs had been the first to place his name in nomination for the presidency. In his reply Clay declared that he had not abandoned his intention to visit North Carolina. He praised the state's party as the first to denounce Tyler, lauded the state's patriotism, and promised to visit in the spring of 1844.[145] By the fall Clay had nearly set a date for his visit. The Chairman of the Whig Central Committee received word from Clay that he intended to visit Raleigh in March 1844. "He expects to come from New Orleans by way of Charlestown," he reported to Mangum.[146]

Though Mangum was in Washington, he was involved in the preparation for the Clay visit. Graham, as the Whigs' gubernatorial nominee, also took part. Mangum urged his Whig friends in Orange County to meet Clay in Raleigh, and he asked Paul Cameron to speak to Badger in Raleigh about asking "the patriotic ladies of Raleigh" to offer a "splendid banner" to the county sending the largest delegation to the Clay rally in Raleigh. Mangum was confident that Clay's popularity would ensure that Whigs would turn out for the rally and make it a success: "I trust, indeed, I am sure, that the hospitalities & affectionate regards of the 'old North' towards her illustrious guest will be neither sparingly nor grudgingly tendered."[147] The New Hanover Clay Club elected William Graham an honorary member and invited him to join them in welcoming Clay in Wilmington. "It seems particularly meet, that the *favorite son of North Carolina* should welcome by his presence the landing of the *favorite son of the Union*, upon the shores of North Carolina," they wrote.[148] Graham accepted that invitation; fearing that Clay might be overtaxed by speaking engagements in Raleigh, he suggested to the Central Committee that they invite Crittenden, Morehead, Foster and Jarnagan to meet Clay in Raleigh for the primary purpose of scheduling his speaking agenda while in the city.[149]

As Mangum's suggestion for a banner award implied, delegations from many counties were expected at the Capitol for the event. Clay's visit to Raleigh was a celebratory event that combined the elements of a political mass meeting, a revival camp meeting, a grand banquet, and a holiday festival. The editor of the *Register* noted that camp grounds would be provided for what was expected to be a large assemblage: "We would suggest, therefore to our friends, the expediency of adopting to as great an extent as possible, the Log Cabin style of traveling, practiced in 1840, with baggage wagons, tents, &c. The necessary wood for cooking will be provided at the respective Camp-grounds, *free of charge*." When Gales learned the date of Clay's arrival in the city, he announced it to his expectant Whig readers as—"the BIG DAY."[150] The day before Clay's arrival, Gales triumphantly reported: "Already is our City crowded with strangers, from all parts of the State, and even from other States, brought here by a desire to see and hear HENRY CLAY."

Before Clay's arrival, prominent Whigs addressed "two or three thousand" persons already assembled on the Capitol grounds. When Clay arrived on Friday evening at 7 o'clock, he was met outside of town by "a countless throng" and welcomed by the official committee of reception. The committeemen and two militia companies, cavalry and infantry, escorted him to Governor Morehead's mansion. Gales styled the visit as a "Whig Jubilee" and projected an image of the event as a great rally of all the Whigs, from all walks of life:

> MR. CLAY'S VISIT. Ten thousand Whigs in Council! Ten thousand Whigs ... were here in Raleigh, as in 1840, with banners and badges, and other insignia of the Whig party to welcome *their* great leader, and the country's benefactor, HENRY CLAY.... North Carolina was represented by the flower of her population ... never yet did any State look out upon a nobler scene than the assembled thousands who listened to the great Speech of HENRY CLAY. From every County, from every Town, from every hill and valley, came forth her gallant and true-hearted sons, to swear anew their allegiance and fidelity to the unaltered and unalterable principles of the Whig party. The Planter ... the Mechanic ... the Lawyer ... the Merchant ... the Physician ... [came] up, one and all, to the grand Council of the State.

A prominent Virginia Whig attending the rally told Mangum that "Clay was in fine spirits, and in the best humour."[151] On Saturday morning a procession escorted Clay's carriage to the Capitol grounds where he addressed the assemblage of Whigs. B.W. Leigh thought that Clay's speech was "excellent," though not up to his standards in the Senate. "[A]s he was not excited by the collision of debate, he did not rise to any of *his* high flights of eloquence." Nonetheless, Leigh could not convince Whig friends who heard the speech that it was not one of Clay's best.[152] Clay addressed an audience that included both male and female. The *Register* specifically pointed out that Whig women were present at the speech to "adorn the scene" and lend their "sanction" to the proceedings. After his speech, Clay was presented with "a Silk Vest pattern" by "Miss Harris, of Granville." Clay's address was followed by a "plain, substantial" barbecue attended by "seven or eight thousand" diners. After the barbecue, more prominent Whigs gave political speeches and on Saturday night there was a display of fireworks and "two Balloons were sent up" under the direction of a "patriotic young Whig, William H. Tucker."[153] Clay told Mangum during his visit, "My reception at the Capital of your State has been cordial and enthusiastic, and attended by numbers, far surpassing my most sanguine anticipations."[154] Shortly after Clay's visit one of Mangum's friends from Granville County wrote him, "I was in Raleigh last week when Mr. Clay was there. Such an assemblage I never saw."[155]

As the account above makes clear, women participated in such celebratory Whig Party rallies. One prominent scholar of the politics of the early republic has argued that by the 1820s the focus of politics had shifted from out of doors to the "internal activities" of the party organizations, thus excluding women from participation in party events. Even if such a general shift occurred, the Clay celebration of 1844 shows that it was not the case among the Carolina Whigs. The rally was the major party event of the 1844 campaign and was decidedly "out of doors." Whigs used the tradition of such a celebratory political culture from the old Republican party in their campaigns. The entire event was characterized by a festive spirit, and Whig women attended the key event of the day: Clay's speech. And they were prominently featured in presentation of banners and the silk vest to Clay (a political act of endorsement). In fact, as earlier chapters indicated, women had been participating in Whig celebratory campaign events since its first campaign in 1835–1836.[156] Women were indeed excluded from the party's political meetings and "mass meetings" where delegates were selected and resolutions were passed, but they participated in all the celebratory events designed to raise party spirits and enthusiasm. Whig politics in North Carolina were conducted in two realms: the private, indoors realm of political meetings and party caucuses where votes occurred, and the public, out of doors realm of celebrations and party rallies. It is the Whigs' continued use of "celebratory" politics that allowed for women's participation. Whig women were integral to the public realm of Whig politics.[157]

Clay's speech at the Raleigh Whig "jubilee" was a major address in his campaign (though, of course, as presidential candidates did not campaign in the 1840s, this was only a "tour"). The *Raleigh Register* took notes on the speech and sent them to Clay for his revision for publication. The speech was thus meant as a campaign document and was published in pamphlet form, in addition to its reprinting in other newspapers. He combined Old Republican and National Republican themes: opposition to executive power, national unity, and Whig measures. "My opinions upon great and leading measures of public policy, have become settled convictions, and I am a Whig because that party seeks the establishment of those measures," Clay explained. The one prominent difference between the two parties, Clay asserted, was "the respect and deference uniformly displayed by the one, and the disregard and contempt exhibited by the other to the constitution, to the laws and to public authority." In contrast to the "destructive and disorganizing tendency of the character, tendency and principles of the Democratic party," Clay emphasized the party unity—"entire concurrence as to the principles and measures of public policy"—the Whigs had achieved, even including assent to "the justice and expediency of the principle of a tariff for revenue, with discriminations for protection"— the old divisive issue of the 1830s.

Clay also spoke to the importance of regional unity and declared it a principle of the Whig Party that facilitated its measures. In decisions on national measures, he insisted, "the interests of the whole Union, as well as all its parts" should be considered "in a paternal and fraternal spirit." No one state or section, he declared, could reasonably expect or desire that the general government should be administered "exclusively according to its own particular interests" without regard to the interests of the other sections. According to Clay such unity could achieve Whig measures such as the "necessity for a United States Bank," the need for "a National Army, a National Navy, a National Post office establishment, National Laws regulating our foreign commerce and our coasting trade," and above all "a National Currency"— essentially the components of his "American System." The Whigs stood for national unity through compromise. Clay denied that compromise and reconciliation were impossible. The United States embodied "the hopes of the world." "The Union must be preserved," he averred.

Clay then turned to executive usurpation of power. Clay declared the Whigs' belief that during the Jackson, Van Buren, and Tyler administrations executive power had been "intolerably abused"; had "disturbed the balances of the Constitution"; and, by its encroachments upon the other branches of the government, had become "alarming and dangerous." The Whigs are therefore desired to "restrain it within constitutional and proper limits." Linking the Whigs' struggle against Jackson, Van Buren, and Tyler to the struggle of the Republicans in 1798–1799, Clay called for the Whigs to follow the course of Jefferson, Macon, and the Old Republicans:

> The Democrats or Republicans of 1798–'9, taught by the fatal example of all history, were jealous and distrustful of Executive power. It was of that department that their fears were excited, and against that their vigilance was directed.... And the Whigs are now in the exact position of the Republicans of 1798–'9.

Clay concluded his speech by predicting that the scenes of "the memorable event of 1840" were going to be "renewed and re-enacted." Clay ridiculed Democrats' complaints that the Whigs' festive and enthusiastic campaign style and their "popular meetings and processions, to the display of banners, the use of log cabins, [and] the Whig songs" had won the election.

"How greatly do they deceive themselves!... All these were the mere jokes of the campaign," Clay claimed. Implying that Whig victory lay on the horizon, Clay asserted that the Whigs won in 1840 not because of their tactics but "by a strong, deep, and general conviction pervading all classes, and impressed by a dear bought experience, that a change of both measures and men was indispensable to the welfare of the country. It was a great and irresistible movement of the people."[158]

Clay's speech seemed designed to appeal to Southern Whigs assembled in Raleigh. Perfectly tuned for the Carolina Whigs, it united National Republican measures, Old Republican opposition to executive usurpation and corruption, and Whig insistence on adherence to the Constitution and the law; and emphasized an overall theme of national unity. The speech thus contained all the ideological elements that were at the center of the Carolina Whigs' ascendancy in the state. Clay's visit was the major campaign event of the Whigs' 1844 campaign. At least in Raleigh, Clay's southern tour was a great success as the Carolina Whigs gathered in Raleigh enthusiastically welcomed him. The rally in Raleigh was probably the grandest celebratory event the North Carolina Whigs ever staged, and it represented the party at the apogee of its ascendancy.

The Clay visit was a success for the North Carolina Whig Party. The Whigs decisively reestablished their ascendancy in the state in the summer elections for governor and the legislature. Graham was elected governor and the Whigs won majorities in both houses of the legislature—by two in the senate and fourteen in the commons. This was a significant turnaround. In the previous legislature the Democrats had had a majority of 30 on joint ballot. Graham's winning margin in the gubernatorial election was 7,859 of the 79,113 votes cast.[159] For the first time since 1840 the Whigs completely controlled the state government.

Ecstatic, the Whig press pointed out the larger, national significance of this triumph. "*North Carolina is Whig to the core!*" the *Register* proclaimed, and in its next issue declared, "NORTH CAROLINA REDEEMED!!!" "Loco Focoism is prostrate in North Carolina," Gales assured his fellow Whigs. The paper asserted that the election results represented "the triumph of Whig principles" and triumphantly asked, "what is it that the gallant Whigs of North Carolina cannot accomplish—*will* not accomplish—for Henry Clay and his principles?" As North Carolina had been the first state to nominate Clay, it was important for the national Whig coalition that the states' Whigs deliver a victory: "The value of this victory to the Whig cause, throughout the Union, cannot be estimated.—Had North Carolina gone for the Loco Focos, we verily believe it would have inflicted a blow upon Whig principles which, with all their recuperative energy, it would have taken them years to recover."[160] The Whig victory was thus seen as important for the national Whig Party and a Democratic victory would have indicated that Clay could not win in the Middle South. P.C. Cameron summed up the Whigs' enthusiasm when he wrote to Mangum, "As in 1840, the old North stands first, foremost, and freest!"[161]

The Whigs hoped the summer victory presaged a Clay victory in the state's fall presidential election. The themes and ideology emphasized by the Central Committee in the fall campaign were in line with Clay's Raleigh speech. A message that the Central Committee placed in the Whig press shows the ideological unity of the Whigs in 1843–1844; it notes that the state election had been fought and won on the great measures of the Whig party. The central committee's address "To the Whigs of North Carolina" also shows the connection between national and state elections: state elections held national significance because they tested the strength of the national party. After congratulating the Whigs on their recent victory in the state, the address drew sharp contrasts between the opposing parties, declaring that in the election the Whig candidates throughout the State, "openly avowed the great measures of the Whig party": a tariff for revenue, with incidental protection to American industry; the distribution of the proceeds of the sales of the public lands among the states; a national bank; and "the one term principle." The conduct of the Democrats, the committee claimed, had been the opposite of the Whigs: "The immediate annexation of Texas, is the only affirmative proposition, which they have supported. In all else, they have but opposed the doctrines of the Whigs."

The Central Committee called for thorough party organization and urged the Whigs to be diligent come November: "to be, every man, at the Polls on that day." The committee reminded the Whigs that victory alone was not enough. Because they were the first to nominate Clay, the Carolina Whigs had the duty to ensure that "no State shall exceed us in the vote by which we shall declare for Clay and our Country"; the victory must be "worthy of our principles" and "worthy of our great leader."[162]

In October Gales reminded the Whigs of the issues in the presidential election. Asking Whigs to "Remember that HENRY CLAY is your candidate," he reviewed the combination of National Republican and Old Republican themes at the foundation of the Whigs' ascendancy in the state: "a sound, well regulated, National Currency," "a fair and just protection to *American* Industry," "an equitable division of the proceeds of the Public Lands, among all the States," "one Presidential Term," "restricting the Veto power to a proper limit," "a strict accountability among Public Officers," and "reducing the expenses of Government, to the *lowest* practicable point," and Whigs should "remember *all the time*, that [Clay] is in favor of the UNION!" And he added a reminder that Clay favored the protection of slavery without the annexation of Texas: "And, never forget that he prefers our union, *as it is*, to all other Governments under the Sun!"[163] The campaign of 1844 was contested on Whig principles and Whig measures.

The Central Committee's emphasis on these themes proved a successful formula for the state's presidential election. The enthusiasm of the Clay visit was confirmed. The Whigs won a victory for Clay and confirmed that North Carolina was a Clay state. Clay received 32,939 votes to 29,549 votes cast for Polk in the state, but Polk narrowly defeated Clay nationally.[164] Clay, as the embodiment of Whig principles, remained popular with a majority of North Carolinians. Twenty-six counties were strong or solidly Whig counties where both Graham and Clay received twice as many or more than 100 votes, respectively, than Hoke and Polk. As it had for a decade, the strength of the Whigs lay in the West and the Piedmont counties.[165] In 1844 the Whigs ran firmly in opposition to Tyler and his policies; the Texas issue did not work for the Democrats in North Carolina. Despite Clay's loss nationally, North Carolina firmly established itself as a Whig Party bastion in the national coalition.

Whigs in North Carolina were disappointed in Clay's narrow loss nationally. Yet, in no sense did they feel beaten. The Carolina Whigs took courage in the fact that they were ascendant in North Carolina and other states across the Union (Clay won in Vermont, Massachusetts, Rhode Island, Connecticut, New Jersey, Delaware, Maryland, Ohio, Kentucky, and Tennessee, in addition to North Carolina; he narrowly lost Louisiana) and that they would control a slim majority (27–25) in the U.S. Senate. The Central Committee continued to stand by Whig principles and the spirit of the party. Gales wrote in the *Register* that the Whig cause was "just" and that Whig principles were "those of the Constitution" and would "console

[Whigs] in adversity, and will prompt them to never ceasing exertions."[166] The Whigs took special pleasure in noting that they had triumphed in Tennessee, Polk's home state.[167]

Despite their disappointment in the national results, the North Carolina Whig leaders remained proud of their party and defiant toward the Democrats. Though the Democrats had proven themselves to be the nation's majority party, Graham explained to fellow Whig James Bryan that he remained a Clay Whig, determined to support the Whig party and its principles. He argued the Whig Party was the only check to the Democrats' radicalism: "Although I shall probably never see a candidate for the Chief Magistracy for whom I shall have as great a personal admiration as I entertain for Mr. Clay, yet I deem the conservative character of the Whig party so essential to the preservation of our institutions, that I should deeply regret its dissolution. Even though unsuccessful, the sense of its vigilance and the rectitude of its principles are a powerful check to the downward course of Locofoco-ism."[168] And Edward Stanley wrote in a defiant mood to Mangum that "the Whigs are still unconquered & feel unconquerable: though heart stricken for our country & our glorious 'old chief'— dearer to us now than if he had been successful.—We shall have a meeting & pass some resolutions in testimony of our high regard … for Mr. Clay."[169] In a second letter, Stanly, then serving in the state legislature, indicated a "disinclination on the part of our political friends to pass political resolutions" because the Whigs did not have majorities in both houses of the legislature. Stanly thought otherwise: "we ought to give 'line upon line & precept upon precept': to let the people understand that Whig principles still exist."[170]

The Carolina Whigs achieved complete ideological and organizational unity with Clay, the embodiment of Whig principles, as the symbolic head of the party and Mangum and Graham as the bridge between the national party and the state party. That unity was critical to the maintenance of the party's ascendancy after setbacks resulting from Tyler's blockage of critical pieces of the Whigs' national financial program. The Whig principle of opposition to executive power, now deployed against Tyler and his efforts to form a third party, facilitated this unity. Yet, the union of Old Republicanism and the National Republican measures of Clay continued to be the foundation of the party's ascendancy in North Carolina. Clay was the perfect symbol of opposition to Presidential power. The party's rhetoric and campaigns were most effective when it projected itself as the opponent of the national executive and the defender of Whig principles and measures against Democratic corruption. And the party's quick recovery after electoral setbacks during the struggle in Washington with Tyler demonstrated how powerful the Whig ideology of opposition could be when the party was unified behind a candidate who embodied its principles.

The apparent disaster of Tyler's apostasy thus actually facilitated the unity of the Whig party in North Carolina. Mangum's rapid move to separate the party from Tyler, place it firmly behind Clay and Whig principles, and emphasize its opposition to the apostate President's claims for executive power allowed the party to quickly recover after the electoral defeats of 1841 and 1842 and maintain its ascendancy in the state. As the statement of the Whig Party at the 1842 convention, Clay's speech at the 1844 rally in Raleigh, and the fall address of the Central Committee all show, the Carolina Whigs contested the campaign of 1844 on the combination of Old Republican and National Republican themes that had been the foundation of their success since 1840.

The Whig ascendancy in North Carolina made the state vital to the national Whig coalition. Mangum's position as leader of the national Whig party reflected the state's importance.

As a proven bastion of Whig power in national politics, the course of Whig politics in North Carolina became increasingly important in the remainder of the decade. After the success of Whig unity achieved under Clay's banner in 1844, the North Carolina Whigs experienced challenges resulting from personal and regional rivalries, increasing factionalism, and the failure to find a candidate both trusted by Southern Whigs and professing true Whig principles. They would also be challenged by a new Democratic revolution in the state and the impact of the northern Free Soil Party on the national Whig coalition.

7

The End of the Whig Ascendancy

"The Whigs are at ease, they are quiet, cherishing no excessive feeling, but as a mass devoted to the principles of their Cause," Willie Mangum reported to friend in Morganton, North Carolina, in February 1845 just before the Senate was to vote on the annexation of Texas and just weeks before his time as president of the Senate was to end with the close of the Twenty-Eighth Congress.[1] Having disapproved Tyler's treaty of annexation on Texas by denying him the constitutionally required two-thirds, Mangum and the Senate Whigs would soon see a foreign country annexed to the United States by the novel procedure of a majority vote of Congress. The Whigs were no doubt devoted to the principles of their cause, but their party, having just suffered the severe blow of their failure to elect Clay, was now about to suffer the additional blow of the annexation of Texas. That act—so long sought by Tyler and championed by the new president, Polk—would have far-reaching consequences for the Whig Party.

As Mangum assessed the state of the Whigs in Washington in January 1845, he found them sensible of their defeat but still sure their party could yet prevail. "Our Whig friends are somber & melancholy, but in no wise, dispirited in regard to the future," Mangum told his wife, "Mr. Clay writes me that he and his family are well, & that he bears with quiet & resignation the unexpected result."[2] Mangum used his power as president pro tem to help raise Whig spirits by directing Senate investigations into voting irregularities. Mangum corresponded with D. Francis Bacon, editor of the Whig paper *New York Daybook*, who was investigating frauds in New York City and he conferred with Kentucky Senator John Crittenden on the Senate's investigation. Mangum felt it had "weight, magnitude, & real importance." Holding that a commission should be appointed to investigate the "portentous frauds," Mangum deemed the enquiry was "within the Constitutional Competency & proper functions of the Senate." Since many rank-and-file Whigs were angry at the frauds they believed had cost Clay the election, the Whig leaders designed it as a partisan investigation to boost Whig spirits. Mangum thought the revelations would be "of very great importance" and would "brace the Whigs to renewed & more desperately energetic efforts." The Senate Judiciary Committee appointed commissioners to investigate the frauds. Little came of it; the investigation was merely a palliative to sooth Whig spirits.[3]

In North Carolina, a rivalry between Mangum and another Old Whig stalwart, George Badger, threatened the unity of the Whig Party. At the same time regional rivalries emerged, particularly against the control of the party by the "Raleigh Clique." Both the state divisions and the national divisions would weaken loyalty to traditional Whig principles. And the Whig ascendancy in North Carolina was threatened by a resurgent Democratic Party with new ideas. The period began with Mangum at the head of a unified Whig Party; at its end the Whig party was divided and Mangum and the old Whig stalwarts had been set aside. As Mangum's assessment in early 1845 indicated, few Whigs could have imagined the severity of the challenges they were to face and the strains it would put on the party.

Rising divisions among the Whigs in North Carolina were nearly as great a danger to the state party as the political defeats in Washington were to Mangum's Senate Whigs and the national party. The defeat of James Graham by fellow Whig Thomas Clingman in the 1843 election for Congress in the Mountain District, one of the strongest Whig districts in the state, seemed an isolated event, but it was just the beginning of the intra-party rivalries of the coming years. Despite his bitterness, James Graham foresaw the danger to the Whigs: "Many of our substantial and influential Whigs have seen so much selfishness and personal advancement in the conduct of those who claim to be leaders in the party that they are disgusted and discouraged.... I regard the Whig cause in N.C. as in imminent danger from the general apathy and personal jelousies [sic] in this District among those who aspire to fill high stations."[4] Graham was wrong about apathy among the district's Whigs, but his prediction of danger to the Whig Party was justified. Whig unity had been critical to the successes of 1840 and 1844. At mid-decade, divisions among the Whigs jeopardized the ascendancy they had won.

Mangum and most of the Raleigh Whig leadership had opposed Clingman's challenge to Graham, and Mangum expressed "deep regret" at Grahams defeat.[5] Clingman soon became the ardent champion of the Whig party and its principles in Congress—a rising Whig star. Yet Clingman himself soon became a source of disruption in the Whig Party. Although none of the Whigs realized it at the time, the division in the Mountain District between Whigs James Graham and Thomas Lanier Clingman was only one of many that followed in the wake of Whig success. The rift between Graham and Clingman was also one of the most bitter, long-lasting, and damaging. James Graham had insisted that his opposition consisted only of Democrats, "ultra whigs," and those "who always desire a change." He did not seem to realize the unpopularity of his vote against distribution.[6] It was an "ultra" Whig that the people of his district wanted—they chose Thomas Lanier Clingman. The division between "ultra" Whigs—those who strongly advocated all the Whig principles and pressed for the implementation of Whig measures—and more moderate Whigs—who, like Graham, opposed aspects of the Whig program and sought less confrontation, and even cooperation, with Democrats—was to be the chief source of division.

These Whig divisions and the resulting loss of Whig unity combined with a resurgent Democratic Party to end the Whig ascendancy in North Carolina. Mangum was involved in the challenges to Whig unity at both the national and state level. Anti–Van Burenism had been one of the greatest unifying factors in the Whig Party coalition ever since the first rumblings of an opposition Anti–Van Buren Party in 1832. In 1844, the North Carolina Whigs lost Van Buren as a unifying foil and had to deal with the populist agitation of Polk's continental expansion and, later, a nominally Whig president who wished to replace the party with a non-partisan organization based on his own fame. All of this occurred in the midst of growing disunity in the national party over slavery in the territories. Southern Whigs temporarily were able to overcome some of their problems on the national level with a popular policy focused on sectional compromise and the Union.

Whig High Tide in North Carolina and the Whig Feud in the West

The period of William Graham's governorship (1845–1848) was the Whig high tide in North Carolina. In his 1845 inaugural address Graham called for an extended system of internal improvements. With an evenly divided state senate and a majority of only twenty in the lower house, the Whigs could do little to implement their state measures; and few Whigs in the legislature had any inclination to press internal improvements or public education. The Whigs rhetorically supported the system of common schools. In 1846 Governor Graham called for greater "intelligence, uniformity, and efficiency" in the execution of the School Law and the appointment of a commissioner to superintend the common schools. But the legislature took little action. The Whigs, though, were pleased with Graham as their standard-bearer.

Declaring their "full confidence" in his "integrity, ability, and devoted patriotism," the 1846 Whig state convention re-nominated Graham for a second term and asked him to canvass the state.[7] In an indication of his popularity with the Carolina Whigs, Graham was reelected by a decisive margin, defeating James Shepard of Raleigh, his Democratic opponent, by a majority of 7,859 votes. This margin was an increase of more than 4,700 votes over 1844.[8] The Whigs also retained control of the legislature, winning a majority in both branches of the legislature—by two in the senate and fourteen in the commons. Graham and the Whig platform of internal improvements, the tariff, and distribution had proved popular.[9]

The Whigs, though, again failed to act on a state program despite their increased majority in the legislature and Graham's decisive victory. Their inaction during this period reflected their opposition ideology and their composition: one-half of the Whig coalition was, like Mangum, Old Republican in background. As a historian of the Whig Party in North Carolina has pointed out, the extremely conservative position of the Democrats on issues of political economy made it possible for the Whigs to maintain their ascendancy without pressing their program.[10] But the influence of the Old Republican ideology was a greater cause of inaction. The opposition ideology of the Whigs was better suited to oppose Democrats than to convince public opinion to support a positive government program. And Mangum, the greatest spokesman of the North Carolina Whigs, was always more focused on national issues where he could oppose a Democratic administration. Mangum would not have opposed a state program, but he and his Old Republican Whigs had little inclination to back one actively.

Even as the Whigs reached the height of their popularity with Graham's resounding reelection victory, divisions had already emerged in the Whig ranks and in the bastion of Whig voting strength—the western counties.

James Graham's defeat by Clingman in 1843 did not end the division in the West. In 1845, Graham and Clingman again confronted each other and once again divided the Whigs; this time, though, Clingman's bold championship of Whig principles in Congress had made him more popular with the state's Whig leaders, and almost all of them favored his reelection. In early 1845, Mangum held a high opinion of Clingman. "He is a fine, bold, decided & talented fellow of great use to us here," he told a friend from Clingman's district.[11] Apparently, when James Graham's Whig friends discovered that most Democrats in the district would vote for Graham to remove Clingman—who had become a Whig star in Washington—they persuaded Graham to revenge his defeat of 1843.[12] In July 1845, shortly after returning from a trip to Louisiana and on the persistent urging of these "old Whig friends," Graham suddenly decided to enter the August contest in opposition to Clingman.[13] The Whig leadership at Raleigh had already expressed support for Clingman's reelection. The *Raleigh Register* declared that "there is a general and very natural wish not only among the Whigs of this State, but among the Whigs of the Union, that Mr. Clingman should again be returned."[14] After Graham declared his intention to challenge Clingman, the Whig leadership, other than Governor Graham, continued to favor their rising star, Clingman, and the Raleigh Whig press continued to back Clingman as well. Graham ran against Clingman chiefly on Southern issues with appeal to Democrats: Clingman's vote against the gag rule, suppressing discussion of anti-slavery petitions in the House, and his vote against the annexation of Texas.[15]

Relying on the united vote of the district's Democrats and a minority of dissident Whig supporters, Graham narrowly defeated Clingman. Among more than ten thousand voters who went to the polls, Graham's vote topped Clingman's by 326 votes. While Clingman received three-quarters of the Whig vote, Graham received approximately 3,600 votes from Democrats added to about 1,600 Whig votes. A correspondent to the Democratic *North Carolina Standard* commented that the Democrats of the district had rallied "almost in solid column" to Graham.[16] The bitterness between the Graham brothers and Clingman continued after the election, and Clingman tried to convince Mangum that William Graham had been damaged in the district by his brother's reliance on the Democrats. In the fall, Clingman told Mangum that many of the district's "best whigs" refused to support William Graham's renomination. James Graham was viewed by three-quarters of the Whigs in the district "in no better light than John Tyler himself." He implied that the "fishy whigs" who had supported Hoke in 1844 and by implication who had helped elect James Graham would not vote for William Graham for governor.[17] In an October 1845 meeting in the Mountain District led by Clingman, the assembled Whigs gave a lukewarm endorsement to William Graham's renomination for governor.[18] The Grahams and their friends bore an equal ill-will to Clingman and sought evidences of his supposed disloyalty to the party. They complained that the October 1845 meeting exhibited a spirit of opposition to William Graham.[19]

The division among Whigs in the Mountain District, however, had implications that went beyond just personal rivalry and bitterness. Graham told his brother that "there was a deep and abiding dissatisfaction among the people with regard to Clingman's course."[20] Yet Governor Graham surely knew that the Whigs of the state and the district preferred Clingman and that the dissatisfaction was among the Democrats. Graham had relied to a far greater extent than Clingman had in 1843 on the districts Democrats to defeat a fellow Whig. And in 1845, James Graham had specifically campaigned in opposition to "ultra" Whiggery. In an effort to revenge his defeat by Clingman in 1843 he cast aside loyalty to the national Whig party. Graham presaged the willingness by nominal Whigs in the environment of Whig ascendancy to cast aside ardent defense of Whig principles to gain office and an election victory. Still the Democrats held a balance of power there if Whigs divided.

State-wide in the 1845 elections, the Whigs won only two other districts, a decline of one from the 1843 delegation's four Whigs and five Democrats. The Whigs' poor showing probably more reflected the depression of Whig spirits after Clay's defeat and the effective reorganization of the districts by the Democrats in the 1842 legislature than a decline in the popularity of the Whig Party. But the defeat of so zealous a Whig as Clingman by Democratic voters in the Whigs' stronghold district did not bode well for the continued ascendancy of the Whig Party.

Opposition to Manifest Destiny: Mangum Against Polk

The Whigs had suffered apostasy at the highest level, yet in many states, like North Carolina, they remained strong and Clay's candidacy was unifying. Texas and Oregon gave Polk and the Democrats a powerful appeal to contest Clay's popularity with Whigs. The Democrats' commitment to continental expansion associated their party with the Jeffersonian ideal of the republican empire; Polk's election was proof of its continuing ideological power forty years after the Louisiana Purchase.

Though it came too late and Tyler was a flawed party leader, he found with the annexation of Texas an ideal issue on which to form the Tyler Party. Of all the issues on which he tried to form his own party, Texas was the most effective. Territorial expansion was Jeffersonian, and the Old Republicans like Macon had approved of the Louisiana Purchase. Tyler could also capture Southern Democrats on the issue of slavery expansion. And by raising the issue of slavery in the territories, an issue the Whigs wished to avoid, Tyler also made life difficult for his Whig opponents.

The Whigs in the Senate resisted Tyler's drive to annex Texas by rejecting the treaty of annexation. Tyler attempted to override the Senate (and the Constitution) with a joint resolution of Congress, which needed only a majority vote and declared Texas annexed to the United States. Texas was ostensibly an independent foreign country, and relations between countries are conducted through treaties. Most Whigs viewed annexation by joint resolution as unconstitutional because it bypassed the Senate's constitutionally appointed role in approving treaties. The two-thirds necessary for approval of treaties by the Senate was a conservative provision to limit executive power; Tyler sought to overcome that conservative limitation on executive power. Some historians have argued that Tyler's determination to annex Texas by joint resolution was democratic and showed "political courage," but whether or not courageous or democratic it was an attempt to overcome a conservative limitation on executive power.[21]

James K. Polk had made Texas annexation and continental expansion the central focus of his campaign. As Joel Silbey points out, Polk was "a dedicated expansionist."[22] The Democratic Party platform of 1844 called for the "reannexation of Texas and the reoccupation of Oregon." With Polk's nomination, territorial expansion became "a central tenet of the Democratic Party's creed."[23]

Continental expansion also became associated with federal internal improvements. On November 12, 1845, an internal improvements convention convened at Memphis, Tennessee. Because of his role as one who had "advocated, with distinguished zeal and ability, the great interests of the South and West," Mangum was invited to the convention.[24] (He did not attend.) Showing that he had never abandoned his "War Department Nationalism," Calhoun presided at the convention attended by six hundred delegates from fifteen states and territories. The convention recommended numerous military and naval projects and river and coastal navigation improvement projects to Congress as "national" projects suitable for federal aid.[25] The convention seems to have received momentum from Polk's ideas of continental expansion which Calhoun also apparently supported. Polk's continental expansion was a reawakening of Calhoun's (and Jefferson's) continental vision.

The Democrats' push for Texas made the annexation of Texas the chief issue facing Congress during its 1844–1845 session. On January 25, 1845, the House approved, by a vote of 120 to 98, the joint resolution that declared Texas annexed to the United States. Whigs in the Senate opposed immediate annexation. On February 4, the Senate Foreign Relations Committee reported unfavorably on the joint resolution. Thomas Hart Benton, Democrat from Missouri, proposed a substitute bill that would have left the boundaries of Texas and the terms of the annexation to negotiation between American commissioners and the Texas government with the settlement submitted to both governments for acceptance or rejection. Benton's bill split the Democrats. If annexation was not accomplished by March 4, Sam Houston, President of Texas, threatened to break off all negotiations. European influence in Texas gave muscle to this threat. After Polk arrived in Washington on February 13, he increased pressure on Senate Democrats to approve the joint resolution. Robert J. Walker put forward an alternative that combined the joint resolution with Benton's bill and left the president free to adopt either method. The Senate approved Walker's bill 27 to 25, and it passed the House 132 to 76.

As he remained president pro tem of the Senate in the second session of the Twenty-Eighth Congress, Mangum took a leading part in the Whigs' resistance to the Democrats' program of continental expansion.[26] He believed that Polk since his arrival in Washington had lent a powerful impulse to "party action" on Texas and that Polk's election had promoted an even greater radical spirit for continental expansion and war. "The War Spirit is high with the democracy, especially the Western Section of it," he reported to a friend from western North Carolina.[27] Immediately realizing that Walker's bill simply authorized the president to annex Texas, Mangum viewed it as a radical act that would excite anger and resentment in predominantly Whig states across the country. He thought it would raise animosity against the South. Immediate annexation by joint resolution, which Mangum did not doubt would be the alternative pursued, would give rise to "deep & dangerous excitement in portions of the North & East." It was, he told Governor Graham, an "outrage upon the Constitution & past precedents" and in the North and East it was certain to "stir deeply the anti Slavery feeling, & shake profoundly the confidence of higher & better men in the perpetuity of our system." Mangum told William Graham that if Polk did not become "firmer & more conservative," he feared war with England, but he thought it far more likely over Oregon than over Texas. Mangum thought the best policy was to remain "quiet" on Oregon and let migration to the territory take its course; eventually the territory would come into possession of the United States "without an effort."[28]

On December 4, 1845, Dr. A.W. Gay, a prominent Whig from Granville County, reminded Mangum that his political course would be the main topic of state political discussion the next summer prior to the elections for the General Assembly that would consider his reelection to the Senate. As Mangum was sure to be "the object of violent attack" by the Democrats, Dr. Gay recommended that Mangum should deliver speeches in the Senate that could be "industriously circulated" by Mangum's friends in North Carolina to help them meet Democratic attacks on Mangum and the Whigs.[29] Mangum may have taken this advice because less than two weeks later he gave a major speech decrying the Senate Democrats' provocative measures in the dispute with Great Britain over the Oregon territory. Early in the first session of the Twenty-Ninth Congress, Senator Lewis Cass of Michigan had introduced resolutions for the Senate committees on military affairs, the militia, and naval affairs to inquire into the means of the defense of the country and the defense of the coasts and commerce, as well as the present condition of fortifications, military supplies, the militia, the navy, and naval supplies. Cass would be the Democrats' nominee in 1848; he therefore represented majority opinion in the party.

Mangum's speech reflected the Whigs' opposition to the Democrats' war spirit and radical policy of continental expansion. Polk had been attempting to cast the burden of restraint in Oregon on Congress. Mangum's second objective was to throw responsibility for the Oregon crisis completely on the administration. Mangum wanted to put the burden for any war decision squarely on Polk and the Democrats while Polk was attempting to put the onus for a negotiated settlement of Oregon on the Senate.[30] Exceedingly regretting the introduction of Cass's defense resolutions, Mangum argued that the resolutions had been "unnecessarily pressed on the Senate" because the committees named already were responsible for inquiring into the conditions of the army, navy, and militia and the state of the country's defenses. He more particularly regretted that Cass had indulged "in the strain of remarks which he had thought proper to use." Calling the public mind "greatly disturbed and inflamed," Mangum thought it was "a most unpropitious time" for Cass to use belligerent language in introducing his resolutions. Cass's resolutions might provoke "an additional exasperation of the public mind"—an exasperation, Mangum insisted, that every man had a duty to check rather than aggravate. Because whatever was said on the floor of the Senate was certain to receive severe scrutiny in Europe, senators should act with "extreme caution and discretion."

Having established that the Senate Whigs favored restraint, Mangum then placed the burden of a settlement on Polk. In contrast to Cass's language, Mangum was pleased with the moderation of Polk's course in the difficult and important negotiation and was "willing to leave it entirely in the hands of the Executive." Mangum insisted that the president—not his subordinates—conduct the whole negotiation and expressed confidence that Polk would use "every method consistent with our dignity and honor" to procure an amicable adjustment of the Oregon boundary. But he took this position "with an ardent desire to see it maintained with moderation, calmness, and justice, and with proper respect and deference on both sides." Mangum wanted Polk to do nothing to precipitate the country into a conflict over Oregon "so long as the slightest hope remains that, by a course of prudent moderation, the existing negotiations may be brought to an amicable conclusion." If it became manifest that that conclusion could not be reached, all would "unite as one man" to provide any military force that should be necessary for the country's defense and the protection of the Oregon immigrants.[31] Mangum criticized Cass's eagerness to stir public sentiment for war with Britain over Oregon, essentially criticizing the Democrats' agitation of public opinion for Manifest Destiny at any price. Mangum thus opposed Cass's war spirit with an appeal for calm and a course of "prudent moderation," but he also made it clear that Whigs would not hesitate to defend American rights. It was a speech reminiscent of Macon's speeches in regard to war with Great Britain thirty-five years earlier.

Mangum claimed to his daughters that he delivered the speech "without warning & without expecting it," but it was popular with Whigs. Thurlow Weed thanked Mangum for the "enlightened and patriotic" speech and expressed the confidence of the New York Whigs in Mangum's "wisdom and firmness in taking the Country and the Whig Party safely through the ordeal.[32] Thomas Clingman, then in Congress, told Mangum that his position on Oregon was "just what it ought to be." He thought Mangum had taken the "true position on that question" and that Mangum had restrained the Northern Whigs from taking "an extreme anti-war position" that would have weakened the Whig Party. Indeed Clingman deemed the course Mangum proposed the only practicable one.[33]

Tyler and Polk found Texas and continental expansion very effective party issues, but the price was increased sectional agitation over the expansion of slavery. Both Tyler and Polk, especially the latter, were convinced Northern Democrats would bend to the will of Southern Democrats. The agitation would cause greater political damage to the Whigs. The Democrats' successful effort to overcome the conservative limitation of executive power embodied in the Constitution's provision for Senate approval of all treaties by a supermajority and their drive for continental expansion at the risk of greater sectional agitation and division, both interpreted by the Whigs as radical and politically dangerous, soon led the latter to identify their party's principles as "conservative."

"The great Conservative principles of the Whig party"

Polk's insistence on continental expansion to California and the Pacific led him to a war with Mexico whose northern provinces of New Mexico and California Polk sought to acquire for the United States. War, Polk reasoned, would force Mexico to make territorial concessions. Expecting a quick victory, Polk ordered the army assembled in Texas under General Zachary Taylor to advance into disputed territory. But the costly (in both blood and treasure) two-year war offered the Whigs an opportunity to counter the popular spirit of Manifest Destiny that Polk had raised.[34] Mangum thought the Democrats' course had increased the danger to the Union.

Like most Whig leaders in Congress, Mangum strongly opposed the war in Mexico. Early in 1847, Mangum declared that the Democratic Congress had stirred up a popular favor for continental expansion and war that they could nor rein in: "The truth is the War is most distasteful—& all would be for a speedy termination of it, upon almost any terms—but for fear of popular opinion—Congress has conjured up a factitious, & in my judgment, a most unsound public, or rather popular opinion, at which they are appalled." Mangum also feared the war was driving the government's finances "into the worst condition."[35] By early 1848, Mangum pronounced public opinion "deeply debauched" with the war spirit and believed the next president would be the candidate who favored the annexation of all of Mexico.[36] Mangum was convinced that Democratic Party expansionists Cass, Buchanan, and Quitman would make "the bold, broad, & unprincipled" issue of the complete conquest and annexation of all of Mexico the centerpiece of their party's platform.[37]

The electoral success of their anti–Mexican War campaign in 1847 and the opposition to Polk's drive for continental expansion by Mangum and the Whigs in Congress led the Carolina Whigs to make opposition to Polk's pursuit of Manifest Destiny the foremost "opposition" of their platform for the 1848 campaign. Like Mangum, the Carolina Whigs perceived Polk's actions as radical. The focus of the Whig Party shifted; they began to emphasize the conservative nature of their principles in contrast to the Democrats' principles. The Whigs had taken advantage of their control of the 1846–1847 General Assembly to redistrict the state's nine congressional districts in their favor. This advantage along with opposition to the war in Mexico and Polk's program in Washington led to the election in North Carolina of six Whigs to Congress in 1847. Adopting the stance of Mangum and the Southern Whigs in Congress against the Mexican War, the Whig candidates insisted that the war had been illegally started by Polk, was a war solely for conquest, and should be fought to a successful conclusion as soon as possible. They combined this stance with opposition to Polk's tariff revision of

1846 lowering rates and to the independent treasury. Instead they advocated a protective tariff and a sound currency.[38]

By 1848, Whigs opposed to Polk's policy of war and continental expansion and the Carolina Whigs were describing their principles as "conservative." They defined these conservative Whig principles in contrast and in opposition to the Democrats' pursuit of increased executive power and continental expansion, which Whigs viewed as radical. This was language they had not used in 1846. Conservative was mainly defined, then, as opposition to Polk's expansionist and war policies that, according to Carolina Whigs, threatened the Constitution and the Union. The declarations of the Whig Conventions of 1846 and 1848 reflected these changes.

In 1846 the Whigs of North Carolina wrote a conventional platform, only adding a statement on their desire for restraint in Oregon. The Whig delegates approved resolutions declaring the party's adherence to the "Whig doctrine" of a revenue tariff with incidental protection for "Commerce, Agriculture, and Manufactures" and distribution and opposition to the Sub-Treasury. The Whigs also declared their preference that the Oregon controversy be settled by "peaceful negotiations" rather than "an appeal to arms." Though there was no presidential election, the convention passed a resolution praising Henry Clay, still the favorite of Carolina Whigs:

> Resolved. That this Convention deem it but a just reflection of the deep and heartfelt feeling of their constituents, to express their admiration and affection for HENRY CLAY, the noblest embodiment of Whig principles, as he is one of the noblest specimens of American character that our nation has produced.[39]

Henry Clay as the embodiment of Whig principles was still the heart of the Whig ideology in 1846, but the subsequent course of Polk and the Democrats added opposition to continental expansion and opposition to the Mexican War to Whig principles.

The Whig convention of February 22, 1848, held at the height of the Mexican War, made opposition to continental expansion the major plank of the party's platform. The resolutions of the convention, drafted by a committee headed by Kenneth Rayner, included in the principles of the party opposition to the Democrats' policy of continental expansion. Indeed, that plank received more attention than any other. Before addressing their objections to specific policies of the Democrats, the Whigs first addressed the importance of Whig principles. Declaring themselves still devoted to "the cause of the great Conservative principles of the Whig party," they argued that the "alarming condition of the Country" which had grown out of the "misrule of the party in power" convinced them of the necessity of "unswerving perseverance in the support and maintenance of those principles." The resolutions then turned to specific measures. The Whigs dedicated one resolution to the "old issues" on which they had combated "the party in power" for years: the Democrats' "warfare upon American industry," "reckless management of the public treasure," "wasteful expenditures," and "prostitution of public office." All these policies were "utterly in conflict with the Constitution" and "destructive of public morals."

The Whigs dedicated most of their resolutions, however, to an explanation for their opposition to the "unnecessary and unconstitutional war." It was begun, they declared, in "a spirit of selfish ambition" and Polk persisted in it "with a view to party triumph." Polk's order to the Army to march into disputed territory between Texas and Mexico was "an unauthorized aggression." Furthermore, because the Constitution reserved to Congress alone power to declare war, the convention viewed Polk's order to General Taylor to invade the disputed territory that had effectively brought about a state of war "as a manifest usurpation of the authority of Congress and as a palpable violation of the Constitution." Asserting that "too many of our sons have already fallen" and "too much of our treasure has already been wasted," the Carolina Whigs declared that the war was "unnecessary, expensive, and unconstitutional" and that should be ended as soon as possible consistent with the country's honor. Though they wanted to establish an equitable boundary line and acquire a "safe and convenient harbor on the Pacific," the convention delegates declared their opposition to the acquisition of Mexican territory by conquest. They declared their "admiration and approval" of the conduct of the officers and men of the army and navy, "who have so gallantly sustained the American Flag."

With an eye to that year's presidential election, the convention delegates declared that the administration's "warfare" on Generals Taylor and Scott, who were Whigs, showed "a spirit of jealousy and ingratitude" inconsistent with "justice and honor." They declared their approbation of the position taken by senators Mangum and Badger against the further prosecution of the war. Finally, the Whigs declared for compromise, harmony, and Union. In a resolution approving of the national Whig convention, they declared: "That the time has arrived when the Whigs of the Union should put forth every effort; that we think upon their success greatly depends the security of our rights, and the perpetuity of our Institutions; that, at this time, above all others, compromise and harmony should prevail in our councils; that Union is the first great pre-requisite to success."[40] Thus, not only did the Whigs declare their principles conservative, as opposed to the radical course of the Democrats, they emphasized as the foremost of their "great Conservative principles" opposition to a war they considered unconstitutional and opposition to the Democrats' policy of territorial acquisition that would jeopardize the spirit of compromise and harmony between the sections essential to maintaining the Union.

Responding to the declared concerns of his state Whig Party and seeking to set out the Southern Whig position on the war and acquisitions of new territory, Mangum made the Democrats' policy of continental expansion the subject of a major speech in the summer of 1848 in the midst of the presidential campaign between Cass and Taylor. Asserting that Polk's war against Mexico was an unconstitutional exercise of presidential power, he portrayed Cass, the Democrats' presidential nominee, as the head of the Democratic Party's expansionist wing. In the first part of his speech Mangum ridiculed the Cass's policy of leaving the question of slavery in Mexico and California up to the people of those territories—popular sovereignty—as a "bungling device" that deceived no one. It was merely an attempt to evade responsibility. Mangum also declared his opposition to the Wilmot Proviso. He stood by "the rights of the South." The proviso implied "an offensive disparagement" to the South and had "no warrant in the Constitution, in good faith, or in equal justice." However, Mangum insisted that as a practical question he regarded it as of "exceedingly slight importance" because New Mexico was highly unlikely to become a slaveholding country. He would rather see New Mexico and California independent than see them disturb "the harmony of this Union."

Mangum then turned to Cass and the new spirit of the Democratic Party. He considered Cass the true representative of "the worst type of Democracy"—that wing of the Democratic Party which was "fraught with most danger to the peace, prosperity, and enduring glory of the country." Mangum critiqued the spirit of this expansionist wing of the Democratic Party:

"aggressive, reckless, grasping, and ... rapacious," it tended to "violence and excess" and its maxims scorned to "count the cost in life, in money, or in good repute in the world." The Democrats had first disclosed that "bold, aggressive spirit" during the Oregon controversy. The Senate, not Polk, had settled Oregon, Mangum insisted. The firmness of the Senate in resisting the war spirit and Polk's "shallow stratagem" of bluster while secretly counting on Congress to moderate the situation had allowed the peaceful resolution of the Oregon dispute. Mangum then accused Polk of seeking "name and fame" in the Mexican War. He expressed the view of the North Carolina Whig convention that in beginning the war on his own initiative, Polk had usurped powers in violation of the Constitution:

> The President moved the army from Corpus Christi to the Rio Grande. That made the war inevitable. It was an act of war—the one-man power in its worst, most dangerous form; and I hold him and his advisors—the country and posterity will hold him and his advisers, General Cass as one of them—responsible for this dangerous violation of the Constitution, and for all the blood and treasure that that war has cost our people.

He accused the administration of prosecuting the war "from the very first" with "views of territorial aggrandizement."

Mangum then returned to the attack on Cass and directly associated him with the Democrats' policies of continental expansion and war. Mangum insisted that Cass as head of the expansionist wing of the Democratic Party, had "encouraged, aided, and stimulated every excess" of the administration. His election would only continue "this incompetent and dangerous Administration." Mangum asserted that the "aggressive ambition of this portion of the Democracy is boundless and unappeasable." In contrast, Mangum opposed "the acquisition of a foot of territory by conquest" unless with the "general concurrence of my countrymen" because above all he prized "the harmony, mutual confidence, and kindly feelings among the States of this Union." (This stance, of course, had been Clay's position on Texas annexation during the 1844 campaign.) In contrast, Cass exhibited a "high war spirit" and he had "little appreciation of any fame but that which is enthroned under the shadow of laurels steeped in blood." Furthermore, Cass was guilty of the offense committed by all the recent Democratic presidents: usurpation of power. In Mangum's observation, Cass was "always ready to augment the Executive power" that was even then "overshadowing and fearful." Cass was "always the apologist of Executive usurpation or abuse." His election, Mangum declared, would be "a great national blunder," even a "catastrophe." The only safety for the country, Mangum insisted, lay in "the great and conservative principles of the Whig party."[41] After the declarations of their convention platform and such a forceful speech from their senior senator, there could be no doubt of the ideological focus of the Carolina Whigs in the 1848 campaign. In contrast with the radical and divisive "war spirit" of the Democrats, the conservative principles of the Whigs now included opposition to territorial expansion and a spirit of harmony among the states—the spirit of Union.

Whig Divisions—Part I: Contest for the Senate and the Taylor Party

In 1840, the Senate elections had been a source of unity for the Carolina Whigs. The elections of 1846–1848 divided the Whigs. Early challenges to Mangum's reelection in 1846 showed that the leadership position he had held from 1835 to 1844 was beginning to erode.

The ambitions of some Whigs to replace him in the Senate also showed the difficulty of maintaining Whig unity. Clingman, after his defeat by James Graham in the 1845 contest, became ambitious for Mangum's Senate seat. In the fall of 1845 Clingman tried to persuade Mangum to run for governor in 1846 rather than support re-nominating William Graham. In Clingman's depiction, Mangum's candidacy would call forth "the western reserve … "in all its whig strength" and give him a larger majority than any other potential candidate.[42] Mangum's indecision about his political future probably contributed to the eagerness to succeed him. In fact, Mangum had not made up his mind to stand for reelection to the Senate; early in 1846 he was contemplating a move to the Oregon territory.[43] Mangum's reply to Clingman's letter may have suggested a reluctance to serve another term, but Mangum may simply have been reluctant to declare his political ambitions in an age when politicians did not openly speak of ambition for high office.[44] When it became clear to Clingman in early 1846 that the party leaders were not considering nominating anyone other than William Graham for governor in 1846, he realized that the Whigs had to reelect Mangum to the Senate unless he intended to retire. Clingman then assured Mangum that he fully supported his reelection and encouraged the Whig candidates for the legislature in his district to come out strongly for Mangum's reelection.[45] In a sign of further division and rivalry, prominent Charlotte Whig James Osborne suggested to his friend Graham that he decline re-nomination for governor so that he could replace Mangum in the Senate.[46] Osborne, however, had his own ambitions about replacing Mangum.

When William H. Haywood unexpectedly resigned from the Senate rather than support an administration measure lowering the tariff, a vacancy was opened that gave the Whigs, with a majority in the legislature, the opportunity to once again have two Whig senators representing the state in the United States Senate.[47] It also gave an opening for ambitious Whigs. The main candidates considered by the Whig caucus were George Badger of Raleigh, a former cabinet officer and long-time party leader; former governor John M. Morehead of Guilford County in the western piedmont; and former congressman Edward Stanly of eastern Beaufort County, one of Mangum's friends. Still other Whigs were ambitious for Senate seats, including Mangum's.

In September Raleigh Whig leader Weston Gales, editor of the *Raleigh Register*, warned Mangum that persons "for reasons of their own" were "very studiously" keeping the idea before the public that Mangum intended to decline reelection. The *Star* had already nominated Badger and Osborne, giving the impression that Mangum had declined reelection (the nomination had been, according to Gales, written by Raleigh Whig Henry W. Miller). Gales informed Mangum that, despite the article in the *Star*, the Whigs intended to nominate Mangum for reelection unless he positively declined. (Knowing that Mangum could not declare himself a candidate, Gales probably wrote the letter to clarify Mangum's intentions by giving him the opportunity to decline or affirm his candidacy by not declining.) Gales preferred Badger or Morehead to fill the remainder of Haywood's term. He considered all other Whigs "small fry" and complained that they were "electioneering" for a nomination.[48]

Clingman was one of those "small fry" who, before the legislature of 1846 met, began to press his claims for consideration by the caucus by writing to Mangum. He addressed his appeal to Mangum "and others whom I know to be personally my friends." Clingman obliquely enquired as to whether Mangum would use his influence with the Whigs of Wake and Orange for him. He clearly understood that the Raleigh Whigs would exert a controlling influence—

he knew Mangum's influence with them and he was lobbying Mangum. His chief arguments were that he was an ardent champion of the Whig Party, that the western counties deserved more representation in the state offices, and that the middle counties unfairly dominated the Whig Party. He reminded Mangum that he had previously "alluded" to Clingman being a candidate for a Senate seat. Realizing that Badger's position in the Whig Party was "eminent," Clingman explained that he did not desire to be brought into a "collision" if Badger desired the Senate seat. Claiming he did not want to be presented "merely as a sectional candidate," Clingman queried Mangum about the degree of support he might receive from the "middle or Eastern part of the state." Specifically, he wanted to know if the delegations from Orange County and the "adjoining counties" (including, of course, Wake County) would support him. Realizing that his feud with the Grahams might hurt him, Clingman insisted that he had rendered Graham "more service than any one Whig in the state" in both campaigns. Clingman concluded his letter by citing as his major qualification his "capacity and zeal in the service of the Whig party."[49]

Clingman's efforts were unavailing; the party stood behind its stalwarts Mangum and Badger. Apparently not receiving the assurance of support from Mangum that he desired, Clingman arranged for a letter to the *Raleigh Register* in October 1846 that, under the pseudonym "Fair Play," set out his case, but Gales refused to publish it. Instead, he critiqued the letter in two articles and attempted to refute the arguments of "Fair Play."[50] The Democrats, however, used the letter to highlight Whig divisions and William Woods Holden editorialized in the *Standard* that Clingman was the victim of a "central clique."[51] Despite his claim of not wishing to challenge Badger, Clingman lobbied the Whig caucus in the legislature, but the Whigs nominated Mangum and Badger. Mangum was elected without challenge to another six-year term and the legislature chose Badger to fill Haywood's remaining term.[52]

Despite Clingman's resentment of the power of the Raleigh Whigs, he continued in early 1847 to consider Mangum an ally. Failing in his bid for a Senate seat, Clingman had decided once again to challenge James Graham for Congress, and in January 1847 he wrote to Mangum to obtain any documents or speeches the senator could provide on Texas annexation and the Mexican War.[53] Showing that the rivalry between Graham and Clingman continued, Graham withdrew from the contest when he learned that Clingman would not be his sole opponent— the race he desired. Despite a three-way race, Clingman won the district.[54]

Whigs were divided about the candidate they wanted to put forward for the 1848 presidential campaign: a party stalwart loyal to Whig principles who would rally old Whigs or a new man who could attract new voters to the party. Daniel Webster, Associate Supreme Court Justice John McLean of Ohio, and General Winfield Scott, hero of the War of 1812, all attracted early interest from various Whig constituencies. It was Henry Clay and General Zachary Taylor, however, who garnered the most support by early 1848. Clay was beloved by Whigs. While Clay had given no clear indication that he was prepared to enter another campaign, many Whigs held to the hope that he would make himself available. General Taylor's early victories in the Mexican War at Palo Alto, Resaca de la Palma, Monterrey, and especially his victory against overwhelming odds at Buena Vista created a powerful boom for his candidacy, especially among those Whigs looking for a candidate who could attract voters outside the party. Mangum preferred Clay; should Clay be unavailable, Mangum was favorably disposed toward to McLean but preferred Scott. He was unalterably opposed to Taylor. Mangum's friend John Crittenden of Kentucky switched from Scott to Taylor and became

Taylor's unofficial campaign manager.[55] In 1848, Mangum wrote that Crittenden was "the head, the heart & soul of Taylorism" in Washington.[56]

Throughout 1847, Taylor was reluctant to endorse Whig principles. He fostered an image as a No Party man, committed only to "republican" principles.[57] In February 1848, he asserted that he would not be the candidate of any political party or "the exponent of their party doctrines."[58] Even Taylor's ardent Whig supporters felt some concern that an absolute renunciation of Whig principles would endanger his candidacy. In February, the Whig caucus in the Senate selected four Southern Whigs—Mangum, Crittenden, Clayton, and C.S. Morehead of Kentucky—to try to gain Taylor's acceptance of a letter of Whig positions. Mangum, who preferred a candidate more committed to Whig doctrines, refused to participate and was piqued that the senators had debated whether to use the word "Whig" in the document.[59] Clay benefited from Taylor's assertions of no-partyism. Enthusiasm among Whigs in stops along his route home after a visit to Washington and reassurances from his ardent supporters convinced Clay to reconsider his availability, and in April 1848 he issued a letter to the papers in Lexington, Kentucky in which he announced his intention to put his name before the national Whig convention as a candidate for the Whig nomination.[60]

In order to shore up his support with Whigs in the face of Clay's entry into the contest, Taylor that same month issued letters from Baton Rouge to clarify his stance on Whig principles and measures.[61] Insisting that his opinions had been "misconceived and misrepresented," Taylor declared that he had no "party projects to build up." He avowed that he held "great cardinal principles" which would regulate his "political life." He declared himself a Whig who was independent of the party. He also asserted that he was a Whig "but not an ultra whig" and would not be a "mere President of a party." Though he intended to act "independently of party domination" and would not be bound by "party schemes," he expressed opinions that pleased Whigs on the veto power, the "injurious influence" of the Executive on Congress, war as a "national calamity" to be avoided, and adherence to the "will of the people" as expressed by Congress on the tariff, the currency, and internal improvements. He would accept the nomination of the Whig Party if he would be free from all pledges. But he threatened to run independently if the Whig convention selected Clay. His only pledge was that he would administer the government guided by "the Constitution in a strict and honest interpretation, and in the spirit and mode in which it was acted upon by our earlier Presidents."[62]

Mangum disliked Taylor's No Party stance. Before Clay's candidacy, he preferred the more reliable Whigs Scott or McLean to Taylor. No doubt with Tyler in mind, Mangum wanted a Whig president committed to Whig principles and Whig measures. Deeming Taylor "objectionable," Mangum feared the effects of Taylor's No Party stance. He thought that Taylor's support from Democrats and from Whigs ready to put "no party" before Whig principles threatened "a destructive fusion of parties & a partial annihilation of organized conservatism." Mangum insisted that he would not support Taylor unless he modified his position. "No man *will* clean out the corruptions accumulated during Tyler's & Polks [sic] time, who ... receives a considerable support from both parties," he told Governor Graham. Fusion of the parties was "absolutely impossible." Support for Taylor was "unwise"; it simply was "blind enthusiasm" motivated by a "virtuous" but "unreflecting" desire to lessen the fierce party conflict.[63] If the Whigs were determined to have a general for their presidential candidate, Mangum told Graham, "I infinitely prefer Scott." Mangum believed Scott "much the abler man" who had exhibited great ability in his Mexican campaign and was "a great man." He was a solidly reliable

Whig. Though wishing to bring Taylor to Whig principles, Mangum thought if the Democrats went for a "military & aggressive" ticket—meaning Cass, it would be necessary for the Whigs to match it "with a certain military 'prestige,'—with Scott or Taylor."[64]

For Mangum, then, Whig principles were the foremost consideration. If Taylor refused to embrace them, Mangum was prepared to rally to Clay as the surest representative of Whig principles. If Taylor did not "deign to avow himself a Whig" and declined to accept the nomination of a Whig convention, Mangum asked Graham whether the Taylor men meant to "abandon the ground we have won & maintained for ten years, after more than ten years of hard & Strenuous contest?" His own mind was made up:

> If they do—I do not & firmly trust a powerful fragment of us for talent, public Virtue & consistent perseverance will be found rallying to the banner that we long ago flung to the breeze & endeavored to uphold by all the efforts of which mortal man was capable.—Yes, we will rally around it, though it may be torn into rags by contempt, trailed in the dust or be-draggled in mud & mire.[65]

Mangum was thus prepared to start a movement for Clay if Taylor could not be brought to run on Whig principles. In February 1848, Mangum had a private "full & frank conversation" with Clay during his visit to Washington. Although Clay emphasized the necessity of Whig principles, he did not indicate to Mangum any resolution to assent to his name being placed in nomination. Mangum reported to Graham that Clay's position was "essential to bring gentlemen to their senses, as well as to Whig principles.—A No-Party stand cannot be held.... I adhere to the opinion—that if Gen T. stands mute, either Clay, Scott, or McLean will be run."[66] The two old Whig warhorses were thus convinced that the Whig candidate had to run on Whig principles to be acceptable to the party.

Clay's declaration of his candidacy in April cleared the way for Mangum to support the old favorite of the Southern Whigs. Though Clay's Lexington letter shocked some Whigs because no candidate had ever shed the fiction of passively awaiting the nomination, Mangum had only waited for the issue of availability to be settled. After Clay's Lexington letter appeared, Mangum declared in favor of Clay: "I am, as ever, in favor of Mr. Clay as my first choice in the union, if the question of availability were settled," he explained to a friend. "I have not looked to him as a probably [sic] candidate until very lately."[67] Though he personally preferred Clay, Mangum thought the old Whig stalwart's prospects for the nomination were doubtful and he regretted Clay's decision to assent to his nomination because of the mortification a failure might give Clay.[68] Nonetheless he supported Clay.

Mangum thought that Taylor's April letters "set him on his legs again" in Washington and encouraged the latter's supporters in regard to his nomination, but he continued to prefer Scott to Taylor, if Clay could not be nominated. Mangum thought that either Scott or McLean were most likely to get the Whig nomination.[69] He explained to a Rhode Island friend why he preferred Scott over Taylor: "If we have to march a President into the White House, with drum & fife, I prefer the abler man, & one who is not only a Whig, but who will respect the usages & become the exponent of the principles of the Party."[70] Mangum clearly had not been pacified by Taylor's letter. A victory that did not include the triumph of Whig principles was not a victory.

Mangum also had another reason for preferring Scott to Taylor if the convention chose a military man. Having already been acting vice-president in 1841–1845, Mangum hoped to attain the official office as Scott's vice-president in 1848. As early as 1846 Whigs in Congress mentioned Mangum as a potential candidate for Vice President,[71] and he also was considered as a running mate for Ohio's John McLean.[72] Given McLean's lack of support for the traditional Whig program, Mangum was unenthusiastic about those overtures. Mangum's friendship with Scott and his own prominence as a leading Southern Whig led him to consider himself a candidate for nomination with Scott.[73] In January 1848 Mangum doubted the "Military feeling" would carry the Whig Party. If it did, and in the spring it appeared increasingly likely that it would, Mangum preferred Scott and himself as Scott's running mate. In the spring of 1848 Mangum told William Graham that he thought the convention would nominate Scott and expressed a hope that he would be placed on the ticket as vice president.[74] Mangum, however, did not have the support of his own delegation to the national Whig Party convention; they opposed his nomination as vice-president.[75] Possibly Mangum's increasing tendency to alcoholism undermined his support. More likely, however, their opposition sprang from the fact that a majority of the delegation (six of eleven) were Taylor men. Also, Mangum would only have been considered if a Northern man were the presidential nominee; all but one of those who did not back Taylor supported Clay and nine of the delegation voted for Abbott Lawrence of Massachusetts for the vice-presidential nominee.[76] The demand of the Southern delegates to have a Southern man as the party's presidential nominee doomed Mangum's chance at the vice-presidency. Scott's failure to win the nomination frustrated Mangum's hopes.

In the end, even with the possibility of nomination with Scott, Mangum preferred Clay to all other candidates; and his reasons combined opposition to the Democratic Party, Polk, and the Mexican War: "If we had soundness enough, it would be a great point to manifest to the world that an infamous war gotten into to make Presidents, not only crushed its projectors, but failed to place any blood-stained laurels in the Executive Chair."[77] The old opponent of Andrew Jackson thought the Whigs' preference for a military hero was weakness.

Taylor's reluctance to put forward an unequivocal endorsement of Whig principles created divisions in North Carolina. The North Carolina Whigs split between Clay and Taylor (and some for Scott). Those placing primary importance on Whig principles backed Clay. Support for Taylor came primarily from Whigs willing to set aside staunch defense of Whig principles. Most North Carolina Whigs remained loyal to Clay in 1847 and early 1848, but as support for Taylor increased in Congress, many began to shift to Taylor. By early 1848, the North Carolina Whig delegation in Congress alone among Southern states preferred Clay. Mangum and four Carolina Whig congressmen opposed Taylor, but the majority sentiment among the other Southern Whig delegations had shifted from Clay to Taylor.[78] Mangum was particularly upset with Crittenden and the Kentucky delegation calling Kentucky "the *Political Yankeedom* of the South."[79] And Mangum tried to reassure Carolina Whigs that Clay was physically able to take on the presidential duties, writing from Washington to one Whig friend in North Carolina during Clay's visit to Washington that Clay was "in fine & vigorous health, feeling beyond all doubt, that he is quite able to take upon himself the burthens of office."[80]

Senator George Badger was Taylor's most prominent supporter in North Carolina, and his difference with Mangum was an example of the rivalry that had developed between the two Whig senators. A personal rivalry, it also was a competition for the leadership of the state party.[81] Badger seemed to chafe at Mangum's leadership and power in the Carolina Whig party. Almost immediately after entering the Senate, Badger gave a speech on the most controversial issue before the country—against territorial acquisitions in the Mexican war in which he acknowledged the authority of Congress to bar slavery in the territories. Although "ultra" Whigs were displeased, many North Carolina Whigs were delighted Badger's performance in the Senate. "Our citizens are very much pleased with Badgers speech, they speak of it as an able effort," Charles Hinton told Mangum.[82] Believing Taylor gave local Whigs a better chance in the legislative elections, Badger sought to bring the state convention to endorse Taylor. But his support of Taylor and Mangum's preference for Clay introduced division at the highest levels of leadership in the North Carolina Whig Party.

With the two senators supporting different candidates, the state convention would inevitably be divided between Taylor Whigs and Clay Whigs. According to Mangum, with Whig opinion so split about their preferred presidential candidate, it would be "unwise" and "inexpedient" for the North Carolina convention to endorse any particular candidate. He advised Governor Graham that the Whig convention should nominate a gubernatorial candidate but leave the presidential question "untouched." Mangum also reported that Badger and other Taylor supporters in the Carolina congressional delegation had written to their friends to advise them to nominate Taylor at the convention.[83] The Whigs followed Mangum's recommendation, but Badger succeeded in having his friends introduce a pro–Taylor resolution at the convention. The delegates to the Whig state convention (held 22 February 1848 at Raleigh) were divided between Clay Whigs and Taylor Whigs. Kenneth Rayner introduced a pro–Clay resolution: "*Resolved*, that our admiration and attachment for the great American statesman, Henry Clay, are unabated; and that we will ever cherish the most profound gratitude for the eminent and distinguished services he has rendered his country." John Kerr introduced a similar pro–Taylor resolution. The convention unanimously adopted both resolutions, thus preserving neutrality (and peace) among the Whigs. Furthermore, the convention pledged to support the nominee of the national convention.[84]

In the *Raleigh Register*, Gales tried to downplay the Clay-Taylor divide among North Carolina Whigs and insisted that the "divisions and bitterness" between the two Whig camps had taken "no foot-hold among the staunch Whigs of old North Carolina." Reflecting the resolutions of the state convention, Gales declared that the Whigs were strongly attached to both Clay and Taylor "but *devoted* to the good of the Whig party—they go for principles rather than men." He acknowledged that "a large majority" of Carolina Whigs preferred Taylor, but he was sure they would rally to Clay were he selected as the party's standard bearer. Gales insisted that those who would remain loyal only to a man were "not *Whigs* at all" because they had "no devotion to the cause." Calling for "the restoration of harmony in our ranks," Gales declared, "We desire, above all things the triumph of our party."[85] In contrast the *Hillsborough Recorder* found Taylor's April letters "perfectly satisfactory" and insisted that it left "no doubt that he is a good Whig."[86]

Despite Gales's assertions to the contrary, the Whigs were divided. In some of the district conventions that met to select delegates to the national Whig convention in Philadelphia Taylor Whigs pushed to gain an endorsement for Taylor. Most districts, however, chose merely to declare support for the nominee of the national convention. For example, the Whigs of the Fifth District[87] resolved to "cheerfully abide the decision of the National Convention." Nevertheless, the Taylor men tried to pass a resolution declaring Taylor the choice of the district. The convention rejected the resolution because there was "some contrariety of opinion among the delegates as to who is the first choice of the district, whether Gen. Taylor or Henry Clay."[88] In language that unmistakably opposed the "no principles" stand of the Taylor men, the Whigs of the southeastern Seventh District[89] declared themselves "still loyal to Whig principles." They resolved that their delegate "be elected more from his known attachment to Whig principles than individual men." Nonetheless, they did not expressly declare their preference for Clay. Instead they left their delegate "free, uninstructed and untrammeled" and declared that the party's nominee would receive their "hearty support." Fitting their declaration of loyalty to principles, though, they selected as their delegate and alternate "true blue Henry Clay men."[90] The Whigs meeting in the Wake County District Convention emphatically favored Taylor. They elected G.W. Haywood, "a decided Taylor man," as their delegate to the national convention. H.W. Miller of Raleigh, "a warm friend of Old Zack's," presidential elector. Other districts simply pledged to support the nominee of the national Whig Convention.[91]

County meetings in all regions of the state showed more specific support for Clay. The Whigs of Brunswick County declared that among "the great men in the Whig ranks," Henry Clay was their choice for the next presidency because he was "best fitted by his commanding influence ... to check the unholy and reckless spirit of conquest and territorial aggrandizement" of the Polk administration and "bring back the Government to the good old Republican track." Similarly, the Whigs of Stanly, Anson, and Macon counties declared for Clay. The Whigs of Davie County endorsed Clay, but they also proclaimed that Taylor was "suitable" and should be "respectfully considered." But the Whigs of Richmond and Randolph counties made no expression of preference for Clay or Taylor and pledged to abide by the decision of the national convention. Similarly, the Whigs of Northampton County seem to have been divided between Clay, Taylor, and Scott: they passed resolutions praising all three of the Whig leaders.[92]

At the national Whig convention, former governor of North Carolina John Morehead was elected president of the convention. Clay and Taylor received the most support from the delegates. Reflecting the sentiments of most of the Carolina district conventions, six of North Carolina's eleven delegates to the convention were Taylor Whigs. The other five, were, like Mangum, Clay Whigs. On the first ballot at the convention Taylor received 111 votes to Clay's 97. Clay had reached his maximum vote, though. On the second ballot, Taylor picked up seven votes; Clay lost eleven. After the first two ballots, the Clay men in the North Carolina delegation joined the movement of the convention away from Clay and slowly went over to Taylor. Taylor was nominated on the fourth ballot. The convention selected Millard Fillmore of New York as their vice-presidential nominee. The national Whig Party thus chose "No Party" over the "embodiment of Whig principles." Although Northern votes were critical to Taylor, it was largely the Southern state delegates who gave Taylor the nomination.[93]

In the days after the national Whig convention, Mangum loyally backed Taylor. After the convention's endorsement and the publication of Taylor's statements in his April letters about his respect for Congress as the representative of the people's will, the limited use of the veto, and his opposition to wars of conquest, Mangum believed he could support Taylor "cordially" as the representative of "all the great conservative characteristics of the Whig Party."[94] In a letter published to reassure Whigs of his support for Taylor, Mangum told Virginia Whig Congressman John S. Pendleton that he was hard at work promoting the Whig cause. He was, he explained, then in Washington "in the rooms of 'the Whig Executive Committee,' where I am and have been for several days aiding in the distribution of matter designed to enlighten and bring up the public mind to the support of Messrs. Taylor and Fillmore." "I am in favor of Gen. Taylor," he assured Whigs, "not only with zeal, but with undoubting confidence."[95]

Taylor carried North Carolina by a sizable margin and won nationally, winning twelve states, in addition to North Carolina—five of them Southern Whig states.[96] Despite the division in the state, the Carolina Whigs celebrated Taylor's victory over Cass. The *Register* ran a triumphant banner filling a whole two columns and a "Grand Whig Rally" was held in Raleigh to celebrate the "glorious triumph."[97]

Opposition Whig and Southern Whig Compromise

As Mangum had feared in the spring, the central agenda of Taylor's presidency became the transformation of the Whig Party into a Whig-Democratic amalgamation. Two of Mangum's Whig friends soon helped to preside over this destruction of the Whig Party. Clayton and Crittenden, Mangum's old friends in the Senate, had been original Taylor men and Taylor appointed them to his Cabinet. The plan of Taylor and "originals" like Clayton essentially was to form a new party based on loyalty to Taylor, not Whig principles, to be known as the Taylor Republican party. In place of "ultra" Whig principles it would seek a middle-ground on issues. The main instrument for building this Taylor party, of course, would be patronage appointments.[98] The recommendations of old party stalwarts and Clay men like Mangum, despite their long service and high position, were unlikely to be heeded by Taylor and his cabinet in such an environment.

Many Whigs who had not originally supported Taylor nevertheless expected him to unite the party in his cabinet. Nicholas Carroll, an influential Whig of New York City, informed Mangum that New York City Whigs wanted Mangum in the cabinet. They wanted the Whig "old Guard" to have the reins of Taylor's cabinet.[99] When Taylor failed to include Clay Whigs in his appointments, dissension arose in the party. In the summer of 1849 William A. Graham detected dissatisfaction with the Taylor administration among the Whigs: "With the discord now prevailing from various causes among the Whigs, we are in great danger of losing our ascendancy in the State," he told James W. Bryan.[100]

And the Whigs in North Carolina were indeed somewhat damaged in the congressional elections of 1849. They were unable to improve on their showing in 1847. Six Whigs and three Democrats were elected, but the Democrats increased their majority in the Fifth District that included Mangum's home county of Orange, formerly a Whig stronghold, by contesting the issue of Southern "honor."[101]

Taylor's appointment policy drove Mangum into opposition. One important appointment is illustrative and also shows how divisions between Mangum and Badger hurt Mangum's influence in Washington. Mangum's preference for Scott and Clay in 1848 curtailed his influence with the Taylor administration. Early on it was clear to Mangum that Taylor would favor his original supporters over old guard Whigs. Mangum and William Graham were determined to secure their friend Hugh Waddell, a long-time leader of the Whig Party in Orange County, an appointment as ambassador to Spain. Graham assured Waddell that he and Mangum and Badger "would leave no stone unturned" in procuring the appointment for Waddell. Although Mangum expected "much difficulty" in getting the appointment, he too was committed to Waddell "against all Comers." Badger, though, was lobbying for diplomatic posts for both his kinsman Edward Stanly and Waddell, and he desired the more prestigious Spanish mission for Stanly.[102] Mangum thought that despite Badger having been an original Taylor supporter, North Carolina was unlikely to receive two diplomatic appointments. Moreover, Congressman Daniel M. Barringer had been lobbying since March for the appointment to Spain for himself. "He has active friends among the *originals*," Mangum explained to Graham.[103] Mangum worked hard to influence the appointment, even remaining in Washington after the Senate adjourned. By mid–April, Mangum was frustrated about his lack of influence with the new administration. "I am unhappy. I am embarrassed. I have suffered *everything*," he lamented to Charity.[104] To a Virginia friend he complained of the "Taylor Concern."[105] In May, Mangum reported to Graham that he had failed: "After the most strenuous efforts, that I have ever made in my life, I am beaten; & our friend Waddell will fail.—He cannot be appointed abroad."[106]

Mangum failed to gain the appointment for Waddell, but ironically could have gotten it for himself or Graham. Despite the combined weight of the recommendations of Mangum, Graham, and Badger, Taylor had refused to appoint Waddell. The chief reason was the rival interests of Badger and Mangum. Mangum insisted on Waddell, Badger insisted on Stanly before Waddell, and Mangum threatened to make difficulties in the Senate if Stanly were appointed in place of Waddell. To solve the difficulty, Taylor seems to have refused the appointment of anyone but a former governor, senator, or congressman based supposedly on past policies of former presidents. He therefore offered appointment as ambassador to Spain or Russia to Mangum or Graham, which neither desired. Mangum thought the "notion" of earlier president's appointment policy was "fudge & foolery." He threatened "dreadful reprisals" on the "appointing power" if Taylor appointed Stanly but not Waddell.[107] Nonetheless, he recognized the "obvious political necessity" of the alternative offer to appoint him or Graham, and he hoped Graham would accept the appointment for North Carolina.[108] In the end, Graham declined and Barringer received the appointment to Spain.

Though he bore no ill will to his old friends Clayton and Crittenden or even to Taylor, Mangum intended by the approach of the 1849–1850 session of Congress to go into opposition, but not with the Democrats. He seems to have envisioned a sort of independent opposition. Mangum wrote a letter to Clayton chiding him and Crittenden for a perceived disrespect in not heeding his judgment in regards to appointments.[109] Mangum also told a friend from North Carolina that, though he felt no personal bitterness toward members of the administration, he was "fettered and hampered in every way" regarding appointments.[110] Mostly, he was angered that North Carolina's position as the strongest Whig state in the South next to Kentucky went unrewarded. He thought the lack of senior appointments for North Carolina showed a disrespect for a strong Whig state and that Taylor had let states that were not Whig states dictate appointments.[111] He told Clayton that the Taylor administration was "gradually losing power."[112] And he let his North Carolina friends know that he intended to oppose the administration, if necessary, on confirmation of their appointments. By the fall he had determined to ask no more favors of the administration. He meant, he said, "to be left 'as free as air,' in the discharge of my Senatorial duties."[113]

Mangum's Old Republicanism was a second reason for his turn to independent opposition. Despite his work for Waddell's appointment, Mangum's Old Republican anti-party sentiments made him regret the numerous other requests he received. "I profoundly regret the growing appetite for patronage in N.C.," he told Clayton. While understanding the reason for a desire to turn out Democrats, he thought pursuit of office hampered the Whigs' effectiveness as an opposition. The "enormities" of Tyler and Polk had aroused "a Vindictive &

retaliating spirit" Mangum explained to Clayton, "We have been *Whig* because we asked & cared for nothing."[114] Mangum revealed his preference for opposition: he preferred to be free to *critique* pursuit of party and patronage. His chief concern about patronage was that North Carolina receive her due of high appointments reflective of the state's importance to electing a Whig president. Thus, even before the first meeting of Congress during the Taylor administration, Mangum had staked out a position of independence.

Mangum's position of independent opposition led him at least temporarily to ally with Southern Whig "ultras" on the issue of slavery in the territories in opposition to Taylor's policy on the admission of California and New Mexico. Taylor wanted California and New Mexico immediately admitted as states without undergoing a territorial stage (to avoid the question of Congress's right to bar slavery from a territory) and independently of any discussion of the slavery question.[115] Mangum joined the "Southern rights" position of the Southern Whig "ultras," who insisted that justice to the South required that the admission of California as a free state be linked to an overall adjustment of the slavery question. Clingman, who had become a leader of the Southern "ultras," spoke on January 22 and stated their position that the South had little to lose by disunion. He also threatened a filibuster.[116] Clay, once again the Whig leader in the Senate, opposed both Taylor's plan and the course of the "ultras." Thus he introduced a compromise plan. In this situation, on February 6, Mangum also gave a speech about the "rights of the South." A day earlier Clay declaimed at length in front of packed galleries in defense of his compromise plan while Southern Democrats, joined by John M. Berrien from Georgia, had criticized it.

Though he did not did not specifically attack Clay's proposals, Mangum assumed an opposition position that seemed to ally him with the "ultras," as he insisted on Southern unity and defended Southern rights. Mangum also gave indications that the speech might have been more gasconade to pressure Taylor and set a strong Southern position for compromise than pure opposition to a settlement. Mangum presented a set of resolutions from a public meeting in Wilmington that proclaimed loyalty to the Union (but not at the sacrifice of principle) and supported a meeting in Raleigh to select delegates to the Nashville convention where respect for Southern rights and Southern unity were to be the principal topics. Mangum's first threat of opposition was a call for a unified Southern party: "Sir, it is no longer a mere question of party policy in the South. An overwhelming proportion of our people believe that this Government has no power to touch the subject of slavery either in the States or in the Territories … all mere questions of party are merged when we are brought to the consideration of this great question." Mangum's second threat of opposition was that of disunion that Clingman had broached. Mangum declared he had heard much about compromises and equivalents and compensation, but these seemed to be based on an "unjust" if not "entirely false" idea of the South's position. "What is compensation for?" he asked. "Have we done anything that the North has a right to complain of?" Was the South to make compensation for "the slanders, for the calumny, for the endangering of our firesides for the exciting of domestic insurrection?" "No, sir," he declared. "We stand by the Constitution and our rights, and we mean to stand by them under Heaven.… Everything or anything will be incurred in preference to dishonor and an ignominious submission to an impudent, arrogant, and unconstitutional interference with our rights." Insisting that North Carolina had always been devoted to the Union, Mangum declared that the state and the South would defy "all enemies who attempt to invade our rights by force or otherwise." In a clear reference to the Wilmot Proviso's demand that slavery be banned from territory acquired from Mexico, Mangum invoked the Old Republican doctrine of state equality: he would not recognize the right of any one to entirely appropriate "the spoils of war" to only one-half of the states when they had come at the "sacrifice of common blood and common treasure."[117]

Still, two aspects of the speech suggested it was more gasconade than absolute opposition to compromise. First, Mangum made a motion that the Wilmington resolutions be referred to the Printing Committee for a decision on printing them (the Senate approved 58–2). And immediately following his speech, Mangum showed support for Clay's position by moving that ladies be admitted to the Senate galleries to hear the second day of Clay's argument for his compromise plan. The speech also appears to have been positioning for compromise: Mangum supported the Senate's Southern Whigs not Taylor. His gasconade, as that of other Southern Whigs, was as much opposed to Taylor as to Northern Whigs and Democrats.

Thus, despite Mangum's flirtation with the Southern Whig "ultras," Clay could reasonably believe that Mangum could be persuaded to return to his national outlook and support the compromise measures. On April 8, the Senate referred Clay's "omnibus" bill embodying his compromise measures to a select committee of thirteen, seven Whigs and six Democrats. Clay chaired the committee and Mangum was appointed to the Committee of Thirteen, which also included Whigs Daniel Webster of Massachusetts and John Bell of Tennessee.[118] Mangum's work on the committee with Clay seems to have moderated his stance. Later, Mangum claimed that he had supported the formation of the Committee of Thirteen with the hope that it might "harmonize ... the distractions and the bad feelings of the country." He declared that his goal on the committee had been to help engineer an adjustment on "practical ground" that would ensure "equal justice" to both sections.[119] Mangum consulted with and coordinated some matters with Webster.[120] And Mangum was instrumental in convincing Webster to support the Compromise Bill.[121] When the committee presented the results of its work to the Senate, Mangum was fully supported the compromise plan.

On May 8, 1850, Mangum appealed to the senators to accept the committee's compromise. Though, as was the case with the other committee members, he found some parts in the compromise that did not accord with his opinions, he approved of the compromise as a whole with "cordiality" and "pleasure." He believed it contained the principle of "equity and justice" and he believed that it would be "cordially and favorably received by a vast and overwhelming majority of the country." Moreover, Mangum predicted that the compromise would defeat the "agitators"—the "abolitionists, freesoilers, renegades"—who would be "unhorsed, defeated, and fall into disrepute." He contrasted their fate with his hopes for the party of the compromise:

> Sir, I hope to see the restoration of that concord and harmony and good feeling which has formerly pervaded every section of this Union. I trust we shall see it; and I trust that the patriotic party, as I regard them—the men who stand up here without any other power to impel them to action except their belief that it is the will of much the greatest portion of the good men of the country, and for their enduring happiness and glory—if, under the favor of Heaven, that party should succeed in bringing this matter to a consummation, they will be regarded by an overwhelming portion of the country as the great patriotic party of the land, standing upon the ramparts of the Constitution and recognizing and sustaining all its principles and guarantees.[122]

Further evidence that Clay viewed Mangum as a critical supporter of the compromise can be found in Clay's lament over his absence from the Senate when Mangum went home to bring his wife to Baltimore. Clay urged Mangum to return "forthwith," declaring, "[w]e shall be hard run, if not defeated in the Senate without your vote."[123] In short, Mangum rapidly returned from his brief association with the Southern Whig "ultras" and their extreme position to work with Clay and became one of the senators urging compromise.

While the committee's compromise plan was under debate in Congress, President Taylor took ill after attending a Fourth of July oration at the Washington Monument. He died on July 9, 1850. Mangum expressed optimism about Whig prospects with Fillmore in the presidency.[124] More favorable to the Southern Whigs' compromise plan, Fillmore actively pushed for the passage of the compromise measures. Though Clay's omnibus compromise failed in the Senate (the exhausted Clay temporarily left Washington), the compromise measures eventually passed individually (as Clay had originally proposed). Separating the measures allowed majority coalitions of pro-compromise Whigs and Democrats to be assembled. Even though Stephen A. Douglas decoupled the bill and oversaw the passage of the individual components and votes of Northern Democrats were critical to its passage, the Compromise of 1850 was the Whigs' work and Southern Whigs—especially Clay, Mangum, and Badger—had been strong advocates for it.[125]

Fillmore's ascension to the presidency seems to have changed Mangum's attitude. Mangum helped secure the appointment as Secretary of the Navy for his friend William Graham, who had retired as governor in January 1849. This appointment to high office seems to have convinced Mangum that North Carolina would fare better on appointments under Fillmore's administration. All the Whigs in the North Carolina delegation joined in recommending Graham for a cabinet appointment and Fillmore appointed Graham Secretary of the Navy. (Later, Mangum went further and recommended Graham be transferred from Navy Secretary to Secretary of War.) Raleigh Whigs and Graham's friends urged him to accept the appointment, which he did on July 25, 1850.[126] North Carolina Whig leaders were pleased with the Fillmore administration, the president's approval of the Compromise, and especially Graham's appointment to the cabinet.[127]

The greatest effect of Fillmore's ascension to the presidency and Graham's appointment to the cabinet was increased federal patronage for the North Carolina party. In the fall, Mangum recommended several individuals to Graham for employment in the Navy Department and he also lobbied for other Carolinians with Treasury Secretary Thomas Corwin.[128] Mangum was pleased at the respect accorded to the state and to his and Badger's recommendations. Early on Mangum believed he would have greater influence with Fillmore than he had had with Taylor, and he was positive about the Fillmore administration. Mangum praised Graham's annual report to Congress as exhibiting "bold originality of conception & a fearlessness of responsibility" and he declared it would give Graham a higher "reputation" in the country than anything he had previously written. Because Graham had recommended an "entire reorganization" of the department and merit promotions for the ranks of captain and above, Mangum praised Graham's willingness to grapple with the problems of the Navy.[129]

When the mission to Havana opened up in the fall of 1850, Mangum pressed Secretary of State Daniel Webster to appoint Waddell. Webster wanted a Southerner but preferred George S. Gaines of Mississippi for the post. Mangum countered that "the dispensing of patronage to a hopeless state was little else than a waste of it." Mangum again was urging that North Carolina receive her due as a Whig bastion. Mangum also told Webster that Waddell's friends would not consent to his receiving a lesser post than Barringer whom they considered "greatly his inferior." With Graham in the cabinet, Mangum did not think it necessary for him to be the chief agent for lobbying for the appointment: "I know of nothing further that I can do & the whole case will have to devolve on you."[130]

Nevertheless, Mangum continued to press the administration for Waddell's appointment during the winter of 1851, but after becoming convinced that Fillmore and Webster were unfriendly to North Carolina, Mangum declared himself in independent opposition to the administration. Disagreement on party patronage was once again creating divisions in the Whig Party. Webster told Mangum that the difficulty with Waddell's appointment lay with President Fillmore, but Mangum suspected Webster was blocking the appointment. Mangum hoped Graham could exert some influence on Fillmore, but Webster's refusal to appoint Waddell led to Mangum's vow to oppose the administration. Webster's "unfriendly" and "insincere" course was, in Mangum's estimation an attempt to reserve the department's patronage for New England and his personal friends. Declaring that he had nothing to fear from opposition because his term did not end until Fillmore's term expired in 1853, Mangum reminded Graham: "If this design be carried out—you may set me down in opposition—remember, I live politically as long as this administration. My opposition will be first disclosed in reference to nominations from the State Department, whenever they are objectionable."

Somewhat in contradiction with his own insistence on the appointment of his friend, Mangum accused Webster of open use of patronage to build his party:

> One difference between Northern & Southern Statesmen (I have long seen it) is that the former suppose the hope or reception of office, is the great power to govern—The latter—not less ambitious—would be ashamed to admit it, or even to think it. That is very much the difference between your colleague & the best specimens of Southern Statesmen.[131]

Evident here was Mangum's suspicion of Northern statesmen's motivations, inherited from his Old Republican background. Southern statesmen were the true proponents of Republican principles; Northern statesmen were spoils men and office seekers. These were the same views Mangum had expressed during his trip to Massachusetts in 1834. Mangum's views also reveal the suspicions that had to be compromised between the Whigs from the two sections. In addition to Webster, Mangum was particularly upset with the "conscience Whigs" of Massachusetts. They were, he complained to Graham, "so timid & so pure that they scarcely ever act—and if they are spurred to action, they are afraid to do right, too pure to do wrong, & usually, or rather, often, seeking the 'medio tutissimus' make themselves a laughing stock or ridiculous." Irate about the course of these Whigs who tried to follow their anti-slavery principles, Mangum thus ridiculed perhaps the most principled group of Northern Whigs. His anger indicates the strains that the slavery issue had begun to place on the Whig Party—the effect of the Democrats' policy of continental expansion.

Finally, in this very revealing letter, Mangum complained that he was as blocked by the Fillmore administration just as he had been by Jackson's administration when he was in "violent opposition." He threatened to place the North Carolina Whig Party in opposition to the Fillmore administration:

> I think it nearly time for you & me & [any] other Whig, who has a just respect for his State to quit the Concern, go home, & as far as we may, enable them to learn more wisdom.—I am extremely hurt to hear that the President accords in this Course of policy.—If so, it will cost me personally, no more to Show resistance to him & his policy, than to the State dept.—My instincts have rarely failed me & that the State (N.C.) will uphold her due pretension by withdrawing Confidence & support from those who treat her with neglect, I feel as sure as that…. I am now living.[132]

Yet Mangum's ability to lead the Carolina party into opposition was now limited by Graham. Once appointed to Fillmore's cabinet, he now stood more at the head of the North Carolina Whig Party than Mangum. Graham's course, not Mangum's, would determine the direction of the party. And perhaps that was the subtext of this letter: Mangum was losing influence in North Carolina as well as with the administration in Washington and resented it. Yet in the nomination of a Whig candidate in 1852 at the national convention Mangum was to demonstrate that he still carried weight in the national Whig Party.

Early on, Graham resisted wholesale purges of Taylor Whigs from his department. However, the complaints and appeals of the Carolina Whigs and Fillmore's desire to purge William Seward's faction from federal posts soon changed his mind. He switched his policy. Taylor, Seward, and Clayton had appointed some Democrats to offices. Many of Seward's friends had been appointed in New York. Shortly after taking office, Graham told his brother that he had already received "numberless applications" for office, "especially from N.C." But he was reluctant to proscribe the Taylor men: "Some changes will be required beyond what were made under the last administration, for the Whigs were greatly disheartened then, but there will be no indiscriminate proscription."[133]

Things soon changed. Raleigh Whig leader Richard Hines told Graham that Taylor's retention of Democrats had hurt the Whigs in the 1850 elections for governor and the legislature. Apparently dissatisfied with Graham's policy, Whig congressmen from North Carolina, Georgia, Ohio, New York, and New Jersey signed a joint letter asking Fillmore to place the Navy Department's bureaus "under the charge and direction of persons connected with the Whig party." Fillmore referred the letter to Graham.[134] By January of 1851 Graham favored a wholesale purge of the Seward faction from the government departments even though "Seward and his faction" were disposed to peace with President Fillmore. "But I think we should not be content with that," he announced to his brother. Convinced that the Seward faction was more of an opposition than the Democrats, he instead thought Fillmore "should eject them from place and strip them of influence of office."[135] By March 1851 Fillmore, according to Graham, had decided that "the feud with the Seward men" was "irreconcilable." Graham himself was convinced that Seward's influence on Taylor had been "disastrous." Calling Weed and Seward "impudent," he told his brother that "nothing but chastising with a bold hand will check them."[136] Caught up in Fillmore's feud with Seward's faction by the spring of 1851, Graham was completely convinced that the battle between Fillmore and Seward was a battle for the soul of the Whig Party.

Despite the difficulty in obtaining an appointment for Waddell, Graham did use his position to dispense patronage appointment to his friends in North Carolina—proving again that he, not Mangum, was now at the head of the Carolina Whig Party. He appointed William Long of Halifax as Naval Storekeeper at Spezzia, Italy, for the navy's squadron of ships in the Mediterranean and gave the post of keeper of naval stores at San Francisco to a son of Raleigh party leader Richard Hines. He procured a clerkship in the Treasury Department for a prominent Whig and member of the legislature from Carteret County. And he was able to secure the appointment of the brother-in-law of his friend James Osborne to the lucrative collectorship at the port of Wilmington. Yet Graham remained as dissatisfied as Mangum with Webster's failure to appoint Waddell to the post of consul in Havana, Cuba. Like Mangum, he thought that Webster gave too much patronage to the North and to his "admirers."[137]

Mangum seems to have expected greater influence with the Fillmore administration, but his old distrust of Webster reemerged, however. As Secretary of State Webster controlled the prestigious diplomatic appointments Mangum wanted to deliver to his old Whig friends like Waddell. Webster was probably more interested in courting allies for his presidential aspirations than in satisfying a state such as North Carolina that he no doubt believed was solidly Whig (North Carolina had not given a majority to Democratic presidential candidate since Martin Van Buren in 1836). Mangum better understood patronage: Ideology might be enough to keep Carolinians from voting for Democrats, but North Carolina Whigs had to receive patronage to keep them enthusiastically working for the Whig Party.

In contrast with Mangum's opposition, William Graham was by 1851 a Fillmore Whig—clearly known and self-identified as such. Graham accepted Fillmore's view of Seward. Because of a lack of closeness to Fillmore Mangum was always more willing to work with Seward's New York Whigs, in spite of their anti-slavery views. Graham objected to Seward on the grounds of the latter's opposition to Fillmore and his anti-slavery views. Mangum only shared the second view.[138]

Mangum was always more comfortable in opposition, which best suited his strong adherence to Whig ideology. His almost constant desire to be in opposition combined with his ardent adherence to Southern Whig ideology shows the Southern Whigs' difficulties with national government. They, not the Southern Democrats, were the true heirs to the Old Republican ideology.

Whig Divisions: Clingman (Again), Mangum and Badger, and the "Raleigh Clique"

In the years 1848 to 1850, the divisions between Clay and Taylor Whigs were not the only fissures in the North Carolina party. Divisions over leadership and high offices split Whigs. The Whig divisions seen in the Clingman—Graham feud in the west were merely the precursor to the state-wide divisions that occurred in these years. Two conflicts were involved. At the center of the party the Badger/Mangum rivalry caused rifts. Yet another problem was the eastern and western Whigs' resentment against the domination of their party by the Whigs of Orange and Wake: Badger, Mangum, and Graham all were from these counties, and the Raleigh Whigs dominated the Whig Central Committee. Some Whigs from the eastern and western counties felt that the Whigs from the counties around Raleigh had too long exerted an unwarranted and controlling influence on the party and held all the chief offices.

The rivalry between Mangum and Badger intruded into the Whigs' selection of a gubernatorial candidate in 1848 and combined with eastern rivalry against the Raleigh Whigs. Though Badger never sought directly to challenge Mangum, he envisioned the latter moving into retirement, allowing him to be senior senator and party leader. Badger intervened in the gubernatorial nomination in 1848. Pushing his kinsman Edward Stanly for the gubernatorial nomination, Badger boasted that Stanly would serve two terms and then replace Mangum as senator in 1852. Mangum, supported by the state's other four Whig congressmen, opposed Stanly.[139] The Raleigh Whigs also opposed Stanly and preferred Kenneth Rayner from northeastern Hertford County.[140] Rayner was a stalwart of the party and an old ally of Mangum, but he declined the nomination. The Whigs failed to settle on a consensus candidate before their

1848 convention. When Rayner refused to support Stanly's nomination, the convention chose a compromise candidate, Charles Manly, a Raleigh Whig who was less popular than Rayner and Stanly. Manly's nomination, however, left many Whigs dissatisfied because victory would mean another capital-region Whig was governor.[141]

Manly's nomination exacerbated the growing resentment of Whigs from the eastern and western counties about the dominance of the Raleigh Whigs. By the end of 1846, with Badger's election to the Senate and the reelection of Mangum and Graham to the Senate and governor's office, respectively, the highest offices were held by Whigs from two counties: Wake (Badger) and neighboring Orange (Mangum and Graham). (Two of the supreme court justices also resided in Wake County.) Additionally, a Raleigh Whig usually presided at the party's state convention, and Weston Gales published the party's principal newspaper, the *Raleigh Register*, at Raleigh. Once the Whig ascendancy was complete, and especially once it appeared to most Whigs that the party would continue to control the state's highest offices, many Whigs began to resent the power of their fellow partisans from the capital region. Badger's bid for control undoubtedly exacerbated the fears of eastern and western Whigs that they would be shut out.

Because of the selection of Manly, the Raleigh Whigs' preference for Rayner, an easterner, was ignored by those who complained of Manly's selection. They argued that the Raleigh Whigs had again chosen one of their own. The eastern Whigs felt that one of their own deserved the nomination (even though a rivalry between Stanly and Rayner had blocked the selection of an easterner). Manly was a Raleigh Whig and a member of the Whig Party's central committee. The Democrats recognized the Whigs' dissatisfaction with Manly.[142]

The western counties felt a stronger resentment against the control of the capital-region Whigs than the east. Some western Whigs complained that even though they would support Manly, they would have preferred a candidate "out of the influence of Raleigh."[143] Governor William Graham's selection of a Whig from Orange County to fill a vacancy on the state supreme court added to the westerner's dissatisfaction with the Whig leadership. Graham had narrowed his candidates to Richard M. Pearson from western Yadkin County and William Battle from Orange County, both superior court judges. Needless to say, western Whigs wanted Graham to appoint Pearson. One of Graham's friends, Joseph Allison, a western attorney who knew Pearson, advised the governor to choose the westerner: "All your friends in the West are the friends of Pearson, & are particularly in favour of his appointment as a man the best qualified & who would be independent of that Raleigh Clique, to which the people are getting strongly opposed, for using power because they have it." He wanted the judge to be one who would not bow "to the Raleigh Dictators."[144] Graham thus ignored advice from his western friends and chose Battle. All three judges on the court then resided in Orange County. When Graham's appointment of Battle came before the legislature for confirmation, the Whigs were too divided between Battle and Pearson to elect either with a united Whig vote. Like the contest between Graham and Clingman, Whig divisions allowed Democratic votes to elect Pearson to the court.[145]

At the same time that the Whig Party was becoming factionalized, the Democratic Party was energized by the Whig divisions and made changes in their own party that were significant enough to be called a "Democratic revolution." Between 1848 and 1850, the Democratic Party of North Carolina reinvented itself—a revolution that helped to end the long period of Whig ascendancy. In addition to exploiting Whig divisions, the Democrats began to support internal improvements, most importantly railroads, and found an issue that allowed them to emphasize their party as the chief proponent of greater democracy: "equal suffrage." (Of course, equal suffrage referred only to white males.) The two most important leaders of this Democratic revolution were William Woods Holden, editor of the Raleigh *North Carolina Standard* and David S. Reid, the party's candidate for governor in 1848 and 1850.[146]

Introduced by Reid at a debate with Manly in New Bern in May during the election campaign for governor in 1848, "equal suffrage" called for an end to the fifty-acre property qualification for voting for state senators. Manly immediately opposed this change. The Democrats defended equal suffrage as part of their commitment to white equality. The Whigs argued against it as another evidence of the Democrats' radicalism that threatened the "conservative principle" of the state constitution. Realizing that a strictly conservative argument might cost them votes among those who did not own fifty acres of land, the Whigs added regional arguments to their opposition to equal suffrage. In the east, they asserted that it would lead to the reorganization of the senatorial districts from the basis of taxation to that of white population, reducing the power of the eastern counties in the legislature.[147] In fact, Governor William Graham wrote an anonymous letter for publication in eastern newspapers setting out that Whig position and defending the conservative property qualifications. Privately, Graham confessed that it was strictly a "sectional appeal."[148] In the west, the Whigs put forward the opposite argument: equal suffrage would not truly give western white men equality with easterners because property would continue to be represented in the legislature.[149] Reid had found an effective counterweight to Whig charges of Democratic radicalism.

The party division between Taylor men and Clay men that had been so evident in the county and district conventions in the spring of 1848 also made an impact on the state elections in August. Despite the unity around Taylor which Mangum and other Clay Whigs tried to promote after the 1848 national Whig convention, persistent divisions between Clay Whigs and Taylor Whigs reportedly had an effect on the legislative elections. From Washington, Badger wrote to Governor Graham in July that the Whig delegation had heard "bad news from N.C. intimating that by division among ourselves we may lose the legislature."[150] Equal suffrage proved to be enormously popular; much of the debate during the campaign centered on the issue.[151]

In the election, the Whigs nearly lost control of the government, and the weakness of the party fueled regional divisions. The Whigs won a very narrow victory in the contest for governor, with Manly receiving 42,536 votes to Reid's 41,682—a slim majority of only 854 votes. And the Whigs lost their majority in the legislature: the legislative elections resulted in an even division of both houses.[152] The issue of equal suffrage continued important after the election. Democrats adopted it as party policy, and it worsened geographical tensions among the Whigs. Western Whigs pushed for white population as the basis for apportioning representation in the legislature.[153] This position became another source of division with the Whigs of the eastern counties. Though Manly won, his poor showing compared to Graham in 1846 probably intensified the resentments of eastern and western Whigs.[154]

The regional rivalries also played a part in the Senate election of 1848. Clingman, who had been one of the first to attack the monopoly of the capital-region Whigs on offices, again challenged Badger for a Senate seat. In 1848 the reward for the successful candidate was higher than in 1846: the General Assembly would elect a senator to fill a full six-year term, a position that could propel the victor to the leadership of the party. Knowing Mangum sympathized with his opposition to Badger, Clingman solicited Mangum's support with an assessment of Badger's intentions. Unless Badger was blocked, Clingman told Mangum, he would use his early support of Taylor to control the federal appointments in the state. It was therefore urgent, Clingman advised, for all those Whigs who did not wish the party to be "the mere property of one family" to oppose Badger or they would soon be "a minority in the State."[155] Despite his appeals to Mangum, Clingman did not hesitate to renounce his "ultra" Whiggery after he realized that he could attract significant support from Democrats in the legislature if he abandoned the Whig program. In a letter that his biographer calls "a masterpiece of evasion and equivocation," Clingman distanced himself from Whig measures and staked out an independent position favorable to the Democrats.[156] In the election, the Democrats voted for Clingman, but the united vote of the non–Clingman Whigs defeated him. The vast majority of Whigs in the legislature supported Badger's reelection. Badger won when Clingman gave up after several ballots and convinced one of his supporters to switch to Badger.[157]

Clingman's abandonment of Whig principles marked the end of his career with the Whig Party, though his position in the Mountain District remained strong. Democratic editor William Woods Holden, of the Raleigh *North Carolina Standard*, the chief organ of the Democratic Party, described Clingman's letter as evidence that the candidate would be "sure and safe" for Democrats as a Senator. Though he had depended on Democratic votes, James Graham had never abandoned Whig principles. (Significantly, he had never been an ardent, or "ultra," Whig, as Clingman was in his Whig heyday.)

Clingman continued to maintain the posture of an "independent" Whig, but his future no longer lay with the Whig Party. After this time, he began to shift to an "ultra" position on Southern rights. The Democrats increasingly began to claim him as one of their own. Clingman's break with the Whig Party was a blow to the party's fortunes because as a rising star of the party, he would certainly have eventually been one of its leaders. His ambition would not let him wait for the retirement of the more senior party members Mangum and Badger before pressing his claims to a Senate seat.

After Manly's poor showing, Graham's appointment of Battle, and the Senate elections of 1846 and 1848, many Whigs in the eastern and western counties sought to end the control of the "center clique" by removing one of its chief means of control over the party—the Whig Central Committee—that was also one of its chief strengths.

Arguably the Whig Central Committee—established every two years by the state Whig convention—had been largely responsible for the organization of the party's campaign rallies, candidates' speaking tours, and the publication and distribution of party "documents" that had won and maintained the Whigs' ascendancy for nearly a decade; now some Whig leaders from outlying counties were prepared to set the Central Committee aside in effort to break the control of the "central clique" that they believed denied them the state's highest offices. During the contest for the Senate in 1848, Clingman told Attorney General Bartholemew F. Moore that the destruction of the "cormorant propensities" of the state's center counties was more important than the preservation of any party.[158] In short, an effective Whig Central Committee became the victim of the jealously of the Whig leaders from the east and west.

The central committees set up by the conventions of 1846 and 1848 were in accordance with the tried and proven organization of past successful state campaigns since 1840. In both cases seven Whigs from Wake County served on the committee. The 1846 committee totaled thirty-eight members, but the 1848 committee was not as large. In addition to the Wake County members, that convention appointed only one member from each of the nine congressional districts.[159] Both years the convention set five members as the quorum of the committee, giving the Wake members the ability to easily meet and conduct the committee's business. In 1846, the Whig convention gave the central committee its typical mandate: "to watch over the interests of the Whig party in [North Carolina] and to promote the election of the present able incumbent of the Gubernatorial chair, by all proper ... means."[160] The organization of 1848 was particularly efficient. The district members then essentially acted as points of contact in each district for the Central Committee in Raleigh. By 1848, the role and duties of the committee were so well established that the convention passed no resolution defining them.

By the meeting of the Whig Convention of 1850, the desire of the eastern and western Whigs to end the power of the Raleigh Whigs had reached the point that the former group were prepared to dispense with the party coordination and organization that the Whig Central Committee had provided. They used their numbers at the convention to replace the central committee with an ineffective "Executive Committee of the Whig party" with twenty-seven members, three from each congressional district, with no additional members from Raleigh. The Whigs seemed to have realized that the committee could never attain a quorum in Raleigh and set no number for a quorum; they provided only for the committee to set up county sub-committees (with no means of coordination). They did give the Executive Committee the usual mandate of the Central Committee to "attend to the general interests of Whig party in the State," but with Richard Hines as the only member from Wake County, it is hard to see how the convention delegates expected this mandate to be fulfilled. The mandate, then, seems pro forma: the eastern and western Whig delegates manifestly did *not* want a strong central committee to conduct the campaign. As one historian of antebellum North Carolina politics notes, these changes to the party's coordinating committee effectively "rendered it impotent."[161]

A resolution put forward by former senator and governor and long-time Whig party leader James Iredell (who ironically was from Wake County) confirms that the Whigs did not want central direction and were probably overconfident about their ability to win without an organized campaign. Iredell, the chief leader of the Anti–Van Buren movement in the East in 1832, proposed a resolution calling for a state canvass by the gubernatorial nominee "unnecessary, unjust, and not in accordance with true republican principles." Some eastern Whigs, who had been National Republicans, had long opposed the gubernatorial candidate traveling the state and giving political speeches.[162] Rayner succeeded in modifying Iredell's resolution to leave the decision on a canvass up to Manly, but the convention gave no mandate.[163] Also, the Executive Committee set up no canvassing schedule and took no action to coordinate Manly's campaign by organizing district mass meetings. Just when the Whigs most needed organization and enthusiasm to aid the unpopular Manly, they removed the central committee that had acted so successfully in those areas for a decade.[164]

As a part of their revolution the Democrats adopted the Whigs' most popular measure of political economy—internal improvements. In 1848, Holden included "a safe, prudent, and judicious system of Internal Improvements, with justice to all parts of the State" as part of the issues on which the party was campaigning under Reid's banner. And in February 1849 he gave an extended defense of his position in favor of internal improvements in the *Standard*.[165]

Holden thus joined the group of Democrats who supported internal improvements by the state government. Because Holden was the editor of the *Standard*, the Democrats' foremost newspaper, his advocacy lent a new weight to party support of internal improvements. Still, the internal improvement Democrats remained a minority in their party and internal improvements were never incorporated into the platform of any Democratic state convention from 1844 to 1850. Even Holden admitted that Democrats had to "agree to disagree" on support of internal improvements.[166] And the Democrats' candidate for governor in 1850, David Reid, opposed the Central Railroad project. Holden assured him that the "Rail Road Democrats"—Holden chief among them—backed his candidacy, and that his opposition to the railroad project would even be an asset to the party as it would give confidence to the "anti–Rail Road Democrats."[167] Yet a minority of Democrats was all that was required to pass internal improvements in the legislature. Holden's support was thus decisive.

In 1848, his last year in office, Governor William Graham strongly backed the construction of a state-funded central railroad between Raleigh and Charlotte to link the existing railroads from Raleigh north to Virginia and Charlotte south to South Carolina. He proposed the plan in his November 1848 message to the General Assembly.[168] In the House of Commons Giles Mebane introduced a bill drafted by Graham incorporating his plan for the central railroad.[169] Some Democrats supported the bill which was passed by the tie-breaking vote of the Democratic Speaker of the Senate. When the railroad and the other internal improvement bills were approved by the legislature, Graham's friends in the legislature immediately wrote to him with the news.[170] The Whigs had finally enacted their internal improvements passed, but the Democrats could claim a large share of the credit.

The Whigs wanted internal improvements, now including railroads, to be their issue. However, the strong involvement of influential Democrats in the railroad projects, their support of internal improvements in the legislature, and Holden's championing of these issues gave them no chance to contrast their position on internal improvements with that of the Democrats as they had done for so long and so successfully before.

With the program of railroads and internal improvements in place and supported by both Democrats and Whigs, the Whigs turned to compromise, Union, and opposition to Democratic agitation of the slavery issue as their chief difference with Democrats in the 1850 campaign. At their convention in 1850, the Whigs did not set out their traditional platform; especially notable was the absence of a resolution on distribution, in the past the Whigs' most popular measure: the Democrats, though not supporting distribution, now backed a program of state internal improvements. Distribution and internal improvements were thus no longer issues with which they could offer a sharp contrast with the Democrats' policy. A general resolution declared the Whigs' "unabated confidence and attachment to the principles of the Whig Party."

The convention was held amidst the debate in Congress on the Compromise of 1850. The Whigs made the Union their platform, resolving to "uphold and defend the integrity of our National Union." They also declared their desire for an end to agitation on the slavery issue:

> *Resolved*, That we believe a large majority of the American People desire the restoration of harmony and concord to our Country by a fair and honorable adjustment of the agitating questions connected with the Institution of Domestic Slavery, and they demand that their peace and comfort shall be no longer disturbed by keeping open, as capital for demagogues and fanatics, those delicate and dangerous questions.

Expressing full support for the work of the Senate Committee of Thirteen to find a compromise resolution to the territorial issue, the Whigs approved the committee's "plan of adjustment" and declared their desire that the compromise settlement "become the law of the land." They passed a resolution of support for Taylor, stating their expectation that his course in administering the government would be "conservative and patriotic." The Democrats' equal suffrage proposal forced the Whigs to adopt a defensive resolution calling for a referendum on amending the state constitution.[171]

The North Carolina Whigs thus identified compromise and Union with the goals of the Whig Party—indeed, these were the major focus of their platform in 1850. Though the convention did not pass the usual platform resolutions, the *Raleigh Register* printed Manly's acceptance speech in full. It addressed the issues of patronage, education, internal improvements, free suffrage, and a comparison of "Whig principles" and "Democratic principles." Nonetheless, it was a poor substitute for a concise statement of Whig principles that could be used by Whig candidates and published in newspapers across the state—as the Whig Central Committee had always done since 1840.

The elections of 1850 for governor and legislature occurred too soon for the approval of the Compromise to factor into the campaign—only the earlier divisions between Taylor, the "ultra" Whigs, and Mangum and Clay's "omnibus" compromise Whigs. The elections were contested largely on the Whig divisions, Whig defense of the work of the Committee of Thirteen, and on equal suffrage. At their 1850 convention, the Whigs addressed the equal suffrage issue by calling for a referendum on an equal suffrage amendment to the constitution in hopes of taking the issue out of the political debate. But their position failed to satisfy even some of the Whigs. Democrats remained solidly behind equal suffrage and it proved just as popular as in 1848, especially with Reid again the Democratic candidate.[172] By 1850, Holden could assure Reid that he was "universally known" in the state as "the author of Equal Suffrage."[173]

The election highlighted the problem of Whig factionalism. The Democrats recognized the divisions in the Whig ranks created by the conflict between Taylor and Clay on the territorial issue; "lukewarmness" was likely to overshadow the Whigs' campaign. Holden rightly predicted that the "divisions and heartburnings" in the Whig ranks would reduce Manly's vote.[174] The election was the culmination of the Holden-Reid Democratic revolution. Reid won the contest for governor, obtaining 45,080 votes to Manly's 42,337 votes. Reid was the first Democrat to win a gubernatorial race since the popular election of governors began in 1836. The Democrats also won a majority in both houses of the legislature: by ten in the commons and four in the senate.[175]

The organization of the Central Committee arguably had been responsible for the effectiveness of the Whig campaigns from 1840 to 1848. The replacement of the Central Committee with an ineffective Executive Committee played a large part in the Whig defeat in 1850, when because of a weak gubernatorial candidate every vote was needed. Historian of the Whig Party Michael Holt calls the destruction of the state central committee and the demolition of the influence of the Raleigh Whigs "far more disastrous to Whig fortunes in the short term than Clingman's defection."[176] By 1852 the fall of the Raleigh leadership was well-recognized. New Bern Whig leader John H. Bryan complained of "an insane jealousy of the Centre" and told William Graham that any party direction or measure would be injuriously affected if it emanated from Raleigh.[177] Western demands for equality in the legislature continued to divide the Whigs after 1850.[178]

With the Whig supremacy and the victory of Mangum's election achieved by 1841, Whigs by mid-decade began to look beyond Mangum: some wished to see him retire or to supplant him as party leader. In 1836, he had been the symbol of a party struggling to overthrow Van Burenism. By mid-decade, with that victory achieved and the Whig ascendancy established, he was no longer needed as the symbol of the party. After his re-election in 1846 and the confirmation of the Whigs' ascendancy in the 1846 state elections, Whig divisions had rapidly expanded and Mangum's defense of Whig principles, like the central committee, was set aside. The combination of the destruction of the central committee, the rupture between Taylor men and Clay men, and the weakening of Mangum's leadership was a far cry from 1844 when the state party had been united under Clay's banner and Mangum as acting vice president. By 1850 the North Carolina Whig Party had been greatly weakened.

The waning of the Whigs' ability to contrast sharply their measures with those supported by the state's Democrats was almost important as the Whig divisions in ending the Whig ascendancy. In 1850, James Graham detected the need for such contrasts among the people in his Mountain District: "The Whig party of our State suffers greatly from the want of an efficient Press in the State, particularly at Raleigh; to which point the Village Papers look for leading articles, stating clearly and concisely and in a popular manner, the issues, reasons and arguments which divide the two parties."[179] As a result of the Democrats' adoption of internal improvements, the Whigs now had difficulty making the contrast. And equal suffrage turned the Whigs' appeal to their conservative principles into what seemed to be opposition to democracy. The final blow to the Whigs came when failures by the Democrats in the congressional elections of 1851—and similar failures of Democrats in other Southern states who attacked the compromise measures—led to the party's adoption of the central Whig message of 1850–1851: Union and the finality of the Compromise of 1850. The Whigs could no longer attack Democratic radicalism.

Mangum and Scott in 1852

In the congressional elections of 1851 "the great conservative principles of the Whig Party" became the defense of the Constitution and the Union. The Whigs' defense of Fillmore, the Compromise of 1850, and the Union were the focus of the congressional election campaign of 1851. All the Democratic candidates criticized the Compromise, and many defended secession.[180] The Whigs' Constitution and Union stance showed appeal: the Whigs won 6 of 9 congressional districts (including Clingman in the Mountain district). Their internal divisions, however, led to the loss of the governor's office and the legislature. The Compromise and the Union appeared to be an effective platform on which to campaign for Congress. The Whigs hoped to use that appeal in the 1852 presidential contest. Yet which of the potential national Whig candidates was best for North Carolina? Whom should the Carolina Whigs back?

Willie P. Mangum believed that General Winfield Scott remained the best national Whig candidate; he had the added credential of his illustrious war record in the War of 1812 and, most recently, his successful campaign to take Mexico City in 1847–1848. Mangum also preferred him as the truest Whig. Mangum's early support of Scott in 1848, before Clay declared his availability, had been no spur of the moment decision—personal friendship convinced Mangum of Scott's soundness. He and Scott had been friends in Washington since the early

1840s. Scott had also been Mangum's second choice (after Clay) in 1844 for the presidential nomination. In 1842, as the party was choosing it nominee for 1844, Mangum reported to Henry Clay: "I have spent three or four evenings at Scott's quarters at whist parties &C.— As I play but little, & Scott none at all, I have had much Conversation with the General.— After placing you first & against the world, & in Case of an unhappy Contingency, then looking to him next & decidedly...."[181]

Yet, despite his friendship for Scott, the Southern Whigs' difficulties with Taylor cooled Mangum's preference for a military candidate. In 1849 Mangum asserted to John M. Clayton of Delaware that there would not soon be another "military administration"; no military man not even their "excellent and illustrious friend, Gen. Scott" could succeed.[182] His view probably also reflected his own and other old guard Whigs' frustration with Taylor's appointments, rather that a strong revulsion against a military leader. Soon Mangum changed his mind. His anger with Fillmore probably contributed to his backing his old friend Scott, whom he had long favored. Mangum also had long hoped to run as Scott's vice-presidential nominee. And as early as 1849, Mangum was adamant that the next president should *not* be from a slave state.[183] Scott fit that criterion. Although born in Virginia, he had long resided in the North. Mangum was meeting with Scott in 1850.[184] Of course, as in 1848 Mangum could also envision himself as Scott's running mate.

In 1852, Mangum was not, however, among the majority of North Carolina Whigs, and his political position had somewhat eroded. He had become embroiled in a confrontation with the Raleigh Whigs. In the spring of 1850, as the Compromise measures were being debated in Congress, Mangum did not communicate with the Whig leaders in Raleigh, and Whig leaders in North Carolina were unsure of his course. They feared he might oppose Taylor on the admission of California. At the same time, some worried that he and Badger might be insufficiently "zealous" in defending slavery and "too tolerant" of the anti-slavery Whigs in the North.[185] Even as he was pressed for patronage appointments, Mangum was criticized in Raleigh for staying in Washington and not returning to North Carolina at the close of the session of Congress in March. He told Graham that while in Washington "the most unmanly reproaches" had been given against him at home which he meant to "settle" on his return. In April 1849, C.L. Hinton had asked Mangum to call in Raleigh on his return from Washington; presumably it was with these Raleigh Whigs' calling for his return that Mangum was angry.[186] The reasons behind the division are not clear, but by late May a rift had developed between the Mangum and the Raleigh Whig leaders of the Central Committee. In the fall of 1849, when Hinton and Paul Cameron passed through Washington, Mangum refused to meet with them.[187]

In North Carolina, most of the Whigs strongly supported Fillmore because, as one leading Whig from the east explained to Graham, he had "passed through the ordeal" and had been "weighed and found to be of sterling metal." Graham insisted that the administration had "shown every disposition to favor Southern interests."[188] Little discussion of Scott's merits had taken place.[189] Some Carolina Whigs opposed Scott because they believed him too closely associated with Seward.[190] Graham's anti–Seward stance on appointments was in accord with the attitudes of the majority of Carolina Whigs, and their hostility to Seward affected the outlook of the presidential nomination in North Carolina. James Osborne of Charlotte told Graham that Scott's position was affected by "a suspicion of Sewardism."[191] In the congressional delegation, however, Stanly and Badger also supported Scott, though Outlaw opposed him.

Southern Whigs' greatest concern about Scott was the extent of his support of the Compromise of 1850, especially the fugitive slave law. Yet Mangum realized that a definitive declaration from Scott might hurt him with Northern Whigs. With more Whig states in the North than in the South, the best hope of a Whig victory was the united vote of Whigs in the northern states, where the Free Soil Party now gave anti-slavery Whigs an alternative. Scott was more popular with Northern Whigs than Fillmore. State conventions in Ohio, Pennsylvania, Indiana, and New York as well as a caucus of Whigs in the Delaware legislature had endorsed Scott. At the same time, important Southern Whigs in Congress supported the general's candidacy. In addition to Mangum, Badger was receptive to his nomination and Edward Stanly supported him as did Senators John Bell and James Jones of Tennessee and William Ward of Kentucky. The Richmond *Whig*, the Louisville *Journal*, and the Nashville *Republican Banner* all announced their support of Scott.[192] And it was fairly certain that a Southerner would be paired with Scott as the Whigs' vice-presidential nominee. Thus, there seemed every prospect that Scott was the best candidate to unite Whigs North and South and garner the maximum Whig vote.

In the interests of the national Whig coalition and to preserve Northern Whigs' flexibility, Mangum was determined that Scott not be held to a declaration on the Compromise. New York free-soil Whigs, led by Seward, Weed, and Horace Greeley at the New York *Tribune*, insisted that the best, most politically effective stance of the Whig Party was for the state parties, North and South, to "agree to disagree" on the slavery question. Mangum realized the importance of the New York party in electing a Whig president, and he wanted to preserve maximum flexibility for Whigs in both sections.[193] Thus, Mangum's strategy was a balancing act: to increase Whig votes in the North while speaking of Scott's loyalty to the spirit of the compromise to hold Whig votes in the South. Moreover, a Southerner (hopefully himself) on the ticket would further reassure the South.

During the meetings of the Whig caucus in April, Mangum showed how far he was prepared to go against the majority of Southern Whigs to preserve this balancing strategy. At the meetings of the Whig caucus on April 9 and on April 20, Mangum sought to prevent Southern Whigs from putting a resolution about the finality of the Compromise before the caucus. Mangum called the caucus to decide upon the time and place for the Whig convention. When the call for the caucus announced that the meeting would "consider matters of importance to the Whig party," the dissident Southern Whigs had an opening to introduce a resolution on the finality of the compromise. They introduced a resolution that had been approved by a lightly-attended caucus the previous December. After a brief debate that promised to turn divisive, Mangum adjourned the meeting to April 20. He cautioned the caucus that if he were chairman of the next meeting, he would rule the reintroduction of the resolution out of order. In the interim, Mangum made a forceful speech endorsing Scott, but he changed no minds among sectional-minded Southern Whigs.

At the April 20 meeting of the caucus, they reintroduced their resolution and Mangum, again in the chair, ruled it out of order. The Whigs sustained his ruling by a vote of 46 to 21. Mangum also ruled out of order another resolution declaring that Whigs were under no pledge to support the nominee of the convention unless he publicly pledged himself to the finality of the Compromise. Mangum was again sustained by a vote of the caucus. Mangum offered to allow debate on resolutions after the regular business of the caucus had been completed, and the Whigs reassembled specifically to debate resolutions. The dissident Southern Whigs rejected the offer and withdrew from the caucus meeting. Thirteen Southern Whigs remained, however, and the caucus completed its business, selecting Baltimore as the site of the convention to be held on June 16.[194] The determined push by this group of Southern Whigs to gain Northern Whig commitment on the finality of the Compromise shows the degree to which sectional considerations had become dominant. For Whigs like Mangum, who prioritized the national Whig party, it became increasingly difficult to maintain party unity.

Mangum made a personal effort to promote unity for Scott's candidacy. In a major speech to the Senate, Mangum declared his preference for Scott, explained why he considered Scott safe for the South, and explained why no resolutions on the Compromise should be introduced by Southern Whigs. Mangum was "a party man" and would act in good faith to support the nominee of the Whig Party as long as the principles of the party remained "pure, national, and conservative of the rights of the States, as well as the rights of the Union." He realized that the majority of the Whigs in North Carolina preferred President Fillmore. Although he intended to retire from public life at the end of his term, Mangum averred that he still intended to pursue the course that was best in his judgment. Mangum asserted that Scott was "the only Whig in this Union who can reach the Presidency by the voice of the people."

Mangum testified that he had spoken with Scott when the "omnibus" bill was under discussion. Scott, Mangum insisted, possessed as "clean a bill of political health" on the finality of the Compromise as Fillmore, Webster, or Clay. Scott had embraced the Compromise with "zeal" and "ardor" when public opinion on the Compromise was doubtful. Scott had done all in his power to assist in the adjustment of the difficulties of 1850. Mangum argued that Scott as acting Secretary of War in 1850 had supported the Union:

> I consider him as national and as patriotic as any man who is named for the Presidency by either of the parties of the country. He would scorn to acquire a triumph for one section of the country over another.... No enlightened patriot or statesman, with enlarged views, would ever desire it.

Mangum denied that either he or General Scott was controlled by the anti-slavery Whigs of the North. Scott, Mangum insisted, "would never be made an unworthy instrument in the hands of any faction, whether South or North." As to his own position, he respected William Seward but declared that their views on slavery were as "wide as the poles asunder." Challenging those who questioned his loyalty to the South to find one instance in which he had failed to defend slavery, Mangum ridiculed his accusers as men whose views were limited merely to town, county, or congressional district. Though he was "a little ultra" in defense of the South, Mangum denied these views made him sectional or led him to forget that he owed "a great duty" to every portion of the Union.

Finally, Mangum dealt with pledges on the Compromise. Declaring that he had no sympathy with agitators—abolitionists of the North and disunionists of the South—whom he accused of acting "recklessly" and seeking merely to gain "a little flash popularity," Mangum expressed his opposition to any reopening of agitation by putting declarations about the Compromise in the Whig platform. He opposed making the Compromise measures "a new article in our political creed." They were compromise measures: "admitted to be more or less unsatisfactory to all." But they were the law, and the questions were now settled. "There is nothing upon which agitation can act." Yet some now wanted to add them to the Whig platform as if they were all equally popular. "I am opposed to *that*," Mangum declared. "I will give neither aid nor countenance to any one who aids, abets, or connives at the reopening of agitation upon these delicate points." He finished his speech by reminding senators that Scott, if elected President, would be sworn to execute all the laws.[195] Mangum thus supported the spirit of the Compromise but not the potentially divisive attempt to incorporate it into the Whig platform. He averred that Scott was for no section, but for Union and for the enforcement of laws.

Nationally, Whigs in the Deep South states denounced Mangum's speech. The proceedings of the Whig caucus were criticized both by disaffected Southern Whigs and Fillmore Whigs in the North.[196] In North Carolina, many Whigs who had already endorsed Fillmore disapproved of Mangum's speech, but most of the Raleigh Whigs stuck by Mangum, Badger, and Stanly in their support of Scott. At the time of Mangum's speech, Stanly had written an open letter to Southern Whigs in support of Scott. Henry W. Miller told Mangum that he was glad to see Mangum's speech because he thought Scott was the only man in the Whig Party who could be elected president. "Believing that he is sound on the Compromise I go with you," he assured Mangum.[197] Seaton Gales, editor of the *Raleigh Register*, explained to Mangum that the Raleigh Whigs thought Mangum had been "harshly judged and unjustly censured" on account of his speech; they were "fully convinced" that Mangum's judgment was correct.[198]

Other Whigs disapproved but accepted Mangum's support of Scott or simply appealed for party unity. Augustine H. Shepperd supported Fillmore, but was inclined to neutrality on Mangum because of Mangum's long-standing friendship with Scott. "[Mangum], so far as I have heard from him & understand him, has all the while stuck to his first love & has only been waiting his time. Scott and Mangum I always looked on as good jolly boon companions—*I have seen them often together*. So let them be."[199] John Kerr, the Whig candidate for governor, regretted the divisions between Fillmore Whigs and Scott Whigs, especially in the western counties where the Whigs needed a strong vote. He wanted Whig leaders to insist on "Union and harmony in the Whig ranks."[200]

Because of the strong commitment to Fillmore among a majority of the state's leading Whigs, though, most reaction to Mangum's endorsement of Scott was negative. William Graham, as would be expected of a cabinet secretary, disapproved, but his chief objection was the embarrassment caused to Fillmore by their endorsing Scott after Fillmore's supporters were already committed to the president's reelection. He thought Mangum's speech and Stanly's pro–Scott letter were "exceeding ill-timed" and had produced "much feeling" among the "National Whigs" (administration supporters) in the North. He especially objected to Mangum making his speech after nearly all the Whig county meetings of the winter and spring had endorsed Fillmore.[201] Charles Hinton, a Raleigh Whig and former member of the Whig Central Committee, reported to Graham that at the Whig state convention, "No one appears to justify Mr. Mangum's speech; it is spoken of very freely—neither do they approve of Stanly's letter."[202] Robert Gilliam, Whig leader in Granville County, thought Mangum's speech had no effect on Fillmore men and had actually strengthened the "universal sentiment" for Fillmore.[203]

One of the harshest critiques of Mangum's course came from James W. Osborne of Charlotte, who had been a rival of Mangum for the Senate in 1846. He thought that Mangum's course had met with "little favor" among the Whigs and that it threatened to be "extremely injurious" to the Whig Party. Indeed, Osborne, deeming the "ill judged and mistaken" speech "a mere political maneuver," argued that Mangum's ambition for the vice-presidency lay at its cause. He predicted that Mangum would find no support among the state's Whigs: "If Mangum aspires to the Vice-Presidency, as is generally believed, he will find North Carolina in the General Convention pressing any other Candidate. To be deserted at home must convince him too late perhaps of his error."[204] Outside North Carolina Mangum's course also received negative attention. From New York Mangum's old friend Nicholas Carroll, an active Fillmore supporter, wrote Graham, "I am deeply mortified to notice the course of Judge Mangum." He still professed his "unabated regard" for Mangum, but he thought Mangum had "damaged himself" with the speech.[205]

Despite the criticism from Southern Whigs, Mangum received what he had hoped for by remaining loyal to Scott. At the national convention in June, Mangum was offered vice-president on the ticket with Scott but declined because of North Carolina's preference for a Fillmore Whig. He received votes on the first ballot. When delegates began to move to Graham to balance Scott with a Southern Fillmore supporter, Mangum made no effort to impede the movement—especially since the delegates from his own state mostly supported Graham. Many Fillmore men in North Carolina had looked to Graham as a vice-presidential nominee since the spring (but of course with Fillmore).[206] Nevertheless Mangum apparently believed that he could have had the nomination if he had pressed for it. "The nominations," Mangum told his wife, "are mine—I might have had it otherwise. It is best as it is." To his daughter, Martha, Mangum explained: "The nominations are made and are right.—I might have been second, but declined—The ill temper of North Carolina is such that I thought it might hazard the vote."[207] Mangum gave up his ambition to unify the state party behind the Scott-Graham ticket.

In regard to the party's doctrines for the 1852 campaign, the Southern Whig "ultras" and Fillmore national Whigs ("silver-grays") received their declaration in favor of the Compromise measures as the price of Scott's nomination. The most important battle occurred over the plank declaring the Compromise a "final settlement" of the issues embraced in its measures. Included at the insistence of the Southern delegations against Northern objections, the plank declared the Compromise settlement "essential to the nationality of the Whig party, and the integrity of the Union."[208] Still, the conservative principles of the party were also incorporated into the platform. Declaring that the Whigs adhered to "the great conservative republican principles" of the party," the Whig platform stated the "limited character" of the United States government. Yet the platform took a middle position on states' rights: the powers of the government were confined to those "expressly granted" and those that "may be necessary and proper" to carry out the granted powers with all others reserved to the states, who should be "held secure in their reserved rights." It declared that the federal and state governments were both "parts of one system" necessary for "the common prosperity, peace, and security" and that the authority and "constitutional measures" of each should be respected. The platform emphasized the Constitution, the Union, and the laws and advocated "strict economy" in government expenditures, and a "just" protective tariff. Although, the Compromise was central, the Whigs also intended to emphasize their conservatism and their traditional principles. But now they gave more emphasis to the Constitution, the Union, and the laws.

Despite his strong opposition to the Seward faction and fears of Scott's closeness to Seward's free-soil Whigs, Graham agreed to run with Scott for the unity of the Whig Party (after the Compromise plank was added). Graham had never had any personal objection to

Scott, having been friendly with him and dined with the general on his arrival in Washington to take up his duties as Navy Secretary.[209] Graham accepted the nomination in a short speech in which he declared his hopes "for the prosperity of this country, the stability of its institutions, and the perpetuity of the Union," all of which depended on "the ascendancy of the Whig measures." In his official acceptance letter, Graham declared his approval of the Whig platform since its planks accorded with the position of the administration. He also praised Scott as "a citizen of tried patriotism and virtue" and "a safe and sagacious counselor" who had ably fulfilled every trust committed to his hands.[210] He immediately tendered his resignation as Navy Secretary, which Fillmore accepted.[211] Mangum's plan worked regarding the nomination, but worked only at the price of the South exacting a Compromise finality plank. Moreover, North Carolina insisted on the vice-presidential nomination going to a Fillmore Whig. His opposition to Fillmore and the divisions in the state had cost him the vice-presidential nomination with Scott that he had so long coveted.

Despite his pending retirement, Mangum actively campaigned that fall. Remaining popular in the state as a speaker at Whig rallies, Mangum was invited to several Whig meetings. He was invited to speak at a Whig mass meeting for Halifax and Northampton counties. A leader in Stanly County reported that the desire among Whig in the area was "universal" to have Mangum speak at the county's mass meeting—he asserted that Mangum and Badger speaking at a mass meeting would be worth eighty additional votes in both Stanly County and neighboring Montgomery County. And the Whigs of Wilmington urged Mangum to visit their city.[212]

Opinions of Whig leaders about the prospects of the Scott-Graham ticket were mixed. Some were confident of success. Prominent Raleigh Whig Charles Hinton, who had preferred Fillmore, believed that though some "very few" were "backward in coming in," the Whigs were "in fine spirits." He reported that Graham's vice-presidential nomination had added strength to the ticket and that those Whigs who might have otherwise been lukewarm to Scott were "now disposed to use every effort" to gain a Whig victory.[213] One Whig told Graham that his name would be "a tower of strength" for the state's Whigs, and a prominent Whig from western Lincoln County thought that the Whigs in the county could "make more noise over Scott" than over either Fillmore or Webster.[214]

On the other hand, some Whig leaders thought that even with Graham on the ticket, the Whigs were in danger of losing because of Scott's unpopularity in the state. Robert Gilliam, a long-time leader of the Whig Party in Oxford, indicated that the Whigs in Granville County had not received Scott's nomination with "the cordiality which is the usual presage of victory." Expressing to Graham his conviction that only Graham's presence on the ticket would allow the Whigs to carry the state, Gilliam expressed "the greatest apprehensions" that even with Graham the Whigs would fail to win a majority in the legislature. Likewise, in Raleigh, Seaton Gales, an editor of the *Raleigh Register*, detected a slackening of Whig enthusiasm. He reported that the Whigs were organizing mass meetings in every section of the state; but he remained concerned that unless the Whigs were able to arouse "a more *active* feeling" in the state, they might lose the presidential election.[215]

In the August 1852 legislative and gubernatorial elections, Reid won reelection as governor and the Democrats retained a slight majority in the legislature.[216] The elections tended to confirm the new Democratic ascendancy in the state, but the Whigs held out hope for the Scott-Graham ticket later that fall. Some Whigs believed that the equal suffrage issue had again hurt their cause. Leading Whigs were convinced that free suffrage had again damaged them in the state elections, but remained optimistic of victory in the presidential contest where free suffrage would not be an issue. Eastern congressman Edward Stanly, who had supported Mangum's endorsement of Scott and who had written a pro–Scott letter in April, identified the greatest problems of the party: Free suffrage had proved "irresistible." Though he believed the adversity would be "beneficial" to the Whigs in the fall as it would encourage then to work harder, Stanly felt the lack of central coordination was damaging the Whig cause: "Something must be done to produce systematic effort." Without it, he feared that the Whigs would lose the presidential contest.[217]

In the general election, even with the divisions and the late unity of the Carolina Whigs on the Scott-Graham ticket, Scott came within 700 votes of defeating Franklin Pierce in North Carolina. Pierce received 39,744 to Scott's 39, 058 votes. Among the Southern states where the Scott-Graham ticket lost narrowly (Louisiana, North Carolina, Delaware, and Maryland), the Whigs came closest to winning in North Carolina, where the Whig ticket lost by less than one percent of the total votes cast. (The Whigs defeated the Democratic ticket in Kentucky and Tennessee).[218] Graham's nomination and the Compromise finality plank probably boosted Scott's support in North Carolina, but lack of enthusiasm for the ticket cost the Whigs a victory in the state.[219] The Democrats' newly moderated stance on the Compromise and the Union combined with their new support for internal improvements cost the Whigs the election. Lacking Van Buren on the Democratic ticket, Henry Clay or a slave-holding military hero on the Whig ticket, and any central coordination, the Whigs could neither organize nor generate party enthusiasm on a scale sufficient to overcome Democratic organization, anti–Scott propaganda, and greater Democratic numbers. The campaign of 1852 was not the Whigs' last campaign in North Carolina, but the state had rejected the old Whig stalwarts, Mangum and Graham. Combined with defeats in state and presidential elections, the election signaled that the Whigs would not recover their dominant position of the 1840s.

The Whig ascendancy that had begun in 1840 had come to an end. The Whigs' successful and popular ideology combining Old Republican and National Republican ideas and their skills at organization and moving public opinion had, after a decade of control of the state government, failed the Whig Party. Or rather, their own divisions combined with national events and the Democrats' revolution had rendered the Whigs incapable of utilizing those advantages as they had so effectively between 1840 and 1846. But the incompatibility of an opposition ideology with governing also brought their ascendancy to an end. Indicating to David Reid in 1850 that the "Buncombe Whigs"—Clingman's district—were calling for "state reform," William Holden had assured Reid that that call posed a problem for the Whigs, and he urged Reid to declare his intention to cooperate with the General Assembly to bring it about. Because the Whigs had controlled the state government for fourteen years, "Manly could not say that, without condemning his own party," Holden told Reid.[220] Holden, the antagonist of the Carolina Whigs, thus identified the Whigs' greatest weakness: their own ascendancy. "Reform" had been the principal call of the Whigs in their rise. Reform is a powerful call for an opposition party. With ascendancy and control of the government, however, the Whigs' opposition ideology could not furnish them with a weapon to counter the Democrats' populist appeal.

The end of the Whig ascendancy in North Carolina had revolutionary implications. A historian of North Carolina politics and parties in the antebellum period has argued that the election of 1850 was not revolutionary and actually changed little.[221] Viewed from a strictly state level and in terms strictly of changes in vote totals between the parties, that analysis is correct. But that assessment ignores the importance of the Whig ascendancy. It ignores the fact that the Whigs lost control of a government that had been theirs with but a single interruption for twelve years. And it ignores the importance of North Carolina being able to send Whigs to the United States Senate—vital for a Whig Senate—and the importance of North Carolina as a solidly Whig state in the South—critical to electing a Whig president and critical in making the Whig Party a national party. Arguably, the challenge of Free Soil during and after 1848 for Northern Whigs made the Southern Whig states even more important to the national coalition. The election of 1850, confirmed by the elections of 1852, was indeed revolutionary for Southern Whigs, the Whig Party, and the nation—its consequences were felt in all three realms.[222]

Mangum foresaw the revolutionary implications of the division of the Whig Party. In 1848 he thought the disunity evident in the inability of the Whigs in Congress to unite on a Whig candidate threatened the party. "We are in a sad condition here—divided & cut up," he had said then. He feared that any dissolution of the Whig Party would lead to the formation of "the worst & most dangerous kind of parties—I mean, sectional."[223] He had imbibed Macon's fear of sectional parties in the 1820s, and his own experience of the Nullification Crisis had convinced him of their dangers. Mangum had always realized the party's unifying role, and he had worked to sustain it as a national party. The defeat of the old defenders of Southern Whig principles in North Carolina signaled the end of the age of the Whig Party in the South and that meant the rise of the sectional parties Mangum had feared.

Conclusion

Clearly disappointed by the Whig failures, Mangum took no part in the debates of the 1852–1853 session of the Senate, other than voting. After having suffered a life-threatening fall in the winter of 1851 from which he never really recovered, he complained to his wife that now on the verge of his retirement from public life he felt like "an old man." In March 1853, he wrapped up his affairs in Washington and left the city for the last time.[1] His retirement from politics preceded the fall of the national Whig Party by only a few years. By 1856 the Whig Party had disintegrated.[2]

Active in Orange County politics in his retirement, Mangum held honorary posts in the county government, but he took no active role in state and national politics. He did not campaign for the Whigs in 1854. In 1856 he suffered a stroke of paralysis from which he never fully recovered. In the years 1860 to 1861, Mangum, as one would suspect of such a staunch Whig, opposed the secession movement. But when Lincoln issued his call to the states for 90,000 troops to put down the rebellion in South Carolina, Mangum encouraged his son to volunteer. William Preston Mangum joined the 6th North Carolina Regiment of the Confederate Army assembling in Virginia during the summer of 1861. At the Battle of Manassas, William was severely wounded while charging a Union battery. He died of his wounds a week later. Heartbroken when he learned of his only son's death, Mangum did not long survive. He died on September 7, 1861, having lived to see all he had worked for his entire life gone: the Whig Party, the Union, and his son.[3]

The rejection of Mangum and the "old guard" Southern Whigs carried significant consequences for North Carolina and the Union. Except for a brief foray into the ranks of the "ultra" Whigs resulting from his opposition to Taylor in 1849–1850, Mangum had worked to preserve the national Whig coalition, Whig principles, and the Union, but his adamant support of Scott eventually cost him the leadership of the North Carolina Whig party. Graham, another of the "old guard" Whigs became the leader of the Carolina Whig Party by 1852 (as a Fillmore Whig). Even the combined influence of Mangum and Graham, represented in the Scott-Graham ticket of 1852, was insufficient to turn the state back to the Whig Party.

Yet, the Whigs offered the nation a path to cooperation and compromise (as the Compromise of 1850 demonstrated). By 1853, though, the success of the Democratic revolution in North Carolina, combined with Whig divisions and Mangum's declining influence in the state, meant the Carolina electorate had foreclosed any chance for the Carolina Old Guard Whigs to deliver a Whig victory that could help hold their national party together. The Carolina Whigs could not hold the government of their state—the key to sustaining the position of the national Whig Party. The Old Guard Whigs stood rejected in North Carolina (and most of the South). Without "the great Conservative principles of the Whig party" to restrain rampant sectionalism, the South was on a trajectory to disunion.

In the end the unity of the states and the Whig Party as a center of opposition to the Democratic presidents depended to a large extent on the Senate of the United States, where the states were represented as equals and the Whigs largely fought their battles to restrain the (Democratic) radicalism of the people's will. Failure to win the presidency in 1844 or 1852 contributed to the Whigs downfall, but the inability of the Whig Party in the slave states to maintain their ascendancy in their state legislatures where they could elect senators also contributed to the fall of the Whig Party and ultimately of the Union. Southern Whig states—Delaware, Kentucky, Louisiana, Maryland, North Carolina, and Tennessee (and sometimes Georgia)—were critical to maintaining the Whig majority in the Senate. In the late 1840s and early 1850s, the loss of Louisiana and, soon thereafter, North Carolina as reliable Whig states severely damaged the Whig cause.

A Whig Senate restrained the radicalism of the Democratic Party. Even a Democratic Senate with a large Whig minority proved to be a restraining power. And as Tyler's inability to annex Texas by treaty showed, Whig control of the Senate could restrain continental expansion, but when Tyler and Polk set aside the inconvenient Constitution, the Whigs could offer little resistance (other than verbal) in the Senate to restrain Polk's continental ambitions. The Compromise of 1850 was the last act by a moderate/Whig Senate. It is no coincidence that even more demonstrations of Democratic radicalism soon followed (Kansas-Nebraska Act, then Kansas statehood). Any loss of Whig senators from these states meant fewer partners for Northern Whig senators on national issues. North Carolina was particularly critical because of the leadership of her senators, Mangum, Graham, and Badger, in cooperation with the moderate Whigs. When they overcame the checking power of the Senate, the presidents did so by unconstitutional or constitutionally questionable means—Jackson's disregard of Congress in destroying the Bank, his war on the Senate, Polk's annexation of Texas by joint resolution. Time and again the Whigs of the Senate proved to be the restraint on radicalism in the executive and to the Democratic Party's radicalism (usually led by Democratic presidents). And this study has shown that Mangum clearly saw the Senate's role—and his own—in checking radicalism.

In the Whig Senate's battles with the Democratic presidents, the ideological issues between the two parties came to the fore. Jefferson introduced the concept of the president exceeding constitutional powers in the name of the good of the people during exceptional circumstances, with actions judged by Congress. Later Democratic presidents expanded this idea and gave no role to Congress: the president and "the will of the people" was all—a conception of the people's representatives that excluded Congress as an embodiment of "the will of the people." The Whig presidents Harrison and Taylor *did* recognize Congress as the representative of the people. The Democrats lauded the concept of the president as people's tribune, and despite Whig resistance the powers of the presidency made major gains in this era. The Whigs' concept of the presidency reflected Jeffersonian Republicanism, and the Jacksonian concept of the presidency was one more example of the Democrats being less Republican than the Whigs.[4]

Mangum and other like-minded "young" Old Republicans split with their fellow Jackson men in the 1830s as a result of this dispute over the Republicanism of Jackson's concept of the presidency: The Constitution and the laws; executive versus legislative government. This is why Jackson's removal of the deposits was critical: it divided those Republicans who placed legislative supremacy (the laws) highest from those who deemed the popular will (unchecked majority rule) most important. Already disliked by opposition men in North Carolina, Van Buren became the symbol for all that the opposition men feared and disparaged about Jackson's new assertive style of presidential supremacy. The Old Republicans had always stood for legislative supremacy and executive deference to Congress; the Whigs followed this principle. The Jacksonians followed Van Buren in the new, radical idea of executive supremacy.

After 1844, the middle ground of the "old guard" Whigs of the Senate—North and South—was slowly eroded. In the North this came from the challenge of the Free Soil Party and other parties and in the South from the Democrats' adoption of the Whig political economy and the Whigs' move to a strident defense of slavery and sectionalism. The combination removed the "Union and harmony" Whigs from the Senate.

The rejection of their goals had significant implications. Writing to encourage his friend William Graham to accept appointment as Secretary of the Navy in Fillmore's cabinet, Whig party leader James W. Osborne of Charlotte asked Graham to accept for the honor it would confer on the state. He believed, though, even higher considerations were at stake:

> But there is a wider and more comprehensive view of this subject which cannot but influence the Patriot Statesman. It cannot be doubted but that difficulties lie in the way of the National Administration, and peril to some extent the National existence. Should moderation, modern conservatism, and an enlarged nationalism (if I may use the phrase) characterize the Administration, it will achieve a glorious destiny. To harmonize sectional discord, to rebuke and if possible stifle, and extinguish, the fanatical spirit which is found every where, to do justice to all interests, and reestablish the energy of the Constitution will be a glorious work.[5]

This was the Whig vision of what they hoped the Fillmore administration could achieve. And it summed up the goals of Mangum and the Southern Whig "old guard."

The fall of the "old guard" Whigs in North Carolina thus had national implications. As the vital core of North Carolina Southern Whig ideology, Old Republicanism's popularity underlaid the ascendancy of the Carolina Whigs—an ascendancy that was critical to the national Whig coalition. Only a few Southern states had "old guard" Whigs willing to seek compromise in the late 1840s: North Carolina was one and Mangum had a national reputation. As a Whig leader in the Senate from 1841 to 1845, Mangum had built the trust of northern Whigs. Southern Whigs were critical to a Whig Senate, and a Whig Senate was important for Whig goals: the key to restraining Democratic/presidential radicalism, it also was critical to the Compromise in 1850.

The Whig Senate was thus a crucial part of the struggle between Whig conservatism and radical "Jacksonism." By the late 1840s, the Whigs (and North Carolina Southern Whigs) were describing their principles as "conservative." Southern Whig conservatism in the late 1840s was primarily defined by the Whigs as conservative compared to the radicalism of the Democratic President Polk—"little Hickory." The Whigs offered an alternative of restraint: legislative supremacy, primarily from the Senate. Mangum and the Carolina Whigs envisioned an ideal government as a Whig Senate leading Congress and a Jeffersonian Republican president in the mold of Harrison in the presidency. But their defeat showed that Southerners were moving to embrace the Democratic concept of the strong president and continental expansion, pro-slavery outlook. Whig conservatism and compromise on slavery was rejected in North Carolina by 1852. The president as the embodiment of "the will of the people" had triumphed.

For nearly twenty years the Whig Party had been the axis of politics in North Carolina. And the immense popularity of Henry Clay with North Carolina's Southern Whigs raises the question: If the politics of slavery was the dominant campaign mode in the South, as Cooper argues, why was Henry Clay, who had almost refused to discuss slavery in his Raleigh speech of 1844, so popular in North Carolina? Both parties employed the "politics of slavery" in their arsenal of measures, issues, and principles, but from 1834 to 1852 North Carolina politics revolved about the Whig Party—sustaining it or destroying it. The Democrats constantly attacked the Whigs as illegitimate Republicans and as closet Federalists; the Whigs attacked the Democrats as untrue to Jefferson's Republicanism and in reality preferring Executive "usurpation." This ideological battle to claim the mantra of Republicanism—was the central axis of North Carolina politics. Slavery was not central to politics (in North Carolina) until the Wilmot Proviso and the rise of Free Soil in the later 1840s.[6]

The ardent Republicanism of North Carolina between 1800 and 1810 was the foundation on which the Southern Whig coalition was built. As North Carolinians' consistent approval of Nathaniel Macon, the state's staunchest defender of the "Principles of '98," showed, Old Republicanism always remained popular in the state, and the popularity of the Old Republican ideology was important to the triumph of the Southern Whigs in the state. The ascendancy of North Carolina's Southern Whigs that the "old guard" built was founded on the (contingent) union of Old Republicanism and National Republicanism that occurred in 1840 with the popularity of Clay in the state and the nomination of Harrison by the national Whig party. And that blend of opposition and active government allowed the Whigs to control the government of North Carolina and put Whigs in the U.S. Senate for ten years, with only one brief interruption in 1843 as a result of Tyler's apostasy. Mangum's confrontation with Tyler in 1841–1842 showed the uniqueness of North Carolina's combination of National Republicanism and Old Republicanism: the Virginia Whigs were still Old Republicans without Clay's National Republican measures.

Despite the "federal" aspects of the Whig political economy (bank, internal improvements, and a protective tariff) Southern Whigs in North Carolina, with former Old Republicans in their ranks, still held to states' rights but found room in their ideology to support the Whig political economy of Henry Clay. The Southern Whigs of North Carolina, and probably Southern Whigs in general, offered an alternative path from that favored by the Democrats (North and South) that reconciled states' rights with a "federal" political economy. The unique nature of their National Republican–Old Republican coalition had made this a necessity since 1840. Mangum personified this alternative path.

Despite the North Carolina Whigs' comfort in opposition, their ideology combining the Whig program with Old Republicanism was compatible with the outlook of the Northern Whigs (excluding, of course, the Conscience Whigs). Mangum's easy cooperation with Northern Whigs throughout the 1840s, his popularity with Whigs during his tenure as President of the Senate, his support for Scott over Taylor in 1848, and William Graham's alliance with Fillmore and Graham's acceptability with Northern Whigs on the Scott ticket in 1852 all demonstrate that these old North Carolina Whigs had successfully combined Southern Jeffersonian ideas with 1840s Whiggery (forming the conservative "Whig principles" of the 1840s).

The Carolina Whigs, as Jeffersonian Republicans, favored democracy and were, like their forebears Jefferson and Madison, willing to contest for supremacy in the realm of public opinion. Gaining support in public opinion had been the entire point of the Kentucky and Virginia Resolutions—the founding documents of the Principles of '98. But even Whigs understood, even from their beginning as an anti-executive, states'-rights opposition, the necessity to capture the public will: thus their campaign for public opinion in 1834–1836. In the instruction controversy Mangum was willing to appeal to the popular will and set out to capture it by organizing an Opposition party in North Carolina. With the Southern Whigs, however, democracy never trumped legislative supremacy, the Constitution, and the laws.

Old Republicanism was an opposition ideology. This fact made it difficult for the Whigs to sustain ascendancy in the state, despite the popularity of "Whig principles," "Whig measures," and members' organizational skills. The Carolina Southern Whigs were a party of opposition with an ideology best suited for opposition. Opposition to the national administration helped sustain their rise and their ascendancy. Victory in a national election once in a decade was probably sufficient to sustain the party and reward its partisans with patronage. Although the opposition Old Republican ideology was one of the foundations of the North Carolina Whigs' success, it was also one of the chief reasons for their fall. More suitable to bring down governments than sustaining them, Old Republicanism, and its heir, Southern Whiggery, were simply not suited for governing—as Macon and Randolph had demonstrated.

The effectiveness of the Whigs' opposition ideology was also their downfall—they had no ideological means of countering the Democratic Party when the Whigs controlled both the state government and the presidency (especially one that, in North Carolina, had co-opted their political economy) and many leaders, like Mangum, felt comfortable only in an opposition stance. Like Monroe had said of the Old Republican Randolph, the Southern Whigs were better at tearing down than building up. Mangum, in particular, had imbibed too much of the spirit of opposition from Macon in the 1820s: Mangum was always more comfortable in opposition. Whigs had no response to Democrats' adoption of their political economy; and without the spirit of opposition, they had trouble generating enthusiasm—their organization and meetings always relied on a spirit of opposition.

In North Carolina the loss of Van Buren as an opponent and Clay as the party's standard bearer was another large part of the Whigs' fall. The loss of Van Buren as an opponent was critical: he was the foundation of Whig unity in the state from the inception of the party in 1832–1834. In North Carolina, the effect of the absence of Martin Van Buren at the head of the Democratic Party cannot be underrated. Opposition to Van Buren had been the birth of the state's Whig Party and opposition to Van Buren had been the chief unifier of the Whig coalition in 1840 and for most of 1844. When Carolina Whigs were presented with the contrast between Clay and Van Buren, they enthusiastically chose Clay. Polk inspired far less opposition (and was far less of a unifying symbol). The year 1844 saw the height of Whig unity in North Carolina—the Whigs with united leadership under Clay's banner. Van Buren's departure from the scene in 1844 removed a vital part of the unity of the state Whig coalition. But their divisions—personal rivalries, regional rivalries, and divisions over Whig presidential candidates—and the inability of their opposition ideology to answer the populist ideology of the resurgent Democratic Party of the late 1840s ended their ascendancy—and the fall of the Whigs in North Carolina had revolutionary implications. Whig divisions began almost from the moment of Clay's departure as the head of the national party in 1845 when Carolina Whigs had to choose between Northern and Southern leaders.

The Whigs could not answer the opposition in 1848–1850 and lost their ascendancy. Their own divisions, generated by their success, hindered the organization and harmony necessary to hold the state government and promote new Whig leaders. The chief divisions stemmed from lack of loyalty to Whig principles and even to the party by some Whigs in 1848. Loyalty to the party was an important part of Whig conservatism. The Taylor Party movement was so damaging because it sought a party without principles. For Taylor Whigs, Whig principles were "ultra"; but Whigs had to campaign on Whig principles to be elected. Mangum's long fight to establish the Opposition in North Carolina made him a party man. And in 1848 and again in 1852 he insisted on loyalty to Whig principles. Moreover, in the larger battle between Whigs and Democrats, the end of compromise coincided with the end of the age of Whig principles: the defenders of Southern Whig principles, like Mangum, who were willing to compromise with Northern Whigs for the Union were eclipsed by the populist agitation of the revitalized Democrats.

The seeds of both union and disunion lay in the ideology of the Jeffersonian Republican party of 1800 to 1804 (the first term). Both Southern Whigs and Southern Democrats evolved from the party. Yet, it was the Southern Whigs who stayed closer to the Old Republicanism of 1810 than the Democrats because of their opposition to presidential power, insistence on the supremacy of Congress, and anti-party outlook. The North Carolina Whigs were more Republican than the Democrats, despite the Democrats' claims to the contrary; Whigs reflected Old Republican ideology more than the Democrats. The Democrats, though, reclaimed the Jeffersonian mantra with their policy of continental expansion after 1845. And of course the Democrats' political economy was more Old Republican, but it was never as popular in North Carolina as the Whigs program of limited nationalism.

Agitation and Whig conservatism were related: the Southern Whigs (and all Whigs) opposed the Democratic presidents' pursuit of the popular will. Democrats sought agitation (Texas; Manifest Destiny; slavery expansion). Continental expansion—Manifest Destiny— was, in Polk's hands, another means to gain the command of the popular will. Whigs necessarily opposed Manifest Destiny because it represented the unchecked popular will; and was an executive strategy. Indeed it was imminently suited to the executive branch (Calhoun showed the way in 1817–1824 as Secretary of War; Tyler revived it as a means of forming his "Tyler Party"; Polk pursued it as a party measure). But by the time of Tyler and Polk expansionism represented radicalism (viewed against Whig conservatism) because it meant agitation over slavery in the territories. Polk knew this aspect but pursued it anyway because he believed the Democracy commanded the popular will (and he believed the Northern Democracy was commanded by the Southern Democracy, as can be seen in his shabby treatment of the Van Buren Democrats).

A president not under control of Congress (which is to say, the law) who insisted he was the embodiment of the "will of the people" must then favor slavery or the South's "peculiar institution" was as good as gone; thus, in the reasoning of Southern Democrats, who did not hold the Whig doctrine of the limited executive, the only Northerner who could be trusted with the presidency was a "Northern man with Southern principles."

If, as I have argued, the Southern Whigs holding to the pragmatic brand of Old Republicanism to which the North Carolina Whigs and Mangum and Graham—and other like-minded

Southern Whigs in the Senate—adhered represented the true spirit of Jeffersonian Republicanism, then their marginalization and disappearance by 1854 meant that all that was left in the South was the ideology and spirit of Jackson and Polk. With no moderate Jeffersonian counter-weight—no Southern Whig opposition—un–Jeffersonian reliance on presidential power and a (Jeffersonian) policy of slavery extension through continental expansion were all that remained in the South. That trajectory led directly to civil war.

Chapter Notes

Introduction

1. Charles Grier Sellers, Jr., "Who Were the Southern Whigs?" *The American Historical Review* 59 No. 2 (Jan. 1954).
2. Sellers himself failed to comprehend the Southern Whigs, especially the influence of Old Republicanism upon them, in his article (see "Republican Principles, Opposition Revolutions, and Southern Whigs: Nathaniel Macon, Willie Mangum, and the Course of North Carolina Politics, 1800–1853," PhD. dissertation, Benjamin Huggins, George Mason University, 2008, 2).
3. See Lawrence Frederick Kohl, *The Politics of Individualism: Parties and the American Character in the Jacksonian Era* (New York: Oxford University Press, 1989), 168, 177–183.

Chapter 1

1. For a full discussion of this period of party formation see Banning, *The Jeffersonian Persuasion* and Richard Hofstadter, *The Idea of a Party System: The Rise of Legitimate Opposition in the United States, 1780–1840* (Berkeley: University of California Press, 1969). For the development of the political economy of the period see McCoy, *The Elusive Republic*.
2. James D. Richardson, ed., *A Compilation of the Messages and Papers of the Presidents* (New York, 1897) 1: 311–312.
3. Jefferson to James Monroe, 12 January 1800; Jefferson to Edward Livingston, 30 April 1800, Thomas Jefferson Papers, Library of Congress (hereafter referred to as LC).
4. Delbert Harold Gilpatrick, *Jeffersonian Democracy in North Carolina 1789–1816* (1933, reprint, New York, 1967), 48.
5. The slackening of Republicanism in the state, though, probably resulted in a decision by Jefferson to turn to the Kentucky legislature instead of the North Carolina legislature to present his Resolutions against the Alien and Sedition Acts. *ROL* 2: 1067; Jefferson to Wilson Cary Nicholas, 5 October 1798, *Papers of Thomas Jefferson* (hereafter cited as *PTJ*), eds. Julian P. Boyd et al., 41 vols. to date (Princeton, NJ: 1950–), 30: 557.
6. Gilpatrick, 127.
7. Nationalism here is used in the sense of the ideology of those in the Republican party favoring a program of national development. Although, as will be shown below, not all nationalists shared all parts of this ideology, domestically nationalists supported commercial and economic development such as federally funded internal improvements, the protective tariff, and support of the Bank of the United States. They also generally believed in the need for a well-funded though not excessive army and navy. In foreign policy many Republican nationalists sought the expansion of national boundaries, maintenance of national prestige, and pursuit of national interests.
8. Henry Thomas Shanks, ed., *The Papers of Willie Person Mangum*, 5 Volumes (Raleigh: State Department of Archives and History, 1950–1956), 1: xv–xvii. Hereafter cited as *PWPM*.
9. *Ibid.*, xviii–xx.
10. Risjord, 187.
11. Mangum's brother Priestly thought Willie stood "pledged in the opinion of the public" to Crawford, but a Raleigh political friend acknowledged that in the campaign Mangum had refused to pledge his vote in advance and had insisted on preserving his "liberty" to change his mind on support for Crawford if cause arose. P.H. Mangum to Willie P. Mangum, 4 January 1824, Seth Jones to Mangum, 7 January 1824, *PWPM*, 1: 97, 101.
12. Mangum to Duncan Cameron, 10 December 1823, *PWPM*, 1: 82–84.
13. Mangum to Duncan Cameron, 10 December 1823, Mangum to Thomas Ruffin, 20 January 1824, *PWPM*, 1: 83–84, 109.
14. William Polk to Mangum, 26 January 1824, *PWPM*, 1: 111.
15. Mangum to Seth Jones, 24 May 1824, *PWPM*, 1: 146.
16. Mangum to Thomas Ruffin, 20 January 1824, *PWPM*, 1: 108–110.
17. Mangum to Seth Jones, 11 February 1824, *PWPM*, 1: 116.
18. *Annals of Congress*, 6th Congress, 2nd session, 803–804.
19. The enslaved girl, Lucy, appears to have still been Macon's property in the last decade of his life, 1825–1837. "Lucy" is listed in the inventory of his adult slaves, but she was not included on the list of taxables, indicating she was an older slave. "Miscellaneous business papers of Nathaniel Macon—1825, 1829, 1833, 1836–1838,

N.D.," Box PC 1444.3, Katherine C. P. Conway Collection, North Carolina Department of Cultural Resources, Division of Archives and History (Hereafter cited as NCDCR-DAH).

20. William S. Price, Jr., "Nathaniel Macon, Antifederalist," *NCHR* Vol. LXXXI, No. 3 (July 2004), 294–295. William E. Dodd, *Life of Nathaniel Macon* (Raleigh: Edwards & Broughton, 1908), 2–3, 25–40.

21. Dodd, *Nathaniel Macon*, 27–40, 44. Dodd, 38, says that Macon "served his apprenticeship" in Willie Jones's school of politics. Price, "Nathaniel Macon. Antifederalist," 295, says Jones was Macon's "earliest political mentor."

22. Price, "Nathaniel Macon, Antifederalist," 294.

23. *Annals of Congress*, 5th Congress, 2nd session, 1672, 1673, 1698; 5th Congress, 3rd session, 2542; 6th Congress, 1st session, 404–406. Gilpatrick, 87–88; M'Dowell quoted in Gilpatrick, 88.

24. *Annals of Congress*, 6th Congress, 1st session, 404–406.

25. Macon to John Gray Blount, 2 February 1802, William H. Masterson, ed., *The John Gray Blount Papers* III (Raleigh, 1965), 494.

26. Jefferson to Levi Lincoln, 25 October 1802, Thomas Jefferson Papers, LC.

27. Scholars have questioned the Republicans' adherence to their principles once they controlled the government. "Minds changed when party leaders were confronted with responsibility," Lance Banning declares in his study of the formation of Jeffersonian ideology during the first years of nineteenth century. Historian Ralph Ketcham, in his study of the presidents of the first decades of the republic, complains that this view has been all too common among historians of the Jefferson presidency. Many Jefferson scholars have, according to Ketcham, "emphasized his 'inconsistency' or 'flexibility' in promptly jettisoning his nostrums about 'legislative supremacy' and 'strict construction' when he attained power." Banning, *Jeffersonian Persuasion*, 284; Ketcham, *Presidents Above Party*, 106. Yet this chapter argues that rather than ideological infidelity, the schism revealed the divisions that arose among Republicans as they attempted to govern the country *in accordance* with their principles. Banning's account ends with the triumph of the Jeffersonian Republicans in 1800 and he deals with the implications of Jefferson's administration on Republican ideology only in his epilogue. Banning does, however, raise the important point that Jefferson and Madison may have believed that a change of men would in large part corrected the major problem of the late 1790s—the Federalists themselves. But this too became a point of tension. Banning, *Jeffersonian Persuasion*, 288–290.

28. See, for example, Macon to Bartlett Yancey, 8 March 1818, 12 December 1823, and 26 December 1824, Kemp P. Battle, ed., "Letters of Nathaniel Macon to James R. Eaton and Bartlett Yancey," in Edwin Mood Wilson, *The Congressional Career of Nathaniel Macon, James Sprunt Historical Monographs* No. 2 (Chapel Hill, 1900), 48–50, 67–70, 71–73.

29. But this was not a rigid division, except with the Quids, after 1806. The Old Republicans were never in complete opposition, and indeed often supported the administration. The tensions, nevertheless, made Jefferson and Madison vulnerable to charges of ideological infidelity from those not sharing their conception of the "principles of '98." As Banning and others have noted, although the number of the Old Republicans was small (the number of Quids was even smaller) their ideological power was great because their rhetoric appealed to the principles of the Democratic-Republicans' political culture that was born in the struggle with the Federalists. Banning, *Jeffersonian Persuasion*, 290. See also Risjord, *Old Republicans*, 62–63; 96–97. Banning, while crediting the influence of the Old Republicans' critique of administration policy on the party, does not believe that the ideological and policy differences rise to the level of a "major theme."

30. Jefferson to Cooper, 9 July 1807, Thomas Jefferson Papers, LC.

31. "Report on the Alien and Sedition Acts," reprinted in Jack N. Rakove, ed., *Madison: Writings* (New York: Library of America, 1999), 608–662; "Virginia Resolutions Against the Alien and Sedition Acts," Rakove, 589–581; "Resolutions Adopted by the Kentucky General Assembly, *PTJ* 30: 550–555.

32. *ROL* 2: 1287. The immediate reason for the purchase of the Louisiana Territory was to head off demands for war with Spain by the western states. Spain's control of the Mississippi River allowed her to strangle western commerce that depended on access to New Orleans. Obtaining Louisiana, and with it New Orleans, would ensure a Mississippi outlet for western products and unfettered access to the port of New Orleans. In the long run, many Republicans, including Jefferson, envisioned the territory as a zone for U.S. economic expansion, including the expansion of plantation agriculture, and with it slavery. On the crisis with Spain over the Mississippi and New Orleans see Smith, *Republic of Letters*, 2: 1254. Hereafter cited as *ROL*.

33. *Annals of Congress*, 7th Congress, 2 sess., 339–343.

34. *ROL* 2: 1286–1290. Believing a constitutional amendment should accompany ratification of the treaty, Jefferson proposed numerous versions to authorize the purchase. He was persuaded to drop the idea only after Madison convinced him that the treaty might be jeopardized if the Federalists in Congress delayed ratification with a debate over the amendment. Eventually Jefferson deferred to the judgment of the Republicans in Congress as to whether an amendment would be required. Jefferson to Madison, 18 August 1803, *ROL* 2: 1278. Jefferson to Wilson Cary Nicholas, 7 September 1803, quoted in *ROL*, 1290. For Jefferson and Madison's correspondence on proposed amendments see *ROL*, 1268–1272.

35. As Ralph Ketcham notes, Jefferson believed that the tasks of the presidency were critical to effective republican government and that the Republican principles did not forbid the federal executive from acting positively in the public interest. Ketcham, *Presidents Above Party*, 105, 113, 108. See also 173.

36. Thomas Jefferson to John B. Colvin, September 20, 1810, Thomas Jefferson Papers, LC.

37. *ROL* 2: 1255.

38. Macon to Jefferson, 3 September 1803, Thomas Jefferson Papers, LC.

39. Gilpatrick, 156.

40. Speech against the Yazoo claims, first session of the 8th Congress, quoted in Russell Kirk, *John Randolph of Roanoke: A Study in American Politics with Selected Speeches and Letters* (Indianapolis, 1978), 294–311.

41. Adams, *John Randolph*, 55.

42. David N. Mayer, *The Constitutional Thought of Thomas Jefferson* (Charlottesville: University Press of Virginia, 1994), 235.
43. Jefferson to Madison, Nov. 28, 1805, ROL 3: 1400-1.
44. ROL 3, 1400n.
45. As Ralph Ketcham points out, "there was indeed in Jefferson's mind a need to balance possibly incompatible goals, but he refused to relinquish either; he insisted on both mild government mindful of the rights of the people and a positive government capable of acting to preserve the state and, in Aristotelian fashion, 'for the sake of the good life.'" Ketcham, *Presidents Above Party*, 173.
46. Ketcham, 109.
47. Mayer, 237-238.
48. Albert Gallatin, on whom the enforcement of the measure largely fell, doubted the administration's ability to enforce so coercive a measure, unless the people thoroughly supported it. "Without ... the full support of the people, such a strong coercive measure cannot be fairly executed," he told Nicholson. "If the embargo is taken off, I do not perceive yet any medium between absolute subjection or war." Gallatin to Nicholson, 18 Oct. 1808, quoted in Adams, *Life of Albert Gallatin*, 375.
49. Quoted in Risjord, 84.
50. Risjord, 84.
51. Risjord, 84.
52. *Annals of Congress*, 5th Congress, 2nd sess., 1672-73, 1699, 1756-58.
53. Dodd, *Nathaniel Macon*, 220-221.
54. *Annals of Congress*, 10th Congress, 1st sess., 1934-38. Macon to Nicholson, 4 April 1808, "Nathaniel Macon Correspondence."
55. Macon to John Steele, 19 January 1805, Battle, ed., "Letters of Nathaniel Macon, John Steele and William Barry Grove," *James Sprunt Historical Monograph* No. 3 (Chapel Hill, 1902). Macon to Jefferson, 2 September 1804, Thomas Jefferson Papers, LC.
56. Macon to Gallatin, 12 July 1807, Albert Gallatin Papers, New-York Historical Society.
57. Macon to Gallatin, 2 August 1807, Albert Gallatin Papers, New-York Historical Society.
58. Macon to Joseph H. Nicholson, 4 April 1808, "Nathaniel Macon Correspondence," 53.
59. Accounts of meetings and their resolutions appear in *Raleigh Register*, 13 August, 1 October 1807. *Raleigh Register*, 24 December 1807, contains the text of the General Assembly's resolution as originally offered, modified in debate only by the deletion of a phrase characterizing the Federalists as a party that "sought to subvert because they could not direct the measures of government." Debate in *Raleigh Register* 24, 31 December, 1807, 7, 14 January 1808. Gilpatrick, 159-160, summarizes the Federalist objections. Jefferson's reply in *Raleigh Register*, 11 February 1808.
60. Barry, 124.
61. Risjord identifies the Quids as: Randolph, James M. Garnett, Philip R. Thompson, and Abram Trigg of Virginia; Richard Stanford of North Carolina; and Thomas Spalding of Georgia (62).
62. Although my analysis of these Republican factions differs slightly from his, Risjord, 58-71, provides an excellent analysis of these divisions in the Republican party.

63. Risjord, 95-100. Jeffersonian splinter factions in New York and Pennsylvania were also called "Quids." For my use of the term to describe the Randolphites in Virginia, see Risjord, 286n1. For the distinctions between these groups see Noble E. Cuningham, Jr., "Who Were the Quids," *Mississippi Valley Historical Review*, L (September 1963), 252-63. For Risjord's excellent account of the Quid Schism, see 40-71. He identifies only thirteen congressmen as members of Randolph's Quids. Risjord points out, though, that they were powerful beyond their numbers because of their unity, their opposition, their political talent, and their skills in debate, especially Randolph's oratorical skills. Risjord places Macon among the Quids, but shortly thereafter points out that Macon never considered himself in opposition to the administration. The foremost defining characteristic of the Quids was their adamant opposition to Jefferson and Madison; therefore Macon (and Joseph H. Nicholson) should not be considered a Quid, but a sometimes ally of the Quids. Richard Stanford of the Warren Junto was a Quid, though. Macon disliked opposing his friend Randolph, but sometimes did. He is better classed as an "independent." Macon could hardly have remained as Speaker if he adamantly opposed Jefferson on all measures. As we shall see, when Macon did place his loyalty to Randolph above the party, he was voted out of the Speaker's chair.
64. Fifth Annual Message, 3 December 1805, Special Message, 6 December 1805, Richardson, *Messages and Papers of the Presidents* 1: 370-78.
65. *Annals of Congress*, 9th Congress, 1st session, 946-950. "Decius," Richmond *Enquirer*, Aug. 15, 1806.
66. Richardson, *Messages and Papers of the Presidents* 1: 314-370, 393-399. In none of his previous annual messages did Jefferson use the procedure of following the annual message with a special message describing the state of diplomacy with a particular country, though he had followed some annual messages with submission of treaties and conventions. Although, he repeated the procedure of December 1805 in his next annual message in 1806, which he followed the next day with a special message on the state of diplomacy with Great Britain, but it was apparently not secret.
67. *Annals of Congress*, 9th Congress, 1st session, 981-986.
68. Risjord, 54-55.
69. Manuscript in Randolph's secretary's hand of Randolph's speech of March 5, 1806. John Randolph Papers, Alderman Library, University of Virginia. Reprinted in Kirk, 323-355. (Kirk mistakenly says that the speech was delivered in opposition to Gregg's motion on non-importation. Risjord makes it clear that the speech was delivered in opposition to Nicholson's bill.)
70. *Annals of Congress*, 9th Congress, 1st session, 981-986.
71. *Annals of Congress*, 10th Congress, 1st session, 1904, 1940-1952.
72. *Ibid.*, 1904-1912.
73. One Virginia Old Republican declared in the debate that he had always "believed that somewhat of a regular force was necessary." Wilson Cary Nicholas (Va.), *Annals of Congress*, 10th Congress, 1st session, 1948; Risjord, 84-86.
74. Risjord, 57; Adams, *John Randolph*, 226-227.
75. Jefferson to Macon, 22 March 1806, Thomas

Jefferson Papers, LC. Jefferson used similar language in a letter to Albert Gallatin of October 12, 1806: "I have so much reliance on the superior good sense and candor of all those associated with me as to be satisfied they will not suffer either friend or foe to sow tares among us." Adams, *Life of Gallatin*, 345.

76. Dodd, *Nathaniel Macon*, 200–201.
77. Ibid., 208–209.
78. Macon to Nicholson, 1 Dec. 1806, quoted in Barry, 112. Nicholson had left Congress for appointment as a federal judge—an appointment Jefferson had offered (most likely to detach another of Randolph's friends); Macon to Nicholson, 2 December 1806, "Nathaniel Macon Correspondence," 49.
79. Barry, 112–113; Risjord, 75–76.
80. Barry, 110. Another issue was Macon's unexplained absence at the start of the 10th Congress. Macon had always been Speaker in the Republican Congress and knew he was not going to be elected in the 10th Congress. Barry says that Macon was late to the 10th Congress, 1st session (Oct. 26, 1807) due to the death of his grandson in September and his own illness (121–122), but Dodd (219–220) says that Macon stayed away to remove himself from the election of Speaker of the House. Macon had never absented himself and never did so again in twenty years of further service in Congress through good health and bad, as Dodd points out.
81. Macon to Nicholson, 26 December 1806, quoted in Risjord, 76–77.
82. Jefferson to W.C. Nicholas, 28 February 1807, Thomas Jefferson Papers, LC.
83. Macon to _____, 26 March 1808, Macon Papers, NCDCR-DAH.
84. Macon to Joseph H. Nicholson, 4 December 1808, "Nathaniel Macon Correspondence."
85. Dodd, *Nathaniel Macon*, 235.
86. Gilpatrick, 51, 127–178 in general and 129, 146–151, 153–154, 160–162; *Raleigh Register*, 8 December 1808.
87. Macon to unknown, 26 March 1808, Nathaniel Macon Papers, NCDCR-DAH.
88. Macon to Nicholson, 4 December 1808, "Nathaniel Macon Correspondence."
89. Macon to Nicholson, 4 December 1808, "Nathaniel Macon Correspondence."
90. Dodd claims that Gallatin, Macon, and Madison cooperated in formulating the resolutions as the administration's preferred policy. Dodd, 235.
91. *Annals of Congress*, 10th Congress, 2nd. sess., 673.
92. *Annals of Congress*, 10th Congress, 2nd sess., 497–498; *Annals of Congress*, 10th Congress, 2nd sess., 669–674.
93. Macon to Nicholson, 28 February 1809, "Nathaniel Macon Correspondence."
94. For a brief discussion of this failed effort of Randolph, the Quids, and some Old Republicans to have Monroe instead of Madison become the successor to Jefferson, see Benjamin Huggins, "Republican Principles, Opposition Revolutions, and Southern Whigs: Nathaniel Macon, Willie Mangum, and the Course of North Carolina Politics, 1800–1853" (doctoral dissertation, George Mason University, 2008), 137–140.
95. *Annals of Congress*, 9th Congress, 1st. sess., 696.
96. *Annals of Congress*, 5th Congress, 1673 (May 1798).
97. *Annals of Congress*, 10th Congress, 1st sess., 1953.
98. Macon to Joseph H. Nicholson, 31 January 1806, quoted in Barry, 127.
99. Macon to Joseph Nicholson, 1 April 1808, quoted in Barry, 131.
100. Taylor to Monroe, 26 October 1810 quoted in Risjord, 25.
101. Macon to Nicholson, 4 December 1808, Dodd, "Nathaniel Macon Correspondence," 56.
102. Macon to Joseph H. Nicholson, 7 March 1808, quoted in Barry, 131.
103. Nicholson to Monroe, 12 April 1807, quoted in Adams, *John Randolph*, 217–218.
104. His charge against Alston as one of the "new men" was inaccurate—Alston had represented North Carolina since 1799 (elected 1798) and Alston had supported Macon's attempts to repeal the Sedition Act. Alston was in the 6th Congress (Dec. 1799)—the same Congress in which Nicholson first served. Nicholson was probably angry with Alston for what he perceived as a betrayal and so he classed Alston with the "new men" whom he believed were the primary opponents of the Old Republicans.

Chapter 2

1. John Randolph, early 1813, quoted in Kirk, *Randolph of Roanoke*, 89.
2. Risjord, 174.
3. Matthew Mason, *Slavery & Politics in the Early American Republic* (Chapel Hill: The University of North Carolina Press, 2006), 162–63, 201, 207, 236. Robert Pierce Forbes, *The Missouri Compromise and Its Aftermath: Slavery and the Meaning of America* (Chapel Hill: The University of North Carolina Press, 2007), 164–65.
4. Macon to Bartlett Yancey, 8 March 1818, Kemp P. Battle, ed., "Letters of Nathaniel Macon to John R. Eaton and Bartlett Yancey," in Edwin Mood Wilson, "Congressional Career of Nathaniel Macon," *James Sprunt Historical Monographs No. 2* (Chapel Hill, 1900), 48–49. Hereafter cited as "Congressional Career of Nathaniel Macon."
5. Macon to Yancey, 15 April 1818, "Congressional Career of Nathaniel Macon," 47. In 1813 Commodore Decatur was blockaded in the port of New London. The British ships off the port were able to frustrate Decatur's attempts to get his ship past the British squadron. He declared that blue lights were burned by Federalist sympathizers in New London to signal the British ships of his movements. The Republicans thus declared that Federalist opponents of the war were "Blue Light Federalists." The Republicans condemned the Federalist convention of delegates from Massachusetts, Rhode Island, Connecticut, Vermont, and New Hampshire held at Hartford December 15, 1814, as a convention of New England secessionists.
6. Jefferson's remarks to Roane after reading the essays are notable not only because he fully agreed with Roane's views but also because Jefferson directly associated them with the Revolution of 1800. "I subscribe to every tittle of them," Jefferson told Roane. "They contain the true principles of the revolution of 1800, for that was as real a revolution in the principles of our govern-

ment as that of 1776 was in form; not effected indeed by the sword, as that, but by the rational and peaceable instrument of reform, the suffrage of the people." Only the judicial branch had not "submitted" to the revolution. It was "still driving us into consolidation." Jefferson to Spencer Roane, 6 September 1819, Merrill D. Peterson, ed., *Thomas Jefferson: Writings* Vol. II (1984, New York: Easton Press Edition, 1993), 1425–1426.

7. Risjord, 223–224. Quote, 224.

8. For the complete story of Clay's role in the Missouri Compromises, see Remini 177–192 and Peterson, *Great Triumvirate*, 59–65. Robert Pierce Forbes, *The Missouri Compromise and Its Aftermath: Slavery and the Meaning of America* (Chapel Hill: The University of North Carolina Press, 2007) is insightful but Forbes spends too much of his study on his questionable interpretation of James Monroe as the behind the scenes mover of the Missouri Compromise.

9. The best treatment remains Glover Moore's *The Missouri Controversy* (Lexington: University of Kentucky Press, 1953).

10. Peterson, *Great Triumvirate*, 59.

11. *Annals of Congress*, 16th Congress, 1st sess., 272–273, 279.

12. Risjord, 204, 213–214, 218.

13. Risjord, 214.

14. Risjord, 215–216. Their position was not shared, though, by Randolph and other Old Republicans who continued to view slavery as an evil.

15. *Annals of Congress*, 16th Congress, 1st session, 97–99.

16. This particular argument would later be used by Southern nationalists.

17. The other Southern senators who made proslavery defenses were William Smith and Charles Pinckney of South Carolina. In *Slavery & Politics*, Matthew Mason points out that the positive-good doctrine became more attractive because Northerners had exposed the flaws in other defenses of slavery such as the doctrine of diffusion and the necessary-evil doctrine. Mason, 204–207.

18. *Annals of Congress*, 16th Congress, 1st session, 219–232.

19. Clay, "Speech on the Admission of Maine," 30 Dec. 1819, *Clay Papers*, 2: 742.

20. Clay to Amos Kendall, 8 Jan. 1820, Clay to Leslie Combs, 5 Feb. 1820, in *Clay Papers*, 2: 752, 774.

21. Clay to Horace Holley, 17 Feb. 1820, *Clay Papers*, 2: 781. Clay to Adam Beatty, 22 Jan. 1820, *Clay Papers*, 2: 766.

22. Glover Moore, *The Missouri Compromise 1819–1821* (Lexington: University of Kentucky Press, 1966), 100, 112. Risjord, 216.

23. Moore, 108–111, quote on 111.

24. Risjord, 217.

25. Macon to Bartlett Yancey, 19 April 1820, "Congressional Career of Nathaniel Macon," 53. As Glover Moore points out in *Missouri Controversy*, 106, these fears were not groundless. Rufus King in New York did want to use slavery as a lever to create a new alignment of parties.

26. Macon to Bartlett Yancey, 20 June 1820, Kemp P. Battle, ed., "Letters of Nathaniel Macon, John Steele and William Barry Grove, with Sketches and Notes," *James Sprunt Historical Monograph No. 3* (Chapel Hill: University of North Carolina Press, 1902), 73. "Shyhog" was a term taken from "beating the woods" for shy, or runaway hogs. Macon used the word to mean political maneuvering for votes and power.

27. Moore, 138–159; Risjord, 220–222.

28. Randolph (in the House) and Macon and Smith (in the Senate) voted against the Compromise.

29. Moore, 94–95.

30. Jefferson to Macon, 19 January 1819, Thomas Jefferson Papers, LC. It is interesting to speculate as to whether Jefferson intended to include Calhoun and John Quincy Adams in this assessment. He certainly meant to include Monroe and Crawford, both sons of Virginia. Jefferson stated that he had such confidence in "the late and present Presidents, that I willingly put both soul & body into their pockets."

31. Jefferson to Macon, 19 August 1821, Nathaniel Macon Papers, NCDCR-DAH. Macon to Jefferson, 20 October 1821, Thomas Jefferson Papers, LC. Jefferson to Macon, 10 October 1823, "Nathaniel Macon Correspondence," 80; Macon to Jefferson, 14 January 1826, Thomas Jefferson Papers, LC. Jefferson's reference to the "Executive administration" in his 19 January 1819 letter to Macon, quoted at the beginning of this section, included Monroe.

32. Jefferson to Macon, 19 August 1821, Nathaniel Macon Papers, NCDCR-DAH. Jefferson to Macon, 23 November 1821, Thomas Jefferson Papers, LC. Macon to Jefferson, 2 February 1822, 21 May 1824, Thomas Jefferson Papers, LC.

33. Jefferson to Macon, 19 August 1821, Nathaniel Macon Papers, NCDCR-DAH. Macon to Jefferson, 20 October 1821, Thomas Jefferson Papers, LC.

34. Macon to Jefferson, 20 October 1821, 21 May 1824, Thomas Jefferson Papers, LC. Jefferson to Macon, 21 February 1821, Thomas Jefferson Papers, LC. In 1827, Macon repeated his claim that Republican principles began to change under Madison in a letter to Bartlett Yancey. Macon to Bartlett Yancey, 3 November 1827, "Congressional Career of Nathaniel Macon," 94.

35. Daniel C. Gilman, *James Monroe* (Boston: Houghton, Mifflin, and Company, 1898), 222. This anecdote of Monroe was given to Gilman by Judge E.R. Watson of Charlottesville, Virginia, who served as Monroe's personal secretary after his retirement. Gilman included it in his biography as part of "Judge Watson's Recollections" of Monroe.

36. Mangum to Charity A. Mangum, 21 January 1826, *PWPM*, 1: 235–236.

37. Macon to Mangum, 14 January 1827, *PWPM*, 1: 305.

38. Hall to Mangum, 4 January 1826, *PWPM*, 1: 221.

39. Mangum to Bartlett Yancey, 15 January 1826, *PWPM*, 1: 233.

40. Macon to Yancey, 31 March 1824, in Kemp P. Battle, ed., "Letters of Nathaniel Macon, John Steele and William Barry Grove," *James Sprunt Historical Monograph No. 3* (Chapel Hill, 1902), 79. Hereafter cited as "Macon Letters."

41. Macon to Yancey, 31 March 1824, "Macon Letters," 79.

42. Macon to Yancey, 12 December 1823, "Congressional Career of Nathaniel Macon," 68.

43. Macon to Yancey, 25 December 1824, "Macon Letters," 82.

44. Macon to Yancey, 26 December 1824, "Congressional Career of Nathaniel Macon," 72.
45. Macon to Yancey, 31 March 1826, "Congressional Career of Nathaniel Macon," 87.
46. *Register of Debates*, 23 December 1825, 19th Congress, 1st session, 847–849. Congress took no action on Monroe's claim before adjourning in 1826. Congress eventually awarded the claim but not until 1831.
47. W.C. Clements to Mangum, 8 March 1826, *PWPM*, 1: 258.
48. Mangum to Charity Mangum, 11 December 1825, *PWPM*, 1: 211.
49. Mangum to Charity Mangum, 15 January 1826, *PWPM*, 1: 229.
50. Mangum to Charity Mangum, 15 January 1826, *PWPM*, 1: 228–229.
51. Mangum to Bartlett Yancey, 15 January 1826, *PWPM*, 1: 231.
52. William C. Clements to Mangum, 8 March 1826, *PWPM*, 1: 258.
53. Priestly Mangum to Mangum, 29 March 1826, *PWPM*, 1: 262.
54. Mangum to Yancey, 15 January 1826, *PWPM*, 1: 231–34.
55. Yancey to Mangum, 25 January 1826, *PWPM*, 1: 240.
56. This election in the House of Representatives, and Mangum's course during the election, will be discussed later in this chapter.
57. Mangum to Bartlett Yancey, 15 January 1826, *PWPM*, 1: 232–34.
58. *Ibid.*, 232.
59. Mangum to Charity Mangum, 8 April 1826, *PWPM*, 1: 268.
60. Mangum to Charity Mangum, 8 April 1826, *PWPM*, 1: 268.
61. Commission from Governor H.G. Burton, 18 August 1826, *PWPM*, 1: 298.
62. Priestly Mangum to Mangum, 1, 7 September 1826, *PWPM*, 1: 299–300.
63. Mangum to Bartlett Yancey, 1 January 1827, *PWPM*, 1: 302.
64. Macon to Mangum, 14 January 1827, *PWPM*, 1: 305–306.
65. Nathaniel Macon to Weldon Edwards, 5 April 1828, Nathaniel Macon Papers, NCDCR-DAH.
66. Note here that Macon had been elected president pro tem of the Senate and was president pro tem when these letters were written, but he did not preside often as Calhoun was generally present in the Senate.
67. Macon to Weldon Edwards, 22 March 1828, Nathaniel Macon Papers, NCDCR-DAH.
68. Macon to John Haywood, 6 April 1826, *PWPM*, 1: 267.
69. Macon to Weldon Edwards, 22 December 1827, Nathaniel Macon Papers, NCDCR-DAH.
70. Macon to Weldon Edwards, 17, 22, 27 February 1828, Nathaniel Macon Papers, NCDCR-DAH.
71. Macon to Weldon Edwards, 22 March 1828, Nathaniel Macon Papers, NCDCR-DAH.
72. Macon to Weldon Edwards, 28 March 1828, Nathaniel Macon Papers, NCDCR-DAH.
73. Macon to Weldon Edwards, 5 April 1828, Nathaniel Macon Papers, NCDCR-DAH.
74. Macon to Weldon Edwards, 12 April 1828, Nathaniel Macon Papers, NCDCR-DAH.
75. Macon to the North Carolina General Assembly, 14 November 1828, "Nathaniel Macon Correspondence," 88–89.
76. Macon to Weldon Edwards, 20 May 1828, Nathaniel Macon Papers, NCDCR-DAH.
77. For a full study of this campaign in North Carolina, see Albert Ray Newsome, *The Election of 1824 in North Carolina* (Chapel Hill: University of North Carolina Press, 1939).
78. Mangum to Seth Jones, 24 May 1824, *PWPM*, 1: 146.
79. P.H. Mangum to Willie P. Mangum, 4 January 1824, *PWPM*, 1: 97.
80. Mangum to Seth Jones, 11 February 1824, *PWPM*, 1: 115.
81. William S. Hoffman, *Andrew Jackson and North Carolina Politics*, James Sprunt Studies in History and Political Science, XL (Chapel Hill: University of North Carolina Press, 1958), 6–7.
82. Mangum to Thomas Ruffin, 15 December 1824, *PWPM*, 1: 160.
83. Mangum to Bartlett Yancey, 25 December 1824, *PWPM*, 1: 160–161.
84. Mangum to Duncan Cameron, 10 January 1825, *PWPM*, 1: 173–174.
85. Mangum to John Robertson, 3 January 1825, *PWPM*, 1: 170.
86. William Ruffin to Mangum, 1 February 1825, *PWPM*, 1: 186.
87. "The Election of 1824, Speech in the House," February 3, 7, 1825, *PWPM*, 5: 487–500.
88. Hoffman, *Andrew Jackson and North Carolina Politics*, 9.
89. David F. Caldwell to Mangum, 4 December 1825, *PWPM*, 1: 207.
90. Hoffman, *Andrew Jackson and North Carolina Politics*, 10.
91. Richardson, *Messages and Papers of the Presidents*, 2: 299–317.
92. Macon to Weldon Edwards, 1 January 1828, Macon Papers, NCDCR-DAH.
93. Macon to Bartlett Yancey, 8 December 1825, "Congressional Career of Nathaniel Macon," 76.
94. Macon to Yancey, [no day] December 1825, "Nathaniel Macon Correspondence," 86.
95. Macon to Bartlett Yancey, 3 November 1827, "Congressional Career of Nathaniel Macon," 94.
96. Risjord, 260–261. Also note historians' arguments that Southern objections (and Van Buren's) also centered on race and defense of slavery issues.
97. Macon to Bartlett Yancey, 3 November 1827, "Congressional Career of Nathaniel Macon," 95.
98. Macon to Bartlett Yancey, 29 January 1826, "Congressional Career of Nathaniel Macon," 73.
99. Macon to Bartlett Yancey, 16 April 1826, "Congressional Career of Nathaniel Macon," 88.
100. Charles Sellers, *The Market Revolution: Jacksonian America 1815–1846* (New York: Oxford University Press, 1991), 111.
101. Risjord, 231 and Peterson, *Great Triumvirate*, 122.
102. Macon to Bartlett Yancey, 26 December 1824, "Congressional Career of Nathaniel Macon," 73.

103. Macon to Bartlett Yancey, 29 January 1826, "Congressional Career of Nathaniel Macon," 80.
104. Macon to Bartlett Yancey, 31 March, 16 April 1826, "Congressional Career of Nathaniel Macon," 86, 88.
105. Hoffman, *Andrew Jackson and North Carolina Politics*, 10.
106. Salisbury *Western Carolinian*, 8 May 1827.
107. Bartlett Yancey to Mangum, 25 January 1826, *PWPM*, 1: 238–241. Romulus Saunders to Bartlett Yancey, 17 April 1826, in Albert R. Newsome, ed., "Letters of Romulus Saunders to Bartlett Yancey, 1821–1828," *NCHR*, VIII (October 1931), 457. Hereafter cited as "Letters of Saunders to Yancey."
108. Mangum to Bartlett Yancey, 15 January 1826, *PWPM*, 1: 234.
109. Romulus Saunders to Bartlett Yancey, 12 February 1827, "Letters of Saunders to Yancey," 460. Hoffman, *Andrew Jackson and North Carolina Politics*,12–13. Calhoun, despite serving as Adams' vice-president, had joined the Jackson-Van Buren coalition against the Naional Republicans and had moderated his nationalism. Since 1819, South Carolina had also been turning against nationalism and this change also moderated Calhoun's outlook. Calhoun was becoming more of a strict-constructionist and South Carolinians opposed the protective tariff as did the North Carolina Old Republicans. Nevertheless, North Carolina's Old Republicans remained wary of him. For South Carolina's turn away from nationalism and Calhoun's changing ideology see Freehling, *Prelude to Civil War: The Nullification Controversy in South Carolina 1816–1836* (New York: Oxford University Press, 1965), 89–133.
110. Hoffman, *Andrew Jackson and North Carolina Politics*, 27.
111. Hoffman, *Andrew Jackson and North Carolina Politics*, 18–19. Saunders to Yancey, 20 January 1827, in J.G. deRoulhac Hamilton, ed., "Letters to Bartlett Yancey," *The James Sprunt Historical Publications* X No. 2 (Chapel Hill, 1911), 60–62. Hereafter cited as "Letters to Bartlett Yancey."
112. Hoffman, *Andrew Jackson and North Carolina Politics*, 13–14.
113. Macon to Bartlett Yancey, 3 November 1827, "Congressional Career of Nathaniel Macon," 95.
114. Macon to Bartlett Yancey, 16 February 1828, "Congressional Career of Nathaniel Macon," 100.
115. Randolph's Speech on Retrenchment and Reform, 1 Feb. 1828 (in Kirk, *John Randolph of Roanoke: A Study in American Politics*, 531).
116. Hoffman, *Andrew Jackson and North Carolina Politics*, 20.
117. Meetings were held in New Bern and Fayetteville and the counties of Washington, Orange, Duplin, Johnston, Onslow, New Hanover, and Bertie. Fayetteville *North Carolina Journal*, 12 Dec. 1827, Raleigh *Star*, 27 Dec. 1827, 10, 24, 31 January 1828.
118. Raleigh *Star*, 3 Jan. 1828.
119. *Raleigh Register*, 13 Nov., 25 December 1827, 1, 5 June and 3 July 1828.
120. Raleigh *Star*, 10 January 1828. "Sheriff's Certification of Results of Presidential Election in Orange County," 14 November 1828, "Sheriff's Certification of Results of Presidential Election in Granville County," 18 November 1828, *PWPM*, 1: 343–346.
121. Beaufort, Brunswick, Carteret, Jones, Pitt, Randolph, Guilford, and Iredell counties.
122. Hoffman, *Andrew Jackson and North Carolina Politics*, 25.
123. "W.P. Mangum's commission to judgeship of Superior Court," James Martin, Jr., to Mangum, 26 Dec. 1828, *PWPM*, 1: 354.
124. Hoffman, *Andrew Jackson and North Carolina Politics*, 15.
125. Hoffman, *Andrew Jackson and North Carolina Politics*, 14, 26–28, 28–29, 31.
126. William M. Sneed to Mangum, 18 November 1830, *PWPM*, 1: 379–381. Fisher was elected by a majority of 9 votes in the House; Caldwell by only 3 votes in the Senate. Hoffman, *Andrew Jackson and North Carolina Politics*, 32.
127. W.M. Sneed to Mangum, 18 November 1830, C.L. Hinton to Mangum, 18 November 1830, *PWPM*, 1: 379–382.
128. Hoffman, *Andrew Jackson and North Carolina Politics*, 32.
129. W. M. Sneed to Mangum, 25 November 1830, *PWPM*, 1: 385–387.
130. C.L. Hinton to Mangum, 2 December 1830, W.M. Sneed to Mangum, 3 December 1830, *PWPM*, 1: 389–390, 393.
131. Mangum to Owen, 1 December 1830, *PWPM*, 1: 388. C.L. Hinton to Mangum, 2 December 1830, *PWPM*, 1: 390.
132. W.M. Sneed to Mangum, 3 December 1830, *PWPM*, 1: 393. See also *PWPM*, 1: xxv–xxvii.
133. W.M. Sneed to Mangum, 3 December 1830, *PWPM*, 1: 392. Vote totals given in this letter indicate that some of the Spaight faction were voting for Owen but intentionally holding him short of a majority in an effort to block the election of both Owen and Mangum, apparently in an effort to get another Spaight faction member elected who was not supported by opposition men. Sneed indicated in a letter to Mangum that Spaight may have initially encouraged Owen to block Mangum, but he indicates in the same letter that once he realized that Owen might be elected, joined the majority of "his" faction and switched to Mangum. W.M. Sneed to Mangum, 3 December 1830, *PWPM*, 1: 393–394. The whole election testifies to the low state of party discipline that then prevailed in the legislature: despite support from Spaight and Saunders, the leaders of "the party" could not keep some members from pursuing their own strategy.
134. Romulus M. Saunders to Mangum, 3 December 1830, *PWPM*, 1: 391–392.
135. A letter Mangum wrote to Owen on December 8 places him in Raleigh on that date, *PWPM*, 1: 395. Mangum's letter to Owen nearly precipitated a duel with Owen, who interpreted it as a challenge to his character. Mangum insisted that he had only commented on Owen's *political principles* and sought "never to touch the character of a Gentleman in any respect." He also explained that his station as a judge and the "moral sense" of his community prevented any idea in his mind of challenging Owen to a duel. Though he remained bitter at his defeat in the election, Owen accepted Mangum's explanation. Later, the two worked together in the Whig Party and apparently held no grudges. See Mangum to Owen, 1 December 1830; Owen to Mangum, 4 Decem-

ber 1830; Mangum to Owen, 8 December 1830; Owen to Mangum, 11 December 1830, *PWPM*, 1: 388, 394–398, *PWPM*, 1: xxvi–xxvii.

Chapter 3

1. Daniel Walker Howe, *What Hath God Wrought: The Transformation of America, 1815–1848* (New York: Oxford University Press, 2007), 274–275.
2. Macon to Weldon Edwards, 22 March, 12 May 1828, Nathaniel Macon Papers, NCDCR-DAH.
3. Mangum to William A. Graham, 16 December 1834, *PWPM*, 2: 243–44.
4. Delivered in the Senate 7–8 February 1832. The speech that appears in *PWPM*, 5: 519–562 is taken from a pamphlet copy of the speech printed in Raleigh in 1832 and thus it is the speech as revised by Mangum for the printing press. But as it is the version of the speech most North Carolinians would have read, I have chosen to use this version.
5. Like other Southern politicians and political economists, Mangum never placed slave-owning planters in this category.
6. Mangum to Charity Mangum, 11 Feb. 1832, *PWPM*, 1: 478.
7. R.M. Saunders to Mangum, 31 March 1832, *PWPM*, 1: 524.
8. John Bragg to Mangum, 4 March 1832, *PWPM*, 1: 505.
9. Mangum to Charity Mangum, 11 February 1832, *PWPM*, 1: 478. Mangum informed Charity that the pamphlet version was not as good as his delivery in the Senate.
10. Francis Jones to Mangum, 7 June 1832, *PWPM*, 1: 551; Robert B. Gilliam to Mangum, 5 April 1832, *PWPM*, 1: 529; John Long to Mangum, 5 April 1835, *PWPM*, 1: 531. See also Adam Lockhart to Mangum, 3 April 1832 and C.P. Mallett to Mangum, 4 April 1832, *PWPM*, 1: 524–25, 527. Lockhart expressed accord with Mangum's views but was surprised that Mangum "knew there was Ever such a man living on earth as A. Lockart…" Mangum distributed the pamphlets to those who he did not know personally but who could influence opinion. Lockhart was a former state legislator.
11. Hoffman, *Andrew Jackson and North Carolina Politics*, 39.
12. Peterson, *Great Triumvirate*, 183.
13. Peterson, *Great Triumvirate*, 184.
14. For more on this dispute and its relation to North Carolina's factional politics see Hoffman, *Andrew Jackson and North Carolina Politics*, 41–43.
15. John Branch to "A Gentleman in This City," New Bern *Spectator*, 21 May 1831 quoted in Hoffman, 41.
16. *Western Carolinian*, 9 May 1831. Hoffman, 41.
17. *Western Carolinian*, 20 June 1831. Hoffman, 42–44.
18. Hoffman, *Andrew Jackson and North Carolina Politics*, 44–45. Also see Jeffrey, *State Parties and National Politics: North Carolina 1815–1861* (Athens: The University of Georgia Press, 1989), 32–48. Jeffrey points out that the ascendancy of the Old Republicans/Crawford men in the Jackson administration was critical to driving original Jackson men like Branch and Polk out of Jackson's party.

19. John Martin to Mangum, 16 March 1832, *PWPM*, 1: 512.
20. See for example "Jackson Anti–Van Buren Meeting," Salisbury *Western Carolinian*, 7 May 1832.
21. Hoffman, *Andrew Jackson and North Carolina Politics*, 47–57.
22. Salisbury *Western Carolinian*, 5 September 1831.
23. Salisbury *Western Carolinian*, 30 April 1832.
24. See for instance, report of a "Jackson meeting" on 21 March 1832 in Rockingham (Richmond County), *Western Carolinian*, 9 April 1832. Hoffman, 47–48.
25. Salisbury *Western Carolinian*, 9 April 1832.
26. "Jackson Anti–Van Buren Meeting," Salisbury *Western Carolinian*, 7 May 1832, quoting the Halifax *Advocate*.
27. *Western Carolinian*, 25 June 1832, printed accounts of meetings in Bertie, Orange, Cumberland, Perquimons, Hyde, and Martin counties.
28. Bertie, Beaufort, Chowan, Cumberland, Edgecomb, Granville, Halifax, Hertford, Hyde, Lenoir, Martin, New Hanover, Northampton, Orange, Pasquotank, Perquimons, Warren, and Wake counties. Pitt County nominated a delegate but he was unable to attend due to illness in his family. A similar Jackson-Barbour convention met in Virginia at Charlottesville on June 12. Salisbury *Western Carolinian*, 2 July 1832.
29. "State Convention," Salisbury *Western Carolinian*, 2 July 1832, from account in the Raleigh *Star*. The account of the convention also appeared in the Tarborough *North Carolina Free Press*, 3 July 1832.
30. "Address of the Jackson & Barbour Convention," Salisbury *Western Carolinian*, 9 July 1832.
31. See for instance, "Anti-Tariff Meeting," Salisbury *Western Carolinian*, 12 September 1831.
32. "Mr. M. Van Buren," Salisbury *Western Carolinian*, 11 April 1831; Salisbury *Western Carolinian*, 25 April 1831, complained of the tariff and the divisions in the party shortly after the break up of Jackson's cabinet; "The Intrigue Developed," Salisbury *Western Carolinian*, 20 February 1832; "To the Original Jackson Men," Salisbury *Western Carolinian*, 12 March 1832, praising the Senate's rejection of Van Buren's appointment as ambassador to Britain; "The Vice Presidency," Salisbury *Western Carolinian*, 30 April 1832.
33. Salisbury *Western Carolinian*, 16 April 1832.
34. Salisbury *Western Carolinian*, 16 April 1832.
35. The resolutions as introduced opposed Missouri's admission, but amendments made the resolutions somewhat ambiguous. See Glover Moore, *Missouri Controversy*, 138–139.
36. "State-Right and Anti-Tariff Meeting," Salisbury *Western Carolinian*, 9 July 1832.
37. John Bragg to Mangum, 4 March 1832, *PWPM*, 1: 505. Mangum received letters from committees conveying laudatory resolutions passed by political meetings. See Dillon Jordan, Jr., to Mangum, 14 March 1832 and T.C. Mathews & J.P. Freeman to Mangum, 20 March 1832, *PWPM*, 1: 510–512, 514–515. The former meeting styled itself an "Administration meeting" and the latter, "a large & respectable assemblage of the friends of the present administration."
38. William S. Ransom to Mangum, 8 February 1832, *PWPM*, 1: 474–476. Ransom noted Mangum's "kind letter to us."
39. Saunders to Mangum, 31 March 1832, *PWPM*, 1: 524.

40. Salisbury *Western Carolinian*. 20 February, 19 March, 16, 23 April 1832. The speech appeared in the editions of 16 and 23 April.
41. James Iredell to Mangum, 4 Feb. 1832, *PWPM*, 1: 470–473.
42. On Saunders and Mangum in the Crawford campaign see above, chapter four and Hoffman, *Andrew Jackson and North Carolina Politics*, 7.
43. R.M. Saunders to Mangum, 23 January 1832, *PWPM*, 1: 462. See also Saunders to Mangum 18 March 1832 and Saunders to Mangum 31 March 1832 for letters in which Saunders addresses Mangum as a fellow partisan and Van Buren man.
44. Saunders used Mangum as a go-between to communicate with Branch during a dispute over Branch's disclosure of supposedly confidential conversations with Jackson, for which Saunders had publicly criticized Branch in the Raleigh *Star*. Saunders to Mangum, 3 March 1832, *PWPM*, 1: 502.
45. Saunders to Mangum, 18 March 1832, *PWPM*, 1: 513–14.
46. Saunders to Mangum, 31 March 1832, *PWPM*, 1: 522–24. Other correspondents of Mangum appeared to consider him a strong Jackson supporter, see for instance William Ransom to Mangum, 8 Feb. 1832, *PWPM*, 1: 474–76.
47. Mangum to William A. Graham, 16 Dec. 1834, *PWPM*, 2: 243–244.
48. Saunders to Mangum, 31 March 1832, *PWPM*, 1: 522–24.
49. Mangum to William A. Graham, 16 Dec. 1834, *PWPM*, 2: 243–244.
50. Mangum to William A. Graham, 16 Dec. 1834, *PWPM*, 2: 243–244.
51. *Ibid.*; Robert Remini, *Henry Clay: Statesman for the Union* (New York: W.W. Norton & Company, 1991), 395–396.
52. Mangum to William A. Graham, 16 Dec. 1834, *PWPM*, 2: 243–244.
53. Charles Fisher to Mangum, 24 August 1832, *PWPM*, 1: 571–572.
54. Robert V. Remini, *Andrew Jackson and the Bank War: A Study in the Growth of Presidential Power* (New York: W.W. Norton & Company, 1967), 75–82; Daniel Walker Howe, *What Hath God Wrought*, 378–379.
55. James Iredell to Mangum, 4 Feb. 1832, *PWPM*, 1: 470–473.
56. Mangum to William Gaston, 19 January 1832, *PWPM*, 1: 454–456. Gaston replied that he too thought the continuance of the Bank was an "almost indispensable necessity." "I am mortified and pained too at the want of stability and permanency which a failure to renew the charter would stamp upon all the institutions of our country." Gaston to Mangum, 23 Jan. 1832, *PWPM*, 1: 460–461.
57. Mangum to William Polk, 11 February 1832, *PWPM*, 1: 480–81.
58. Mangum to Duncan Cameron, 24 May 1832, *PWPM*, 1: 548.
59. Duncan Cameron to Mangum, 3 June 1832, *PWPM*, 1: 549. Henry Seawell to Mangum, 14 Feb. 1832, and S.F. Patterson to Mangum, 11 March 1832, *PWPM*, 1: 483–484, 508–510.
60. Hoffman, *Andrew Jackson and North Carolina Politics*, 53. Only one member, Augustine Shepperd, crossed the factional lines. Despite being Branch's friend, he voted in favor of the Bank.
61. Jackson's message is in Richardson, ed., *Messages and Papers of the Presidents*, 3: 1153.
62. Remini, *Andrew Jackson and the Bank War*, 81.
63. Hoffman, *Andrew Jackson and North Carolina Politics*, 48–49.
64. Richard E. Ellis, *The Union at Risk*, 81–95.
65. Macon to Samuel P. Carson, 9 February 1833, "Nathaniel Macon Correspondence," 92.
66. Macon to Jackson, 26 August 1833, Jackson to Macon, 2 September 1833, Macon to Jackson, 25 September 1833, in John Spencer Bassett, ed., *Correspondence of Andrew Jackson* (Washington, D.C.: Carnegie Institution of Washington, 1931), 171–172, 176–178, 208–209.
67. Though he had retired from the Senate in 1828, Macon returned to the political scene in 1835 as president of the North Carolina constitutional convention of 1835. As the chief prophet of conservatism, Macon used one of his few speeches at the convention to warn the delegates against tampering too much with the old constitution: "Patriots formed this venerated Constitution and we ought to approach it with awe. It was the great work of our fathers; but we are about to treat it as many of the thoughtless young are apt to treat their paternal estates" (Harold J. Counihan, "The North Carolina Constitutional Convention of 1835: A Study in Jacksonian Democracy," *North Carolina Historical Review* XLVI No. 4 [October 1969], 358–359). Under Macon's presidency, the convention amended the constitution to change the meeting of the General Assembly (and thus legislative elections) to once every two years. The most far-reaching provision shifted the election of the governor from the legislature to a state-wide popular election and changed the governor's term to two years. The delegates also voted to strip free black men of the franchise, one of the few remaining rights of free men of color in the state. The new constitution was ratified by a vote of 26,771 to 21, 606 (Counihan, 361). During the last decade of his career in politics, Macon had been the ultimate oppositionist. Still, the founder of the Republican party viewed him as the champion of the true Republican creed. In Thomas Jefferson's last letter to Macon, written four months before the former's death, the leader of the Revolution of 1800 declared Macon "the strictest of our models genuine republicanism" and suggested an epitaph for Macon's tomb: "Ultimus Romanorum" (Jefferson to Macon, 24 March 1826, Thomas Jefferson Papers, LC. The letter was a letter of introduction to Macon for Jefferson's grandson, Thomas Jefferson Randolph). Nathaniel Macon died at Buck Spring on June 29, 1837, and was buried beside his wife and son in a plot not far from his house. As he had requested in his will, Macon's grave was marked only by a large pile of stones. He has no mausoleum.
68. John Chavis to Mangum, 8 August 1832, *PWPM*, 1: 566.
69. Mangum to Charity Mangum, 15 Dec. 1832, *PWPM*, 1: 589.
70. J.L. Bailey to Willie P. Mangum, 25 Dec. 1832, *PWPM*, 1: 590–591. Mangum's letter to Priestly is not in the Mangum Papers but Bailey wrote Mangum that Priestly had shown him the letter.
71. *Register of Debates*, 22nd Congress, 2nd Session, 21–24.

72. *Register of Debates*, 22nd Congress, 2nd Session, 174–175.
73. Ellis, *Union at Risk*, 168–177.
74. Barbour's letter printed in the *Tarborough Free Press*, 6 November 1832.

Chapter 4

1. *Register of Debates*, 22nd Congress, 2nd Session, 799–800.
2. Richardson, *Messages and Papers of the Presidents*, 3: 7.
3. Howe, *What Hath God Wrought*, 388.
4. Howe, *What Hath God Wrought*, 388.
5. Mangum to David L. Swain, 22 December 1833, *PWPM*, 2: 51–56.
6. *U.S Telegraph*, 2 January 1834, quoted in Cole, 31.
7. Ellis examines Van Buren's continued loyalty to states' rights in *The Union at Risk* and specifically his "Report on Nullification" for the Joint Committee of the New York legislature. Ellis finds Van Buren to be more loyal to states' rights than Mangum and the Southern opposition did.
8. William Montgomery to Mangum, 27 December 1833, *PWPM*, 2: 59.
9. *Register of Debates*, 23rd Congress, 1st Session, 472–474.
10. Mangum to Duncan Cameron, 7 and 9 Feb. 1834, *PWPM*, 2: 72–79.
11. Howe, *What Hath God Wrought*, 393.
12. Mangum to Duncan Cameron, 7 and 9 Feb. 1834, *PWPM*, 2: 72–79.
13. *Register of Debates*, 23rd Congress, 1st Session, 529–532.
14. Isaac T. Avery to Mangum, 28 February 1834, *PWPM*, 2: 107–111. On Avery, see John C. Inscoe, *Mountain Masters: Slavery and the Sectional Crisis in Western North Carolina* (Knoxville: University of Tennessee Press, 1989), 44, 49, 68.
15. Samuel Hillman to Mangum, 1 March 1834, *PWPM*, 2: 112–15.
16. "Copy of Burke County Resolutions," 27 March 1834, *PWPM*, 2: 127–130.
17. *Register of Debates*, 23rd Congress, 1st Session, 1140, 1205–06.
18. *Register of Debates*, 23rd Congress, 1st Session, 1259–60.
19. *Register of Debates*, 23rd Congress, 1st Session, 1767–1769.
20. "Resolutions of Hillsboro Citizens," 30 May 1834, *PWPM*, 2: 157–158.
21. *Register of Debates*, 23rd Congress, 1st Session, 1187.
22. Remini, *Andrew Jackson and the Bank War*, 142.
23. Richardson, *Messages and Papers of the Presidents*, 3: 1224–1238.
24. Richardson, *Messages and Papers of the Presidents*, 3: 1298, 1309. The follow-up message to the protest changed very little in regard to these arguments because Jackson still ignored the fact that Congress had never changed the law directing the place of deposit and he still claimed to have exclusive control over all executive officers.
25. Remini, *Andrew Jackson and the Bank War*, 143–144.
26. Harry L. Watson, *Liberty and Power: The Politics of Jacksonian America* (New York: Hill & Wang, 1990), 155.
27. Remini, *Andrew Jackson and the Bank War*, 144–147.
28. Clement Eaton. "Southern Senators and the Right of Instruction, 1789–1860," *The Journal of Southern History* 18 (1952), 316.
29. Jackson to Andrew Jackson, Jr., 6 April 1834, in Basset, *Correspondence of Andrew Jackson*, 5: 259; Jackson to Livingston, 27 June 1834, *Correspondence of Andrew Jackson*, 5: 272.
30. Mangum to David L. Swain, 22 Dec. 1833, *PWPM*, 2: 53.
31. R.H. Alexander to Mangum, 29 Nov. 1834, *PWPM*, 2: 224–226.
32. William A. Graham to Mangum, 8 Dec., 1834, *PWPM*, 2: 230–231.
33. Graham, "Address of the Republican Whig members of the General Assembly of 1838 to the People of North Carolina," n.d., in J.G. deRoulhac Hamilton, ed., *The Papers of William Alexander Graham* (Raleigh: State Department of Archives and History, 1957), 2: 39–48. 337–363. Hereafter cited as *PWAG*.
34. Mangum to William A. Graham, 16 Dec. 1834, *PWPM*, 2: 241.
35. Mangum to William A. Graham, 17 Dec. 1834, *PWPM*, 2: 245.
36. Mangum to William A. Graham, 16 Dec. 1834, *PWPM*, 2: 241.
37. Mangum to John Beard, 7 Oct. 1834, *PWPM*, 2: 218. John Beard was the editor of the Salisbury *Western Carolinian*.
38. Mangum to William A. Graham, 17 Dec. 1834, *PWPM*, 2: 245.
39. Mangum to William A. Graham, 28 December 1834, *PWPM*, 2: 260–61.
40. *North Carolina Standard*, 26 Dec. 1834.
41. Howe, *What Hath God Wrought*, 411. Also see Kohl, *The Politics of Individualism*, 179–184.
42. Potter to Mangum, 31 December 1834, *PWPM*, 2: 263–266; William Albright to Mangum, 8 January 1835, *PWPM*, 2: 278–279; J.S. Smith to Mangum, 26 January 1835, *PWPM*, 2: 293–294. The Whigs commonly referred to the Democrats as unthinking "collar men," led on a collar by their party masters, like slaves.
43. Thomas Clingman to Mangum, 30 January 1835, *PWPM*, 2: 295–296. See also P.W. Kittrell to Mangum, 1 January 1835, *PWPM*, 2: 266–268; B.S. King to Mangum, 1 January 1835, *PWPM*, 2: 268–269; John B. Bobbitt to Mangum, 3 January 1835, *PWPM*, 2: 270–271; R.H. Alexander to Mangum, 6 January 1835, *PWPM*, 2: 275–276; Michael Holt to Mangum, 11 January 1835, *PWPM*, 2: 280; and Henry Seawell to Mangum, 7 February 1835, *PWPM*, 2: 306–309.
44. Jones to Mangum, 22 August 1834, *PWPM*, 2: 186–190. In this letter Jones also wrote of the Senate and Jackson: "Both have sinned, passion and prejudice have prevailed too extensively—the Country will feel it, and therefore not forget this wayward course of their rulers for years to come." Jones also told Mangum, "I have given, as our old friend Mr. Macon says, some tests and if you dispute my orthodoxy, I propose that we discuss

them..." Jones to Mangum, 25 February 1835, *PWPM*, 2: 317–318. Jones also informed Mangum that he had given a speech at an assembly of Van Buren supporters at the Warren court house, but had wished Mangum had been there "and had said a word against Van Buren—I would roasted you in a good humour but with great severity." For letters advising Mangum to obey the instructions and resign, see James Somervell to Mangum, *PWPM*, 2: 281–282 and Burton Craige to Mangum, 21 January 1835, *PWPM*, 2: 287–289. Both Somervell and Craige supported Mangum's opposition to Jackson, but thought he was required to obey the instructions of the legislature. Somervell was a wealthy planter from Warrenton and operated a ferry across the Roanoke River. He described himself as "an old fashioned Republican."

45. Priestly Mangum to Willie P. Mangum, 6 Feb. 1835, *PWPM*, 2: 302–303.

46. Sam P. Carson to Mangum, 4 Jan. 1835, *PWPM*, 2: 272.

47. D.L. Swain to Mangum, 2 January 1835, *PWPM*, 2: 269–270.

48. *Register of Debates*, 23rd Congress., 2nd sess., 722.

49. William P. Hoffman, "Willie P. Mangum and the Whig Revival of the Doctrine of Instructions." *The Journal of Southern History* 22 (August 1956): 338–354. Mangum to David L. Swain, 22 December 1833, *PWPM*, 2: 54.

50. "Resolutions of Fayetteville Public Meeting," [1835], *PWPM*, 2: 299–300. The copy of the resolutions sent to Mangum was followed by the annotation "A true copy from the Minutes" and "Isham Blake Jr. Secretary."

51. John H. Brownrigg to Mangum, 24 January 1835, *PWPM*, 2: 290–291.

52. D.C. Freeman et al. to Willie P. Mangum and enclosure of resolutions, 16 April 1835, *PWPM*, 2: 332–334.

53. *Fayetteville Observer*, 24 Feb. 1835.

54. Quoted in Cole, *Whig Party in the South*, 34–35.

55. William A. Graham to Mangum, 8 Dec., 1834, *PWPM*, 2: 230.

56. Graham, "Speech on Instruction to Mangum," Dec. 1834, *PWAG*, 1: 337–363. The speech was published in the *Raleigh Register*, 27 January 1835 and the *Hillsborough Recorder*, 30 January 1835. On the importance of the speech to the Opposition and to Graham's rise, see *PWAG*, 1: 337n60.

57. "Vindex" appeared in the *Raleigh Register*, 2 Feb. 1835 and "Civis" answered in the *North Carolina Standard*, 27 Feb. 1835.

58. Lawrence Frederick Kohl, *The Politics of Individualism: Parties and the American Character in the Jacksonian Era* (New York: Oxford University Press, 1989), 168–169, 179–181, explains that Democrats in general tended to hold this view that the popular will trumped the Constitution and how Whigs in general placed the Constitution first as a limit on majority tyranny.

59. Jackson to Joseph Conn Guild, 24 April 1835, in Basset, *Correspondence of Andrew Jackson*, 5: 339. Jackson to Polk, 3 August 1835, in Basset, *Correspondence of Andrew Jackson*, 5: 359.

60. Tyler's letter was dated from Washington 29 February 1836. It was printed in the *Raleigh Register*, 15 March 1836. Leigh's letter was dated from Washington 2 March 1836 and was printed in the *Raleigh Register* 22 March 1836.

61. The occasion for the speech was in response to Jackson's special "War Message" of January 15, 1836, on the French diplomatic situation.

62. *Register of Debates*, 24 Congress, 1 Sess., 367–383. The speech is reprinted in *PWPM*, 5: 586–611.

63. Robert B. Gilliam to Mangum, 1 April 1836, *PWPM*, 2: 416–417. John A. Anderson to Mangum, 20 June 1836, *PWPM*, 2: 456. *Raleigh Register*, 5 April 1836.

64. Neither Wilentz, Holt, Watson, *Liberty and Power*, nor Howe, *What Hath God wrought*, discusses Jackson's war on the Senate. Howe and Wilentz discuss Jackson's claims for executive power. Only Eaton, "Right of Instruction," discusses Jackson's attempts to remove his opposition in the Senate.

65. Lawrence Frederick Kohl, *The Politics of Individualism: Parties and the American Character in the Jacksonian Era* (New York: Oxford University Press, 1989), 83.

66. Kohl, 179–180.

67. Kohl, 84.

68. In addition to the claims in Jackson's messages to Congress, see Jackson to Joseph Conn Guild, 24 April 1835, in Bassett, *Correspondence of Andrew Jackson*, 5: 338–341.

69. Wilentz, *Rise of American Democracy*, 399. Wilentz argues that Jackson's protest reflected changed the changed political realities of the 1830s whereby in most states the voters elected the presidential electors. One fails to see the difference, though, between senators being elected by electors—the state legislators—and presidents being elected by electors. Wilentz further argues that Jackson's aim's were in part defensive: not to establish a new "imperial presidency" but to prevent Clay from establishing an "imperial Congress" and ward off the threat of repeated harassment by censure that would dilute the president's power.

70. Jeffrey, *State Parties and National Politics: North Carolina 1815–1861* (Athens, Georgia, 1989), 128.

71. Michael O'Brien, *Conjectures of Order: Intellectual Life and the American South, 1810–1860* Vol. 2 (Chapel Hill: University of North Carolina Press, 2004), 836–849. O'Brien also makes the important point that Jackson favored executive action and had an imperialist/nationalist outlook because of his long service in the War Department administering the American Empire as a soldier and territorial governor.

72. Kohl, 158–159.

73. Refer to chapter two, specifically Jefferson's 1810 letter on the power of the president to exceed the Constitution, his correspondence with Madison on the possible invasion of Florida, and his correspondence and messages to Congress on the Louisiana Purchase.

74. The best example is the series of letters from "Lucius" that appeared in the Raleigh *North Carolina Standard* between 14 November and 19 December 1834. See also Robert H. Jones to Mangum, 16 December 1834 and William H. Haywood to Mangum, 30 December 1834, *PWPM*, 2: 239–240, 261–262. Jones and Haywood denied being the author of the letters.

75. Eaton, "Right of Instruction," 315.

76. Cole, 33–34, quote on 33.

77. Mangum to John Beard, 7 Oct. 1834, *PWPM*, 2: 218.

78. Howe, *What Hath God Wrought*, 6.

79. Harry L. Watson, *Jacksonian Politics and Community*

Conflict: The Emergence of the Second American Party System in Cumberland County North Carolina (Baton Rouge: Louisiana State University Press, 1981), 274, 243–245, quote, 244.

80. Herbert Dale Pegg, *The Whig Party in North Carolina*. (Chapel Hill: Colonial Press, 1968), 24–25.

81. The invitation from the committee of E.H Eure, Thomas M. Crowell, Michael Ferral, and William L. Long is in *PWPM*, 2: 319–320. The account in the *Roanoke Advocate* added R.J. Hawkins and E.C. Pittman to the committee of invitation. The account was, of course, reprinted in the central party newspaper, the *Raleigh Register*.

82. The dinner was held in the Eagle Hotel, where North Carolina's first constitution had been framed—a point the speakers at the dinner made sure to bring out. The county's Whigs were eager to get a copy of Mangum's speech on the occasion to print with the account of the dinner in the *Roanoke Advocate*. Two days after the dinner, the committee of invitation, addressed a request to Mangum for a copy of his remarks and on the 19th Robert Bond, one of the vice-presidents of the dinner, sent a letter to Mangum explaining the order in which the speeches and toasts would appear in print and asking him to emphasize his opposition to the resolutions of instruction in his copy for print. Both letters in *PWPM*, 2: 321–322.

83. David L. Swain to Mangum, 7 April 1835. *Raleigh Register*, 21 April 1835.

84. *Raleigh Register*, 14 and 21 April 1835.

85. Philo White announced the celebration in his *Standard* and seemed to believe that it would be a strictly patriotic affair, but the Whigs, in a demonstration of their organizational skills, appear to have assumed control of this celebration and made it their own. (Philo White announced in the *Standard* on 24 April, but all toasts were Whig toasts).

86. Salisbury *Western Carolinian*, 6 June 1835.

87. Franklin Smith of the celebration's committee wrote in his invitation to Mangum that Mangum might think it improper to introduce political subjects at the celebration; thus he offered Mangum the venue of another, openly political, forum to be held the day after the Celebration, where Mangum could speak to political topics and make "such an impression on the public mind as the uprightness of your course and your abilities so well enable you." Mangum, though, decided that the celebration offered the best opportunity to make such an impression on the people of Mecklenburg and delivered a political speech.

88. The oration at the celebration was only mentioned and the political speeches at the dinner by Mangum and Swain were summarized but all the toasts were printed. The toasts were mixed political themes with praise of North and South Carolina. The *Western Carolinian* and the *Register* both carried accounts of the celebration, but the *Register* did not print the full list of toasts. *Western Carolinian*, 6 June 1835; *Raleigh Register*, 9 June 1835. The toasts noted here were published in both. Indicating that the parties considered them effective campaign devices, toasts were often revised and/or submitted especially for publication in the account.

89. Salisbury *Western Carolinian*, 29 Aug. 1835.

90. Salisbury *Western Carolinian*, 29 Aug. 1835.

91. Salisbury *Western Carolinian*, 29 Aug. 1835. Because names were not given with these toasts we cannot know whether these toasts were given by the same lady of two different ladies.

92. Elizabeth R. Varon, *We Mean to Be Counted: White Women and Politics in Antebellum Virginia* (Chapel Hill: University of North Carolina Press, 1998), finds that in Virginia women were "marginal" to the rituals of partisan politics before 1840. The Whigs of North Carolina appear to have given women a prominent place in their celebrations earlier than the Whigs of Virginia.

93. Pegg, 44n35.

94. Isaac Croom to Mangum, 18 August 1835, *PWPM*, 2: 355–356.

95. Moore, et. al. to Mangum, enclosure to David Outlaw to Mangum, 10 September 1835, *PWPM*, 2: 359–361. The invitation was also printed by Beard in the Salisbury, *Western Carolinian*, 17 October 1835. Beard introduced the invitation with the comment: "Thus, while hired calumniators are pouring their abuse upon Judge Mangum for the patriotic stand which he has taken in defence of the Constitution and the liberties of his country, the genuine PEOPLE are rewarding him by public manifestations of their approbation"; Allen Rogers & Others to Willie P. Mangum, 6 October 1836, *PWPM*, 2: 469–470.

96. See Albert Ray Newsome, *The Presidential Election of 1824 in North Carolina* (Chapel Hill, 1939), 138.

97. Pegg, 35.

98. Watson, *Jacksonian Politics and Community Conflict*, 271.

99. The *Western Carolinian* stated that the meeting was called by the Grand Jurors of the Superior Court, but the officers of the meeting were all Opposition leaders in the county.

100. The Southern Whigs thus attacked Van Buren for what may have been his greatest achievement—the organization of the Democratic Party. See Richard Hofstadter, *The Idea of a Party System: The Rise of Legitimate Opposition in the United States, 1780–1840* (Berkeley: University of California Press, 1969), 212–238.

101. Charles Fisher to Mangum, 30 April 1835, *PWPM*, 2: 340–341.

102. The committee of five that was appointed to prepare the meeting's resolutions consisted of Graham, Federick Nash, James Mebane, Hugh Waddell, and Dr. James S. Smith. Graham made the report of the committee to the meeting and it is safe to assume the report reflected his views. Graham's report to the Orange meeting and the resolutions of the meetings in Warren, Halifax, and Hertford counties were reported in the *Raleigh Register*, 15 March 1836.

103. Both the Stokes County and Granville County resolutions are in the *Raleigh Register*, 12 April 1836. Other similar resolutions were passed in meetings in Davidson County and Wake County (*Register* 23 Feb. 1836) and Nash County and Chowan County (*Register* 24 May 1836). And these were not all, the *Register* carried them weekly from April 1836 through June.

104. See Norton, 85, for North Carolina Democrats' attitude to White.

105. William J. Cooper, Jr., *The South and the Politics of Slavery 1828–1856* (Baton Rouge, 1978), 74–96.

106. Pegg, 63.

107. Salisbury *Carolina Watchman*, 20 August 1836.

108. *Raleigh Register*, 6 September 1836.

109. Allen Rogers & Others to Mangum, 6 October 1836, *PWPM*, 2: 469–471.
110. Graham to Mangum, 4 November 1836, *PWPM*, 2: 474–475.
111. Allen Rogers & Others to Mangum, 6 October 1836, *PWPM*, 2: 469–471.
112. James Graham to William Graham, 29 Dec. 1836, *PWAG*, 1: 471.
113. Salisbury *Western Carolinian*, 1 March 1834.

Chapter 5

1. Remini, *Jackson and the Bank War*, 165–168.
2. Mangum to Charity Mangum, 19 August 1834, *PWPM*, 2: 183.
3. Mangum to Charity Mangum, 20 August and 2 September 1834, *PWPM*, 2: 183–86, 193–95.
4. Mangum to Charity Mangum, 20 August 1834, *PWPM*, 2: 183–186.
5. Mangum to Charity Mangum, 2 Sept., 1834, *PWPM*, 2: 193–199.
6. Mangum to Charity Mangum, 13 September 1835, *PWPM*, 2: 201.
7. Mangum to Charity Mangum, 13 Sept., 1834, *PWPM*, 2: 200–204.
8. Mangum to William Gaston, 24 Sept. 1834; Daniel Webster to Mangum, 7, 8, 9 Oct. and 4 Nov. 1834; John Tyler to Mangum, 22 Oct. 1834; Mangum to William A. Graham, 16 Dec. 1834, all *PWPM*, 2: 205–6, 219–24, 240–44.
9. Mangum to John Beard, 7 October 1834, *PWPM*, 2: 212–219. The *Western Carolinian* was a Calhoun State Rights Party newspaper.
10. Mangum to Beard, 7 October 1834, *PWPM*, 2: 217.
11. Calhoun to Mangum, 8 Feb. 1837, *PWPM*, 2: 490–492.
12. Duff Green to Mangum, 6 March 1837, *PWPM*, 2: 493–494.
13. Charles P. Green to Mangum, 20 April 1837, *PWPM*, 2: 495.
14. Holt, *Rise and Fall of the American Whig Party*, 61.
15. Pegg, 95.
16. Pegg, *Whig Party in North Carolina*, 95.
17. *Raleigh Register*, 21 August 1837.
18. Weston R. Gales to *WPM*, 1 June 1837, *PWPM*, 2: 498–500; C.L. Hinton to Mangum, 10 June 1837, *PWPM*, 2: 503–04; William A. Graham to Mangum, 25 May 1837, *PWPM*, 2: 497–98.
19. *PWPM*, 2: 497n18.
20. Giles Mebane to Graham, 20 June 1837, John W. Norwood to Graham, 23 June 1837, M. McGehee to Graham, 27 June 1837, Graham to Susan Washington Graham, 28 June 1837, *PWAG*, 1: 504–505, 507–508, 508–509, 509–510; William A. Graham to Mangum, 25 May 1837, Weston R. Gales to Mangum, 1 June 1837, *PWPM*, 2: 497–98, 498–500.
21. *Raleigh Register*, 24 July 1837; *Hillsborough Recorder*, 28 July 1837.
22. Peterson, *Great Triumvirate*, 270–273.
23. Mangum to Duncan Cameron, 24 February 1834, *PWPM*, 2: 101–02. See the discussion in Chapter Two of Calhoun's role in establishing the Second Bank of the United States, as well as Nathaniel Macon's total opposition to Calhoun at that time for his nationalism (showing that all Mangum's thought did not derive from Macon's Old Republicanism.)
24. William W. Freehling, *Prelude to Civil War: The Nullification Controversy in South Carolina, 1816–1836* (New York: Oxford University Press, 1965), 158, 173. Freehling identifies Preston as a S.C. "radical" leader (217), but a "perceptive nullifier" (356) who knew its futility.
25. William C. Preston to Mangum, 4 Oct., 1837, Preston to Mangum, 7 April 1838, *PWPM*, 2: 508–510, 519–520. See also Preston to Mangum, 28 March 1838, *PWPM*, 2: 517. In this letter Preston was more decided in his views of Calhoun's motives. He wrote to Mangum: "Mr. Calhoun spares no exertion to bring his corps of nullifiers to the support of the administration that upon the junction he may assume the truncheon of command—I hope in God that you will all avoid the union in No Carolina."
26. J.J. Crittenden to Mangum, 11 October 1837, *PWPM*, 2: 511–12.
27. Mangum to Henry Clay, 26 March 1838, in Seager, ed., *Papers of Clay*, 9: 166.
28. Mangum to John Beard, 7 October 1834, *PWPM*, 2: 217. This was the same letter in which Mangum set out his "views" of the Boston Whigs.
29. William C. Preston to Mangum, 4 Oct., 1837, *PWPM*, 2: 508–510. In early 1838 Preston was more bitterly divided in his views of Calhoun's motives. He wrote to Mangum: "Mr. Calhoun spares no exertion to bring his corps of nullifiers to the support of the administration that upon the junction he may assume the truncheon of command—I hope in God that you will all avoid the union in No Carolina." Preston to Mangum, 28 March 1838, *PWPM*, 2: 517.
30. Mangum named his only son after Preston. William Preston Mangum was born July 13, 1837. It was William C. Preston who persuaded Vice-President Calhoun in the fall of 1828 to write the *Exposition* that established the principles of the South Carolina doctrine of nullification. See Freehling, *Prelude to Civil War*, 158–159.
31. Henry Clay to Mangum, 17 November 1837, *PWPM*, 2: 512.
32. *Carolina Watchman*, 25 November 1837. Pegg, 29. Pegg notes that at times the newspaper's circulation extended to 40 counties.
33. Hamilton C. Jones to Mangum, 22 December 1837, *PWPM*, 2: 513.
34. Hamilton C. Jones to Mangum, 22 December 1837, *PWPM*, 2: 513–15.
35. *Raleigh Register*, 5 March 1838.
36. Preston to Mangum, 7 April 1838, *PWPM*, 2: 519–520.
37. Mangum to Henry Clay, 26 March 1838, in Seager, ed., *Papers of Henry Clay* 9: 166–167.
38. *Raleigh Register*, 27 August 1838. County by county returns for governor and Whig gains and losses in the legislature are in the 20 and 27 August *Raleigh Register*.
39. *Raleigh Register*, 20, 27 August 1838.
40. Paul C. Cameron to Mangum, 23 August 1838, *PWPM*, 2: 528.
41. Graham to the Representatives from North

Carolina (draft), 12 January 1839, *PWAG*, 2: 35–37. A copy of the resolutions is enclosed with the draft letter.

42. Mangum to Thomas D. Bennehan, 9 December 1838, *PWPM*, 2: 534–535.

43. Pegg, 66.

44. Quoted in the *Raleigh Register*, 22 October 1838.

45. *Raleigh Register*, 10 September 1838.

46. Washington (NC) *Whig* quoted in the *Raleigh Register*, 1 October 1838.

47. *Carolina Watchman* quoted in the *Raleigh Register*, 17 September 1838.

48. *Raleigh Register*, 26 November 1838.

49. William C. Preston to Mangum, 7 April 1838, *PWPM*, 2: 520.

50. Mangum to Thomas D. Bennehan, 9 December 1838, *PWPM*, 2: 534–535. In this letter Mangum makes it clear that he authored the resolutions.

51. *Hillsborough Recorder*, 28 January 1841.

52. See chapter five for discussion of Mangum's vote on re-charter of the Second Bank of the United States.

53. Mangum, in referring to the resolution asking that the expunging resolution be rescinded, stated, "I express the wish that the Senate will rescind it" (Mangum to Bennehan, 9 Dec. 1838). This is more evidence that Mangum designed the resolutions; though Rayner referred to them as "my resolutions" in a letter to Mangum, 31 Dec. 1838, at least indicating joint authorship of the resolutions; cooperation between the two would not be unexpected as Rayner backed Mangum in the caucus for election as Senator—see Rayner to Mangum, 31 Dec. 1838.

54. The resolutions are recorded in the *Raleigh Register*, 10 December 1838.

55. Mangum to Thomas D. Bennehan, 9 December 1838, *PWPM*, 2: 534–535.

56. James Graham to William A. Graham, 4 January 1839, *PWAG*, 2: 30–31.

57. *Raleigh Register*, 28 January 1839.

58. Pegg, 66.

59. In October 1839, William A. Graham wrote Mangum with advice about the Whig convention to be held in Raleigh the following month and at the end of the letter urged Mangum to dedicate the whole power of his "faculties and services" to "the promotion of the great & good cause in which we are engaged." Graham to Mangum, 11 October 1839, *PWPM*, 3: 20. Mangum also referred to the Whigs' campaigns as "the good cause." See Mangum to Charles P. Green, 1 April 1842, *PWPM*, 3: 308.

60. James Graham to William A. Graham, 22 December 1839, *PWAG*, 2: 73. James Graham to William A. Graham, 4 September 1840, *PWAG*, 2: 114–116.

61. William C. Preston to Mangum, 7 April 1838, *PWPM*, 2: 519.

62. William H. Battle to William A. Graham, 24 April 1840, *PWAG*, 2: 87.

63. *Raleigh Register*, 27 March 1840.

64. Weston R. Gales to William Graham, 16 April 1839, *PWAG*, 2: 55. Gales was preparing for a "large edition," which is consistent with an address discussing all the principles at length. For Graham's "Address," the only completed portion of which was a condemnation of the Democrats' 1837 expunging resolution, see Chapter Four.

65. Kenneth Rayner to William A. Graham, 5 April 1840, *PWAG*, 2: 79–80.

66. Pegg, 96.

67. Kenneth Rayner to Mangum, 31 December 1838, *PWPM*, 2: 535–537. Mangum's friend Kenneth Rayner was behind the move to declare the caucus a Whig convention. In this letter he explained to Mangum that he had organized a meeting of the Whig caucus on December 30, 1838, at which he introduced resolutions stating that the Whig caucus should assemble in "convention" that week (essentially declaring itself a Whig convention) and nominate Clay for the presidency subject to the decision of a national convention. However, Rayner discovered "that a large majority was against me—all avowing their preference for Mr. Clay, but expressing fears that a nomination here, would operate to our injury." The resolutions were published in the (Raleigh) *Star and North Carolina Gazette*, 27 February 1839.

68. Cole, *Whig Party in the South*, 88. Elliott, *The Raleigh Register*, 28–29, 57.

69. Howe, *What Hath God Wrought*, 584.

70. Mangum to Henry Clay, 26 March 1838, in Seager, ed., *Papers of Henry Clay*, 9: 166. Mangum's opposition to sending a delegation to the national convention may have been ameliorated by Clay's pleas for him to reconsider. See Clay to Mangum, 31 May 1838, *PWPM*, 2: 525.

71. William A. Graham to Mangum, 11 October 1839, *PWPM*, 3: 18–20.

72. Pegg, 97. *Raleigh Register*, 14 Dec. 1839.

73. Pegg, 97. *Raleigh Register*, 14 December 1839. *National Intelligencer*, 10 December 1839.

74. Cooper, *South and the Politics of Slavery*, 132–134. Howe, *What Hath God Wrought*, 574–578, refutes the claims of some historians that the Whigs' campaign of 1840 was merely "mindless hoopla."

75. See Hardy Herbert et.al. to Mangum, 17 Sep. 1840, *PWPM*, 3: 55.

76. James Graham to William A. Graham, 14 December 1838, *PWAG*, 2: 24.

77. Pegg, 44.

78. *Raleigh Register*, 27 March, 2, 17, 24 April, and 1, 8 May. The paper reported mass meetings in Orange, Brunswick, Beaufort, Davie, Iredell, New Hanover, Edgecombe, Washington, Wayne, Cumberland, Richmond, Robeson, Warren, Montgomery, Granville, Burke, Pasquotank, Perquimons, Halifax, Franklin, New Hanover, and Gates counties.

79. *Raleigh Register*, 27 March 1840.

80. *Raleigh Register*, 27 March 1840.

81. Pegg, 44–45.

82. *Raleigh Register*, 8 May 1840.

83. *Hillsborough Recorder*, 28 May 1840. Kenneth Rayner to Mangum, 30 June 1840, *PWPM*, 3: 35.

84. The final tally was 44,484 to 35,903 (*PWPM*, 3: 46n25).

85. *Raleigh Register*, 18 August and 21 August 1840.

86. *Raleigh Register*, 21 August 1840.

87. Rayner to Graham, 5 April 1840, *PWAG*, 2: 81.

88. Kenneth Rayner to Mangum, 30 June 1840, *PWPM*, 3: 35–38.

89. *Raleigh Register*, 28 August, 4, 18, 22 September 1840.

90. The prominent place of women in this Whig party rally at Raleigh conforms with Elizabeth Varon's description in *We Mean to Be Counted* of the prominent place of Whig women in 1840s Virginia Whig politics.

91. A full description of the procession and all the

other events of the convention were printed in the *Raleigh Register*, 9 October 1840.

92. William A. Graham to Willie P. Mangum, 11 October 1839, *PWPM*, 3: 19.

93. *Raleigh Register*, 9 October 1840.

94. "The Unanimous Declaration of the Whigs of North Carolina in Convention Assembled, 5th October, 1840," printed in the *Raleigh Register*, 9 October 1840.

95. Resolutions of the Whigs of Moore County, *Raleigh Register*, 1 May 1840.

96. William Cooper argues in his *South and the Politics of Slavery* that the campaign of 1840 "confirmed the politics of slavery as the primal force in southern politics." And he asserts that in 1840 "the politics of slavery dwarfed all economic issues even though Van Buren's administration had been consumed by the panic and the concomitant debate over banks and the Independent Treasury." Cooper, *South and the Politics of Slavery*, 132–141, esp. 132–133, quotes, 132. The resolutions of the Whig meetings and the "The Unanimous Declaration" refute Cooper's argument for North Carolina. Though slavery as an issue had been prominent in 1836, the Whig central committee and the Whig convention did not use it in 1840. They preferred to concentrate on the core opposition ideology of the party and the Whig measures. The resolutions are heavy with condemnation of the administration's party corruption, the seizure of unauthorized executive power, and measures of political economy. Likewise, the "Declaration" is concerned with political economy, corruption, and abuse of executive power. Kruman, *Parties and Politics in North Carolina*, points out that the absence of the proslavery argument in the press reflected "a broad consensus within the state in favor of protecting slavery" (Kruman, 106). It was therefore not a point that would help the Whigs distinguish themselves from the Democrats.

97. *Hillsborough Recorder*, 12, 19 November 1840. *Raleigh Register*, 13 November 1840.

98. Pegg, 101.

99. 12 November 1840 quoted in the *Raleigh Register*, 24 November 1840.

100. *Fayetteville Observer*, 2 December 1840.

101. Pegg, 66n103.

102. Charles P. Green to Mangum, 22 August 1840, *PWPM*, 3: 46–47.

103. Graham to James Bryan, 21 November 1840, *PWAG*, 2: 121–122.

104. James W. Osborne to William A. Graham, 26 August 1840, *PWAG*, 2: 111. C.L. Hinton to Mangum, 22 September 1840, *PWPM*, 3: 57–58. Charles p. Green to Mangum, 8 October 1840, *PWPM*, 3: 64–65.

105. Speech of Thomas Clingman in the legislature printed in the *Hillsborough Recorder*, 21 January 1841.

106. Graham to James Bryan, 21 November 1840, *PWAG*, 2: 121–122.

107. Graham to James Bryan, 21 November 1840, *PWAG*, 2: 121–122.

108. C.L. Hinton to Mangum, 22 September 1840, *PWPM*, 3: 57–58.

109. James W. Bryan to Mangum, 9 December 1840, *PWAG*, 2: 129.

110. William A. Graham to James W. Bryan, 18 November 1840, *PWAG*, 2: 118–120. Graham to Bryan, 21 November 1840, *PWAG*, 2: 121–123.

111. Mangum used this description of Whigs following Clay's banner in the presidential campaign of 1844; it is used here as the best short description of Whigs, including the Carolina Whigs, who backed Clay as their preferred presidential candidate in this earlier period. See Mangum to John M. Clayton, 16 March 1844, *PWPM*, 4: 67.

112. Wilentz, *Rise of American Democracy*, 482.

Chapter 6

1. Mangum to Charity Mangum, 9 December 1840, *PWPM*, 3: 79. William Graham reported to his wife Susan that Thompson had gotten out of the car and was walking ahead of the train as it moved slowly through the snow. Thompson "being muffled up in his cloak, & not hearing very well, the front car ran on him, knocked him down just along side of the rail, and the whole train passed over him, ripping his cloak & clothes along the back and pressing him down so as to bruise and lacerate his face, but without material injury except a severe stunning." Graham to Susan Washington Graham, 7 December 1840, *PWAG*, 2: 127. In the 1839–1840 session of Congress, Waddy Thompson had introduced what William Freehling calls the "uncompromising gag rule." Freehling, *Road to Disunion*, 346.

2. William Graham to Susan Washington Graham, 21 December 1840, *PWAG*, 2: 136.

3. William Graham to Susan Washington Graham, 25 January 1841, *PWAG*, 2: 148.

4. Holt, *American Whig Party*, 126.

5. Graham to Susan Washington Graham, 10 December 1840, *PWAG*, 2: 130–131.

6. Mangum to Charity A. Mangum, 13 February 1841, *PWPM*, 3: 113.

7. Graham to William Gaston, 16 December 1840, *PWAG*, 2: 131. William Graham to James W. Bryan, 20 December 1840, *PWAG*, 2: 134.

8. Graham to James W. Bryan, 13 February 1841, *PWAG*, 2: 161.

9. Holt, *American Whig Party*, 124–127.

10. Richardson, *Messages and Papers of the Presidents*, 4: 1860–1876.

11. Robert J. Morgan, *A Whig Embattled: The Presidency under John Tyler* (Lincoln: University of Nebraska Press, 1974 [orig. pub. 1954]), 6–12, discusses the importance and significance of this act. Though his oath as vice-president was adequate for him to act as president, Tyler chose to take the presidential oath as symbolic that he *was* now the president.

12. Richardson, *Messages and Papers of the Presidents*, 4: 1889–1892.

13. *National Intelligencer*, 7 April 1841, quoted in *Hillsborough Recorder*, 15 April 1841.

14. *Hillsborough Recorder*, 15 April 1841.

15. George E. Badger to William A. Graham, 28 April 1841, *PWAG*, 2: 189.

16. Richardson, *Messages and Papers of the Presidents*, 4: 1893–1904.

17. Holt, *American Whig Party*, 129.

18. *Hillsborough Recorder*, 15 July 1841.

19. Mordecai M. Noah to Mangum, 13 June 1841, *PWPM*, 3: 167.

20. *Hillsborough Recorder*, 15 July 1841. Mangum made his assertions as to the popularity of the bank among the Whigs in North Carolina in the course of a two-day

exchange with Calhoun in the Senate, when Calhoun had claimed that "the South" was against the establishment of any national bank. Mangum objected to Calhoun speaking for North Carolina, and declared that his opinion was "exactly the reverse of that expressed by the Senator, so far as North Carolina was concerned." The debate appears in the *Hillsborough Recorder*, 15 July 1841 and *Congressional Globe*, 27th Congress, 1st sess., 103, 115–116. The two one-time allies had already quarreled over the pre-emption bill during the short session. "I am sorry to say my old friend Calhoun has quarreled with me, & perhaps, made as little by it, as any man ever did." Mangum to Charity A. Mangum, 13 February 1841, *PWPM*, 3: 113–114. See Shanks, 113n45 [Ref. *Hillsborough Recorder*, 18 Feb. 1841; *Raleigh Register*, 26 Jan. 1841].

21. Henry W. Miller to William A. Graham, 9 June 1841, *PWAG*, 2: 195–196.

22. Edward B. Dudley to William A. Graham, 10 July 1841, *PWAG*, 2: 212. Dudley believed that the people of North Carolina were indifferent to the Bank and that only the businessmen—both Whig and Democrats—wanted the Bank.

23. Richard Smith to Mangum, 19 July 1841, *PWPM*, 3: 203–205. Smith was a member of the first Whig Central Committee organized in December 1835 [Ref. *Raleigh Register* 29 Dec. 1835]. See also the letters of Reverdy Johnson to Mangum, 13, 15, 28 July and 24, 27, 29 August 1841, *PWPM*, 3: 198–199, 200, 207–208, 219, 222, 225–226.

24. Holt, *American Whig Party*, 129–130.

25. Holt, *American Whig Party*, 130, discusses this interpretation.

26. Mangum to Duncan Cameron, 26 June 1841, *PWPM*, 3: 184. Mangum noted to Cameron that Clay, though his positions were well known by the Senate Whigs, and spoken little in the caucus.

27. Ibid.

28. Richard Smith to Mangum, 19 July 1841, *PWPM*, 3: 203–205. Smith was a member of the first Whig Central Committee organized in December 1835. *PWPM*, 2: 412n86.

29. Ibid.

30. Holt, *American Whig Party*, 129.

31. Mangum to Duncan Cameron, 26 June 1841, *PWPM*, 3: 181–188.

32. Mangum to Duncan Cameron, 26 June 1841, *PWPM*, 3: 181–188.

33. Mangum to William A. Graham, 10 and 11 July 1841, *PWPM*, 3: 193–195. Graham had temporarily returned to North Carolina because of the illness of his wife. Graham wrote at the bottom of the latter letter: "Tyler's defection and others."

34. Graham to James W. Bryan, 30 July 1841, *PWAG*, 2: 222. Also see Graham to Susan Washington Graham, 28 July 1841, *PWPM*, 2: 219.

35. Holt, *American Whig Party*, 133.

36. Holt, *American Whig Party*, 133.

37. Graham to Susan Washington Graham, 13 August 1841, *PWAG*, 2: 227. Graham to Susan Washington Graham, 16 August 1841, *PWAG*, 2: 228.

38. Mangum to C.L. Hinton, 13 August 1841, *PWPM*, 3: 215–216.

39. Richardson, *Messages and Papers of the Presidents*, 4: 1916–21.

40. Graham to William Gaston, 17 August 1841, *PWAG*, 2: 229. Holt attributes the "discovery" of this formula to Attorney General Crittenden. Whig Congressmen discussed the issue with Tyler on the 17th and Graham's comments indicate that relayed Tyler's receptivity to such a change to the congressional Whigs the same day. Holt, *American Whig Party* 133–134.

41. Statements of Ewing, Bell, and Badger in the *National Intelligencer* quoted in *Hillsborough Recorder*, 22, 30 September 1841.

42. Holt, *American Whig Party*, 134.

43. Richardson, *Messages and Papers of the Presidents*, 4: 1921–1925.

44. Mangum to Duncan Cameron, 26 June 1841, *PWPM*, 3: 181–182.

45. Mangum to Duncan Cameron, 26 June 1841, *PWPM*, 3: 181–188.

46. Graham to Susan Washington Graham, 8 August 1841, *PWAG*, 2: 225.

47. Mangum to C.L. Hinton, 13 August 1841, *PWPM*, 3: 215–216.

48. Graham to Susan Washington Graham, 27 August 1841, *PWAG*, 2: 235. Graham to Susan Washington Graham, 29 August 1841, *PWAG*, 2: 237.

49. Holt, *American Whig Party*, 126.

50. Mangum to Charity A. Mangum, 5 September 1841, *PWPM*, 3: 230–231.

51. Graham to Susan Washington Graham, 29 August 1841, *PWAG*, 2: 236.

52. Letters of Bell and Badger in the *National Intelligencer*. Reprinted in the *Hillsborough Recorder*, 30 September 1841.

53. *Hillsborough Recorder*, 30 September 1841, quoting Badger's letter to the editors of the Washington *National Intelligencer*.

54. The address was printed in *Hillsborough Recorder*, 23 September 1841.

55. Richardson, *Messages and Papers of the Presidents*, 4: 1860–1876.

56. Richardson, *Messages and Papers of the Presidents*, 4: 1889–1892.

57. Richardson, *Messages and Papers of the Presidents*, 4: 1893–1904.

58. By 1842, Tyler did not even claim constitutional objections to Clay Whig measures; the president, not Congress, would be the source of national economic policy. Tyler claimed in his bank vetoes that the Whigs' Bank failed to meet his constitutional scruples, but Morgan points out in *Whig Embattled*: "But this practice was soon dropped in favor of a frank admission that the President did not agree with Congress on policy and, therefore, would not sign an objectionable bill. Such was the case with Tyler's disapproval of the tariff and distribution bills in 1842.... Tyler became the first President to cast off the cloak of constitutional argument and openly to base his veto on the ground that Congress' action was unwise" (181).

59. *Hillsborough Recorder*, 23 September 1841. Seager, *Papers of Henry Clay* 9: 590–592 gives only a summary. The full text of Clay's speech rebutting Rives defense of Tyler was printed in full in the *Hillsborough Recorder*, 23 September 1841, notably the same issue that printed the address of the Whig caucus that read Tyler out of the Whig Party (see below).

60. William Gaston to William A. Graham, 19 August 1841, *PWAG*, 2: 231–232.

61. C.P. Green to Mangum, 10 December 1841, *PWPM*, 3: 253.
62. *Hillsborough Recorder*, 25 November 1841.
63. Pegg, *Whig Party in North Carolina*, 148.
64. *Hillsborough Recorder*, 25 November 1841.
65. S.H. Harris to Mangum, 10 January 1842; Jeremiah Whedbee to Mangum, 13 January 1842; Jeremiah Hatch to Mangum, 14 January 1842; S.H. Harris to Mangum, 27 January 1842; *PWPM*, 3: 264–265, 268, 269, 280–281.
66. Reverdy Johnson to Mangum, 31 December 1841, *PWPM*, 3: 258.; S.D. Caufield to Mangum, 3 January, 1842, and C.P. Kingsbury to Mangum, 6 January 1842, *PWPM*, 3: 261, 263–264.; *North Carolina Standard*, 12 January 1842; *Hillsborough Recorder*, 20 January 1842.
67. Charles P. Green to Mangum, 17 November 1841, *PWPM*, 3: 251–252.
68. William A. Graham to James W. Bryan, 10 February 1842, *PWAG*, 2: 257.
69. William A. Graham to Priestly H. Mangum, 9 March 1842, *PWPM*, 3: 302.
70. Mangum to Charles P. Green, 2 March 1842, *PWPM*, 3: 291–292.
71. *Ibid.*; Willis Hall to Mangum, 31 January 1842, *PWPM*, 3: 282–83. Hall was a friend of New York Whig editor and Whig Party activist Thurlow Weed.
72. William A. Graham to James W. Bryan, 8 March 1842, *PWAG*, 2: 276.
73. William A. Graham to Priestly H. Mangum, 9 March 1842, *PWPM*, 3: 301–303.
74. C.P. Green to Mangum, 10 December 1841, *PWPM*, 3: 253–255. The newspaper clipping enclosed in the letter is printed with this letter.
75. *Raleigh Register*, 29 March 1842.
76. *Raleigh Register*, 1 March 1842.
77. *Raleigh Register*, 5 April 1842.
78. Charles P. Green to Mangum, 2 March 1842, *PWPM*, 3: 292–293.
79. C.P. Green to Mangum; H.W. Miller and others to Mangum, 8 March 1842, *PWPM*, 3: 300–301.
80. Charles P. Green to Mangum, 23 March 1842, *PWPM*, 3: 306–307. "What is the reason that Mr. Clay does not answer either of the letters of invitation—All of his friends regret that he has delayed so long—the cause is thought to be unwise as the excitement is & has been for weeks very high to hear from him even if he will not accept. I hope you will urge him to give an answer without waiting another moment." Green advised Mangum that he should attend the convention.
81. William A. Graham to James W. Bryan, 8 March 1842, *PWAG*, 2: 276. William A. Graham to Priestly H. Mangum, 9 March 1842, *PWPM*, 3: 301–303.
82. Ralph Gorrell to William A. Graham, 22 March 1842, *PWAG*, 2: 282.
83. *Raleigh Register*, 29 March 1842. *Raleigh Register*, 5 April 1842.
84. Mangum's letter is cited in H.W. Miller to Mangum, 3 April 1842, *PWPM*, 3: 311.
85. H.W. Miller to Mangum, 3 April 1842, *PWPM*, 3: 311–312.
86. Pegg, 118. The events of the convention and its report were printed in *Raleigh Register*, 8 April 1842. *Raleigh Register*, 22 April 1842 and *Hillsborough Recorder*, 5 May 1842.
87. Willie Mangum to Charity Mangum, 11 April 1842, *PWPM*, 3: 315–316.
88. H.W. Miller to Mangum, 3 April 1842, *PWPM*, 3: 311.
89. The members of the central committee were: Charles Manly, Thomas Hicks, John Ligon, Richard Hines, E. B. Freeman, John W. Harris, Willie J. Fuller, G. W. Haywood, George E. Badger, H. W. Montague, A. J. Foster, Thomas J. Lemay, Weston R. Gales, Johnston Busbee, Henry W. Miller, R. W. Haywood, Stephen Stevenson, James Litchford, John H. Bryan, Alfred Jones, and Samuel F. Patterson.
90. C.L. Hinton to Mangum, 5 April 1842, *PWPM*, 3: 314–315.
91. *Raleigh Register*, 22 April 1842.
92. Both quoted in the *Raleigh Register*, 22 April 1842.
93. Graham to James W. Bryan, 11 April 1842, *PWAG*, 2: 285–286.
94. Charles P. Green to Mangum, 18 April 1842, *PWPM*, 3: 321.
95. John M. Morehead to William A. Graham, 7 April 1842, *PWAG*, 2: 284.
96. Pegg, 121.
97. Pegg, 122–123. Clarence Clifford Norton, *The Democratic Party in Antebellum North Carolina 1835–1861* (Chapel Hill: University of North Carolina Press, 1930), 81. Hamilton, *Party Politics in North Carolina*, 89. *Hillsborough Recorder*, 9 February 1843 quoting the *Fayetteville Observer*.
98. All the Whigs except Bayard and White.
99. Mangum to Henry Clay, 15 June 1842, *PWPM*, 3: 358–361.
100. William A. Graham to Priestly H. Mangum, 4 June 1842, *PWPM*, 3: 354.
101. Henry Clay to Mangum, 7 June 1842, *PWPM*, 3: 355–356.
102. Mangum to Henry Clay, 15 June 1842, *PWPM*, 3: 358–361.
103. *Hillsborough Recorder*, 9 June 1842.
104. Hugh Waddell to William A. Graham, 8 June 1842, *PWAG*, 2: 339.
105. Charity A. Mangum to Willie P. Mangum, 14 June 1842, *PWPM*, 3: 357. For indications of concern that Mangum was moving too far from state politics see John W. Norwood to William A. Graham, 13 June 1842, *PWAG*, 2: 340 and Charles L. Hinton to William A. Graham, 12 July 1842, *PWAG*, 2: 352.
106. Carroll to Mangum, 8 September 1844, *PWPM*, 4: 180–184; John W. Syme to Mangum, 4 November 1843, *PWPM*, 3: 473–474.
107. Carroll to Mangum, 8 September 1844, *PWPM*, 4: 180–184; John W. Syme to Mangum, 4 November 1843, *PWPM*, 3: 473–474; Ferdinand Henery Finck to Mangum, 30 January 1843, *PWPM*, 3: 423–426; R.G. Fairbanks to Mangum, 8 February 1843, *PWPM*, 3: 429–430; "Resolutions of Florida Legislature for Florida Canal," 18 March 1843, *PWPM*, 3: 438; for Mangum's invitations during the campaign of 1844 see *PWPM*, 4: xi–xiv; Charles C. Fulton to Mangum, 21 December 1842, *PWPM*, 3: 410–411. Fulton requested appointment as a clerk to one of the Senate's standing committees. Fulton was a reporter covering the Senate and also wrote Mangum in the same letter pointing out his availability for partnering in the establishment of a Whig newspaper in Washington.

108. Mangum to John M. Clayton, 16 March 1844, *PWPM*, 4: 65–68.
109. Clayton to Mangum, 30 March 1844, *PWPM*, 4: 85–86.
110. B.W. Leigh to Mangum, 28 March 1844, *PWPM*, 4: 79–83. Reverdy Johnson to Mangum, 23 March 1844, *PWPM*, 4: 74–75.
111. Richard H. Atwell, 17 April 1844, *PWPM*, 4: 104–106.
112. The issues in the Whig Party raised by Tyler's push to annex Texas to the United States will be fully discussed in Chapter Nine.
113. William Hayden to Mangum, 6 April 1844, *PWPM*, 4: 92–94.
114. Mangum to Duncan Cameron, 26 June 1841, *PWPM*, 3: 187.
115. Mangum to C.L. Hinton, 13 August 1841, *PWPM*, 3: 215.
116. Graham to James W. Bryan, 13 June 1841, *PWAG*, 2: 198.
117. Graham to William Gaston, 17 August 1841, *PWAG*, 2: 230. Graham to Susan Washington Graham, 5 September 1841, *PWAG*, 2: 239. Graham to James W. Bryan, 22 December 1841, *PWAG*, 2: 246.
118. William A. Graham to David L. Swain, 6 January 1842, *PWAG*, 2: 249.
119. William A. Graham to David L. Swain, 6 January 1842, *PWAG*, 2: 249. William A. Graham to James W. Bryan, 10 February 1841, *PWAG*, 2: 256.
120. Graham to James W. Bryan, 11 April 1842, *PWAG*, 2: 286. See also William A. Graham to Priestly Mangum, 9 March 1842, *PWPM*, 3: 302. "In a few weeks, we shall have a trial, as to whether the Whig party can longer stand together. Mr. Webster, and the conservatives are no doubt in consultation at present, and hope to drag after them, the residue of the quondam Whig party..."
121. Mangum to John M. Clayton, 16 March 1844, *PWPM*, 4: 66–67. See Holt, *American Whig Party*, 149–150, for the September 1842 convention in Massachusetts.
122. Confirmed by Webster's Faneuil Hall speech— see Remini, *Webster*. A brief reconciliation between Mangum and Webster may have occurred in the winter of 1844 when Webster visited the national capitol, but if so, it was fleeting. The Mangum Papers contain a letter from Mangum inviting Webster to a festive dinner where a "saddle of mutton" sent to Mangum by a friend was to be the main course. Webster accepted. Shanks speculates that the invitation was part of reconciliation attempted by Choate. Mangum to Webster, 8 January 1844, Webster to Mangum, 8 January 1844, *PWPM*, 4: 9, 9n7.
123. Holt, *American Whig Party*, 150.
124. Holt, *American Whig Party*, 416.
125. Holt, *American Whig Party*, 416–418. Holt is specifically describing the impatience of Whigs with Taylor's slow and often non-partisan patronage process in 1849 but his statement is applicable to the partisan contest throughout the 1840s.
126. *Raleigh Register*, 27 March 1840.
127. *Raleigh Register*, 17 April 1840.
128. "The Unanimous Declaration of the Whigs of North Carolina in Convention Assembled, 5th October, 1840," printed in the *Raleigh Register*, 9 October 1840.
129. Robert Ransom's son Robert graduated from West Point eighteenth in his class in 1850, served as a Captain in the 1st U.S. Cavalry Regiment and was a Major General in the Army of Northern Virginia in the Civil War. See Douglas Southall Freeman, *Lee's Lieutenants: A Study in Command* (New York: Charles Scribner's Sons, 1942), I, 273ff and I, 273n48.
130. Robert Ransom to Mangum, 27 December 1840, *PWPM*, 3: 84–85. Ransom's reference to his "recorded votes" also is a reminder that in this age in which ballots were not secret, voters openly demonstrated their fealty to a party.
131. James Harvey to Mangum, 22 January 1841, *PWPM*, 3: 99–100.
132. James Harvey to Mangum, 22 January 1841, *PWPM*, 3: 99–100. James Harvey to Mangum, 14 June 1841, *PWPM*, 3: 169–171.
133. Hoffman Whithouse to Mangum, 28 May 1842, *PWPM*, 3: 346–347.
134. See *Raleigh Register*, 7 April 1835 and above Chapter Six, 382–3.
135. Robert C. Bond to Mangum, 14 February 1841; Thomas L.B. Gregory to Mangum, 20 February 1841; William L. Long to Mangum, 27 February 1841; *PWPM*, 3: 114–115, 119–120, 124. Long was not appointed to either of the diplomatic posts. *PWPM*, 3, 114n47.
136. William Kerr to Willie P. Mangum and William A. Graham, 13 January 1841, *PWPM*, 3: 93.
137. John Van Hook, Jr., to Mangum, 1 February 1841, *PWPM*, 3: 103–104. Hook did not receive the appointment as postmaster at Huntsville. *PWPM*, 3: 103n25.
138. Edward Stanly to Mangum, 15 December 1843, *PWPM*, 3: 483–484.
139. John F. Poindexter to William A. Graham, 1 March 1841, *PWPM*, 3: 125–126. Though addressed to Graham the letter is in the Mangum Papers.
140. Graham to Susan Washington Graham, 15, 23 February 1841, *PWAG*, 2: 163, 169.
141. Mangum to Henry Clay, 15 June 1842, *PWPM*, 3: 358–361.
142. Willie P. Mangum to Henry Clay, 4 July 1842, Seager, ed., *Papers of Henry Clay*, 9: 724–728. See Peterson, *The Great Triumvirate*, 337–339, for an analysis of Calhoun's flirtation with city democrats in the Northeast.
143. Cole, *Whig Party in the South*, 99–102.
144. Charles P. Green to Mangum, 22 January 1843, *PWPM*, 3: 420.
145. *Raleigh Register*, 21 July 1843 (summary in Seagar, 833); To B.F. Moore et al., 10 July 1843, in Seager, ed. *Papers of Clay*, 9: 833.
146. Richard Hines to Mangum, 18 October 1843, *PWPM*, 3: 471.
147. Mangum to Paul C. Cameron, 10 February 1844, *PWPM*, 4: 43. The Whig ladies of Raleigh followed through on Mangum's suggestion: The 9 April *Raleigh Register* reported on a "Clay banner" prepared by the women of the capital city: "The Ladies of Raleigh, with that patriotic ardor which has ever distinguished them, have had prepared a splendid Banner for the occasion of Mr. Clay's contemplated visit to this City." The paper provided a detailed description of the banner, its motto (in Latin) was, "The good old times will return."
148. Committee of the New Hanover Clay Club (Edward Dudley, Robert H. Cowan, and Frederick C. Hill

(editor of the Whig Wilmington *Advertiser*) to William A. Graham, 4 February 1844, *PWAG*, 2: 470–471.

149. Graham to New Hanover Committee, 16 February 1844, *PWAG*, 2: 474; William A. Graham to Mangum, 17 February 1844, *PWPM*, 4: 49. An illness prevented Graham from meeting Clay and participating in the rally. See Graham to Richard Hines, 11 April 1844, *PWAG*, 2: 489.

150. *Raleigh Register*, 26 March, 5 April.

151. B.W. Leigh to Mangum, 22 April 1844, *PWPM*, 4: 114.

152. B.W. Leigh to Mangum, 22 April 1844, *PWPM*, 4: 114.

153. From the accounts in the *Raleigh Register*, 26 March, 5, 9, 12, 16, 19 April 1844. Add here that Clay's slave dropped his keys during the celebration and that they were returned to Mangum. Wesley Hollister to Mangum, 23 April 1844, *PWPM*, 4: 117.

154. Henry Clay to Mangum, 14 April 1844, *PWPM*, 4: 103

155. A.W. Gay to Mangum, 20 April 1844, *PWPM*, 4: 113.

156. See the 1835 Mecklenburg celebration and the Whig barbecue at Buffaloe Springs in Virginia, Chapter Six and the 1840 party rally in Raleigh, Chapter Seven.

157. Rosemarie Zagarri, *Revolutionary Backlash: Women and Politics in the Early American Republic* (Philadelphia, 2007), 156–157, 164. Zagarri recognizes that Whigs were the exception to her rule but she characterizes the period of women's participation in the Whig Party's activities as "brief." In what may be an oversight in stating the period of the Whig Party, she says that the space for women's participation opened only in the "the late 1840s and early 1850s." While the Whigs' general status as the minority party may have meant their practices were the exception in American politics, not the rule, this celebration and earlier activities support the view that space for women in the public realm of Whig politics was large and lasted longer. As we have seen the Whig Party's first campaign began in 1835 and the party continued in American politics to 1854, a span of twenty years. This is hardly "brief." (It is as long as the period examined in Zagarri's book.) Zagarri does not sufficiently account for the two realms of politics: The Whigs were superb party organizers, but organization did not exclude the celebratory realm of Whig politics and Whig women were full participants there. Elizabeth Varon has pointed out women's participation in Virginia Whig politics in the 1840s in *We Mean to Be Counted: White Women and Politics in Antebellum Virginia* (Chapel Hill, 1998).

158. *Raleigh Register*, 25 June 1844. Notably in such an extensive statement of policy, Clay did not feel that is was necessary (or he did not want) to address the issues of abolition and the extension of slavery. He merely referred to his opinions expressed in Congress and his letter to Mr. Mendenhall, of Richmond, Indiana.

159. *Raleigh Register*, 9, 23 August 1844.

160. *Raleigh Register*, 9 August 1844, 13 August 1844.

161. P.C. Cameron to Mangum, 7 August 1844, *PWPM*, 4: 169.

162. *Raleigh Register*, 23 August 1844. See also calls for organization in *Raleigh Register*, 30 August 1844 and *Raleigh Register*, 29 October 1844. And circular on Whig organization issued by the Maine Whig Central State Committee on 16 September 1844 in *PWPM*, 4: 193–196.

163. *Raleigh Register*, 11 October 1844.

164. Pegg, 151.

165. Strong Whig counties (counties where Graham and Clay received more than twice the votes of Hoke and Polk): Anson, Burke, Camden, Guilford, Iredell, Montgomery, Pasquotank, Randolph, Richmond, Rutherford, Stanly, and Wilkes. Solidly Whig Counties (counties where the Whigs had comfortable [in excess of 100 votes in both elections] majorities): Beaufort, Buncombe, Cabarrus, Caldwell, Chatham, Cherokee, Davidson, Henderson, Hyde, Northampton, Perquimons, Pitt, Tyrell, and Washington. Narrowly Whig counties: Ashe, Bertie, Brunswick, Carteret, Chowan, Craven, Greene, Halifax, Haywood, Hertford, Jones, Macon, Moore, Orange (Mangum's county), and Surry. Narrowly Democratic counties: Gates, Granville, Johnston, Robeson, Stokes, and Wake.

166. *Raleigh Register*, 15, 19 November 1844.

167. *Raleigh Register*, 22 November 1844. And they also trumpeted the "monstrous frauds committed on the ballot box" in Plaquemines County, Louisiana that gave that predominantly Whig state to Polk. *Raleigh Register*, 19 November 1844. The *Register* noted that although the 1840 census listed 1351 men, women, and children resident in the parish of Plaquemines, the count of the ballots in the parish had yielded a majority for Polk of 1195 votes.

168. Graham to James W. Bryan, 25 November 1844, *PWAG*, 2: 526.

169. Edward Stanly to Mangum, 2 December 1844, *PWPM*, 4: 224–225.

170. Edward Stanly to Mangum, 10 December 1844, *PWPM*, 4: 229–230.

Chapter 7

1. Mangum to Tod R. Caldwell, 20 February 1845, *PWPM*, 4: 269.

2. Mangum to Charity A. Mangum, 14 January 1845, *PWPM*, 4: 252.

3. Mangum to D. Francis Bacon, 2, 11 January 1845, D. Francis Bacon to Mangum, 16 January 1845, *PWPM*, 4: 244–245, 250–251, 254. Holt, *Whig Party*, 228. John M. Berrien of Georgia, the committee's chairman, did introduce a naturalization reform bill in January 1845.

4. James Graham to William A. Graham, 5 November 1843, *PWAG*, 2: 451.

5. William A. Graham to James Graham, 1 September 1843, *PWAG*, 2: 441.

6. James Graham to William A. Graham, 25 May 1843, *PWAG*, 2: 426.

7. "Whig State Convention," *Hillsborough Recorder*, 22 January 1848.

8. Pegg, 123, 125.

9. Pegg, 125.

10. Pegg, 102.

11. Mangum to Tod R. Caldwell, 20 February 1845, *PWPM*, 4: 269.

12. Jeffrey, *Clingman*, 52–53.

13. James Graham to William A. Graham, 19 August 1845, *PWAG*, 3: 63.

14. *Raleigh Register*, 18 April 1845, quoted in Jeffrey, *Clingman*, 52.
15. Jeffrey, *Clingman*, 53.
16. Jeffrey, *Clingman*, 54–55. Raleigh *North Carolina Standard*, 20 August 1845, quoted in Jeffrey, *Clingman*, 338n53.
17. Clingman to Mangum, 21 February 1846, *PWPM*, 4: 395–396.
18. Jeffrey, *Clingman*, 57–58.
19. James W. Osborne to William A. Graham, 22 October 1845, *PWAG*, 3: 79–80. John Gray Bynum to William A. Graham, 4 November 1845, *PWAG*, 4: 84.
20. James Graham to William A. Graham, 19 August 1845, *PWAG*, 3: 63.
21. Morgan, *Whig Embattled* (188) refers to Tyler's "political courage," but this is just a euphemism for Tyler's resisting the known will of the majority of the people. Like most historians infatuated with the presidency, Morgan invokes the presidential appeal to the people to overcome the veto of Congress as "democratic" but then praises presidential resistance to the majority's will as "political courage" and personal fortitude. In reality both were, and are, simply means to enforce presidential power against Congress. Morgan declares it was democratic to seek the annexation of Texas by appealing to the people after the Senate vetoed Tyler's treaty. But was it constitutional? Did it respect the law? Morgan, *Whig Embattled* (183), states: "When the Senate rejected the annexation treaty, he took his case in a unique manner to the House and to the country, where it can be said that the question was fairly settled through the democratic process." I disagree: This was the President using the people—a plebiscite—to bypass the Constitution.
22. Joel Silbey, *Storm over Texas: The Annexation of Texas and the Road to Civil War* (New York: Oxford University Press, 2005), 69.
23. Ibid., 70.
24. J. Pope, Jr., et al. to Mangum, 15 September 1845, *PWPM*, 4: 310–312.
25. *Hillsborough Recorder*, 4 December 1845. The resolutions approved by the convention declared improvements to the navigation of the Mississippi River and its tributaries "national" projects, recommended federal aid to such projects, recommended the improvement of the St. Louis harbor, recommended a ship canal to connect the Great Lakes with the Mississippi River, called for military and naval defenses and additional aids to navigation along the Gulf Coast, recommended construction of a navy yard on the Mississippi to build war steamers and a dry dock on the Gulf of Mexico, called for the establishment of a national armory and foundry at some point on "the western waters," called for improved mail service in the West and South and the introduction of the telegraph in the Mississippi Valley, recommended construction of marine hospitals on "the Western and Southwestern waters," called for construction of levees on the Mississippi River, called for grants of public land to projected western railroads, and called for the completion of a military road from the Mississippi opposite Memphis to the highlands of Arkansas in the direction of army posts on the western frontier.
26. With the close of the second session of the Twenty-Eighth Congress on March 4, 1845, Mangum's three-year service as president of the Senate came to a close, as did the Whigs' control of the Senate.

27. Mangum to Tod R. Caldwell, 20 February 1845, *PWPM*, 4: 267–270.
28. Mangum to William A. Graham, 21 February 1845, *PWPM*, 4: 271–272.
29. A.W. Gay to Mangum, 4 December 1845, *PWPM*, 4: 329–331.
30. See William Dusinberre, *Slavemaster President: The Double Career of James Polk* (New York: Oxford University Press, 2003), 139–140.
31. "National Defence," Speech in the Senate, 15 December 1845, *PWPM*, 5: 649–658. Webster and Crittenden also spoke against Cass's resolutions. Crittenden proposed a resolution authorizing the president to notify Great Britain that the Oregon convention of 1827 was abrogated. Mangum proposed an amendment that the notice of abrogation of the agreement be accompanied with a proposal to submit the claims of the two countries to arbitration. A second provision in his amendment authorized the Senate Committee on Territories to report a bill organizing a territorial government for Oregon upon the expiration of the joint U.S.–British occupation (see *PWPM*, 4: 381n43). Mangum was considering a move to Oregon at the time and may have wanted the government in place so he could be in it. Mangum appears to have been unconcerned with the issue of slavery in Oregon. He viewed it as a free state above the 36–30 line.
32. Mangum to Sally, Patty, & Mary Mangum, 1 January 1846, Thurlow Weed to Mangum, 18 December 1845, 19 January 1846, *PWPM*, 4: 344–345, 337–338, 368–369. For other praise of the speech see Daniel Mallory to Mangum, 22 December 1845, Alexander F. Vache to Mangum, 22 December 1845, C.P. Kingsbury to Mangum, 22 January 1846, and Abraham W. Venable to Mangum, 22 January 1846, *PWPM*, 4: 339–340, 340–342, 369–371, 372.
33. Clingman to Mangum, 21 February 1846, *PWPM*, 4: 395.
34. Dusinberre, *Slavemaster President*, 133–136; Silbey, 113–115.
35. Mangum to William A. Graham, 7 January 1847, *PWPM*, 5: 10.
36. Mangum to David L. Swain, 12 January 1848, *PWPM*, 5: 91.
37. Mangum to William A. Graham, 23 January 1848, *PWPM*, 5: 95.
38. Pegg, 153.
39. "Whig State Convention," *Hillsborough Recorder*, 22 January 1846.
40. "Whig State Convention!" *Raleigh Register*, 26 February 1848.
41. "Democratic Platform, Speech in the Senate," 3 July 1848, *PWPM*, 5: 658–690.
42. Clingman to Mangum, 5 October 1845, *PWPM*, 4: 315–317.
43. Mangum to Sally A. Mangum, 5 January 1846, *PWPM*, 4: 347–348. As late as November 1846 Mangum told Paul Cameron that he had "southern notions" because of his financial difficulties (complained of lacking sufficient "accumulated capital" to support both his slaves and his family [Mangum to Paul C. Cameron, 8 November 1846, *PWPM*, 4: 514]—he seems to have looked for the better plantation profits of the Deep South; his earlier contemplated move to Oregon shows he was considering selling his slaves and using the money to buy land and move to Oregon).

44. Clingman to Mangum, 25 August 1846, *PWPM*, 4: 477.
45. Clingman to Mangum, 21 February 1846, *PWPM*, 4: 396. Clingman to Mangum, 25 August 1846, *PWPM*, 4: 477.
46. James W. Osborne to William A. Graham, 9 December 1845, *PWAG*, 3: 88.
47. Norton, *The Democratic Party in Ante-bellum North Carolina* (Chapel Hill: University of North Carolina Press, 1930), 120–124. Haywood refused to support the Polk administration on the Walker tariff mainly due to his belief that the Mexican War had made it necessary for the United States to have a high tariff in order to meet the country's war debt.
48. Weston R. Gales to Mangum, 22 September 1846, *PWPM*, 4: 496–497.
49. Clingman to Mangum, 25 August 1846, *PWPM*, 4: 478.
50. "Fair Play" and "Fair Play-Again," *Raleigh Register*, 20, 23 October 1846. Jeffrey, *Clingman*, 59.
51. Jeffrey, *Clingman*, 60.
52. *Ibid.* Badger had served on the Whig Central Committee in the recent campaign, but, despite his claims of central domination and ignoring of the west, Clingman had also been appointed to the committee by the state convention. *Hillsborough Recorder*, 22 January 1846.
53. Clingman to Mangum, 15 January 1847, *PWPM*, 5: 15.
54. Graham intended to again oppose Clingman. In fact, he told his brother that despite poor health he was "*determined* to be a candidate again, *if* Clingman were my only opponent." But when Bynum, another Whig, made it clear that he intended to run, Graham declined to run in a four-way contest with Whigs Clingman and Bynum and Democrat Samuel Fleming. He thought that three Whigs in the race would give the election to the Democrat. "All I desired was a single race with Clingman," he declared to his brother. James Graham to William A. Graham, 10 May 1847, *PWAG*, 3: 193–194.
55. Holt, *Whig Party*, 260–263, 269. Mangum to William A. Graham, 23 January 1848, *PWPM*, 5: 93. Crittenden, who had been ardent for Clay in 1844, was convinced that Clay was unavailable and firmly in retirement Mangum's friend Clayton from Delaware also switched from Scott to Taylor. Mangum to James F. Simmons, 11 May 1848, *PWPM*, 5: 105; Holt, *Whig Party*, 269.
56. Mangum to James F. Simmons, 11 May 1848, *PWPM*, 5: 105.
57. Holt, *Whig Party*, 271.
58. Holt, *Whig Party*, 307.
59. Mangum to William A. Graham, 15 February 1848, *PWPM*, 5: 98.
60. Holt, *Whig Party*, 309.
61. See Holt, *Whig Party*, 309–310 for the circumstances and details of the drafting of these letters.
62. *Fayetteville Observer*, 9 May 1848.
63. Mangum to William A. Graham, 23 January 1848, *PWPM*, 5: 92–94.
64. Waddy Thompson to Mangum, 29 October 1847, *PWPM*, 5: 85; Mangum to William A. Graham, 23 January 1848, *PWPM*, 5: 95.
65. Mangum to William A. Graham, 23 January 1848, *PWPM*, 5: 96.
66. Mangum to William A. Graham, 15 February 1848, Mangum to James F. Simmons, 11 May 1848, *PWPM*, 5: 98, 104.
67. Mangum to James F. Simmons, 11 May 1848, *PWPM*, 5: 104.
68. *Ibid.*, 105.
69. Mangum to James F. Simmons, 11 May 1848, *PWPM*, 5: 105.
70. *Ibid.*
71. James Graham to William A. Graham, 20 February 1846, *PWAG*, 3: 107.
72. Some newspaper articles spoke of the two as Whig candidates for president and vice-president See F.H. Davidge to Mangum, 30 March 1847, *PWPM*, 5: 58–59. In an effort to gain Mangum's influence with Southern Whigs for their candidate, McLean's lieutenants wrote Mangum promising him the vice-presidential nomination if he abandoned Clay and supported McLean. See J.B. Mower to Mangum, 2 August, 17 November, 13 December 1846, 2, 23 January, 12 March, 21 September, 18 October 1847, Rush Peters to Mangum, 2 January 1847, *PWPM*, 4: 468–470, 515–517, 523–525; 5: 3–7, 18–20, 56–58, 81–85. Holt, *Whig Party*, 262. See also James E. Harvey to Mangum, 24 October 1846, *PWPM*, 4: 500–502. And McLean himself tried to persuade Mangum to back his candidacy and made it clear that he desired Mangum as his vice-president. "I sink or swim with you," he wrote Mangum. John McLean to Mangum, 30 January 1847, *PWPM*, 5: 23.
73. When Polk was finally persuaded by his cabinet and Benton to send Scott to lead a campaign in Mexico, Scott immediately informed Mangum and signed the letter, "your friend." Winfield Scott to Mangum, 20 November 1846, *PWPM*, 4: 519.
74. William Graham to James Graham, 9 June 1848, *PWAG*, 3: 229.
75. William Graham to James Graham, 9 June 1848, *PWAG*, 3: 229.
76. Mangum's biographer raises the problem of his excessive drinking. Thompson, "Willie Person Mangum: Politics and Pragmatism in the Age of Jackson" (Ph.D. Dissertation, University of Florida, 1995), 379–380. From Washington, James Graham wrote to William Graham early in 1846 that Mangum was "not improving his habits." James Graham to William Graham, 20 February 1846, *PWAG*, 3: 107.
77. Mangum to James F. Simmons, 11 May 1848, *PWPM*, 5: 105.
78. Holt, *Whig Party*, 285.
79. Mangum to William A. Graham, 23 January 1848, *PWPM*, 5: 95.
80. Mangum to David L. Swain, 12 January 1848, *PWPM*, 5: 91.
81. Holt, *Whig Party*, 306.
82. C.L. Hinton to Mangum, 22 January 1847, *PWPM*, 5: 17.
83. Mangum to William A. Graham, 23 January 1848, *PWPM*, 5: 96.
84. "Whig State Convention!" *Raleigh Register*, 26 February 1848.
85. "Taylor Men—Clay Men," *Raleigh Register*, 8 April 1848.
86. *Hillsborough Recorder*, 10 May 1848.
87. Granville, Person, Caswell, Orange and Chatham, with 34 of 37 delegates from Orange County.

88. "District Convention," *Hillsborough Recorder*, 10 May 1848. *Fayetteville Observer*, 16 May 1848.
89. Bladen, Brunswick, Columbus, Cumberland, Duplin, New Hanover, Onslow, Robeson, and Sampson counties.
90. *Fayetteville Observer*, 2, 9 May 1848.
91. *Raleigh Register*, 15, 29 April 1848; *Fayetteville Observer*, 16 May 1848.
92. *Fayetteville Observer*, 2 May 1848; *Raleigh Register*, 12 April 1848; "Taylor Meeting in Orange," *Raleigh Register*, 29 March 1848; "Northampton County," *Raleigh Register*, 17 March 1848, "Whig Meeting in Brunswick," *Raleigh Register*, 22 March 1848.
93. Holt, 323–325; William A. Graham to James Graham, 9 June 1848, PWAG, 3: 229.
94. Speech on the Democratic Platform, 3 July 1848, PWPM, 5: 685, 689.
95. Mangum to John s. Pendleton, 26 August 1848, PWPM, 5: 108–109. The letter was published in Whig papers to refute a rumor that had arisen in Virginia that Mangum had returned to North Carolina to work for Cass's election.
96. New York, Pennsylvania, Connecticut, Rhode Island, Massachusetts, New Jersey, Vermont, and the Southern Whig states Maryland, Georgia, Tennessee, Kentucky, and Delaware.
97. *Raleigh Register*, 15 November 1848.
98. Holt, *Whig Party*, 414.
99. Nicholas Carroll to Mangum, 15 November 1848, PWPM, 5: 124. Also Carroll to Mangum, 18, 23 November 1848, PWPM, 5: 125–130.
100. William A. Graham to James W. Bryan, 26 August 1849, PWAG, 3: 311.
101. Pegg, 202–203. The Democratic candidate in that contest had campaigned on the insistence that the slave states should insist on enforcement of the fugitive slave law, declaring that, though he was a friend to the Union, he preferred "disunion to dishonor" and "resistance to degradation."
102. In 1848, Clingman had warned Mangum that Badger would try to provide for himself and Stanly. If one was appointed to the cabinet and the other received a foreign mission, they would "absorb about all that North Carolina can hope to receive for her share of ... offices" (Clingman to Mangum, 1 September 1848, PWPM, 5: 110).
103. Hugh Waddell to Mangum, 13 December 1848, PWPM, 5: 134. Mangum to William A. Graham, 1 March 1849, PWPM, 5: 136. For another reference to "the originals" see Nicholas Carroll to Mangum, 18 November 1848, PWPM, 5: 125.
104. Mangum to Charity A. Mangum, 15 April 1848, PWPM, 5: 141.
105. W.S. Archer to Willie P. Mangum, 22 April 1849, PWPM, 5: 143.
106. Mangum to William A. Graham, 25 May 1849, PWPM, 5: 149–150.
107. Mangum to William A. Graham, 25 May 1849, PWPM, 5: 149–150. Also Mangum to William A. Long, 21 October 1849, PWPM, 5: 167 where Mangum admits "the difficulty of reconciling rivals interests" for an ambassadorship for North Carolina.
108. Mangum to John M. Clayton, 9 June 1849, PWPM, 5: 155.
109. Mangum to John M. Clayton, [n.d.] May 1849, PWPM, 5: 151.
110. Mangum to William L. Long, 21 October 1849, PWPM, 5: 166, 168.
111. *Ibid.*
112. Mangum to John M. Clayton, [n.d.] May 1849, PWPM, 5: 151–152. Clayton to Mangum, 17 June 1849, PWPM, 5: 156–157.
113. Mangum to William L. Long, 21 October 1849, PWPM, 5: 167.
114. Mangum to John M. Clayton, 9 June 1849, PWPM, 5: 155.
115. Cole, 154–157.
116. Cole, 163–164.
117. *Congressional Globe*, 6 Feb 1850, 31st Congress, 1st session, 300.
118. Other members of the Committee of Thirteen were: Lewis Cass of Michigan, Bright, Dickinson, Downs, William R. King, Cooper, Phelps of Vermont, John Berrien of Georgia, and Mason of Virginia.
119. *Congressional Globe*, 8 May 1850, 31st Congress, 1st session, 950.
120. Webster to Mangum, [1850], PWPM, 5: 456–457.
121. Cole, 165.
122. *Congressional Globe*, 8 May 1850, 31st Congress, 1st session, 950.
123. Henry Clay to Mangum, 25 June 1850, PWPM, 5: 178; Missouri Senator David Atchison also urged Mangum to return to the Senate. "We cannot get on without you," he told Mangum, "and even with you the fate of our Bill, the 'Compromise' is doubtful." D.R. Atchison to Mangum, 28 June 1850, PWPM, 5: 179.
124. Mangum to Charity A. Mangum, 10 July 1850, PWPM, 5: 181.
125. Holt, *Whig Party*, 532–543.
126. Willie P. Mangum and others to President Fillmore, July 1850, PWPM, 5: 185. The letter was signed by George Badger, Mangum, A.W. Shepperd, E. Deberry, David Outlaw, and J.P. Caldwell. Mangum to Millard Fillmore, 6 August 1850, PWPM, 5: 186; Charles L. Hinton to Graham, 14, 20 July 1850, Augustine H. Shepperd to Graham, 11, 16, 22 July 1850, James W. Osborne to Graham, 22 July 1850, PWAG, 3: 326–327, 330–335. William Graham to James Graham, 19, 24 July 1850, PWAG, 3: 329–330, 338–337; Millard Fillmore to William Graham, 22 July 1850, William Graham to Millard Fillmore, 25 July 1850, PWAG, 3: 333, 337–338; William A. Graham to James Graham, 25 August 1850, PWAG, 3: 371.
127. Richard Hines to William A. Graham, 16 September 1850, PWAG, 3: 392. Robert B. Gilliam to William A. Graham, 24 September 1850, PWAG, 3: 401.
128. Mangum to Graham, 3, 16 September 1850, PWPM, 5: 187–88, 190; Mangum to Corwin, 7 August, 26 September 1850, PWPM, 5: 187, 191.
129. Mangum to Graham, 3 December 1850, PWPM, 5: 195–196.
130. Mangum to William A. Graham, 19 December 1850, PWPM, 5: 198–197.
131. Mangum to William A. Graham, 27 February 1851, PWPM, 5: 203–204.
132. Mangum to William A. Graham, 27 February 1851, PWPM, 5: 203–205.
133. William Graham to James Graham, 25 August 1850, PWAG, 3: 372.
134. Richard Hines to William A. Graham, 16 Sep-

tember 1850, *PWAG*, 3: 393 . "From Whig Representatives to Millard Fillmore," 20 September 1850, *PWAG*, 4: 396. Fillmore also referred to Graham a similar letter asking for the replacement of the Navy agent at Norfolk, Virginia. *PWAG*, 3: 398.

135. William A. Graham to James Graham, 6 January 1851, *PWAG*, 4: 3.

136. William A. Graham to James Graham, 12 March 1851, *PWAG*, 4: 52.

137. William A. Graham to James Graham, 12 March 1851, *PWAG*, 4: 53. James W. Osborne to William A. Graham, 13 June 1851, *PWAG*, 4: 122.

138. Fillmore's New York tour in May 1851. Graham accompanied Fillmore on the tour. During the tour Graham made speeches to people gathered at various stops along the tour route in which he "took occasion to present distinctly to their attention the duties of Northern men in suppressing abolition sentiments." William Graham to James Graham, 30 May 1851, *PWAG*, 4: 109.

139. Holt, *Whig Party*, 306–307.

140. Raleigh Whig Richard Hines, perennial member of the Central Committee, preferred Rayner for governor to succeed Graham. Hines thought Rayner would be acceptable "to every section of the state." C.L. Hinton had been pleased with Rayner's leadership in the 1846–1847 General Assembly and thought he was the only member who had "made much political capital" during the meeting of the legislature. Richard Hines to Mangum, 19 January 1847, *PWPM*, 5: 16; C.L. Hinton to Mangum, 22 January 1847, *PWPM*, 5: 17.

141. Kruman, 145–146.

142. William W. Holden to A.W. Venable, 12 March 1848, *Papers of William Woods Holden*, 1: 23–24. Graham indicated to a friend from the east that it was "generally understood" by the Whigs that the gubernatorial nominee should be from one of the eastern counties and that the convention delegates from the east would have it in their power to chose the nominee "if they can agree." Graham to James W. Bryan, 11 January 1848, *PWAG*, 3: 212–213. The inability of the easterners to agree more than the controlling influence of the Raleigh Whigs resulted in Manly's selection.

143. Joseph Allison to William A. Graham, 5 March 1848, *PWAG*, 3: 216.

144. Joseph Allison to William A. Graham, 5 March 1848, *PWAG*, 3: 215. One of Graham's Hillsborough friends also recommended Pearson, who had the support of many Whigs. John W. Norwood to William A. Graham, 26 February 1848, *PWAG*, 3: 213–214.

145. Kruman, 146–147.

146. Norton, *The Democratic Party in Ante-Bellum North Carolina*, 155.

147. Kruman, *Parties and Politics in North Carolina*, 87–89.

148. William Graham to James W. Bryan, 13 July 1848, and enclosure, James W. Bryan to William Graham, 18 July 1848, *PWAG*, 3: 232–235, 238.

149. Kruman, 89.

150. George E. Badger to William Graham, 13 July 1848, *PWAG*, 3: 236.

151. Kruman, 89–90.

152. Pegg, 126–127.

153. Kruman, 91.

154. *Ibid.*, 146.

155. Clingman to Mangum, 1 September 1848, *PWPM*, 5: 110.

156. Thomas E. Jeffrey, *Thomas Lanier Clingman: Fire Eater from the Carolina Mountains* (Athens: The University of Georgia Press, 1998), 67. "Mr. Clingman's Address," Raleigh *North Carolina Standard*, 24 January 1849. Jeffrey, *Clingman*, 66–67. In his letter, Clingman found "decisive objections" to a national bank, rejected the Whig Tariff of 1842, declared that only "modifications" were required to the Democratic Walker Tariff of 1846 that had drastically lowered the rates of the 1842 tariff, and renounced outright opposition to the Sub-Treasury system which only needed "some alterations." In regard to slavery in the territories, he avoided stating his belief that Congress had the power to prohibit slavery in the territories and emphasized his opposition to the Wilmot Proviso as "a gross violation of the Constitution." (A position on which almost all Southerners agreed.)

157. Kruman, *Parties and Politics*, 149.

158. Quoted in Kruman, *Parties and Politics*, 148–149. Clingman seems to have identified the Raleigh Whigs of the central committee more with Badger than Mangum because in the fall of 1848 he complained to Mangum about "the clique at Raleigh" opposing western interests. Clingman to Mangum, 1 September 1848, *PWPM*, 5: 109–110.

159. In 1846, the Wake County committee members were: Richard Hines, Weston Gales, George Badger, Henry W. Miller, Alfred Jones, Charles Manly, and H.W. Husted—and another, Hugh Waddell, was from neighboring Orange County. In 1848, the Wake County committee members were W.R. Gales, Alfred Jones, G.W. Haywood, Richard Hines, T.J. Lemay, H.W. Husted, and H.W. Miller. In 1848, the district representatives appointed by Richard Hines, president of the convention, were: N. Woodfin, N.L. Williams, T.S. Galloway, Rufus Barringer, Hugh Waddell, C.L. Hinton, Kenneth Rayner, Edward Stanly, and E.J. Hale. Additionally, John H. Bryan was nominated and approved with the Wake County members as a representative of the two far-western counties of Cherokee and Haywood.

160. "Whig State Convention," *Hillsborough Recorder*, 22 January 1846.

161. Kruman, 149.

162. For instance, see James W. Bryan (of Beaufort) to William A. Graham, 13 October 1843, *PWAG*, 2: 446. Bryan, writing to Graham in the context of the latter's expected nomination as governor, told Graham: "I think the office of Gov'r has become somewhat degraded by the miserable system of demagogueism which by a sort of common consent is now attached to it in seeking popular favour on the stump at every grog-Shop and carttail in the Country. It is asking too much in my humble estimation of a gentleman to 'stump it' throughout the State. We would give any gentleman the same vote down here without these appeals to popular prejudice."

163. "Whig State Convention," *Raleigh Register*, 15 June 1850.

164. Kruman, 150.

165. "Our Position—Its Difficulties," Raleigh *North Carolina Standard*, 7 February 1849.

166. Raleigh *North Carolina Standard*, 20 December 1843, 14 January 1846, 19 April 1848, 19 June 1850; "Our Position—Its Difficulties," Raleigh *North Carolina Standard*, 7 February 1849. Support for state-funded internal

improvements was not added to the platform of the Democratic Party until 1854. See Kruman, 76–77.

167. Holden to D.S. Reid, 1 June 1850, *PWWH* 1: 31.
168. "Extract from Message," 27 November 1848, *PWAG*, 3: 255–259.
169. Giles Mebane to William A. Graham, 18 January 1849, *PWAG*, 3: 267.
170. Hugh Waddell to Graham, 26 January 1849, Charles L. Hinton to Graham, 26 January 1849, *PWAG*, 3: 271–273.
171. "Whig State Convention," *Raleigh Register*, 15 June 1850.
172. Kruman, 92–93.
173. Holden to Reid, 1 June 1850, *PWWH* 1: 31.
174. Holden to D.S. Reid, 1 June 1850, 7 July 1850, *PWWH* 1: 31, 36.
175. Pegg, 169–170.
176. Holt, *Whig Party*, 393.
177. John H. Bryan to William A. Graham, 5 April 1852, *PWAG*, 4: 281.
178. Kruman, 94–96.
179. James Graham to William A. Graham, 21 April 1850, *PWAG*, 3: 320.
180. Pegg, 203.
181. Willie P. Mangum to Henry Clay, 4 July 1842, Seager, ed., *Papers of Henry Clay*, 9: 724–728.
182. Mangum to John M. Clayton, [n.d.] May 1849, *PWPM*, 5: 151.
183. Mangum to John M. Clayton, [n.d.] May 1849, *PWPM*, 5: 151.
184. General Winfield Scott to Mangum, 25 November 1850, *PWPM*, 5: 192.
185. William A. Graham to James Graham, 24 March 1850, *PWAG*, 3: 319.
186. C.L. Hinton to Mangum, 17 April 1849, *PWPM*, 5: 143. Mangum to William A. Graham, 25 May 1849, *PWPM*, 5: 149.
187. William A. Graham to James Graham, 24 March 1850, *PWAG*, 3: 319.
188. William A. Graham to James Graham, 6 January 1851, *PWAG*, 4: 4.
189. John H. Bryan to William A. Graham, 5 April 1852, *PWAG*, 4: 281.
190. Augustine H. Sheperd, 26 April 1852, *PWAG*, 4: 295; James W. Osborne to Graham, 26 May 1852, *PWAG*, 4: 303–304; Joseph B. Hinton to Graham, 23 June 1852, *PWAG*, 4: 321.
191. James W. Osborne to William A. Graham, 13 June 1851, *PWAG*, 4: 122.
192. Cole, 224–232.
193. Cole, 234–236.
194. Cole, 236–238.
195. "Speech in the Senate," 15 April 1852, *PWPM*, 5: 725–745.
196. Cole, 232, 240.
197. Henry W. Miller to Mangum, 17 April 1852, *PWPM*, 5: 225.
198. Seaton Gales to Mangum, 23 September 1852, *PWPM*, 5: 242.
199. Augustine H. Shepperd to William A. Graham, 26 April 1852, *PWAG*, 4: 295.
200. John Kerr to William A. Graham, 22 May 1852, *PWAG*, 4: 301.
201. William A. Graham to James H. Bryan, 17 April 1852, *PWAG*, 4: 290. Pegg, 204.

202. Charles L. Hinton to Graham, 28 April 1852, *PWAG*, 4: 297.
203. Robert B. Gilliam to Graham, 2 June 1852, *PWAG*, 4: 306.
204. James W. Osborne to William A. Graham, 26 May 1852, *PWAG*, 4: 302–3.
205. Nicholas Carroll to Graham, 29 April 1852, *PWAG*, 4: 297.
206. Charles L. Hinton to William A. Graham, 28 April 1852, *PWAG*, 4: 297; Edward J. Hale to William A. Graham, 21 April 1852, *PWAG*, 4: 292; Augustine H. Sheperd, 26 April 1852, *PWAG*, 4: 295; James W. Osborne to Graham, 26 May 1852, *PWAG*, 4: 304; Robert B. Gilliam to Graham, 2 June 1852, *PWAG*, 4: 306–7; Joseph B. Hinton to Graham, 23 June 1852, *PWAG*, 4: 321.
207. Mangum to Charity A. Mangum, 23 June 1852, Mangum to Martha P. Mangum, 23 June 1852, *PWPM*, 5: 233–234. Also see Holt, *Whig Party*, 723–724.
208. "The Official Platform of the Whig National Convention," [n.d.], *PWAG*, 4: 317–20.
209. William A. Graham to James Graham, 25 August 1850, *PWAG*, 3: 370.
210. "Speech in Washington," 21 June 1852, *PWAG*, 4: 313. Graham to J.G. Chapman, 24 June 1852, *PWAG*, 4: 325–326.
211. Graham to Millard Fillmore, 28 June 1852, Fillmore to Graham, 30 June 1852, *PWAG*, 4: 328–329, 333.
212. W.T.G. Alston to Mangum, 21 September 1852, *PWPM*, 5: 240–241. E. F Lilly to E.J. Hale, 22 September 1852, *PWPM*, 5: 241–242. Martha Person Mangum to Mary S. Mangum, 29 September 1852, *PWPM*, 5: 244.
213. Robert B. Gilliam to William Graham, 8 July 1851, Charles L. Hinton to William Graham, 9 July 1851, *PWAG*, 4: 344–346.
214. Thomas Mutter Blount, 16 August 1852, *PWAG*, 4: 371. J.T. Alexander to Graham, 24 June 1852, *PWAG*, 4: 324–325.
215. Seaton Gales to William A. Graham, 12 September 1852, *PWAG*, 4: 397.
216. Pegg, 173.
217. Edward Stanly to William A. Graham, 17 August 1852, Thomas Mutter Blount, 16 August 1852, *PWAG*, 4: 371–373.
218. Holt, *Whig Party*, 757, Table 30.
219. Holt, *Whig Party*, 758, argues that this was the case not just in North Carolina but across the South..
220. Holden to Reid, 1 June 1850, *PWWH* 1: 32.
221. Kruman, 151.
222. William Cooper, *The South and the Politics of Slavery*, 311–312, agrees with my interpretation of the election as revolutionary, but I differ with Cooper somewhat as to the reasons why the fall of the Whigs in North Carolina was revolutionary. Cooper emphasizes the "politics of slavery" and ignores Whig divisions.
223. Mangum to James F. Simmons, 11 May 1848, *PWPM*, 5: 104.

Conclusion

1. Willie P. Mangum to Charity A. Mangum, 25 January 1853, Mangum to Robert P. Anderson, [March 1853], *PWPM*, 5: 264, 271. On Mangum's fall and the difficulties of his long recovery, see Mangum to Charity

A. Mangum, 19 May 1851, 29 September 1851, 3 February 1852, *PWPM*, 5: 207, 216, 220.

2. See Holt, *Whig Party*, 765–985, for the story of the final years of the Whig Party.

3. Thompson, "Willie Person Mangum," 394–396; *PWPM*, 1: xli.

4. A fact pointed out by Merrill Peterson, *The Jefferson Image in the American Mind*, 87.

5. James W. Osborne to William A. Graham, 22 July 1850, *PWAG*, 3: 334.

6. Arguably he Whig Party preempted this sort of party division on slavery/no slavery lines for two decades (1830s and 1840s). Forbes, *Missouri Compromise and Its Aftermath*, argues that Van Buren formed the Jackson party on the division over slavery—exactly what Macon had predicted. But Jackson and Van Buren's radical pursuit of executive power diverted politics (national and state) to a different track: Whig opposition to Executive power; Democrats' battle to de-legitimatize the Whig Party—the Whig Party, not slavery/antislavery became the axis of politics in North Carolina (and probably other states where the Whig Party was powerful). Only the fall of the Whigs—brought about in part by the rise of Free Soil—would put politics everywhere back on the axis predicted by Macon and designed by Van Buren.

Bibliography

Archives and Manuscript Collections

Library of Congress, Washington, D.C.
Thomas Jefferson Papers
Mangum Papers
Joseph H. Nicholson Papers
John Randolph Papers

New York Historical Society
Albert Gallatin Papers

North Carolina Department of Cultural Resources, Division of Archives and History, Raleigh, NC
Katherine Clark Pendleton Conway Collection
Weldon N. Edwards Papers
Governor's Letter Book
Nathaniel Macon Papers
Mangum Papers
Martin Van Buren Papers

Government Documents

United States Congress. *Annals of the Congress of the United States.*
United States Congress. *The Congressional Globe.*
United States Congress. *Register of Debates in Congress.*

Published Primary Sources

Bassett, John Spencer, ed. *Correspondence of Andrew Jackson.* Volume 5. Washington, D.C.: Carnegie Institution of Washington, 1931.
Battle, Kemp P., ed. "Letters of Nathaniel Macon, John Steele and William Barry Grove, with Sketches and Notes." *James Sprunt Historical Monographs No. 3.* Chapel Hill: University of North Carolina, 1902.
Battle, Kemp P., ed. "Letters of Nathaniel Macon to John R. Eaton and Bartlett Yancey" in Edwin Mood Wilson, "Congressional Career of Nathaniel Macon." *James Sprunt Historical Monographs No. 2.* Chapel Hill: University of North Carolina, 1900.
Dodd, William E., ed. "Macon Papers." *The John P. Branch Historical Papers of Randolph-Macon College.* Vol. 3 No. 1, June 1909. Richmond: Richmond Press, 1909.
Hamilton, J.G. de Roulhac, ed. *The Papers of William Alexander Graham*, Volumes I–IV. Raleigh: State Department of Archives and History, 1957–1961.
Hamilton, J.G. de Roulhac, and Henry McGilbert Wagstaff, eds. "Letters to Bartlett Yancey," *The James Sprunt Historical Publications* Vol. 10 No. 2. Chapel Hill: University of North Carolina, 1911.
Hopkins, James F., Mary W. M. Hargreaves, Robert Seager II, Melba Porter Hay, eds. *The Papers of Henry Clay.* 10 volumes. Lexington, Kentucky: University of Kentucky, 1959–.
McPherson, Elizabeth G., ed. "Letters from Nathaniel Macon to John Randolph of Roanoke." *North Carolina Historical Review*, 39 (1962).
McPherson, Elizabeth G., ed. "Unpublished Letters from North Carolinians to Thomas Jefferson." *North Carolina Historical Review*, 12 (1935).
McPherson, Elizabeth G., ed. "Unpublished Letters from North Carolinians to Van Buren." *North Carolina Historical Review*, 15 (1938).
Newsome, Albert R. ed. "Letters of Romulus M. Saunders to Bartlett Yancey, 1821–1828," *North Carolina Historical Review,* 8 (October 1931).
Rakove, Jack N. *James Madison: Writings.* New York: Literary Classics of the United States, 1999.
Raper, Horace W., ed., and Thorton W. Mitchell, assoc. ed. *The Papers of William Woods Holden*, Vol. I. Raleigh: Division of Archives and History, North Carolina Department of Cultural Resources, 2000.
Richarson, James D., ed. *A Compilation of the Messages and Papers of the Presidents, 1789–1897.* 10 volumes. Washington: Government Printing Office, 1896–99.
Shanks, Henry Thomas, ed. *The Papers of Willie Person Mangum.* 5 volumes. Raleigh: North Carolina State Department of Archives and History, 1950–1956.

Smith, James Morton, ed. *The Republic of Letters: The Correspondence Between Thomas Jefferson and James Madison 1776–1826.* 3 vols. New York: W.W. Norton & Company, 1995.

Wagstaff, H. M., ed. "The Harris Letters." *James Sprunt Historical Publications* Vol. 14 No. 1. Chapel Hill: University of North Carolina, 1916.

Newspapers

Fayetteville *North Carolina Journal*
Fayetteville *Observer*
Hillsborough *Recorder*
Newbern *Carolina Sentinel*
Newbern *Federal Republican*
North Carolina Standard (Raleigh)
Raleigh *Minerva*
Raleigh *Register*
Raleigh *Star*
Salisbury *Western Carolinian*
Tarboro *North Carolina Free Press*
Wilmington *Journal*

Contemporary Writings

Clingman, Thomas L. *Selections from the Speeches and Writings of Ho. Thomas L. Clingman of North Carolina with Additions and Explanatory Notes.* Raleigh: John Nichols, 1877.

Edwards, Weldon Nathaniel. *Memoir of Nathaniel Macon, of North Carolina.* Raleigh: Raleigh Register Steam Power Press, 1862.

Secondary Sources

Adams, Henry. *John Randolph.* Boston: Houghton, Mifflin and Company, 1882.

Adams, Henry. *The Life of Albert Gallatin.* Philadelphia: J.B. Lippincott & Co., 1879.

Allen, W.C. *History of Halifax County.* Boston, 1918.

Ashworth, John. *"Agrarians" and "Aristocrats": Party Political Ideology in the United States, 1837–1846.* London: Royal Historical Society, 1983.

Atkins, Jonathan M. "The Presidential Candidacy of Hugh Lawson White in Tennessee, 1832–1836." *The Journal of Southern History,* 58 (February 1992), 27–56.

Banning, Lance. *The Jeffersonian Persuasion: Evolution of a Party Ideology.* Ithaca: Cornell University Press, 1978.

Berlin, Ira. *Slaves Without Masters: The Free Negro in the Antebellum South.* New York: The New Press, 1974.

Blassingame, John W. *The Slave Community: Plantation Life in the Antebellum South.* Revised and Enlarged Edition. New York: Oxford University Press, 1979.

Brown, Thomas. "Southern Whigs and the Politics of Statesmanship, 1833–1841." *Journal of Southern History,* 46 (August 1980), 361–380.

Bruce, Dickson D., Jr. *The Rhetoric of Conservatism: The Virginia Convention of 1829–30 and the Conservative Tradition in the South.* San Marino, CA: The Huntington Library, 1982.

Carroll, E. Malcolm. *Origins of the Whig Party.* Duke University, 1925.

Censer, Jane Turner. *North Carolina Planters and Their Children 1800–1860.* Baton Rouge: Louisiana State University Press, 1984.

Cole, Arthur Charles. *The Whig Party in the South.* 1914. Gloucester, MA: Peter Smith, 1962.

Cooper, William J. *Liberty and Slavery: Southern Politics to 1860.* 1983. Columbia: University of South Carolina Press, 2000.

Cooper, William J. *The South and the Politics of Slavery 1828–1856.* Baton Rouge: Louisiana State University Press, 1978.

Cornell, Saul. *The Other Founders: Anti-Federalism & the Dissenting Tradition in America, 1788–1828.* Chapel Hill: The University of North Carolina Press, 1999.

Counihan, Harold J. "The North Carolina Constitutional Convention of 1835: A Study in Jacksonian Democracy." *North Carolina Historical Review,* 46 (1969), 335–64.

Cunningham, Noble E., Jr. "Nathaniel Macon and the Southern Protest against National Consolidation." *North Carolina Historical Review,* 32 (July 1955), 376–384.

Dawidoff, Robert. *The Education of John Randolph.* New York: W.W. Norton & Company, 1979.

Dodd, William E. *The Life of Nathaniel Macon.* Raleigh: Edwards & Broughton, 1903.

Dodd, William E. "The Place of Nathaniel Macon in Southern History." *The American Historical Review,* 7 (July 1902), 663–675.

Dusinberre, William. *Slavemaster President: The Double Career of James Polk.* New York: Oxford University Press, 2003.

Earle, Jonathan H. *Jacksonian Antislavery & the Politics of Free Soil, 1824–1854.* Chapel Hill: University of North Carolina Press, 2004.

Eaton, Clement. "Southern Senators and the Right of Instruction, 1789–1860." *Journal of Southern History* 18 (1952), 303–19.

Elliott, Robert Neal, Jr. *The Raleigh Register 1799–1863.* Chapel Hill: University of North Carolina Press, 1955.

Ellis, Joseph J. *American Sphinx: The Character of Thomas Jefferson.* New York: Alfred A. Knopf, 1997.

Ellis, Richard E. *The Jeffersonian Crisis: Courts and Politics in the Young Republic.* New York: W. W. Norton & Company, 1971.

Ellis, Richard E. *The Union at Risk: Jacksonian Democracy, States' Rights and the Nullification Crisis.* New York: Oxford University Press, 1987.

Foner, Eric. *Free Soil, Free Labor, Free Men: The Ideology of the Republican Party before the Civil War*. [1970] New York: Oxford University Press, 1995.

Forbes, Robert Pierce. *The Missouri Compromise and Its Aftermath: Slavery & the Meaning of America*. Chapel Hill: The University of North Carolina Press, 2007.

Formisano, Ronald P. "The 'Party Period' Revisited." *Journal of American History*, 86 (June 1999), 93–120.

Formisano, Ronald P. *The Transformation of Political Culture: Massachusetts Parties, 1790s–1840s*. New York: Oxford University Press, 1983.

Franklin, John Hope. *The Free Negro in North Carolina 1790–1860*. Chapel Hill: University of North Carolina Press, 1943.

Freehling, William W. *Prelude to Civil War: The Nullification Controversy in South Carolina 1816–1836*. New York: Oxford University Press, 1965.

Freehling, William W. *The Road to Disunion, Volume I, Secessionists at Bay, 1776–1854*. New York: Oxford University Press, 1990.

Gilman, Daniel C. *James Monroe*. Boston: Houghton, Mifflin and Company, 1898.

Gilpatrick, Delbert Harold. *Jeffersonian Democracy in North Carolina 1789–1816*. New York: Columbia University Press, 1931.

Greenberg, Amy S. *Manifest Manhood and the Antebellum American Empire*. New York: Cambridge University Press, 2005.

Hamilton, J.G. De Roulhac. *Party Politics in North Carolina 1835–1860*. The James Sprunt Historical Publications, XV, Nos. 1–2. Chapel Hill: The University of North Carolina Press, 1915.

Hargreaves, Mary. *The Presidency of John Quincy Adams*. Lawrence: University of Kansas Press, 1985.

Harris, William C. *William Woods Holden: Firebrand of North Carolina Politics*. Baton Rouge: Louisiana State University Press, 1987.

Hill, C. William, Jr. *The Political Theory of John Taylor of Caroline*. Cranbury, NJ: Associated University Presses, 1977.

Hoffman, William S. *Andrew Jackson and North Carolina Politics*. James Sprunt Studies in History and Political Science, XL. Chapel Hill: University of North Carolina Press, 1958.

Hoffman, William S. "The Election of 1836 in North Carolina." *North Carolina Historical Review*, 32 (1955), 31–51.

Hoffman, William S. "John Branch and the Origins of the Whig Party in North Carolina." *North Carolina Historical Review*, 35 (1958), 299–315.

Hoffman, William S. "Willie P. Mangum and the Whig Revival of the Doctrine of Instructions." *The Journal of Southern History*, 22 (August 1956), 338–354.

Hofstadter, Richard. *The Idea of a Party System: The Rise of Legitimate Opposition in the United States, 1780–1840*. Berkeley: University of California Press, 1969.

Holt, Michael F. *The Rise and Fall of the American Whig Party: Jacksonian Politics and the Onset of the Civil War*. New York: Oxford University Press, 1999.

Howe, Daniel Walker. *The Political Culture of the American Whigs*. Chicago: The University of Chicago Press, 1979.

Howe, Daniel Walker. *What Hath God Wrought: The Transformation of America, 1815–1848*. New York: Oxford University Press, 2007.

Hoyt, Elizabeth S. "Reactions in North Carolina to Jackson's Banking Policy, 1829–1832." *North Carolina Historical Review*, 25 (1948), 167–78.

Inscoe, John C. "Mountain Masters: Slaveholding in Western North Carolina." *North Carolina Historical Review* 61 (April 1984): 143–73.

Inscoe, John C. *Mountain Masters, Slavery, and the Sectional Crisis in Western North Carolina*. Knoxville: University of Tennessee Press, 1989.

Jeffrey, Thomas E. "Internal Improvements and Political Parties in Antebellum North Carolina, 1836–1860." *North Carolina Historical Review*, 55 (1978), 111–56.

Jeffrey, Thomas E. *State Parties and National Politics: North Carolina, 1815–1861*. Athens: University of Georgia Press, 1989.

Jeffrey, Thomas E. *Thomas Lanier Clingman: Fire Eater from the Carolina Mountains*. Athens: University of Georgia Press, 1998.

Jeffrey, Thomas E. "'Thunder from the Mountains': Thomas Lanier Clingman and the End of Whig Supremacy in North Carolina." *North Carolina Historical Review*, 56 (1979), 366–95.

Ketcham, Ralph. *James Madison: A Biography*. Charlottesville: University Press of Virginia, 1990.

Ketcham, Ralph. *Presidents Above Party: The First American Presidency, 1789–1829*. Chapel Hill: University of North Carolina Press, 1984.

Kirk, Russell. *John Randolph of Roanoke: A Study in American Politics with Selected Speeches and Letters*. Indianapolis: Liberty Press, 1978.

Kirk, Russell. *Randolph of Roanoke: A Study in Conservative Thought*. Chicago: University of Chicago Press, 1951.

Kohl, Lawrence Frederick. *The Politics of Individualism: Parties and the American Character in the Jacksonian Era*. New York: Oxford University Press, 1989.

Kruman, Marc W. *Parties and Politics in North Carolina 1836–1865*. Baton Rouge: Louisiana State University Press, 1983.

Kruman, Marc W. "Thomas L. Clingman and the Whig Party: A Reconsideration." *North Carolina Historical Review*, 64 (1979), 1–18.

Lipsky, George A. *John Quincy Adams: His Theories and Ideas*. New York: Thomas Y. Crowell Company, 1950.

Malone, Dumas. *Jefferson and His Time*, 6 vols. Little, Brown and Company, 1948–1977.

Mason, Matthew. *Slavery & Politics in the Early Amer-*

ican Republic. Chapel Hill: The University of North Carolina Press, 2006.

McCormick, Richard P. "Was There a 'Whig Strategy' in 1836." *Journal of the Early Republic*, 4 (Spring 1984), 47–70.

McCoy, Drew R. *The Elusive Republic: Political Economy in Jeffersonian America*. Chapel Hill: University of North Carolina Press, 1980.

McCoy, Drew R. *The Last of the Fathers: James Madison and the Republican Legacy*. Cambridge, U.K.: Cambridge University Press, 1989.

Miller, Zane L. "Senator Nathaniel Macon and the Public Domain, 1815–1828." *North Carolina Historical Review*, 38 (October 1961), 482–499.

Monroe, Dan. *The Republican Vision of John Tyler*. College Station: Texas A&M University Press, 2003.

Moore, Glover. *The Missouri Controversy 1819–1821*. Lexington: University of Kentucky Press, 1953.

Morgan, Robert J. *A Whig Embattled: The Presidency under John Tyler*. Lincoln: University of Nebraska Press, 1974 (orig. pub. 1954).

Morrill, James R. "The Presidential Election of 1852: Death Knell of the Whig Party in North Carolina." *North Carolina Historical Review*, 44 (1967), 342–59.

Newsome, Albert Ray. *The Presidential Election of 1824 in North Carolina*. The James Sprunt Studies in History and Political Science, XXIII, No. 1. Chapel Hill: The University of North Carolina Press, 1939.

Niven, John. *John C. Calhoun and the Price of Union: A Biography*. Baton Rouge: Louisiana State University Press, 1988.

Niven, John. *Martin Van Buren and the Romantic Age of American Politics*. New York: Oxford University Press, 1983.

Norton, Clarence Clifford. *The Democratic Party in Ante-bellum North Carolina 1835–1861*. The James Sprunt Historical Studies, XXI, Nos. 1–2. Chapel Hill: The University of North Carolina Press, 1930.

Oakes, James. *The Ruling Race: A History of American Slaveholders*. New York: W.W. Norton & Company, 1982.

O'Brien, Michael. *Conjectures of Order: Intellectual Life and the American South, 1810–1860*. 2 Vols. Chapel Hill: The University of North Carolina Press, 2004.

Pasley, Jeffrey L. *"The Tyranny of Printers": Newspaper Politics in the Early American Republic*. Charlottesville: University of Virginia Press, 2001.

Pegg, Herbert Dale. *The Whig Party in North Carolina*. Chapel Hill: Colonial Press, 1968.

Peterson, Merrill D. *The Great Triumvirate: Webster, Clay, and Calhoun*. New York: Oxford University Press, 1987.

Peterson, Merrill D. *The Jefferson Image in the American Mind*. New York: Oxford University Press, 1960

Peterson, Merrill D. *Olive Branch and Sword—The Compromise of 1833*. Baton Rouge: Louisiana State University Press, 1882.

Price, William S., Jr. "Nathaniel Macon, Antifederalist." *North Carolina Historical Review*, 81 (July 2004), 288–312.

Price, William S., Jr. "Nathaniel Macon, Planter." *North Carolina Historical Review*, 78 (April 2001), 187–214.

Remini, Robert V. *Daniel Webster: The Man and His Time*. New York: W.W. Norton & Company, 1997.

Remini, Robert V. *Henry Clay: Statesman for the Union*. New York: W.W. Norton & Company, 1991.

Remini, Robert V. *Martin Van Buren and the Making of the Democratic Party*. New York: Columbia University Press, 1959.

Risjord, Norman K. *The Old Republicans: Southern Conservatism in the Age of Jefferson*. New York: Columbia University Press, 1965.

Rothman, Adam. *Slave Country: American Expansion and the Origins of the Deep South*. Cambridge, MA: Harvard University Press, 2005.

Sacher, John M. *A Perfect War of Politics: Parties, Politicians, and Democracy, 1824–1861*. Baton Rouge: Louisiana State University Press, 2003.

Sellers, Charles. *James K. Polk: Jacksonian, 1795–1843* and *James K. Polk: Continentalist, 1843–1846*. Princeton: Princeton University Press, 1957 and 1966.

Sellers, Charles. *The Market Revolution: Jacksonian America 1815–1846*. New York: Oxford University Press, 1991.

Sellers, Charles. "Who Were the Southern Whigs?" *American Historical Review*, 59 (1954), 335–346.

Shade, William G. *Democratizing the Old Dominion: Virginia and the Second Party System 1824–1861*. Charlottesville: University Press of Virginia, 1996.

Shalhope, Robert E. *John Taylor of Caroline: Pastoral Republican*. Columbia: University of South Carolina Press, 1980.

Shalhope, Robert E. "Thomas Jefferson's Republicanism and Antebellum Southern Thought." *Journal of Southern History*, 42 (1976), 529–56.

Shankman, Andrew. *Crucible of American Democracy: The Struggle to Fuse Egalitarianism & Capitalism in Jeffersonian Pennsylvania*. Lawrence: University Press of Kansas, 2004.

Silbey, Joel H. *Storm Over Texas: The Annexation Controversy and the Road to Civil War*. New York: Oxford University Press, 2005.

Simms, Henry Harrison. *The Rise of the Whigs in Virginia 1824–1840*. Richmond: The William Byrd Press, 1929.

Sinha, Manisha. *The Counterrevolution of Slavery: Politics and Ideology in Antebellum South Carolina*. Chapel Hill: University of North Carolina Press, 2000.

Tate, Adam L. *Conservatism and Southern Intellectuals 1789–1861: Liberty, Tradition, and the Good Society*. Columbia: University of Missouri Press, 2005.

Thornton, J. Mills III. *Politics and Power in a Slave Society*. Baton Rouge: Louisiana State University Press, 1978.

Varon, Elizabeth R. *We Mean to Be Counted: White Women and Politics in Antebellum Virginia.* Chapel Hill: The University of North Carolina Press, 1998.

Vinson, John Chalmers. "Electioneering in North Carolina, 1800–1835." *North Carolina Historical Review,* 29 (1952), 171–88.

Waldstreicher, David. *In the Midst of Perpetual Fetes: The Making of American Nationalism, 1776–1820.* Chapel Hill: University of North Carolina Press, 1997.

Watson, Harry L. "Conflict and Collaboration: Yeomen, Slaveholders, and Politics in the Antebellum South." *Journal of Social History,* 10 (1985), 273–98.

Watson, Harry L. *Jacksonian Politics and Community Conflict: The Emergence of the Second American Party System in Cumberland County, North Carolina.* Baton Rouge: Louisiana State University Press, 1981.

Watson, Harry L. *Liberty and Power: The Politics of Jacksonian America.* New York: Hill & Wang, 1990.

Watson, Harry L. "Squire Oldway and His Friends: Opposition to Internal Improvements in Antebellum North Carolina." *North Carolina Historical Review,* 54 (1977), 105–19.

Wellman, Manley W. *The County of Warren, North Carolina, 1586–1917.* Chapel Hill: University of North Carolina Press, 1959.

Wells, Jonathan Daniel. *The Origins of the Southern Middle Class, 1800–1861.* Chapel Hill: University of North Carolina Press, 2004.

Wilentz, Sean. "On Class and Politics in Jacksonian America." *Reviews in American History,* 10 (December 1982), 45–63.

Wilentz, Sean. *The Rise of American Democracy: Jefferson to Lincoln.* New York: W.W. Norton & Company, 2005.

Williams, Max R. "The Foundations of the Whig Party in North Carolina: A Synthesis and a Modest Proposal." *North Carolina Historical Review,* 47 (1970), 115–29.

Williams, Max R. "William A. Graham and the Election of 1844: A Study in North Carolina Politics." *North Carolina Historical Review,* 45 (1968), 23–46.

Young, Jeffrey Robert. *Domesticating Slavery: The Master Class in Georgia and South Carolina, 1670–1837.* Chapel Hill: University of North Carolina Press, 1999.

Zagarri, Rosemarie. *Revolutionary Backlash: Women and Politics in the Early American Republic.* Philadelphia: University of Pennsylvania Press, 2007.

Dissertations

Barry, Stephen J. "Nathaniel Macon: The Prophet of Pure Republicanism 1758–1837." Ph.D. Dissertation, State University of New York at Buffalo, 1996.

Helmes, James Marvin, Jr. "The Early Career of Nathaniel Macon: A Study in 'Pure Republicanism.'" Ph.D. Dissertation, University of Virginia, 1962.

Thompson, Joseph Conan. "Willie Person Mangum: Politics and Pragmatism in the Age of Jackson." Ph.D. Dissertation, University of Florida, 1995.

Index

Numbers in **_bold italics_** refer to pages with photographs.

abolition and abolitionists 101, 110, 127, 191, 205
Adams, John 15, 23
Adams, John Quincy 42–43, 48, 52–56, 74–75, 107, 109, 114
Adams, Peter 161
Alabama 93, 125, 132, 161
Alabama territory 17
Albright, William 88
Alexander, William J. 57–58
Alien and Sedition Acts 7, 12, 15, 27
Allison, Joseph 196
Alston, Willis 25, 48, 64–65, 68
Annapolis, Maryland 137
Anson County, North Carolina 124, 187
Anti-Federalists 8, 11–12, 106
Anti–Van Buren party 3, 59, 62, 64–71, 74–75; origins 4, 63
Appleton, Nathan 109
Avery, Isaac T. 81

Bacon, D. Francis 170
Badger, George 125, 128–129, 133–134, 137, 139, 148, 150–151, 163, 170, 179, 181–182, 185–186, 188–189, 192, 195–198, 203–204, 206, 208, 212
Baker, Blake 21
Baltimore, Maryland 64–65, 67–69, 102, 108, 148, 159, 191, 205
bank, national 134–142, 146–147, 156–157, 167, 214
Bank of the United States 32, 40, 70–71, 74, 76–84, 107, 112, 118, 126, 149, 165, 212
Barbour, Philip Pendleton 63–66, 74
Barringer, Daniel 9, 189, 192
Baton Rouge, Louisiana 183
Battle, William 120, 196, 198
Bayard, Richard 153
Beard, John 87, 97, 106, 110–111

Beaufort County, North Carolina 65, 82, 89, 181
Bell, John 93, 133, 139, 191, 204
Benton, Thomas Hart 85, 153, 175
Berrien, John M. 190
Biddle, Nicholas 70, 107
Bill of Rights 8
Black, John 93
blacks 35–36
Bladen County, North Carolina 56–57
Blount, William 65, 118
Bond, Robert 160–161
Boston, Massachusetts 108–111, 156
Botts, John Minor 138–139
Bragg, John 62, 67
Branch, John 57, 62–64, 68, 71, 100
Brooklyn, New York 160
Brown, Bedford 57, 75, 80–82, 89, 105, 117–118, 120, 127
Brunswick County, North Carolina 187
Bryan, James 125, 129, 148, 152, 157, 168, 188
Bryan, John H. 201
Buchanan, James 177
"Buck Spring" 12
Buffaloe Springs, Virginia 100
Buncombe County, North Carolina 209
Burke County, North Carolina 81–82

Cain, William 9
Caldwell, David 52, 57
Caldwell, Joseph 128
Calhoun, Floride 63
Calhoun, John C. 9–10, 38, 43, 55, 57, 66–67, 72, 74–75, 97–99, 107, 110, 112, 116, 128–129, 138, 174, 216; joins Democrats 113–115, 130; political principles 64; political views 84–85,
90; supporters 48, 70, 101–102; as vice president 54, 63
California 177, 179, 190, 203
Cameron, Duncan 9–10, 49, 71, 79–80, 136, 157
Cameron, Paul C. 116, 163, 166, 203
Carolina Watchman (Salisbury) 97, 104, 114–115, 117
Carroll, Nicholas 188, 207
Carson, Charles 88
Carson, Samuel P. 63, 72, 88
Carteret County, North Carolina 194
Cass, Lewis 175–176, 179–180, 184, 188
Caswell County, North Carolina 21, 56
Charleston, South Carolina 163
Charlotte, North Carolina 57, 99, 160, 181, 200, 203, 206, 213
Charlotte County, Virginia 17
USS _Chesapeake_ 18–23
Chowan County, North Carolina 89
Clarksville, North Carolina 147
Clay, Clement C. 132
Clay, Henry 3, 5, 9, 43, 48–49, 56, 61, 64, 69–70, 73, 75, 77, 82, 85, 89, 97, 100, 107, 112, 114, **115**, 116, 132–138, **_143_**, 144, 153, 160, 170, 173–174, 178, 182–188, 190–192, 201–203, 205, 209, 214–216; American System 59–60, 66, 116, 131, 165; and "corrupt bargain" 52; and election of 1832 74; and election of 1840 117–119, 121–124, 127–130; and election of 1844 155–157, 167–169; in Missouri Compromise 32–33, 36, 38; nomination as presidential candidate 145–152; political principles 141–142, 165; political talents 10; political views 84, 180; as secretary of

state 42, 54; supporters 70; visit to North Carolina 162–166
Clay, Joseph 25
Clayton, John M. 155, 183, 188–190, 194, 203
Clingman, Thomas 88, 171–173, 176, 181–182, 190, 195, 197–198, 201–202, 209
Clinton, DeWitt 55, 103
Coffeeville, Mississippi 161
Colvin, John B. 16
Compromise of 1820 36–37
Compromise of 1833 74–76, 110–111, 118
Compromise of 1850 192, 201–209, 211–213
Congress 5–6, 8–9, 11–18, 21–23, 26–27, 29, 33–34, 37, 40, 42, 45–46, 50–51, 59, 63, 65, 69–73, 76–77, 82, 92, 100, 112, 114, 116, 120, 129, 133–136, 138–141, 148–149, 151–152, 154, 157, 160, 171, 176–177, 180, 182–185, 187, 189–190, 192, 202–204, 210, 212–213, 216; powers of 31–32, 35, 38–39, 41, 53, 60, 83–84, 90–91, 93–96, 113, 136, 142, 144–146, 170, 174, 178–179; *see also* House of Representatives; Senate
Connecticut 125, 167
Constitution 13, 19, 23, 34–35, 37, 39, 42, 44, 51–53, 55–56, 60, 65, 72, 78, 86–87, 89–90, 92–96, 98–100, 102–103, 106, 124, 126, 134, 138–142, 144, 149, 159, 165–167, 174–175, 177–180, 183, 190–191, 202, 207, 212–213; strict construction of 28, 30–31, 33, 36, 38, 41, 45, 50, 57, 66, 73, 91, 137
Constitutionalist (Raleigh, N.C.) 67
Cooper, Thomas 15
Cooper, William 104, 214
Corwin, Thomas 192
Crawford, William Harris 9–11, 42, 52, 56, 65, 68, 115; supporters of 43, 48–49, 54–55
Crittenden, John 113–114, 133, 153, 163, 170, 182–183, 185, 188–189
Cumberland County, North Carolina 65, 98, 124
Cushing, Caleb 157

Daily Atlas (Boston, Mass.) 156
Davidson County, North Carolina 67
Davie County, North Carolina 123–124, 158, 187
Davis, John 155, 157
Declaration of Independence 35
Delaware 48, 155, 167, 203–204, 209, 212

USS *Delaware* 137
Democrats and Democratic Party 3–6, 51, 79–80, 86, 88, 96–98, 100, 102, 104–107, 112, 116–119, 121, 123–126, 151, 153–154, 157–161, 165, 167–169, 171, 174–180, 184–185, 188–189, 191–194, 209, 212–213, 215–216; conventions 68–69, 103; doctrines 87, 92, 95; *see also* Northern Democrats; Southern Democrats
disunion 21, 33, 36, 212, 216
Donnell, John R. 57
Douglas, Stephen A. 192
Duane, William J. 77, 90
Dudley, Edward B. 65, 104–105, 116, 128, 135

Eaton, Clement 97
Eaton, John Henry 62–63
Eaton, Margaret O'Neale Timberlake 62–63
Edgecombe County, North Carolina 82, 85
Edwards, Weldon 44–47, 59
Election of 1800 7, 8, 11, 14
Election of 1824 9, 48–50
Electoral College 50
Embargo Act 18, 21, 24, 26–27, 72–73
Ewing, Thomas 109, 133–134, 136, 139
executive power 16–17, 22, 39, 71, 77, 79–80, 83–84, 90, 95–96, 119–120, 134, 177–178, 180; opposition to 15, 23, 28, 30, 53, 76, 81–82, 90, 94, 98–100, 102–103, 105, 107, 123–124, 126–127, 130, 133, 140–141, 147, 165–166, 168, 174, 215–216

Fayetteville, North Carolina 21, 89
Fayetteville Academy 9
Fayetteville Observer 114, 122, 152
Federalism 12, 14, 17, 20, 28
Federalists and Federalist party 3–4, 7–8, 10–12, 15–16, 19–21, 26–27, 29–30, 37, 40, 42, 54–55, 106, 123, 214; doctrines 31, 73
Fillmore, Millard 6, 155, 187, 192–195, 202–208, 213–214
Fisher, Charles 55, 57, 63, 66, 70, 72, 102
Florida 17, 21–24
Foster, Ephraim 163
France 16–18, 22–23, 26–27; in "quasi war" 7–8
Free Soil Party 169, 191, 204, 210, 213–214

Gaines, George S. 192
Gales, Joseph, Jr. 48, 121

Gales, Joseph, Sr. 121
Gales, Seaton 206, 208
Gales, Weston 48, 99, 104, 112, 114, 116–117, 119–121, 126, 163–164, 166–167, 181–182, 186, 196
Gallatin, Albert 17, 20, 26
Garnett, James 25
Garrison, William Lloyd 101
Gaston, William 57, 128–129, 137, 144
Gay, A.W. 175
Georgia 9, 48, 133, 155, 190, 194, 212
Gholson, J.H. 101
Gilliam, Robert B. 62, 206, 208
Gilmer, Thomas R. 138, 157
Gorrell, Ralph 150
Graham, James 81, 105, 119, 122, 125, 132, 171–173, 181–182, 194–195, 198, 202
Graham, Susan 162
Graham, William A. 4, 69, 85–86, 88, 90–91, 95, 103, 105, 113, 116–117, 119–122, 124–126, 128–129, 132–139, 141, 144, 146, 148–150, 152–153, 156–157, 159, 161–163, 166–168, 172–173, 175, 181–186, 188–189, 192–198, 200–201, 203, 206–209, 211–214, 216
Granger, Francis 133
Granville County, North Carolina 56, 62, 103, 147, 149–150, 164, 175, 206, 208
Great Britain 14, 17–18, 21, 25–27, 60, 67, 175–176
Greeley, Horace 204
Green, Charles P. 112, 125, 128, 145, 148–149, 152, 163
Green, Duff 112
Greensboro, North Carolina 150
Guilford County, North Carolina 181

Hale, Edward J. 152
Halifax, North Carolina 62, 66, 82, 98–99, 103, 160–161, 194
Halifax *Advocate* 64
Halifax County, North Carolina 11, 57, 65, 208
Halifax district 48, 63
Hall, Thomas H. 41
Hamilton, Alexander 28
Hampden essays 32
Harris, S.H. 147–148
Harrisburg, Pennsylvania 121
Harrison, William Henry 5, 114, 121–127, 130–131, 133–134, 138–142, 145, 151–152, 157, 161, 212–214
Harvard University 109
Harvey, James 159–160
Hatch, Jeremiah 147
Havana, Cuba 192, 194

Hayden, William 156
Haywood, G.W. 187
Haywood, William Henry, Jr. 152, 181–182
Hertford County, North Carolina 21, 65, 103, 195
Hillman, Samuel 81
Hillsboro Academy 9
Hillsborough, North Carolina 103, 113, 120, 145
Hillsborough Convention (1788) 12
Hillsborough district 85
Hillsborough Recorder 90, 127, 134, 146, 148, 153, 186
Hines, Richard 194, 199
Hinton, Charles L. 57–58, 128, 151, 186, 203, 206, 208
Hoffman, William 52, 55–56
Hoke, Michael 167, 173
Holden, William Woods 182, 197–201, 209
Holt, Michael 137, 157–158, 201
House of Representatives 10–13, 17, 19, 22, 24–26, 29, 32–33, 36–38, 42, 47, 75, 83, 112–113, 137, 140, 174–175; and presidential election of 1824 48–49, 51–52
Houston, Sam 175
Howe, Daniel Walker 77, 79, 87, 97, 121
Hunter, Robert M.T. 138
Huntsville, Alabama 161

Illinois 36
Indiana 125, 127, 204
internal improvements 31–33, 40, 46, 52–53, 64, 103, 118, 123, 144, 172, 174, 183, 196–197, 199–202, 209, 214
Iredell, James 57, 63, 65, 67–68, 70, 199
Iredell County, North Carolina 123, 158

Jackson, Andrew 3–4, 10, 42, 46, 51, *54*, 55–59, 61–69, 74–76, 79–82, 86–87, 89–92, 97–98, 100–103, 107, 109, 111, 117, 119–120, 125, 130, 139–140, 142, 144–145, 147, 155–156, 161, 165, 193, 212–213, 217; attacks on Whig opposition 5, 83–85, 93–94; opposition to 76–77; political principles 95–96; political views 70–73, 84–85; supporters of 43, 48–50, 52, 88, 101, 110
Jarnagin, Spencer 163
Jefferson, Thomas 4, 6, 11, 13, *14*, 15, 20–26, 28, 32, 54, 106, 109, 122, 127, 129, 131, 165, 174, 212, 215; election as president 7, 53; political principles 3, 8, 14, 16,
18, 39–40, 72, 96; presidential administration 9, 17, 19
Jeffrey, Thoma 96
Johnson, Reverdy 148
Jones, Francis 62
Jones, Hamilton 114
Jones, James 204
Jones, Robert S. 88
Jones, Seth 48
Jones, Willie 11–12
Journal (Louisville, Kentucky) 204
Judiciary Act (1801) 14

Kansas 212
Kansas-Nebraska Act 212
Kendall, Amos 76–77
Kentucky 9, 32, 75, 113–114, 125, 149–150, 153, 158, 167, 170, 182–183, 185, 189, 204, 209, 212
Kentucky Resolutions 15, 31, 64, 106, 215
Kerr, John 186, 206
Kerr, William 161
King, Rufus 10
Kohl, Lawrence 95–96

Lawrence, Abbott 155, 157, 185
legislative power 15
Leigh, Benjamin Watkins 93–95, 99–101, 119, 164
Lenoir County, North Carolina 102
HMS *Leopard* 18, 21
Lexington, Kentucky 183–184
Liberty Party 101
Lincoln, Abraham 211
Lincoln, Levi 14
Lincoln County, North Carolina 208
Livingston, Edward 85
Livingston, Robert 16
Long, John 62
Long, William 99, 160–161, 194
Long Island Sound 108
Louisiana 34, 158, 167, 172, 209, 212
Louisiana Purchase 15–17, 20, 35, 174
Louisiana Territory 14–17, 35
Louisville, Kentucky 204
Lowell, Massachusetts 109

Macon, Gideon Hunt 11
Macon, Harrison 11–12
Macon, John 11–12
Macon, Nathaniel 3, 10–11, 14–17, 22–25, 32, 38, 41, 43, 48, 50, 52, 58, 60, 74, 144, 165, 174, 176, 214–215; early political career 12; election to Senate 30; as opposition leader 6; political principles 4–5, 12–13, 18, 28–31, 39–41, 44–47, 61, 130, 141;
political views 19–21, 26–27, 33–37, 53–56, 59, 62, 66, 72, 73, 210; resignation from Senate 47
Macon, Priscilla 11
Macon, Seigniora 41
Macon County, North Carolina 187
Madison, James 9, 15, 17–18, 26, 40, 65, 67, 100, 103, 122, 127, 129, 142, 144, 215; administration 28–29; political principles 3, 16; presidency 4
Madisonian (Washington, D.C.) 153
Maine 33, 36, 79, 157
Mallory, Francis 138
Mangum, Arthur 9
Mangum, Catherine Davis 9
Mangum, Charity Alston 9, 42–43, 62, 73, 107–109, 132, 150, 154, 189, 191, 207, 211
Mangum, Martha 207
Mangum, Priestly 9, 42, 48, 57, 73, 88, 153
Mangum, Rebecca 9
Mangum, Walter 9
Mangum, William Person 9
Mangum, William Preston 211
Mangum, Willie P. 3–5, 7, 14–15, 34, 36, 41, 43, 45, 54–56, 63, 75–76, 98, 104, 107, 173, 181, 196, 198, 201, 209, 212, 214–216; early political career 9–10; election to Senate 57–58; and Henry Clay 43, 114–116, 146, 149–151, 162–164, 166, 168; impressions of New England 108–111; in opposition 6, 42, 67–70, 77–78, 85–95, 97, 189–191, 193–195; opposition to him 44; and political patronage 159–162; political principles 10, 47, 49–51, 74, 88–89, 130, 135, 141, 144–145, 172; political views 59–62, 71–73, 79–84, 112–113, 170–171, 175–177, 179–180, 182–188, 192, 210, 213; praise of 99–103; as president pro tem of the Senate 152–157; presidential election of 1824 48–52; as representative 48–52; resignation from Senate 105–106; retirement 211; return to Senate 117–122, 124–125, 128–131; Whig leader in Senate 132–134, 136–140, 142, 147–148; and Winfield Scott 202–208
Manly, Charles 65, 196–199, 201, 209
Marshall, John 31–32
Martin, John 63
Maryland 167, 209, 212
Massachusetts 27, 155–157, 167, 185, 191, 193

Mayer, David 18
McCulloch v. Maryland 31
McDuffie, George 49–50, 99
McIver, the Rev. Colin 9
McLane, Louis 76–77
McLean, John 97, 182–185
McPheeters, the Rev. William 9
Mebane, Giles 200
Mecklenburg County, North Carolina 98–100
Mecklenburg County, Virginia 100
Memphis, Tennessee 174
Mexico 177–179, 191
Michigan 175
Miller, Henry W. 135, 150–151, 181, 187, 206
Mississippi 93, 192
Mississippi River 15–17, 34
Missouri 32, 34–39, 103, 175
Missouri Compromise 32, 37–38
Missouri Controversy 32–38, 45, 65, 67, 101
Monroe, James 9, 16, 28–29, 40, 42, 215; administration 39, 53
Montgomery, William 78
Montgomery County, North Carolina 67, 208
Moore, Bartholemew F. 198
Moore, Gabriel 93
Moore, Glover 37
Moore, Robert G. 127
Moore County, North Carolina 124
Moorehead, C.S. 183
Moorehead, John M. 124, 146, 149, 151–152, 163–164, 181, 187
Morganton, North Carolina 170
Mountsville, North Carolina 82

Napoleon I 16–17
Nashville, Tennessee 190, 204
National Intelligencer (Washington, D.C.) 121, 134
National Republicans and National Republican party 5, 46, 54–57, 70, 72, 74–77, 80, 90, 97, 104–108, 111–112, 115, 124, 135, 144; doctrines and measures 52–53, 123, 127, 130, 147, 165–168, 209, 214
Navy, United States 13
Nebraska 212
neutral rights 21, 23, 26
New England 60, 72, 107–111, 156, 193
New Hampshire 79
New Hanover County, North Carolina 65, 163
New Jersey 153, 167, 194
New Mexico 177, 179, 190
New Orleans, Louisiana 16, 163
New York 32, 54–55, 59, 67–69, 79, 103, 148–149, 154–155, 176, 187, 194–195, 204, 207

New York City 108, 110, 134–135, 148, 160, 170, 188, 204
New York Courier 152
New York Daybook 170
Newbern, North Carolina 201
Newbern Spectator 114–115, 127
Newport, Rhode Island 108
Nicholson, Joseph 21, 23, 25–26, 28–29
Niles Register 72
Noah, Mordecai M. 135
non-importation 21, 23, 25, 27
North Carolina 10, 15, 20, 27, 31, 38, 40–43, 49, 74, 78, 109, 119, 189–190, 193; Democrats and Democratic Party in 3, 98, 104–107, 112, 117–118, 121, 123–125, 128–130, 152, 154, 166–167, 169, 171–173, 175, 182, 188, 196–202, 208–209, 211, 214–216; legislature 8–9, 12, 15, 21, 26, 30, 57–58, 86–90, 92, 99–100, 103–105, 116–117, 120, 123, 128, 163, 166, 168, 172, 175, 177, 181–182, 197–198, 200–201, 208–209; National Republicans in 57, 71, 104, 107, 116, 128–129, 199; Old Republicans in 9, 36, 39, 52, 54–59, 63, 67–69, 71, 74, 90, 113, 129; political meetings 21, 81–82, 89, 102–104, 123; politics in 47–48, 52, 56, 59, 62–67, 71, 75–76, 83, 85, 97–98, 102, 114–115, 120, 125, 144, 157–158, 162, 169, 209, 212, 214; Republicanism in 8; Western Republicans in 55, 57–58, 63, 66–68, 70–72, 75, 90
North Carolina Standard (Raleigh) 87, 92, 173, 197–200
North Carolina Whigs 3–6, 65, 75, 82, 86, 89, 92–93, 95, 97–108, 111–113, 115–135, 138, 145–155, 157–159, 162–164, 166–172, 174–175, 177–180, 182, 192, 194, 200, 208, 212–215; divisions 173, 181, 185–188, 193, 195–199, 201–203, 205–207, 209–211, 216
Northampton County, North Carolina 57, 102, 187, 208
Northern Democrats 177, 192
Northern Whigs 3, 176, 191, 193, 210, 204–205, 213–214, 216; *see also* Whigs
Norton, Clarence Clifford 104
nullification 72–77, 79, 110–112, 210

O'Brien, Michael 96
Ohio 79, 121, 126, 167, 182, 185, 194, 204
Old Republicans 6–7, 15, 22, 24, 26–27, 30–32, 37, 43, 46, 48, 56, 59, 62, 68, 74, 76–78, 90, 95, 106, 111, 122, 124, 174; doctrines and ideology 3–5, 9–11, 28–29, 32–33, 36, 38–42, 44–45, 47, 57, 59, 61, 64, 66, 71–73, 75, 93, 96, 100–102, 105, 107, 116, 118, 123, 127, 130–133, 135, 141, 144–145, 147–148, 165–168, 172, 189, 191, 195, 209, 213–214, 215–216; in opposition 52–53, 55
Orange County, North Carolina 9–10, 41, 70, 88, 90, 103, 112, 120, 124, 128, 145–146, 148–149, 153, 163, 181–182, 188, 195–196, 211
Oregon 174–176, 178, 180–181
Osborne, James 181, 194, 203, 206–207, 213
Outlaw, George 48, 203
Owen, John 57–58, 63, 122, 128
Oxford, North Carolina 62, 208

Pamlico Sound 152
Pearson, Richard M. 196
Pegg, Herbert Dale 102
Pendleton, John S. 187
Pennsylvania 25, 79, 155, 204
Perquimons County, North Carolina 147
Person County, North Carolina 9, 56, 112
Petersburgh, Virginia 132, 154
Petersburgh Intelligencer 117
Peterson, Merrill 54
Philadelphia, Pennsylvania 66, 108, 110, 186
Pierce, Franklin 209
Poindexter, George 93
Poindexter, John 161
Polk, James K. 5, 93, 167–168, 170–171, 174–180, 183, 185, 187, 189, 212–213, 215–217
Polk, William 63, 71
Potter, Henry 88
Potts, John W. 85
president 6, 37; patronage 28–30, 46–47, 76, 80, 99, 103; powers of 5, 13, 16, 28, 53, 83–84, 87, 90–91, 93–96, 123, 140, 142
Preston, William C. 99, 113–114, 116, 118, 120, 153
Preuss, Mrs. 132
Princeton University 12
proslavery philosophy 4, 60, 110
Providence, Rhode Island 108–110

Quids 21–26, 28
Quincey, Josiah 27
Quincy, Massachusetts 109
Quitman, John A. 177

Radicals 9
Raleigh, North Carolina 8, 48, 55–56, 58, 64–67, 70, 82, 95,

98–99, 113, 118, 121, 125, 128, 135, 148–152, 157, 162–164, 166, 168, 170, 172–173, 181–182, 186–188, 190, 192, 194–203, 206, 208, 214
Raleigh Academy 9
Raleigh *Register* 48, 90–92, 95, 104, 112, 114, 116–117, 119, 121–122, 123, 125, 127, 149, 152, 163–166, 173, 181–182, 186, 196, 201, 206, 208
Raleigh *Standard* 99, 119, 148
Raleigh *Star* 64, 122, 181
Randolph, John of Roanoke 17, 19, 21, 25–30, 38, 40, 44, 56, 215; political views 22–24
Randolph County, North Carolina 62, 187
Ransom, Robert 159
Ransom, William S. 67
Rayner, Kenneth 65, 119–120, 122, 125, 132, 139–140, 178, 186, 195–196, 199
Reid, David S. 197, 199–201, 208–209
Remini, Robert 71, 84
Republican Banner (Nashville, Tennessee) 204
Republicanism 13–15, 17–18, 20–22, 24–28, 38, 41–42, 47, 53, 56, 64, 109, 126, 129, 214, 217
Republicans and Republican Party 4, 11, 20, 25, 47, 56, 62, 65, 67–69, 71, 73–75, 213–214, 216; divisions in 6, 17, 21–23, 26–30, 33, 38–40, 45; factions 43, 54; nationalists 11, 39–40, 51, 53; political principles 3, 5, 7–9, 13–16, 18–19, 23–24, 30, 39, 92, 96, 111, 193; southern 31–32
Revolution of 1800 *see* Election of 1800
Rhode Island 125, 167, 184
Richmond, Virginia 132, 204
Richmond County, North Carolina 124, 187
Richmond *Enquirer* 22, 32
Richmond *Whig* 152, 204
Risjord, Norman 10, 19, 22, 30, 32
Ritchie, Thomas 32
Roane, Spencer 32
Roanoke River 11–12, 57, 64, 67, 70
Robeson County, North Carolina 124, 158
Rowan County, North Carolina 66–67, 82, 102
Russia 189

Salisbury, North Carolina 52, 55, 57, 66, 70, 88, 97, 102–103, 106, 110, 114
Sandy Grove, North Carolina 88
Saunders, Romulus M. 48, 56–58, 62, 68–69, 82, 85, 125

Scott, Winfield 179, 182–185, 187–188, 202–209, 211, 214
Seaton, William Winston 121
secession 72–73
sectionalism 32
Sellers, Charles Grier, Jr. 3
Senate 3, 5–6, 9, 15, 30, 32–33, 36–38, 44, 46, 56–58, 61–62, 69, 71, 73, 81, 85–86, 89, 92, 97, 103, 105, 107, 113, 117–119, 128–132, 134–138, 142, 146–147, 150, 152–157, 159, 162, 164, 167, 170–171, 175–176, 180–183, 185–186, 188–192, 196–198, 205–206, 210–211, 213–214, 217; as check on presidential power 53, 78–79, 82–83, 91, 212; powers of 84, 86, 91, 96, 174, 177; "war" on 76–77; Whig defense of 90, 93–95, 99–102
Seward, William 194–195, 203–205, 207
Shepard, James 172
Shepard, William 128–129
Shepperd, Augustine H. 206
Silbey, Joel 174
slavery 38, 41, 60, 66–67, 103–104, 110, 120, 122, 129, 153, 155, 167, 171, 173–175, 177, 179, 185, 190–191, 193, 195, 203–205, 200, 213–214, 216–217; defense of 65, 98, 127; gradual emancipation 32; as moral evil 34; positive-good argument (pro-slavery argument) 33, 35, 61–62; restriction 32–37, 65
Smith, James S. 88
Smith, Richard 135
Smith, William 33, 38
South Carolina 9, 31, 33, 38, 41, 49, 66, 69–70, 74, 99, 110–111, 113, 133, 138, 153, 200, 211; and nullification 72, 75–76
Southard, Samuel 153
Southern Democrats 38, 157, 174, 177, 190, 195, 216; doctrines and ideology 3, 36, 95; *see also* Democrats and Democratic Party
Southern Whigs 5–6, 9, 38, 93, 97, 101, 107, 111, 113–116, 119, 130, 138, 141, 144–147, 153, 155–157, 162–163, 166, 169, 171, 177, 179, 183–185, 188, 190–192, 195, 203–207, 210–211, 213, 217; doctrines and ideology 3–4, 36, 90, 94–95, 122, 151, 215–216; *see also* Whigs and Whig Party
Spaight, Richard Dobbs 56–58, 104
Spain 15, 17–18, 22–25, 188–189
Stanly, Edward 125, 161, 168, 181, 188–189, 195–196, 203–204, 206, 209

Stanly County, North Carolina 187, 208
states' rights 6, 33, 39, 65, 67, 69, 71–72, 76–77, 96, 100, 102, 105–106, 112, 123, 136–137, 205; political philosophy of 4, 27, 30–31, 38, 41, 50, 57, 61–62, 66, 94–95, 118, 120, 133–135; supporters of 73–75, 79, 90–91, 93, 97–99, 101, 104, 107–111, 113–114, 116, 127, 129, 143, 157
Stokes County, North Carolina 103, 161
Strange, Robert 105, 117–118, 120, 127–128
Supreme Court 39, 42
Surrey County, North Carolina 128
Sussex County, Virginia 9
Swain, David L. 77–78, 85, 88–89, 99, 102, 128–129

Tallmadge, James, Jr. 32, 34–35, 37
Taney, Roger 76–77
Tappan, Benjamin 101
Tarboro, North Carolina 82
Tariff of 1828 45, 59–60, 62, 64–65, 67–68, 74–75, 103, 111
Tariff of 1832 69, 72, 75, 103
tariffs 11, 32, 40, 46, 57, 73–75, 78, 110–111, 114, 156, 172, 177–178, 183; opposition to 61, 63, 66, 69–70; protective 10, 31, 59, 65, 118, 165, 167, 207, 214
Tayloe, Joshua 161
Taylor, John of Caroline 19, 28
Taylor, Zachary 6, 177, 179, 182–192, 194, 197–198, 201, 203, 211–212, 214
Tazwell, Lyttleton 100
Tennessee 92–93, 97, 99, 155, 167–168, 174, 191, 204, 209, 212
Texas 156, 167, 170, 173–178, 180, 182, 212, 216
Thomas, Jesse 36–37
Thompson, Waddy 132
Trenton, New Jersey 148
Tribune (New York City) 204
Tucker, William H. 164
Tyler, John 5–6, 93–94, 99–100, 108, 110, 119, 123–124, 127, 131–142, 144–151, 153, 155–159, 162–163, 165, 167–168, 170, 173, 176–177, 183, 189, 212, 214, 216
Tyrrell County, North Carolina 89

United States Telegraph (Washington, D.C.) 78
University of North Carolina 9, 52
Upshur, Abel P. 100

Van Buren, Martin 3–4, 6, 54–55, 58–59, 62, 72, 74–80, 92, 105, 107, 112–115, 119–120, 140, 142, 145–147, 149, 156, 158, 161, 165, 195, 209, 213; opposition to 63–70, 97–104, 116, 123–127, 129–130, 133, 157, 171, 215; supporters 70, 111
Van Hook, John 161
Vermont 167
Virginia 3, 6, 11, 20, 25, 31, 48, 63, 82, 93–94, 98–100, 108, 132–133, 136–138, 141–142, 144–145, 147, 155, 187, 200, 203, 211; Old Republicans in 54–55; politics in 85, 97, 125; Republicans 32; Whigs in 101, 214
Virginia Resolutions 31, 64, 100, 106, 215

Waddell, Hugh 153, 188–189, 192–195
Wake County, North Carolina 9, 42, 56–57, 65, 70, 82, 98, 102, 104–105, 112, 125, 128, 149, 153, 181–182, 187, 195–196, 198–199
Walker, Robert J. 175
Ward, William 204
Warren County, North Carolina 11–12, 44, 56–57, 62, 88, 103, 149, 159

Warrenton, North Carolina 62, 67
Washington, George 11, 21
Washington, District of Columbia 10–11, 40, 43, 45–46, 59, 63, 68, 78, 81, 98, 105, 108, 110, 120, 129, 133–134, 148, 153–154, 158, 168, 170–172, 175, 183–185, 187–189, 192, 194, 197, 203, 208, 211
Washington, North Carolina 161
Watson, Harry 84, 98, 102
Webster, Daniel 84, **108**, 109–112, 114, 133, 136, 139, 156–157, 182, 191–195, 205, 208
Weed, Thurlow 176, 194, 204
Western Carolinian (Salisbury, N.C.) 55, 63–64, 66, 68, 100, 102, 106, 110
Whedbee, Jeremiah 147
Whig (Washington, D.C.) 117
Whigs and Whig Party 3–5, 34, 65, 69, 75–76, 78, 85–86, 88–90, 93–95, 97–102, 104–117, 123–126, 131–135, 137–141, 144–146, 148–149, 151–155, 157–166, 168–170, 174, 176–178, 182, 185–186, 191–192, 194, 201, 203–205, 209, 211–212, 214–216; conventions 121–122, 186–187; divisions 171, 188–189, 193, 206, 210; doctrines and ideology 6, 84, 87, 92, 96, 103–104, 118–122, 129–130, 136, 142, 147, 156, 167, 179, 183–184, 187, 202, 207, 213; *see also* North Carolina Whigs; Northern Whigs; Southern Whigs
White, Hugh Lawson 92–93, 97, 99, 101, 103–106
Wilentz, Sean 96, 130
Wilkes County, North Carolina 63, 65
Wilkesboro, North Carolina 82
Williams, Lewis 128–129
Wilmington, North Carolina 163, 190–191, 194, 208
Wilmington *Advertiser* 114
Wilson, Louis D. 118–119
Winslow, Warren 65
Wise, Henry 138
women 99, 101, 109, 125, 163–165, 191

Yadkin County, North Carolina 196
Yancey, Bartlett 37, 41–44, 47–48, 53, 55–56
Yazoo land claims 17, 22

www.ingramcontent.com/pod-product-compliance
Lightning Source LLC
Chambersburg PA
CBHW081548300426
44116CB00015B/2798